D1238898

A Chorus of CULTURES™

Developing Literacy Through Multicultural Poetry

Alma Flor Ada ✦ Violet J. Harris ✦ Lee Bennett Hopkins

illustrated by

Morissa Lipstein ✦ Jane McCreary ✦ Christine McNamara ✦ DJ Simison

HAMPTON-BROWN BOOKS®
Creative Materials for Active Learning™

EAST CHICAGO PUBLIC LIBRARY
EAST CHICAGO, INDIANA

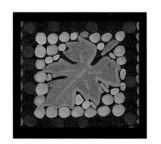

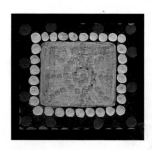

RAP | 3971613✓

Multicultural Review Board

We gratefully acknowledge the contributions of our board in reviewing reams of manuscript over the months it took to develop the Anthology. Members reviewed the poems, explanatory text, and activities for accuracy, cultural authenticity, child-appropriateness, and soundness of instruction. It is the publisher, however, who accepts final responsibility for the accuracy of the material.

◆ Susan Matoba Adler
Associate Lecturer
University of
     Wisconsin–Madison
Madison, WI

◆ María Acosta
Assistant Director
Bilingual Education
Hartford Public Schools
Hartford, CT

◆ Christine Duthie and
Ellie Zimet
First-Grade Teachers
Trumansburg Central School
Trumansburg, NY

◆ Darwin L. Henderson, Ed.D.
Associate Professor
Purdue University
Lafayette, IN

◆ Tou Meksavahn
Area Supervisor
Portland Public Schools
Portland, OR

◆ Amadita R. Muñiz, Ph.D
Elementary Bilingual/ESL
Coordinator
Spring Branch ISD
Houston, TX

◆ Lupe Soltero-Nava
Bilingual Teacher
Migrant Education Resource
Pajaro Valley USD
Watsonville, CA

◆ Doris Seale and
Beverly Slapin
Oyate
Berkeley, CA
     The publisher would also like to acknowledge the additional contribution made by Oyate—a nonprofit organization of Native Elders, artists, activists, educators, and writers—in submitting for consideration approximately 100 original poems written by Native peoples.

ACKNOWLEDGMENTS

Every effort has been made to secure permission, but if any omissions have been made, please let us know. We gratefully acknowledge the following permissions:

"Ears Hear" by Lucia and James Hymes, Jr. from OODLES OF NOODLES © 1964 by Addison-Wesley Publishing Company, Inc. Reprinted with permission of the publisher.

"I Am Sansei" by Susan Matoba Adler. All rights reserved. © 1981 Susan Matoba Adler. Reprinted by permission.

"A Word from the Poet" for September 9 and December 7 used by permission of Arnold Adoff. © Arnold Adoff, 1993.

"Son del pueblo trabajador" by David Chericián is from CAMINITO DEL MONTE. All rights reserved. Reprinted by permission of Agencia Literaria Latinoamericana.

Acknowledgments continued on page 298

Copyright © 1993 Hampton-Brown Books

All rights reserved. No part of this book may be reproduced or transmitted in any form or by any means, electronic or mechanical, including photocopying, recording, or by an information storage and retrieval system, without permission in writing from the Publisher.

Hampton-Brown Books
P.O. Box 22322
Carmel, California 93922

Printed in the United States of America
ISBN 1-56334-325-8

96 97 98 99 00 01 10 9 8 7 6 5 4 3

Cover illustration by: Raphaelle Goethals

CONTENTS

YAQ
370.19341
A191c

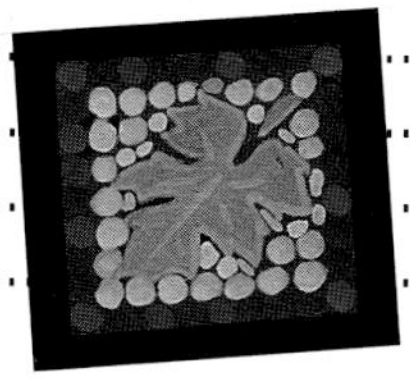

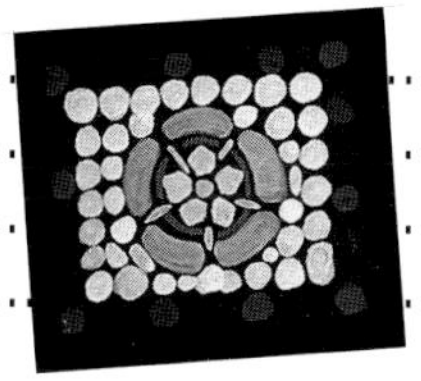

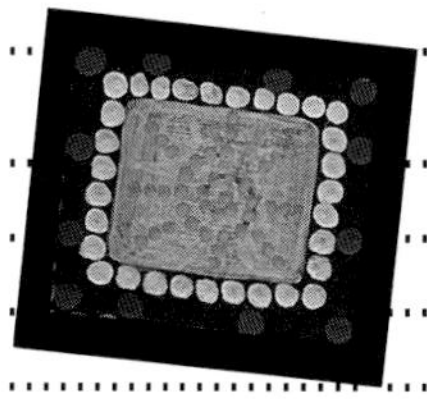

AND THANKS ALSO TO . . .

A program of this size—especially one with the goal of representing the wide cultural diversity of the U.S.—requires the input of many, many people. We'd like to acknowledge our debt to all those people who answered our questions, steered us to helpful resources, translated and interpreted material, and otherwise gave us advice and encouragement.

Poetry Consultants

Arnold Adoff, for poetic criticism and suggestions on much of the manuscript

Ginny Moore-Kruse of the Children's Cooperative Book Center, for recommending multicultural resources

Judah L. Magnes Museum , Berkeley, CA, for submitting poetry by and about Jewish Americans

Luis Kong, Executive Director, CA Poets in the Schools

Dr. Amy Ling, University of Wisconsin–Madison, for leads on poets in the Asian American community

NECA (Network of Educators on the Americas), New York, NY, for suggesting Central American poets

Dr. Barry Wallenstein, Professor of English, The City College of New York, NY

Classroom Teachers

And to the teachers who spent time in their classrooms encouraging their students to become **Young Voices:**

Linda Ben-Zvi, McCreery ES, Marion Center, PA

Mary Boxley and **Claudia Schulte,** University City HS, Philadelphia, PA

Mary Carden, Santa Ana USD, Santa Ana, CA

Paul D. Christiansen, Multicultural Specialist, Tempe School District, Tempe, AZ

Debra Green, Vare MS, Philadelphia, PA

Carolyn Lau, Lincoln ES, Oakland, CA

Dr. Paul Nava, Migrant Director, Pajaro Valley USD, Watsonville, CA

Julie Patton, Teachers and Writers Collaborative, New York, NY

Robin Roy, Furness JHS, Philadelphia, PA

Barbara VandeCreek, McCreery ES, Marion Center, PA

Deborah Wei, Office of Curriculum Support, School District of Philadelphia, PA

Cultural and Linguistic Consultants

AWAIR (Arab World and Islamic Resources), particularly Audrey Shabbas, Sophia Husain, and Jennifer Smith

Yvonne Beamer, Director, New York City Board of Education, Native American Education Program, New York, NY

The Bishop Museum, Honolulu, HI

Joseph Bruchac, publisher of the Greenfield Press, for help in locating Native American poetry

Amy Catlin, ethnomusicologist, UCLA, Los Angeles, CA

Congregation Beth Israel, Carmel, CA

The Defense Language Institute: Chinese, Japanese, and Vietnamese departments, Monterey, CA

Dan Duffy, Southeast Asian Studies, Yale University, New Haven, CT

Kelli Gary, Director, Center for Multicultural Children's Literature, New York, NY

Joan Gilmore, Prinicipal, Leupp School, Flagstaff, AZ

Angele Guerbidjian, of A. G. State Interpreters, Pacifica, CA (Armenian language)

Shabbir Mansuri, Executive Director of the Council of Islamic Education, Tustin, CA

Kevin Minkoff, Carmel, CA (Hebrew language)

Kim-Ahn Nguyen Phan, Administrator of Bilingual Education, San Jose USD, San Jose, CA

Isabel Schon, Center for the Study of Books for Children and Adolescents, California State University, San Marcos, CA

Research

Lisa Poole of the Global Village Press for innumerable leads, and our wonderful Monterey Peninsula librarians, especially **Janet Bombard,** Reference Librarian, of the Harrison Memorial Library in Carmel, CA, for assisting us in locating poems, facts, and source material.

Product Development

For participating in initial product development and critiquing early prototypes of the program:

Dr. Milo Campbell, Associate Professor of Elementary Education and Coordinator of Multicultural Education, Brigham Young University, Provo, UT

Holly Carroll, teacher, Watertown, MA

Marilyn Chin, Department of English and Comparative Literature, San Diego State University, San Diego, CA

Dr. Sara Garcia, Division of Counseling Psychology and Education, University of Santa Clara, Santa Clara, CA

Carla Herrera, teacher, Cerritos, CA

Janice Knight, teacher, Brooklyn, NY

Carolyn Leonard, Coordinator of Multicultural/ Multiethnic Education, Portland Public Schools, Portland, OR

Ana Matiella, educator and author, Santa Fe, NM

Dr. Evelyn Reid, Coordinator of Multicultural Programs, Ohio University, Athens, OH

Dr. Shawn Wong, Director of Asian American Studies, University of Washington, Seattle, WA

The Hampton-Brown Staff

Editorial Staff: **Julie Cason, Suzanne Crain, Sherry Long, Juan Quintana, Josh Weinstein**

Design and Production Staff: **David Kirby, Curtis Spitler, Margaret Tisdale**

Permissions Staff: **Jill Campbell, Valerie Lauer, Barbara Mathewson**

A Chorus of CULTURES™

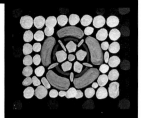

This section is dedicated to learning—the continuing education you undertake as a teacher and the literacy development you work toward with your students.

The authors of this program, all teachers themselves, discuss the power of poetry and its value as an integral part of the curriculum. Also included are valuable techniques for selecting poems, presenting poetry, developing literacy through poetry, and infusing multiculturalism into your classroom—techniques that will help you inspire and motivate each and every one of your students.

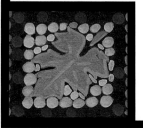

The one who teaches is the giver of eyes.
—Tamil (Asian Indian) proverb

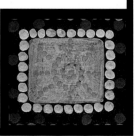

FROM THE AUTHOR: Lee Bennett Hopkins

Voices

Lee Bennett Hopkins, *recipient of the University of Southern Mississippi Medallion (1989) for "lasting contributions to children's literature," has also been honored with four American Library Association Notable Books. He has authored scores of books for children and young adults, as well as professional articles and texts. In 1993, he established the Lee Bennett Hopkins Poetry Award, to be given annually under the aegis of The Children's Literature Council of Pennsylvania.*

Here he comments on the power — and necessity—of poetry in our children's lives.

Were it in my power, I would wrap all children in the arms of poetry—bundle them warm, encircle them tight—for no other form of literature can fit so snugly throughout their school experience, or throughout their lives, as does poetry.

From the time I entered the teaching profession in 1960, I have given children poetry. And I continue to do so today. I see what poetry does to them, for them. I hear the *ooh's* and *ah's*. I see the smiles, the choked-back tears. I witness the wonder, the magic, the power of poetry.

The voice of poetry is strong, mighty; it is a voice that instructs, entertains, enlightens; indeed, it is *A Chorus of Cultures.*

Living in a culturally diverse society, it is of utmost importance that the literature we present to children reflects and builds upon their cultural and linguistic backgrounds—that literature respects the dignity of *all.*

A Chorus of Cultures satisfies this thesis by providing educators and children with works written by a wide array of poets—a plethora of poetry.

Poetry is the voice of people. It mirrors one's culture, moods, emotions; it presents great thoughts in few words; it causes children to laugh, cry, wonder, ponder; it explores and explodes the senses so that children can see, hear, taste, smell, and touch words that have been placed together in forms unique to literature and life.

Voices—voices shouting, singing, whispering, chanting; this is what poetry is all about.

It is a chorus of children, like those in Margot Pepper's first-grade class in San Francisco, ringing out:

Si los niños fuéramos
el año nuevo
seríamos un corazón con alas . . .

If children were
the new year
we'd be a heart with wings . . .

It is the voice of Ramson Lomatewama, who tells us "we are truly different/and yet/we are truly the same"; the melody from the Jewish folk song: *"Hineh ma tov, shevet achim gam yachad*/Oh, how good it is, living in unity"; the music of the Caribbean, which Lynn Joseph captures: "hearing the pan man/pom da de de de dom pom/sweet on that steel drum!"; the wit of poets such as Karla Kuskin and Shel Silverstein; the wisdom of poets like Langston Hughes, when he tells us to:

Hold fast to dreams
For if dreams die
Life is a broken-winged bird
That cannot fly.

Hold fast to dreams
For when dreams go
Life is a barren field
Frozen with snow.
                —*Langston Hughes*

One question I am often asked in workshops is, "How can I find time to get poetry into the curriculum on a daily basis?" My answer is, "It's easy. *Make* time."

Most poems are quite short and can be shared within seconds, or a minute or two. With the poem-a-day format, you might share a poem at the beginning of the school day; before, during, or after a recess or story hour; when children are lining up to go to the library, gymnasium, lunch room. We *can* find time for poetry. We *must*. And *A Chorus of Cultures* will help you share poetry with a multitude of children, so they can hear the voices and perhaps ring out new works on their own.

For me, any day without a poem is an empty day. Moments I take for poetry make my life richer, fuller. I hope you and your students will find time for poetry, because *every* day is poetry time.

Raise voices—for, as the dedication in *A Chorus of Cultures* tells us, we are "all part of the song."

We *are*!

We can find time for poetry. We must.

7

FROM THE AUTHOR: Violet J. Harris

Dr. Violet J. Harris *is an associate professor at the University of Illinois at Urbana–Champaign. Editor of the noteworthy book,* Teaching Multicultural Literature in Grades K-8, *Dr. Harris specializes in children's literature and multiethnic children's literature.*

Here she comments on language: standard and nonstandard language forms, and the value of teaching children to tap into the power of language.

Literacy and Language

Children are active language learners, and we ensure that they continue to learn when we share language used in creative ways. My facility with different language forms comes, in part, from reading at a young age writers and poets such as Nikki Giovanni, Langston Hughes, Gwendolyn Brooks, and Maya Angelou. I imitated their writings in my attempts to capture their cadences, rhythms, forms, truths, and images. I am a better writer because I have read writers and poets who manipulated, created, recreated, and stretched the boundaries of linguistic forms. Because of the diversity of writers and poets that I have read, I recognize the similarities in language forms as well as the differences forged by cultural and historical experiences.

Yet, how many children have had the opportunities to share poetry that represents the disparate poetic voices found in the United States? Not many, and they need it now more than ever. *A Chorus of Cultures* will go a long way toward acquainting children with dynamic, distinct voices. I realize, though, that poetry won't solve all of society's problems. But it will give children moments of respite, joy, and beauty—the things that make life hopeful.

I enjoy sharing poems with children, especially those poems in which the *way* language is used is as important as the meaning of the language. Two of my favorites are "Dreams" (January 19 in the Anthology) by Langston Hughes and "Things" (October 16) by Eloise Greenfield. The short, sharp command to "Hold fast to dreams" is inspirational and empowering, just as its message reminds us that dreams themselves are inspirational and empowering. Conversely, its stark, spare language mirrors the poem's message that a life bereft of dreams and hopes is cold, lonely, and stifling.

In contrast, "Things" is a celebration of creativity, especially of poetry and its power. The language in "Things" is youthful and vibrant. The poem is fun; it is light-hearted and whimsical. In this way it reflects the experiences and developmental stances of children. The child in the poem builds sandcastles on the beach or plays on the floor at home. There is no adult nostalgia in the poem. It is a fine example of the ways in which poets play with and manipulate language to capture a moment, convey a mood, or evoke a certain response.

Standard vs. Nonstandard Language

Poetry is an ideal art form for encouraging children to perceive the functions of language. They can discover that poets possess different "voices" and that those voices are dynamic and create certain moods and evoke myriad responses. For example, when reading "Things," some children hesitate before uttering the line, "ain't got it no more." I say the line with gusto, and many of the children mimic my recitation. I surmised that students do not expect an adult, particularly a teacher, to say *ain't* in school. Teachers react in a similar fashion when I share the poem with them. A typical question is, "Will the use of nonstandard language in poetry or fiction reinforce the use of 'bad English,' nonstandard English, or bad speech?"

Absolutely not. Poetry is art. Painters capture the colors and forms of the world around them in unique, interesting ways. So, too, poets capture the rhythms, cadences, and language of the world around them in unique, interesting ways. Through poetry, children become acquainted with many different worlds, condensed in evocative, connotative language. We cannot limit children's access by validating or sharing only those poems that conform to standard forms. We must provide them with poems that reflect and validate the different realities in which they live.

Language reflects human experience in another, very important, way. We must recognize that, linguistically, one language form is not inherently better than or superior to another, just as no one group of people is inherently superior to another. We should provide children with opportunities not only to hear poems that capture different language forms, but also to speak, read, perform, analyze, and play with all forms of language. Students need to experience the breadth of language to connect with and appreciate their own culture and that of others.

Does this mean that the use of standard language is not important? Of course it is. In our classrooms, we speak—or at least should speak—standard language nearly 100% of the time. And we need to inform children of the benefits of standard language because language, in all its forms, is power.

THINGS

Went to the corner
Walked in the store
Bought me some candy
Ain't got it no more
Ain't got it no more

Went to the beach
Played on the shore
Built me a sandhouse
Ain't got it no more
Ain't got it no more

Went to the kitchen
Lay down on the floor
Made me a poem
Still got it
Still got it

—Eloise Greenfield

Language is Power

How can we as teachers help children tap into the power that comes from effective language use?

✦ We can help children understand that language varies among different contexts, among different situations. For example, the language children use on the playground with their friends is appropriate for the context; however, if the context is a teacher conference or perhaps an interview for a babysitting job, a different register, or type of language, is called for.

✦ We can also make them aware that listeners form judgments about individuals based on their language use and that choosing appropriate registers helps them achieve their goals.

✦ To help remove the mysteries about how and why language works, we need to give children opportunities to experience all kinds of language, with deliberate focus on how language varies by context and situation. Many students decide not to use the forms that we model or the language of the text we use because there is not much incentive to do so. Having them role play different situations in which they use different language forms, and observe others doing the same can help them see the benefits of each form. It also helps to make this insider knowledge explicit in open discussions. *What is their goal? How does their goal influence what they say and how they say it?* For example, children could pretend that they're Bryant Gumbel, Connie Chung, or Oprah Winfrey interviewing the president of the United States. This kind of safe, supported practice and discussion is what conveys the power of language to children.

My experience is that many students have an intuitive understanding of when standard language is required. While some will not produce the form all of the time, they will give viable approximations. And, if they are given opportunities to acquire a variety of registers that are situationally appropriate, ones that they can reproduce with ease and confidence, they will acquire the full power that language can wield.

Children can then take that knowledge from their own lives and use it to create artistic products, in the "voice" of their own choosing. Our job is simply to provide them with the very best poetry so that they will know the pleasure that results from a poem that touches their minds, their hearts, their funny bones, or, indeed, their lives.

> *Safe, supported practice and discussion is what conveys the power of language to children.*

Violet J. Harris

FROM THE AUTHOR: Alma Flor Ada

Poetry and the Oral Tradition

Poetry begins orally. It arises as a way to relate a people's myths and creation stories and the feats of its heroes, as well as to express profound feelings. From its beginnings, poetry intermingles with song, seeking the musicality of rhythm and rhyme in order to create an enduring effect upon human memory.

Poetry has served to raise spirits for work, accompany the solitary shepherd in the mountains, and chronicle the history of a people. Sung by a parent or a grandparent, poetry can become a lullaby to soothe a child to sleep; sung by children, an invitation to join in the game.

Often, such poetry has been passed down from generation to generation as part of the oral tradition. It not only creates an emotional bond between family members, but also connects the family with their heritage and culture. Because poetry from the oral tradition remains alive in many communities, recognizing and valuing its importance is one of the best ways to encourage children's appreciation for written poetry and to build a bridge between the home and the school.

Dr. Alma Flor Ada, an authority on children's literature in Spanish and author of Días y días de poesía *and a number of children's books, has been writing for children for almost 30 years. Committed to bilingual and multicultural education, Dr. Ada is currently a professor in the School of Education at the University of San Francisco.*

Here she comments on the value of poetry and folklore in strengthening the home/school connection and in developing literacy.

Poetry—A Bridge Between the Home and the School

By valuing traditional poetry and folklore, which is part of parents' life experience, schools value parents. When their parents are valued, children sense the school's appreciation for the experiences of their family and community and avoid the kinds of conflicts that can result from feeling forced to choose between the values of the home and those of the school. Consider, for example, the children of an immigrant family. Such families often regard education as the sole means of advancement and communicate to their children that they should accept what the school teaches. If these children then become part of a school that excludes or devalues their family, heritage, and culture, the children will encounter an inevitable conflict. As a result, some children distance themselves from their own parents and become ashamed of them. Other children, who identify with their parents, feel personally rejected; in turn, they respond by rejecting school. Neither of these is a welcome alternative.

> *By valuing traditional poetry and folklore, which is part of parents' life experience, schools value parents. When their parents are valued, children sense the school's appreciation for their family and community.*

Yet neither alternative is necessary, because valuing parents and connecting the curriculum to children's cultures is within reach of all teachers. It requires only a clear and committed awareness that all parents, regardless of their level of formal education, have accumulated much valuable experience and knowledge throughout their lives. Their cultural traditions can enrich not only their own children's lives, but those of all children in the classroom.

When you encourage children to ask their parents to teach them riddles, rhymes, or lullabies, you are promoting communication between parents and children. And when children bring these expressions of folklore to the classroom and you copy, illustrate, and bind their work together to create a book for the classroom library, which is then taken home to share with their families, you are using the power and prestige of the written word to reaffirm the value of the family's contribution.

Connecting the curriculum to children's cultures requires broadening your knowledge and providing numerous opportunities for children to see themselves in the curriculum as well as to value the cultures of other students. As a compendium of culturally connected poetry and background information, *A Chorus of Cultures* will make this process easier for you. Whether you use its calendar format to present poems daily as the year progresses, or whether you select poems from the many indexes to fit your themes or lessons, you will find hundreds of ways to validate the family, heritage, traditions, and experiences of your students.

Validating the experiences of students from homes where a language other than English is spoken means celebrating language diversity as well as cultural diversity. Even when we do not speak that language, we can discuss the importance and value of speaking two or more languages. And when we encourage children to teach poems and songs in home languages to the whole class, we send a powerful message.

It is also our responsibility to support children in maintaining their mother tongue so that they keep open meaningful communication with their parents, as well as future career options in fields such as translation, international business, and teaching.

Poetry Awakens the Poet in Each Child

Children can read, recite, sing, and play along to poetry; they can also create poetry. Children are natural poets, with their openness, their wonder, their capacity to see truth, and their inventiveness at creating metaphors.

In order to awaken the poet's voice within each child, it is important to surround children with poetry. A new poem can be introduced each day, while familiar poems are remembered, re-read, and recited as well. One learns to write by reading and by listening to stories that are told or read aloud. Likewise, one learns to create poetry by reading, listening to, memorizing, and retelling good poetry.

It is also important to validate the variety of expression, to assure all children that they are poets, and to invite them to express themselves freely through poetry. It can help to set aside a special part of each day for creating poetry. Minimize interruptions with a sign on the door that says SILENCE: POETS AT WORK and create a quiet atmosphere with soothing background music. It is especially important for children to see you reading your favorite poets and writing your own poetry during this time.

Among the poems included in *A Chorus of Cultures*, many are effective frameworks for children's own writing: haiku, cinquains, acrostics, etc. But it is important to encourage free expression. Once they have listened to and recited some poems, children can simply be invited to write their own poetry.

Children can create their own anthology along the way, collecting the poems written throughout the year. Accept all poems as a form of self-expression and respond to the authenticity and sincerity of that expression, whether one verse or many, whether based upon models or the result of free-form writing.

Poetry can be a life-long, loyal friend and companion. If, in their search for poetic expression, children learn to recognize their own feelings, open themselves to the information brought to them by their own senses, and learn to observe carefully the world around them, they will also be preparing themselves to become poets of life itself, creators of the verse of daily living.

Alma Flor Ada

> *One learns to create poetry by reading, listening to, memorizing, and retelling good poetry.*

PROGRAM COMPONENTS

Anthology

Organized like a calendar, with a poem-a-day format, the **Anthology** is a rich resource of multicultural poems, songs, and folklore. The 365 entries span a wide variety of levels and topics, from seasons and celebrations to self-concept and siblings.

Thematically grouped selections feature classic, award-winning poets, contemporary poets writing for *A Chorus of Cultures*, and the fresh perspective of children and young people from around the U.S. (our "Young Voices"), as well as traditional folklore from many cultures.

Whole-language activities based on the poems and themes develop literacy and extend concepts across the curriculum. Special tips for involving students acquiring English and for incorporating a multicultural focus in your classroom are included throughout.

Poetry Charts and Small Books

Thirty-six poems from the **Anthology**—one for each week of the school year—also appear on 17" x 22" charts. Beautifully illustrated by culturally connected artists, these charts vividly illustrate that diversity is a concept worth celebrating.

The flip-chart easel that houses the charts has three rings at the top to allow for removal of individual poems so that they can be displayed separately. With the **Small Book** versions of the charts, students can read and enjoy the poetry on their own.

Music Tapes

Four tapes, one for each season, contain authentic and engaging arrangements of selected songs and poems from the **Anthology.** Each song is presented with a vocal rendition, followed by a repetition of the instrumental version—perfect accompaniment for your children's own voices.

A LOOK INSIDE THE ANTHOLOGY

Literary Content

Here in the pages of the **Anthology** you will find the most exciting collection of contemporary multicultural poetry and folklore ever assembled for use with children. The **Anthology** contains entries selected for:

✦ literary merit and variety

✦ appeal to children

✦ representation of many different authors from a variety of cultures

✦ cultural authenticity

✦ significant themes

✦ instructional value

The folklore selections come from the traditions of a wide variety of cultures. Such folklore is important to include not only for its popularity but also because its use in the classroom validates the cultural heritage that children have experienced at home.

Classic and contemporary selections by renowned poets also abound throughout the **Anthology.** Great care was taken in selecting these poems to present works by many different authors. More than 200 authors are represented in the **Anthology,** including such poets as Alma Flor Ada, Arnold Adoff, Marilou Awiakta, Gwendolyn Brooks, Joseph Bruchac, Lucille Clifton, John Ciardi, Ernesto Galarza, Nikki Giovanni, Eloise Greenfield, Lee Bennett Hopkins, Langston Hughes, Myra Cohn Livingston, Eve Merriam, Gary Soto, Mitsuye Yamada, and Charlotte Zolotow. *A Chorus of Cultures* also has the distinction of presenting new voices—such as those of Sarah Chan, Carmen Tafolla, and Doris Seale—poets whose works speak of cultural heritage and diversity. The chorus wouldn't be complete without Young Voices—the schoolchildren living everywhere from Philadelphia and New York City to San Francisco's Chinatown and the desert Southwest who are featured throughout *A Chorus of Cultures.*

> *Great care was taken in selecting culturally authentic poems that represent the cultural diversity of the United States.*

The Calendar Format

Organized into seasons and months, the **Anthology** presents selections in a poem-a-day format.

The **Season Opener** sets the tone for the upcoming season and suggests related multicultural literature, both fiction and nonfiction. Recommendations for related multicultural trade books are also made throughout the **Anthology.**

AUTUMN

Fall is green leaves changing to rust—
Earth turning into a cold, hard crust.
—*Lee Bennett Hopkins*

MULTICULTURAL TRADE BOOKS

Anno, Mitsumasa. **Anno's U.S.A.** (Philomel, 1983). A traveler recounts his journey from the East to the West.

Caines, Jeannette. **I Need a Lunch Box** (HarperCollins, 1988). A boy wants a lunch box because his sister, who is entering first grade, gets one.

Delacre, Lulu. **Arroz Con Leche: Popular Songs and Rhymes from Latin America** (Scholastic, 1989). A resource of folk culture, in Spanish and English.

Haskins, Jim. **Count Your Way Through . . .** (Carolrhoda). A series of counting books. Titles include **Africa** (Swahili), **Arabia, Canada** (French), **China, Germany, India, Israel, Japan, Korea, Mexico,** and **Russia.**

Dorros, Arthur. **Abuela** (Dutton, 1991). A girl and her grandmother take an amazing tour of New York City.

Greenfield, Eloise. **Grandpa's Face** (Philomel, 1988). A girl visits her grandfather at the theater and is surprised by the man she sees.

58

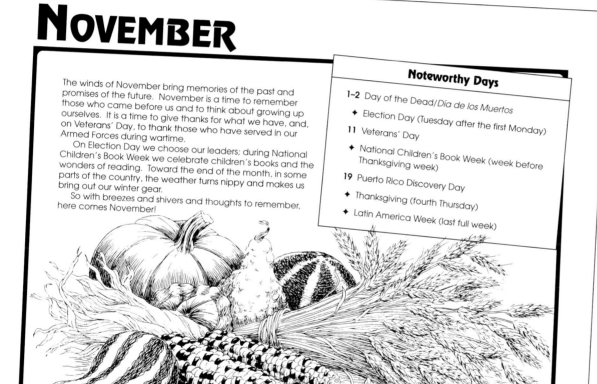

NOVEMBER

The winds of November bring memories of the past and promises of the future. November is a time to remember those who came before us and to think about growing up ourselves. It is a time to give thanks for what we have, and, on Veterans' Day, to thank those who have served in our Armed Forces during wartime.

On Election Day we choose our leaders; during National Children's Book Week we celebrate children's books and the wonders of reading. Toward the end of the month, in some parts of the country, the weather turns nippy and makes us bring out our winter gear.

So with breezes and shivers and thoughts to remember, here comes November!

Noteworthy Days

1–2 Day of the Dead/*Día de los Muertos*

✦ Election Day (Tuesday after the first Monday)

11 Veterans' Day

✦ National Children's Book Week (week before Thanksgiving week)

19 Puerto Rico Discovery Day

✦ Thanksgiving (fourth Thursday)

✦ Latin America Week (last full week)

85

The **Month Opener** summarizes the noteworthy themes, days, and seasonal activities of the month. The entries in **Noteworthy Days** appear in the **Anthology** with related poetry.

Holidays and events that do not fall on a consistent date are represented by a diamond and are listed in the order in which they appear in the **Anthology** and at the approximate time of the month when they occur. You can use the tables on page 265 of the **Anthology** to determine the exact date of the moveable cultural/religious celebrations through the year 2003.

The daily selections are grouped by themes—celebrations, heritage, and family, for example—that reflect the seasonal activities and noteworthy days in the month.

A *This **lead-in** sparks the theme.*

B ***Teaching Notes** give tips, when appropriate, for the successful presentation of poems.*

C *Entries with this symbol are available on the **Poetry Charts** and in the **Small Books** for students, with four-color illustration and enlarged text.*

D *Entries with this symbol are available on the **Music Tapes**.*

E ***Explanatory text** gives additional information about the entry, the date, or the theme.* **As a Matter of Fact** *provides factual information,* **CultureShare** *provides cultural context, and* **A Word from the Poet** *presents commentary by the poem's author.*

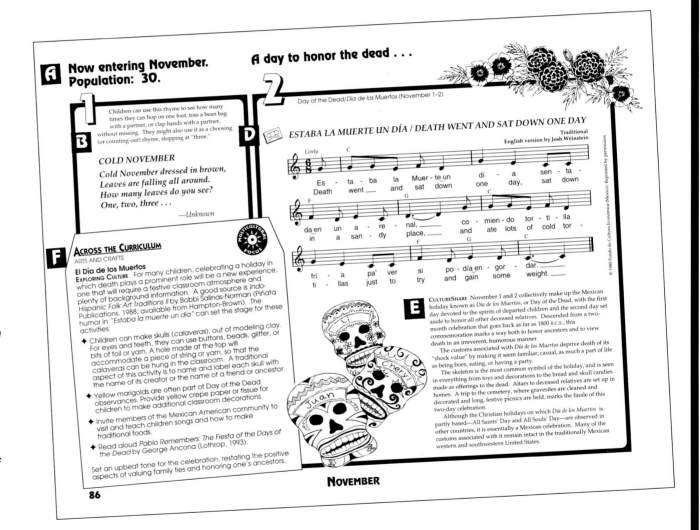

Instructional Activities

Whole-language activities based on the poems and themes develop literacy and extend concepts across the curriculum.

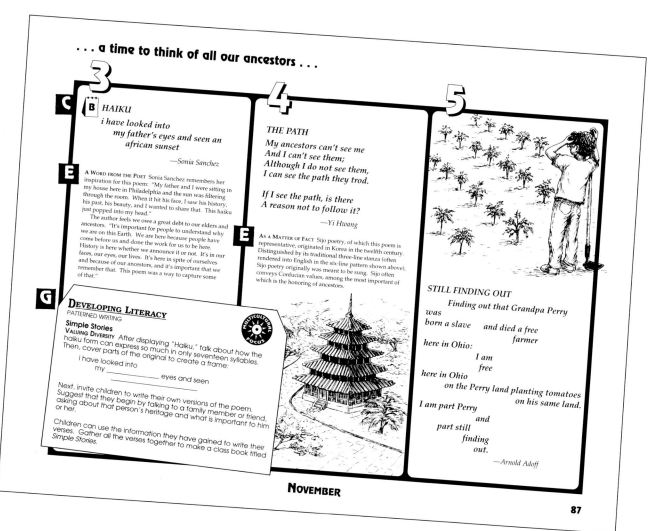

. . . a time to think of all our ancestors . . .

3

B HAIKU

i have looked into
my father's eyes and seen an
african sunset

—Sonia Sanchez

A WORD FROM THE POET Sonia Sanchez remembers her inspiration for this poem: "My father and I were sitting in my house here in Philadelphia and the sun was filtering through the room. When it hit his face, I saw his history, his past, his beauty, and I wanted to share that. This haiku just popped into my head."

The author feels we owe a great debt to our elders and ancestors. "It's important for people to understand why we are on this Earth. We are here because people have come before us and done the work for us to be here. History is here whether we announce it or not. It's in our faces, our eyes, our lives. It's here in spite of ourselves and because of our ancestors, and it's important that we remember that of that."

G

DEVELOPING LITERACY
PATTERNED WRITING

Simple Stories
VALUING DIVERSITY After displaying "Haiku," talk about how the haiku form can express so much in only seventeen syllables. Then, cover parts of the original to create a frame:

i have looked into
my _____ eyes and seen

Next, invite children to write their own versions of the poem. Suggest that they begin by talking to a family member or friend, asking about that person's heritage and what is important to him or her.

Children can use the information they have gained to write their verses. Gather all the verses together to make a class book titled *Simple Stories.*

4

THE PATH

My ancestors can't see me
And I can't see them;
Although I do not see them,
I can see the path they trod.

If I see the path, is there
A reason not to follow it?

—Yi Hwang

AS A MATTER OF FACT Sijo poetry, of which this poem is representative, originated in Korea in the twelfth century. Distinguished by its traditional three-line stanza (often rendered into English in the six-line pattern shown above), Sijo poetry originally was meant to be sung. Sijo often conveys Confucian values, among the most important of which is the honoring of ancestors.

5

STILL FINDING OUT

Finding out that Grandpa Perry
was
born a slave   and died a free
farmer
here in Ohio:
I am
free
here in Ohio
on the Perry land planting tomatoes
on his same land.

I am part Perry
and
part still
finding
out.

—Arnold Adoff

F **Activities Across the Curriculum:**
Arts and Crafts
Mathematics
Music
Reading
Science
Social Studies
Sports & Games
Writing

G **Activities for Developing Literacy:**
Dramatic Interpretation
    Choral Reading
    Pantomime
    Poems for Two Voices
    Readers' Theater
    Sound Effects
    Story Theater
Listening for Language
Listening to Visualize
Memorizing and Reciting
Collecting and Relating Words
Discussion: "Group Talk"
Patterned Writing
Oral Composing
Writing
Reading
Interviewing
Role Play

The **Anthology** includes special features to help you infuse multiculturalism into your classroom in an authentic and effective way.

H Entries with this symbol are poems written by *Young Voices,* school-age children and young people from a variety of cultural backgrounds, U.S. and foreign locations, and ages.

I Activities with this symbol incorporate one of three *Multicultural Focuses*: Promoting Self-Esteem, Exploring Culture, or Valuing Diversity. Many include discussion prompts that give suggestions for dealing with sensitive topics.

J *Especially for Students Acquiring English:* Special tips in activity directions will help you include second-language learners.

K *Footnotes* give meanings and pronunciations for non-English words in the poems.

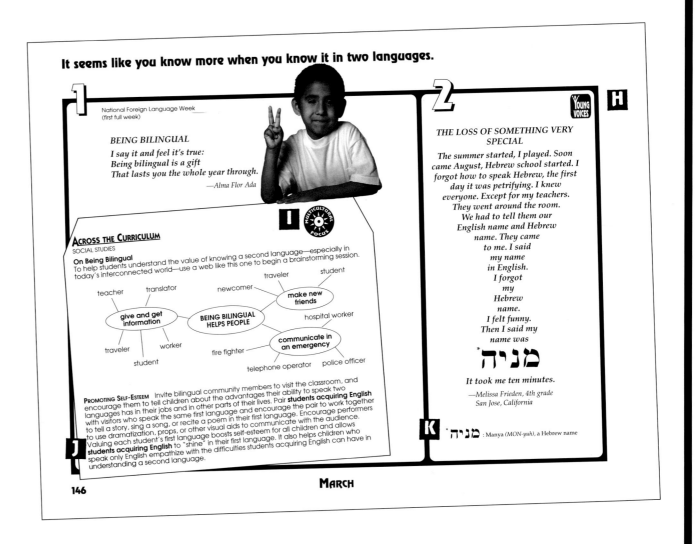

SELECTING POEMS

Looking for a poem for a particular day of the year? Or, perhaps you need poetry for a thematic unit, a poem or two to illustrate onomatopoeia, or just the right song to introduce an important concept. This section will help you access the selections in the **Anthology** for a variety of purposes.

For Daily Use: A Poem a Day

Traditionally, cultures have been very attuned to the seasons, following their lead for planting and harvesting or looking to the weather to guide times for rest or work or celebration. In our fast-paced, technological society, we sometimes forget the importance that seasons and months have had throughout history and still have for children.

Because *A Chorus of Cultures* includes a poem, song, or important thought for each day of the year, you'll find more entries than school days. This allows you to select your favorites for daily readings and to tailor your selections to the time you have available each day and to the age of your students. You'll find poems that delight all ages, poems that challenge students to think, poems that have different meanings to students with different experiences and backgrounds.

Most poems in the **Anthology** can be shared within a minute or two. You might share a poem at the beginning of the school day, to awaken creativity. Or, you might send children off to recess, lunch, or home with a chuckle or a big idea to ponder. Take advantage of those extra minutes when children are lining up to go to the library or the gym.

Some activities that accompany the poems take just a short while to complete; those that are more time-consuming can be saved for when the poem is revisited as part of a thematic unit, as a complement to a reading selection, or within the instruction planned for the rest of the day.

Because the poets represented in the **Anthology** include a wide diversity of ages and ethnic backgrounds, incorporating poems from the **Anthology** in your daily routine is also an easy way to infuse multicultural perspectives and issues on a regular basis—the most effective way to reinforce the value of diversity.

The monthly organization of **A Chorus of Cultures,** *with its poem-a-day format, puts poetry at your fingertips.*

For Thematic Units

The poems in the **Anthology** are grouped according to themes that reflect seasonal activities and noteworthy celebrations and commemorations. Most poems, however, relate to several other themes besides the one that was used to place them into a particular month. All important literary and curricular themes represented by the selections were therefore identified and are presented in the **Index of Themes** on pages 284–296. Use of this index will allow you to select poems to relate to thematic units, to trade-book or basal literature, or to topics of study in content-area lessons.

The **Index of Themes** will also help you design your own themes and units. For example, you might use all of the subthemes indexed under "Family"—siblings, grandparents, parents, aunts and uncles—for your own family unit. Or, you could group the poems for all the cultural celebrations together into a unit that highlights similarities and differences in how people celebrate.

A *Theme names* designate general topics from Activities to Zoo.

B Many general themes have *subthemes* that will help you find just the right poem.

C Each entry consists of the *date* on which the poem appears and the *title* of the poem.

D The *music note* signals entries that are on the *Music Tapes*. A *rectangle* signals entries that appear on the *Poetry Charts* and in the *Small Books* for students.

E Occasional *additional labels* give further details about the entry.

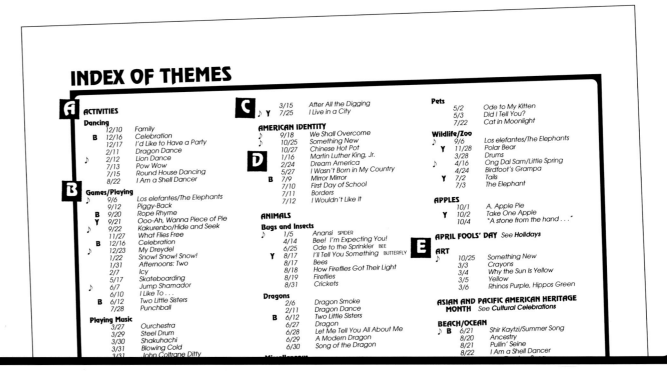

INDEX OF THEMES

A ACTIVITIES

Dancing
	12/10	Family
B	12/16	Celebration
	12/17	I'd Like to Have a Party
	2/11	Dragon Dance
♪	2/12	Lion Dance
	7/13	Pow Wow
	7/15	Round House Dancing
	8/22	I Am a Shell Dancer

B Games/Playing
♪	9/6	Los elefantes/The Elephants
	9/12	Piggy-Back
B	9/20	Rope Rhyme
Y	9/21	Ooo-Ah, Wanna Piece of Pie
♪	9/22	Kakurenbo/Hide and Seek
	11/27	What Flies Free
B	12/16	Celebration
♪	12/23	My Dreydel
	1/22	Snow! Snow! Snow!
	1/31	Afternoons: Two
	2/7	Icy
	5/17	Skateboarding
♪	6/7	Jump Shamador
	6/10	I Like To . . .
B	6/12	Two Little Sisters
	7/28	Punchball

Playing Music
	3/27	Ourchestra
	3/29	Steel Drum
	3/30	Shakuhachi
	3/31	Blowing Cold
	3/31	John Coltrane Ditty

C ♪ Y
	3/15	After All the Digging
	7/25	I Live in a City

AMERICAN IDENTITY
♪	9/18	We Shall Overcome
♪	10/25	Something New
	10/27	Chinese Hot Pot
	1/16	Martin Luther King, Jr.
	2/24	Dream America
	5/27	I Wasn't Born in My Country
B	7/9	Mirror Mirror
	7/10	First Day of School
	7/11	Borders
	7/12	I Wouldn't Like It

D ANIMALS

Bugs and Insects
♪	1/5	Anansi SPIDER
	4/14	Bee! I'm Expecting You!
	6/25	Ode to the Sprinkler BEE
Y	8/17	I'll Tell You Something BUTTERFLY
	8/17	Bees
	8/18	How Fireflies Got Their Light
	8/19	Fireflies
	8/31	Crickets

Dragons
	2/6	Dragon Smoke
	2/11	Dragon Dance
B	6/12	Two Little Sisters
	6/27	Dragon
	6/28	Let Me Tell You All About Me
	6/29	A Modern Dragon
	6/30	Song of the Dragon

Miscellaneous

Pets
	5/2	Ode to My Kitten
	5/3	Did I Tell You?
	7/22	Cat in Moonlight

Wildlife/Zoo
♪	9/6	Los elefantes/The Elephants
Y	11/28	Polar Bear
	3/28	Drums
♪	4/16	Ong Dal Sam/Little Spring
	4/24	Birdfoot's Grampa
Y	7/2	Tails
	7/3	The Elephant

APPLES
	10/1	A. Apple Pie
Y	10/2	Take One Apple
	10/4	"A stone from the hand . . ."

APRIL FOOLS' DAY See *Holidays*

E ART
♪	10/25	Something New
	3/3	Crayons
	3/4	Why the Sun Is Yellow
	3/5	Yellow
	3/6	Rhinos Purple, Hippos Green

ASIAN AND PACIFIC AMERICAN HERITAGE MONTH See *Cultural Celebrations*

BEACH/OCEAN
♪ B	6/21	Shir Kaytzi/Summer Song
	8/20	Ancestry
	8/21	Pullin' Seine
	8/22	I Am a Shell Dancer

For Students Acquiring English

More than 100 poems in the Anthology are appropriate for ESL instruction, so that students acquiring English can reap the benefits and power of multicultural poetry along with the rest of the class. The **Index of Poems Appropriate for ESL Instruction** on pages 266–267 organizes poems by their appropriateness to these stages of language acquisition: Pre-Production (Level 1), Early Production (Level 2), Speech Emergence (Level 3), and Intermediate Fluency (Level 4).

INDEX OF POEMS APPROPRIATE FOR ESL INSTRUCTION

Students acquiring English may be at any one of four stages in their progression toward fluency. This index lists the poems from *A Chorus of Cultures* appropriate to each of these stages of language acquisition: Pre-Production (Level 1), Early Production (Level 2), Speech Emergence (Level 3), and Intermediate Fluency (Level 4).

POEMS ESPECIALLY APPROPRIATE FOR LEVELS 1 AND 2

Poems in this category have simple language and concrete content.

Y	10/2	Take One Apple
Y	10/19	Ears Hear
	10/29	Wouldn't You?
♪	2/16	I Love Everybody
	2/25	Birthday Candles
	3/5	Yellow
	4/17	The Rabbit
B	4/25	I Love the World
Y	5/1	Maytime Magic
Y	7/23	Sleeping Outdoors
Y	8/26	Ravioli
	8/28	Chocolate Rhyme

Poems in this category have predictable text and a regular rhythm and rhyme scheme that makes them easy to memorize and recite. Many songs and raps fall into this category.

Y	9/5	One, Two, Three, Four, Five
♪	9/6	The Elephants
	9/10	Abuelito
	9/12	Piggy-Back
B	10/18	Sampan
Y	10/20	Song of the Train
♪	10/24	Under One Sky
	10/28	Brooms
	11/1	Cold November
	11/9	Good-Bye, Six—Hello, Seven
Y	11/14	Books to the Ceiling
Y	11/28	Polar Bear
	11/29	The Mitten Song
	12/11	Star-Light, Star-Bright
♪	12/15	Great Big Stars
Y	12/19	Bursting
♪	12/23	My Dreydel
	12/25	Must Be Santa
	12/28	Black Is Beautiful
	1/22	Snow! Snow! Snow!
	1/23	January
	1/24	Snow, Snow
Y	2/14	I Love You Little
	2/27	My First Birthday Gift
♪	3/13	We've Come to the Land
	4/6	April
♪	4/16	Little Spring
B	4/22	The Beautiful
	5/3	Did I Tell You?
	5/8	Rainbows

♪	5/19	Train Is a-Comin'
	5/22	Growing Old
♪	6/7	Jump Shamador
	6/10	I Like To . . .
Y	6/19	Daddy
	6/26	The Dragon Boats
	7/5	I Am Freedom's Child
♪	7/21	Rabbit
	8/16	August Heat
Y	8/17	I'll Tell You Something
	8/17	Bees

[column from page 267]

		in a City
		e Did the Baby Go?
		n Annie Was Adopted
		e Poem

APPROPRIATE FOR

ry include some
nd more-complex, less
able for the increasing
Intermediate English
s also offer more
tured discussion and
ward more complex

r School
mber
h, Wanna Piece of Pie
verybody
n

Gifts
ia Is . . .
ple
r
v Year
Future
g a New Year Means
Song

ound

ngual

urple, Hippos Green
h

lors

B	3/25	If They Hate Me
Y	4/4	I Am Running in a Circle
Y	4/7	Spring Rain
	5/15	Preferred Vehicles
Y	5/18	Subways Are People
	5/23	Old Friends
	5/27	I Wasn't Born in My Country
B	6/12	Two Little Sisters
B	6/18	My Father
	7/3	The Elephant
	7/16	Another Kid
B	7/17	The Palet Man
	7/24	The Prairie
Y	7/26	Sunrise
	7/29	Rudolph Is Tired of the City
	8/15	The Feast of Lanterns

For Author Awareness

The **Index of Authors** on pages 275–281 can help you locate works by the poets included in *A Chorus of Cultures* for special author studies.

For Literary Appreciation

The **Index of Genres** on pages 282–283 references poems in the **Anthology** that represent different types of poetry such as cinquain, haiku, and narrative poetry.

For Special Activities

An activity involving a poem can sometimes be the perfect way to spark a lesson or kick off Parents' Night. To locate a poem suitable for a specific kind of activity, such as choral reading or interviewing, see the **Activities Index** on page 297.

A poem can sometimes be the perfect way to spark a lesson.

PRESENTING POETRY

Poetry is meant to be read aloud—and there are many ways to give a poem its say! Here are some tips for presenting the poems in *A Chorus of Cultures*.

✦ Read the poem to yourself several times before reading it to the group, planning oral reading techniques that will reinforce the meaning and beauty of the poem. When you read, be expressive, but don't exaggerate unnecessarily.

✦ Let the meaning guide your pacing and rhythm. It's not necessary, for example, to stop at the end of each line. Consider "There Is a Place," in which the title is part of the poem and the line breaks do not indicate pauses, or "I Am Running in a Circle," which should be read quickly and breathlessly.

THERE IS A PLACE

on
the couch
    for
     grandma
and
a place on
     grandma
for
  me
  in front
of
the
  fire
    and pop
      ping
     corn

—*Arnold Adoff*

I AM RUNNING IN A CIRCLE

I am running in a circle
and my feet are getting sore,
and my head is
spinning
spinning
as it's never spun before,
I am
dizzy
dizzy
dizzy.
Oh! I cannot bear much more,
I am trapped in a
revolving
. . . volving
. . . volving
. . . volving door!

—*Jack Prelutsky*

Other poems need to be read slowly. With "Listen," a slower pace creates an air of mystery and gives children time to create a mental picture:

LISTEN

every
landscape

a wondrous
story

—Francisco X. Alarcón

Still others require their own special pace and beat. Consider this poem, in which the stress on the non-italicized words and the proper pacing will allow children to hear the "train" build up speed:

SONG OF THE TRAIN

1st Stanza: Slowly	2nd Stanza: Increase Rate	3rd Stanza: Quickly
Clickety-clack,	*Clickety-clack,*	*Riding in front*
Wheels on the track,	*Over the crack,*	*Riding in back,*
This is the way	*Faster and faster*	*Everyone hears*
They begin the attack:	*The song of the track:*	*The song of the track:*
Click-ety-clack,	*Clickety-clack,*	*Clickety-clack,*
Click-ety-clack,	*Clickety-clack,*	*Clickety-clack,*
Click-ety, **clack-ety**	*Clickety, clackety,*	*Clickety-clickety,*
Click-ety	**Clackety**	*Clackety*
Clack.	*Clack.*	**Clack.**

—David McCord

◆ Let the inner music of the poem come out. By reading this poem with an emphasis on the *s* sounds, you can create the sound of slipping and sliding.

ICY

I slip and I slide
On the slippery ice;
I skid and I glide—
Oh, isn't it nice
To lie on your tummy
And slither and skim
On the slick crust of snow
Where you skid as you swim?

—Rhoda W. Bacmeister

◆ Use the **Music Tapes** to present entries in the **Anthology** that appear with a cassette logo. Songs have a vocal rendition, followed by an instrumental version. Use the vocal rendition to present the song. Once children know the words, use the instrumental version to accompany their singing.

◆ Vary the presenter—a child in your class, an older student, a parent, a staff member, a puppet, a cassette recording, the principal over the P.A.—and keep your students hooked on poetry. An effective technique is to establish a pool of community members—especially as language and culture "experts"— that you can call on regularly to participate in poetry readings and activities.

◆ Vary the presentation. Some poems just need a whisper.

POEM

I loved my friend.
He went away from me.
There's nothing more to say.
The poem ends,
Soft as it began—
I loved my friend.

—Langston Hughes

Other poems need to be read with animation and different voices for the characters and narrator.

TOMMY'S MOMMY

Mommy did you bring my flippers
Tommy asked his mommy

Is that all you have to say
Mommy asked her Tommy

Did you bring my diving mask
Tommy asked his Mommy

Is that all you have to say
Mommy asked her Tommy

Did you bring my snorkel
Tommy asked his Mommy

Is that all you have to say
Mommy asked her Tommy

I love you Mommy
Tommy said Did you bring them Did you

I love you Tommy Mommy said
Yes I brought them to you

—Nikki Giovanni

◆ For mood poems, set the scene with music, lighting, or sound effects. For example, when you present "Just a Fire" (12/4)*, you might make the room as dark as possible and read the poem by flashlight (or candlelight, if possible). Or, when you present "John Coltrane Ditty" (3/31), you might play jazz music to enhance its meaning:

JOHN COLTRANE DITTY

John be playin'
I be swayin'
help me git dat jazz

He be tootin'
I be hootin'
help me git dat jazz

I be crowin'
while he blowin'
funky razamataz

John be screechin'
I be reachin'
reachin' out for jazz!

—*Dakari Kamau Hru*

Teaching notes that precede some of the poems in this **Anthology** will give you further ideas for effective presentations and sources for "mood" music to use.

*Dates in parentheses refer to the date in the **Anthology** on which the poem appears. For example, "Just a Fire" appears on December 4.

29

Presenting Poems to Students Acquiring English

Almost all classrooms include some students who are on the road to fluency in English. A careful selection of poems (see pages 266–267) along with strategies that make the poems comprehensible, add up to success for students acquiring English (as well as for other students who would benefit from multimodal instruction and language support). Here are some effective teaching strategies.

✦ To provide visual context for the meaning:

— point to pictures and photographs, or draw sketches, as you read a poem. See, for example, "Ears Hear" (10/19). Some **Activity Sheets,** such as those on pages 246 and 255, contain reproducible picture cards for several poems.

— use realia—actual objects—to accompany a reading of the poem. For example, bring in an apple and an apple core for "Take One Apple" (10/2).

— use pantomime, gestures, facial expressions, body movements, sound effects, and intonation to reinforce meaning and increase enjoyment with poems like "Bursting" (12/19) and "I Am Beside Myself" (12/20).

✦ To increase verbal clues, restate text, define words, or give synonyms. For example, with "Success" (10/6), you could read the poem once, then restate its meaning: "I can do anything I try to do; I am wonderful; I can do things that are hard to do." Finally, read the poem again.

✦ To reinforce meaning, use activities like Total Physical Response (TPR) and Directed Drawing. TPR involves whole-body movements that match oral cues. For example, after children have heard (and seen) you read "Subways Are People" (5/18), invite them to move with you as you read the poem again. In Directed Drawing activities, you draw something as you read a poem or as you are giving directions. Students simultaneously draw the same thing, step by step, with you. The activity for October 30 is an example of a Directed Draw.

SUCCESS

I think I can succeed in anything I want to do. Myself—I am a surprising human being.

—Unknown

DEVELOPING LITERACY THROUGH POETRY

Because poetry is printed language meant to be read aloud, it touches all the language arts—listening, speaking, reading, and writing. In fact, poetry invites so much involvement with language that it has great instructional power in developing literacy. Along the way, it can also serve as a literature base for exploring the content areas: science, social studies, mathematics, music, arts and crafts, and sports and games.

The activity "cards" throughout this **Anthology** will give you specific ideas for content-area connections and literacy experiences. Activities that connect to the content areas appear on the Across the Curriculum "cards." The literacy experiences, which appear on the Developing Literacy "cards" and in some teaching notes, cover the following:

✦ Dramatic Interpretation

✦ Listening for Language

✦ Listening to Visualize

✦ Memorizing and Reciting

✦ Collecting and Relating Words for Vocabulary Development

✦ Discussion: "Group Talk"

✦ Patterned Writing

✦ Oral Composing

✦ Writing

✦ Reading

This section describes each of these literacy experiences, offering general strategies to promote their success in your classroom and to give you ideas for your own activities.

> *Because poetry is printed language meant to be read aloud, it touches all the language arts — listening, speaking, reading, and writing.*

Dramatic Interpretation

Dramatic interpretation involves children physically with poetry. Not only is physical involvement especially engaging to children, but it also puts them at ease and encourages listening comprehension. Dramatic interpretation includes:

✦ movement (whole body or gesture) that reflects the meaning of the poem

✦ pantomime

✦ puppetry

✦ story theater

✦ and dramatic vocal interpretations, such as choral reading, poems for two voices, and Readers' Theater

In planning dramatic interpretations, look for actions that can be easily represented. For example the actions in "I Like To . . ." could be represented through movement or pantomime.

Actions are not the only things that can be represented. In the example below, gestures can reinforce the *feelings* in the poem. Children can put a fist on one hip for line 1, the other fist on the other hip for line 2, and both thumbs pointed at the chest for line 3, before they act out the action in line 4.

I LIKE TO . . .

This is the way I like to swim,
Over at the pool.
This is the way I roller skate,
When I'm not in school.
This is the way I fly my kite,
When the wind begins to blow.
This is the way I play jump rope,
See how fast I can go.

—Unknown

PIÑATA
Don't want silver and
Don't care for gold.
But I just gotta
Break that piñata!

— Spanish traditional rhyme
English version by Juan Quintana

Dramatic interpretation can involve listening only or listening and speaking. Listening activities such as pantomimes and story theater are especially effective with shy children and students acquiring English because they allow silent participation.

Dramatic interpretation continues to have value for children who are accomplished speakers, offering the challenge of staging puppet shows or a play.

Any poem whose text suggests multiple parts lends itself to a choral reading, such as "Pullin' Seine" (8/21), in which one group reads the verbs in the left-hand column and another reads the words in the right-hand column.

from *PULLIN' SEINE*

Splash!   *Afternoon tide roll in.*
Heave!   *Fishermen pullin' seine.*
Come on! *Jasmine pulls me along.*

          —Lynn Joseph

Listening activities are especially effective with shy children and students acquiring English because they allow silent participation.

Other good candidates for choral readings are poems with repetitive lines, such as "Chant of the Working People" (9/4).

from *CHANT OF THE WORKING PEOPLE*

When the sun comes up
I set out
to build our life,
when the sun comes up,
for I am the people,
the working people,
when the sun comes up,
when the sun
when the sun
when the sun comes up.

  —David Chericián (original in Spanish)

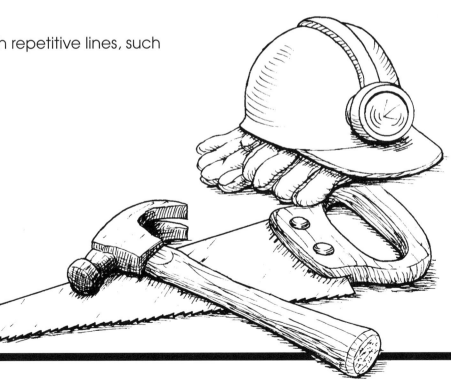

from *LION DANCE*

Drum drum gong drum
gong gong cymbal gong
gong she fah chai
cymbal clang drum clash

—*Trevor Millum*

Drum drum gong drum

gong gong cymbal gong

gong she fah chai   gong she fah chai

cymbal clang

drum clash

Poems for two voices and Readers' Theater provide effective language experiences for older children.

In poems for two voices, lines are assigned to one or both voices to achieve dramatic effect. Students read from scripts like the one at left prepared for "Lion Dance" (2/12). Voice 1 reads the lines in the left column. Voice 2 reads those in the right column. The two voices come together on the boldfaced lines. Voices can be represented by individuals or groups.

Readers' Theater requires poems such as "Rice and Rose Bowl Blues" (3/11) that allow roles to be assigned for different characters. Again, students read from specially prepared scripts. Usually, they sit in a circle to perform the poem and do not use props, costumes, or dramatic effects other than their voices. One student reads the narrator's role, while others read the parts of the characters.

Listening for Language

When children listen for the sounds, rhyme, repetition, and cadence of poetry, they develop careful listening habits and gain an appreciation for language.

Poems with a clear rhyme such as "Spring Rain" (4/7), or a repeating line such as "Sea Timeless Song" (8/23), or a strong beat such as "The Dragon Boats" (6/26), or interesting sound words such as "Sampan" (10/18) are good choices for listening experiences, which can, of course, be enhanced by:

✦ fingerplay, pantomime, and other dramatic interpretations

✦ rhythmic clapping or tapping

✦ voice changes that reflect the meaning of sound words

✦ oral cloze readings, in which children supply a rhyming word

✦ choral recitations in which children chant the repetitive text

Listening to Visualize

The ability to visualize, or create mental images, is an important thinking strategy that affects conceptualization and comprehension as well as oral and written expression. Listening to poetry gives excellent experience in visualizing.

The content and language of poetry, especially the compression that is characteristic of many poems, affect the nature and difficulty of the visualizing experience. Some poems with rich, descriptive detail such as "Cat in Moonlight" (7/22) allow children to form a single, composite picture. Story poems like "Bubie Annie" (12/9) involve children in visualizing sequential action. Metaphoric poems with abstract images like "Borinquen" (9/27) present more-challenging opportunities, but often produce even greater imaginative results.

Like all thinking processes, visualizing is invisible. To help make it more visible, encourage children to describe their mental pictures in discussions or to reproduce them through art.

Memorizing and Reciting

Poetry encourages fluent oral expression because it is so natural to say a poem aloud. When presenting a poem for memorization and recitation, give children several opportunities to hear it, encouraging them to chime in when they can.

Length and language affect the difficulty of poems for memorization. Chants and short poems with clear rhyme, repetition, and/or a consistent beat are easier to remember than longer poems or ones with varying language patterns.

Children may feel more comfortable reciting poems in a group at first. Dramatic interpretation techniques also put children at ease and serve as an aid to remembering the poem. Once children have plenty of group experience, they will be eager to choose a poem of their own for independent presentation.

Each week you might choose one poem for the group to learn, moving from group recitations to individual ones as the week goes along. The **Poetry Charts** and **Small Books** that accompany *A Chorus of Cultures* are ideal for this purpose since 36 poems are included, one for each week of the school year.

BORINQUEN

Borinquen, my little island,
Like a seashell in the sun—
On the outside, like a flower;
On the inside, there's a song.

—Isabel Freire de Matos
(original in Spanish)
English version by
Juan Quintana

Collecting and Relating Words for Vocabulary Development

The distinctive language of poetry cannot help but enrich children's vocabularies. As you share poems with children, encourage them to collect words from the poems in a variety of ways:

◆ using personal journals to record words that they particularly like

◆ categorizing and filing words for special purposes; for example, delicious descriptive words in a file for the Writing Center or a mural dictionary of rhyming words

◆ making class lists of words that fit a particular theme and displaying them prominently on butcher paper or the bulletin board so that they can add to the lists throughout the thematic unit.

Most poems can also serve as a springboard to expanding vocabulary by relating words. The four underscored words in "Preferred Vehicles," for example, can be used to start a word web about transportation.

PREFERRED VEHICLES

A <u>bicycle</u>'s fine for a little trip
   Up the street or down;
An <u>automobile</u> for a longer trip,
   Off to another town;
An <u>airplane</u>'s fine for around the world,
   To many a far-out place;
And a <u>rocket</u>, oh, for the longest trip
   Away into outer space.

          —Leland B. Jacobs

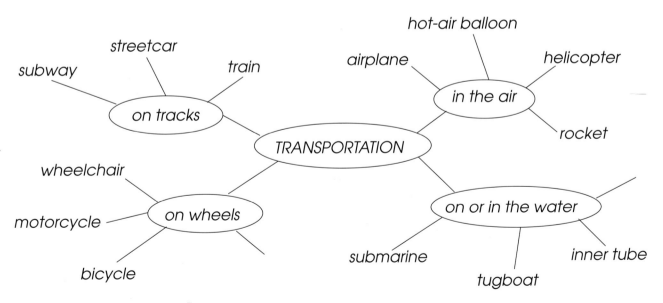

As children suggest words for the web, add category names, such as *land, air, water*, so that the relationships of the words are sharpened in the completed web. Seeing these relationships helps children clarify meanings and remember them. This type of categorization is a useful strategy for students acquiring English.

Often activities on relating words lead to patterned-writing or oral-composing activities (see pages 38–40) because they are an effective way to help children generate the language and ideas they need to express themselves creatively.

Discussion: "Group Talk"

Poetry is about ideas and ideas are worth talking about. *A Chorus of Cultures* contains scores of poems and themes guaranteed to spark substantive discussions—from sharing personal experiences to generating questions and expressing opinions. Sometimes a short poem like "Image" (3/24) can set forth a big idea, worthy of thought and discussion. This three-line poem can be a powerful self-esteem booster for children who have been on the receiving end of prejudice and discrimination, as well as an eye-opener for all students. Here are a few good rules of thumb to follow for effective Group Talks:

IMAGE

I cannot be hurt anymore.
I see that their arrows
are really boomerangs.

—Henry Dumas

+ Once children are familiar with the poem, allow them to "warm up" for the discussion by jotting down responses first or by asking their own questions.

+ Then, ask a few open-ended questions to generate a variety of responses.

+ Acknowledge all responses and make sure children know that there are no "right answers." A safe, caring environment produces the best discussions.

+ Try Think-Pair-Share, where children consider a question, discuss it with a partner, and then partners share their thoughts with the whole group.

+ When children need to work through a problem or generate a lot of questions about a topic, form buzz groups of 5–6 children.

+ If discussions bog down in misunderstanding, you might try a role play, where students with differing viewpoints take on the opposite perspective. Walking in someone else's shoes can make a powerful impression.

Patterned Writing

Many poems, due to their rhyme, rhythm, repetition, or structure, have a pattern to their lines that children can follow to create new poems. These new poems, called *innovations,* are powerful evidence to children of their ability to write.

Innovations can vary from simple substitutions of a single word to the creation of an entirely new poem that uses the pattern but little of the language of the original. Consider these innovations on "Being Bilingual" (3/1):

BEING BILINGUAL
I say it and feel it's true;
Being bilingual is a gift
That lasts you the whole year
  through.

  —Alma Flor Ada

BEING HAPPY
I say it and feel it's true;
Being happy is a gift
That lasts you the whole year
  through.

Simple innovation:
one-word substitution

HAVING FRIENDS
I say it and feel it's true;
Having friends is a joy
That lasts you the whole year
  through.

More complex innovation:
new example

MAKING FRIENDS
I say it and feel it's true
Becoming your friend is a gift
A gift for me and for you.

Entirely new poem

As you evaluate poems for patterned writing, look for a language pattern that can be duplicated. Try inserting blank lines in the poem and check that you can see many different possibilities for filling them. Applying that approach to "Teasing" (1/29), for example, helps you see that the frame will be fertile ground for children to create new poems about their own experiences.

from *TEASING*

Teasing is being laughed at.
It feels like a needle.

Teasing is being told your clothes are ugly.
It looks like tears in your eyes.

  —José Jiménez, 5th grade

Teasing is _____
It feels like _____

Teasing is _____
It looks like _____

Before involving children in innovations, be sure they have internalized the pattern of the original poem through hearing it read aloud several times. Then:

✦ display the frame with blank lines for the innovation

✦ lead the group in brainstorming their ideas

✦ record the ideas on chart paper

Once the brainstorming is complete, individuals or groups can write or dictate their innovations, and soon you'll have a wealth of new poems to read!

Oral Composing

For experiences in oral composing, children create oral innovations in much the same way as with patterned writing. These experiences, however, can be quicker and often involve songs, such as "Ravioli" (8/26), or rhymes, such as "I Love You Little" (2/14), with the kind of language play that is so much fun to say out loud.

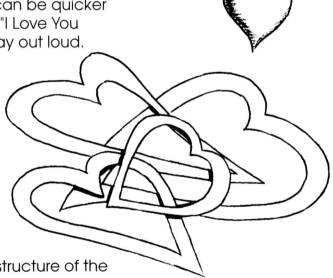

I LOVE YOU LITTLE

I love you little,
I love you lots,
My love for you would fill ten pots,
Fifteen buckets,
Sixteen cans,
Three teacups
and four dishpans.

—*Unknown*

In addition to patterned innovations that use the language and structure of the poems, oral composing also includes creating an original oral response to a poem: making up and telling new episodes, new endings, or related stories, for example. Story poems such as "Birdfoot's Grampa" (4/24) or poems and songs with substantive content, such as "We Shall Overcome" (9/18) or "Something New" (10/25), lend themselves to this type of oral composing.

A special kind of oral composing activity, called poetic dialogue, is especially effective in restoring faith among older children in their ability to compose. To prepare for a poetic dialogue, write a poem unfamiliar to the children on a transparency, leaving space between the lines. When you conduct the first poetic dialogue, work with the group in this way:

✦ Display the lines on the transparency one at a time and ask children to suggest the next line.

✦ Write each new line in place.

✦ Then, read the new poem aloud, supplying the lines of the original poem, while the group reads the ones they have created.

When children are familiar with the process, they can record their own lines on their own papers. Then you can choose a variety of partners to participate in the poetic dialogue. Try reading your lines before your partner's and vice versa; poems with new meaning will be created just by varying the order of the lines. Try reading with more than one partner: You read the first line of the poem; child 1 reads a line, child 2 reads a line; the process then repeats with the second line of the poem.

Here is an example of a poetic dialogue created through this process for "I Am Sun Shining" (10/9).

I am sun shining
I am moon gleaming.
I am the warm sun that shines on the earth.
I am the rain that makes things grow.
I am the hot warm sun shining in the sky.
I am the cool breezes blowing by.

I AM SUN SHINING

I am sun shining.
I am the warm sun that shines on the earth.
I am the hot warm sun shining in the sky.
I am the clouds moving in the sky.
I am the bright clouds that shine.
I am the sun setting.
I am the clouds moving away.
I am myself.

—Marla Want, age 11

In selecting poems for poetic dialogues, look for ones with unity of thought and clear images.

Writing

Poetry promotes writing in dozens of ways. When children write innovations on poems, they gain confidence in writing and begin to view themselves as authors. Poetry can also inspire a variety of original writing—from recording personal responses in a journal, to writing a letter, to composing new poetry.

Suggestions for writing activities are included on both Developing Literacy and Across the Curriculum activity "cards." Be sure to spend ample time in the prewriting phase, using the poetry to build content for the writing activity, brainstorming ideas and language, and encouraging children to plan their compositions before writing their first drafts.

The next stages of the writing process—revising and proofreading—will help children polish their work.

The final stage—publishing—involves producing the composition in a finished way, ready to share. It is important that this final product always have a tangible form, so that the children's work receives the respect it deserves.

Keep in mind that the intensely personal nature of poetry means that frequent opportunities for written personal response will arise. You might consider having older children keep poetry journals to chart their feelings, opinions, and experiences with the poetry and themes in the **Anthology.** Types of journals include:

◆ literary journals, in which children express their feelings about and responses to the poetry

◆ dialogue journals, between you and each child, in which you write responses to students' reflections and questions on a daily or weekly basis

◆ buddy journals, between two children, in which they share ideas and give each other feedback

Reading

Any instructional program whose mission is to develop literacy has, at its core, reading—not only the ability to read, but the desire to read. Poetry, especially multicultural poetry, can inspire even the youngest of children to read books to get to know themselves and others better.

The poetry in *A Chorus of Cultures* can foster a love of reading. Children can read and reread favorite poems from the **Poetry Charts** as a group, or privately in the **Small Books.** They can go off into poetry anthologies to read more poems by poets they love. Or, children might be inspired by a theme—or an activity within a theme—to read more about their own or others' cultural customs and traditions.

Throughout the **Anthology**—on the pages that open a new season, on the activity cards, in Teaching Notes and explanatory text—appropriate, authentic, multicultural trade-book titles are suggested. Before beginning a theme, you might scan for titles you'd like to have on hand—in your Reading Center or in your school library—as children begin their explorations.

Of course, the most important goal is that children read—for pleasure, for information, for a broader world view—and that the books they read accurately reflect their own culture and the cultures of others. Here are some sources of books and some books *about* books—to help you broaden and build your classroom library collection.

Sources of Multicultural Literature

- AWAIR (Arab World and Islamic Resources and School Services), 2095 Rose Street, Suite 4, Berkeley, CA 94709
- Anti-Defamation League of B'nai B'rith, 823 UN Plaza, New York, NY 10017
- *A Hispanic Heritage: A Guide to Juvenile Books about Hispanic People and Culture,* Isabel Schon (Scarecrow, 1980)
- *Literature for Children About Asians and Asian Americans,* Esther C. Jenkins and Mary C. Austin (Greenwood, 1987)

- *Multicultural Literature for Children and Young Adults,* Ginny Moore Kruse and Kathleen T. Horning (Cooperative Children's Book Center, 1991)
- *Our Family, Our Friends, Our World: An Annotated Guide to Significant Multicultural Books for Children and Teenagers,* Lyn Miller-Lachman (Bowker, 1991)
- *Shadow and Substance: Afro-American Experience in Contemporary Children's Fiction,* Rudine Sims (National Council of Teachers of English, 1982)
- *Teaching Multicultural Literature in Grades K-8,* Violet J. Harris, ed. (Christopher-Gordon, 1992)
- *Through Indian Eyes: The Native Experience in Books for Children,* edited by Beverly Slapin and Doris Seale (New Society, 1992)
- *Where I Come From!* Victor Cockburn and Judith Steinbergh (Talking Stone Productions, 1992) Available from Hampton-Brown Books.

Including Students Acquiring English

In our multicultural society, it makes good sense for all students' interests and needs—including those of linguistically diverse students—to be reflected in the curriculum *and* in each day's instruction. Inclusion means acknowledgment, which can foster respect and understanding of cultural and linguistic diversity.

Inclusion has an additional benefit. *All* students are enriched by the wealth of experiences brought to the classroom by children of culturally diverse backgrounds. Perspectives widen and children learn to value their own culture as well as those of others.

A Chorus of Cultures celebrates the contributions students acquiring English make to the classroom, while recognizing the unique needs these students have. Throughout the **Anthology,** you'll see special tips for tailoring the activities to include **students acquiring English.** See the activity below and the ones on pages 78, 95, 152, and 184 for examples.

These tips, summarized below, will help you adapt the good teaching strategies you already use for students at various stages of language proficiency.

> **A Chorus of Cultures** *celebrates the contributions students acquiring English make to the classroom, while recognizing the unique needs these students have.*

DEVELOPING LITERACY
WRITING

Kindred Spirits
After reading these proverbs, challenge children to write their own proverb, using *A friend is* as a beginning. Younger children can illustrate an act of friendship, while **students acquiring English** might start with a drawing and then work with a more-fluent partner to put their proverbs into words.

General Strategies

✦ Build fluency in a low-anxiety setting through echo readings, choral readings, repeated listenings to audiocassettes. As students' fluency improves, have them make their own recordings of poems, songs, and chants.

✦ Always model fluent reading and reciting. The most effective technique is to release responsibility gradually to students, from teacher readings to group readings to paired readings to individual performance.

✦ When assigning poems for memorization and recitation or other dramatic interpretation techniques, break the poem into manageable chunks.

✦ Emphasize rhythm and rhyme—it's what makes language exciting and memorable. And select themes, poems, and activities appropriate to students' development level, ones that reflect their needs, interests, and life experiences.

✦ Provide manipulatives and other props to children as they engage in dramatic interpretation to aid memorization and provide more meaningful context.

✦ Pair or group less-proficient students with more-proficient learners.

✦ In pantomimes and dramatizations, assign the least language-dependent roles to students at the earliest levels of language acquisition.

✦ Allow students to discuss key concepts in small groups first, perhaps in native-language groups, before joining a class discussion.

✦ Include students in heterogeneous groups, especially for activity-oriented tasks.

✦ Ask students to label and manipulate pictures and/or real objects.

Strategies for Level 1—Pre-Production

✦ Respect students' silent period, inviting nonverbal responses such as pointing.

✦ Make poetry charts with repetitive poems and conduct shared readings.

✦ Have students use art, mime, music, and other forms of creative expression to represent meaning and increase their sense of aesthetics.

Strategies for Level 2—Early Production

✦ Ask questions that provide response choices (*Is it big or small?*), that require *yes/no* or 1-2 word answers, and that begin with *Who? What? Where?*

✦ Use dramatic-interpretation techniques—especially movement, pantomime, and fingerplay—with songs, chants, rhymes.

✦ Use semantic maps for collecting and relating words.

Strategies for Level 3—Speech Emergence

✦ Ask open-ended questions *(Why do you like this poem?)*, focusing on communication, not language form.

✦ Use dramatic interpretation, especially well-rehearsed choral readings and poems for two voices, and retellings with puppets, flannel boards, etc.

✦ Assign role plays with dialogue to heterogeneous groups.

✦ Create word banks (through brainstorming) for students to use in their own writing, especially patterned writing and writing innovations.

✦ Help students create their own books through collaborative chart stories and Language Experience activities.

Strategies for Level 4—Intermediate Fluency

✦ Have students use drama—especially Readers' Theater—art, music, and other forms of creative expression to increase their sense of aesthetics.

✦ Structure discussions for heterogeneous groups through the use of discussion outlines and roles for participants, such as Notetaker, Questioner, Encourager.

✦ Use more-complex semantic maps for collecting and relating words.

✦ Guide the use of reference material for independent and group research.

✦ Provide opportunities for students to write new poetry and publish their works.

INFUSING MULTICULTURALISM INTO YOUR CLASSROOM

> *Infusing multiculturalism doesn't mean adding yet another set of requirements or prescribed content to your already full curriculum. Instead, it means using a more inclusive way of teaching.*

Multiculturalism is a way of seeing the world—of seeing peoples and cultures in such a way that their diversity is valued. Infusing multiculturalism into your classroom doesn't mean adding yet another set of requirements or prescribed content to your already full curriculum. Instead, it means using—on a regular and consistent basis—a more inclusive way of teaching. It adds another dimension to *what* you teach and *how* you teach it.

This section will suggest ways to infuse multiculturalism into your classroom by examining and adapting the:

✦ themes around which you build units of instruction

✦ holidays you recognize and teach

✦ authors you read aloud and include in your classroom library

✦ types of activities you emphasize

✦ classroom visitors you regularly invite

✦ classroom environment you create.

Multiculturalism and Themes

What makes a theme an effective way to infuse multiculturalism? Almost any topic or theme can be presented in a multicultural way, but the following types of themes are often the most fertile.

✦ Themes that are universal—that is, that apply to all people—make excellent multicultural themes. For example, the theme for Grandparents Day (9/9 through 9/13) presents five poems about grandparents, each written by a poet with a distinct, culturally connected voice. There are poems by well-known poets, and by children; as well as poems by people who are Jewish American, Hispanic American, Chinese American, African American, and Native American. Through theme explorations like this, children learn that we, as members of the human race, have important things in common—like grandparents—but that we may have different experiences and perspectives.

◆ Another effective type of theme is one that allows you to explore a culture or a perspective in-depth. In the **Anthology,** you will find themes built around heritage observations, such as Jewish Heritage Week (April) and Asian and Pacific American Heritage Month (May); as well as history celebrations, such as Black History Month (February) and Women's History Month (March). These have been included for three reasons. First, these themes help children hear diverse voices from *within* a given group and understand that *individuals* make up groups. Secondly, children from the group being studied and celebrated are able see themselves clearly reflected in the curriculum. And, lastly, all children benefit from hearing the voices of peoples who have all too often been left out of educational materials.

◆ A third type of fertile theme involves values and issues. Research shows that young children are aware—even if unconsciously—of such social issues as racism, prejudice, discrimination, and homelessness, and such social values as cooperation and protecting the environment. Exploring these issues through age-appropriate poetry, trade books, and activities promotes discussion and fosters many "teachable moments"—times when you can model appropriate responses for children.

◆ Of course, you can create your own themes, tailored to your students' needs and interests, by drawing from across the year's worth of poems. For example, you might design your own theme on History or Heritage and present all of the poems for the different observances at one time, rather than in chronological order. Family, feelings, food, and holidays also make terrific themes to explore through poems across the **Anthology.**

Through theme explorations children learn that we have important things in common—like grandparents—but that we may have different experiences and perspectives.

Multiculturalism and Holidays

You may have heard the debates about including holiday celebrations in school. You may have even heard the term "holiday syndrome," which describes the overuse of holidays as a way of introducing multiculturalism to children.

There are drawbacks in presenting holidays. Too often they are handled superficially—as an isolated arts-and-crafts project or the time to eat a special food. Another drawback is that not all children celebrate holidays. Some schools have banned holiday celebrations in an attempt to eliminate this potentially exclusive classroom practice. However, ignoring the religious and cultural diversity of students in this way can be just as problematic as celebrating holidays.

Banning holidays can make some children from non-Christian, non-European American families feel excluded—especially if most of the people they know celebrate a holiday, such as Christmas, that is unfamiliar to them. Other children, whose families *do* celebrate Euro-Christian holidays, lose out as well. They don't have the opportunity to learn that their holidays are *not* universally celebrated or that their own traditions are related to others.

Because the benefits outweigh the drawbacks, holidays have been included in this **Anthology.** They have been carefully selected to represent significant cultural celebrations of peoples in the U.S. To guard against superficial treatment, each holiday in the **Anthology** includes background information to explain the *why* behind the day. While children are having fun making dreydels for Hanukkah, they can also learn why the holiday is celebrated and how it is like or unlike other holidays they celebrate.

You can also choose to treat holidays in a more global way, by creating your own unit about holidays. With the **Theme Index** (pages 284–296), you can locate all of the holiday poems in the **Anthology.** Activities like "Congregate and Celebrate" (12/17) can help children compare and contrast related holidays to see patterns.

One further note—there are several calendars used to determine the dates of holidays from year to year. To help you be responsive to all of your students, you'll find a **Calendar Correlation** section on pages 262–265.

Multiculturalism and Authors

Another way to infuse multiculturalism into your classroom is to include authors from many cultures in the materials you read to, and provide for, children. Authors should be both male and female, young and old, African and Asian American, Hispanic and Native American, Jewish and Arab American, as well as European American.

Whenever possible, authors should be members of the group that they're writing about. That's not to say that good authors can't write effectively about things outside their own experience. They can and do! But often the poems and stories that "ring true" are those written from an insider's perspective. These are the poems that really allow children to see themselves reflected in the literature. Poems that include stereotypes or other inaccuracies are more likely to have been written by authors unfamiliar with daily lives, language patterns, and values.

A Chorus of Cultures includes the works of more than 200 poets from many cultures—poets whose voices speak to both cultural and universal issues; poets who, in short, speak to all of us. You can use the Index of Authors (pages 275–281) to find the works of poets who seem to connect most directly with various cultures. You might come across "My Horse, Fly Like a Bird" (5/16) in the **Anthology** and use the index to find another Virginia Driving Hawk Sneve poem; her work "Another Kid" (7/16) might give a Native American student a boost in self-esteem. "By Myself" (10/7) might similarly prompt an African American student to ask for more Eloise Greenfield poems. For a Chinese American child, "Sister" by Amy Ling (5/26) might provide an emotional release. Arnold Adoff's "Borders" (7/11) could be just the motivation for a European American child to explore his or her heritage.

Of course these poets, while speaking of one culture, often convey feelings common to many. For example, Hispanic students might be delighted to see their emotions reflected in the Alma Flor Ada poems "Orgullo/Pride" (10/13) or "Being Bilingual" (3/1). But who in your class can't appreciate the pride and happiness these poems describe, regardless of culture? *All* children benefit from hearing the authors' varied voices that make up *A Chorus of Cultures* (in fact, to truly accomplish this, you don't need an index—simply begin on September 1 and keep reading!).

ANOTHER KID

I was just another kid
in T-shirt and blue jeans
until Grandmother gave me
new beaded moccasins.

—*Virginia Driving Hawk Sneve*

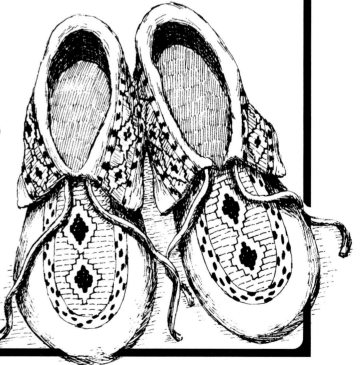

Multiculturalism and Activities

Throughout the **Anthology,** you'll see activities that have a special "Multicultural Focus" logo. These activities have been designed to accomplish three main goals: promoting self-esteem, exploring culture, and valuing diversity.

Promoting Self-Esteem

At first glance, self-esteem may not seem to be a component of multicultural education, but it is arguably its very foundation. A child with a healthy sense of self-esteem knows that she is unique, that he has the power to overcome obstacles and face adversity, and that she is connected to a larger group—a family, a school, a community, a cultural and religious heritage.

Activities with the label "Promoting Self Esteem," such as the one below (from 1/12), address aspects of healthy self-esteem. These activities often include sample validations and discussion prompts (see the last two lines) to help you bring home the message of the activity.

When spider webs unite,
they can tie up a lion.

—*Ethiopian proverb*

ACROSS THE CURRICULUM
SOCIAL STUDIES

Connections
PROMOTING SELF-ESTEEM When children can see that they are connected to, and important to, a group, self-esteem can soar. Use this proverb to demonstrate how each student is an important part of the class.

Have students sit on the floor in a circle and give one child a large ball of yarn (or string). Have that child hold on to one end of the yarn and roll the ball to a child who has helped him or her or who has made a positive contribution to the class, telling about what happened. The second child then relates another story and rolls the ball of yarn on to a third, and so on, until everyone is connected by the "spider web" of yarn.

To ensure that all children are included, you may need to recall special deeds or moments: *Remember the time when Jaime shared the good news about his brother? That made us all feel good that day.* Then, point out how each member is important to the whole class, as shown by the web.

Exploring Culture

The exploration of culture—from the surface level of food, customs, and clothing to deeper levels like values and beliefs—is probably the most obvious multicultural activity.

Activities labeled "Exploring Culture" often extend concepts presented in the **CultureShare** and **As a Matter of Fact** features in a hands-on, experiential manner. Other Exploring Culture activities allow you to draw on the cultural diversity of your class and community to explore, compare, and contrast several cultures.

ACROSS THE CURRICULUM
SOCIAL STUDIES & ARTS AND CRAFTS

So Many Ways To Tell Stories
EXPLORING CULTURE Songs, poetry and prose in spoken and written form, dances, plays, paintings, drawings, needlework—people have found many ways to tell stories. The Hmong people of Southeast Asia have created story cloths—appliqued or embroidered panels called *pa ndau* (pan-DOW)—to tell stories. These cloths are like history books, preserving folktales and contemporary stories for a culture that has not needed or used written language. *Pa ndau* have been brought to the U.S. by Hmong refugees from Laos in recent years.

Children can make their own story cloths from squares of felt and felt scraps or paper in different colors. Show students an actual story cloth and point out how the events in the story are told in sequence as the "reader's" eye travels along a path. You might also consult *Creating Pa ndau Applique: A New Approach to an Ancient Art Form* by Carla Hassel (Wallace-Homestead, 1984). Set up an Author-Artist Chair in which individuals can share their story cloths.

ACROSS THE CURRICULUM
SOCIAL STUDIES & SCIENCE & READING

Pancakes Everywhere!
EXPLORING CULTURE Tortillas, crepes, focaccia bread. Poori, blintzes, blini. Flapjacks, lefse, langos. Lavash, pita, pancakes. People all over the world eat flat, round breads in many variations. When children learn about such similarities, they discover common threads in the daily lives of people everywhere and begin to put their own cultures in a wider perspective.

Make a list of all the types of pancakes the class can think of; include the country (or countries) where each version is made. Groups of children can then work with adult leaders to prepare various kinds of pancakes; sharing the results in a tasting session. Encourage children to compile copies of the recipes into cookbooks, with additional information about traditions or history.

Content-Area ESL
Students acquiring English can demonstrate a recipe and cooking techniques with which they are familiar, while more-fluent speakers narrate the demonstration.

To learn more about how people cook the same types of staple foods in many different ways, read aloud or have children read *Bread, Bread, Bread* by Ann Morris (Lothrop, Lee & Shepard, 1989) and *Everybody Cooks Rice* by Norah Dooley (Carolrhoda, 1991).

Valuing Diversity

The recognition and celebration of diversity is the ultimate goal of education that is multicultural. When children are able to recognize that each person is unique (as they themselves are), that culture is an important part of people's lives, and that the differences among people and cultures are worth learning about and appreciating, you have infused multiculturalism into your classroom.

For multicultural education to be most effective, diversity—of opinions, of ideas, of beliefs, of customs—needs to be celebrated continuously. Isolated activities won't ensure that children internalize the concept. Throughout the **Anthology,** you'll see many Valuing Diversity activities, but take advantage of all opportunities to reinforce this goal. Adapt activities and use validations that celebrate diversity (see "The Wide World of Grandparents" below) in group discussions throughout the school day.

ACROSS THE CURRICULUM

SOCIAL STUDIES

The Wide World of Grandparents

VALUING DIVERSITY This activity explores the diversity of children's relationships with their grandparents. Draw a four-column chart on the chalkboard and label the columns *Where Do They Live?*, *How Many Can We Have?*, *When Do We See Them?*, *What Do We Do Together?* Talk about the possibilities for each column:

◆ In some families, grandparents live in the same home; in others, they live on the other side of the world.

◆ Children may have step-grandparents or "honorary" grandparents or no living grandparents.

◆ Children may see their grandparents every day, only on holidays, or not at all.

Record children's contributions, encouraging them to recall activities they have shared with their grandparents or to brainstorm ones they think would be fun.

Comment on how many different ways of being grandparents and grandchildren there are. For example: *Families come in lots of shapes and sizes, don't they? And even though they're different, every family is special and important.*

Or you might share a personal anecdote about your own grandparent(s) that took place when you were the age of your students, adding, *It's interesting to learn that some of you do similar kinds of things with your grandparents as I did—and some do very different things.*

Multiculturalism and Classroom Visitors

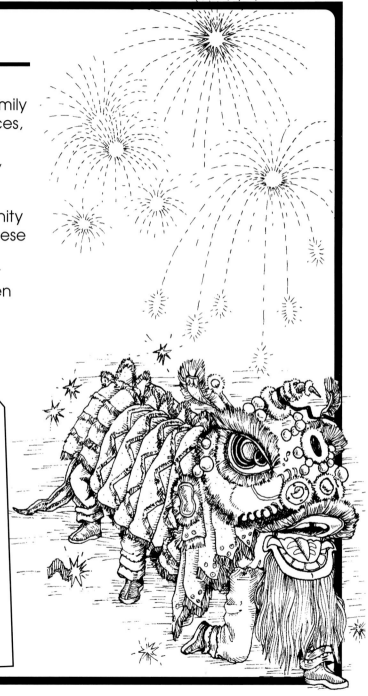

What is one of the most efficient and effective ways to bring many different cultural perspectives into your classroom? Invite classroom visitors—parents, family members, and community members—to share their knowledge and experiences, from retelling folktales and making traditional foods to recounting stories of growing up or immigrating to the U.S. As Alma Flor Ada noted on pages 11–13, inviting parents and family members strengthens the home-school connection *and* provides rich educational opportunities for students.

Activities throughout the **Anthology** contain suggestions for inviting community and family members into the classroom to share specific aspects of culture. These exchanges work best when they are part of an ongoing program of involving visitors. When community members are invited on a regular basis to share their knowledge of culture—as well as of their work, their hobbies, their lives—children learn to see the visitors as well-rounded individuals, not just as members of one particular group.

Across the Curriculum
ARTS AND CRAFTS & SOCIAL STUDIES

Welcoming the New Year
VALUING DIVERSITY All cultures celebrate the new year as a symbol of a new beginning. The celebrations take different forms in different cultures. Explore the diversity of new-year's customs, while emphasizing the universality of the celebration. Here are some ideas:

◆ Read aloud all the new-year poems and background information in this anthology: Rosh Hashanah (9/15), New Year's Day (1/1), and the Lunar New Year (2/11–13).

◆ Encourage children to research new-year celebrations. You might make available *Happy New Year Round the World* by Lois S. Johnson (Rand McNally, 1966), *Happy New Year* by Emily Kelly (Carolrhoda, 1984), and *Joy Through the World* by the U.S. Committee for UNICEF (Allen Bragdon Publishers, 1985).

◆ Invite community members from various cultures to teach children more about holiday foods, songs, decorations, apparel, greetings, games, and other traditional activities.

◆ Help children synthesize all the information they've found. Using **Activity Sheets 10** and **11**, children can make "culture wheels" to compare and contrast the names, greetings, and traditions of different new-year traditions.

Multiculturalism and the Classroom Environment

As you've seen, there are a number of ways to infuse multiculturalism throughout your curriculum—from themes and holidays to authors, activities, and visitors. But, what kind of environment will support these activities? The climate of the classroom, from what you include in the physical surroundings to the way feelings and issues are discussed and resolved, is crucial in promoting multiculturalism.

Here are some guidelines to help in your selection of materials, displays, visuals—and even in your own thinking, for one of the first things that multiculturalism will do is challenge you to examine your own biases and assumptions. These guidelines will help you create a classroom environment in which multiculturalism can thrive. As this will be an ongoing learning process for you and your students, don't be afraid to make some mistakes. One of the best lessons we can model for children is how to learn from our mistakes.

The climate of the classroom is crucial to promoting multiculturalism.

✦ **Portray people, past and present, as fully, richly human.**

When you present folklore or other traditional material, balance it with a contemporary view by reading and discussing good poetry and fiction by contemporary writers. Sometimes, the only exposure children get to certain cultures is a historical view; children don't realize that descendants of ancient cultures are living in today's world.

✦ **Strive to be inclusive and balanced.**

Think about the people students are exposed to in reading materials, on bulletin-board displays, as subjects of research projects, etc. Is there a balance of male and female? Different ages? Different racial, religious, and ethnic backgrounds? Different socioeconomic levels? Different abilities? And are the lifestyles of the students in your class represented?

Use materials that present multiple perspectives—especially in social studies. There's always more than one way to look at a historical event or an issue. (See October 12–14 for multiple perspectives on Columbus.)

There's no formula for achieving balance; it's simply important not to overemphasize any single perspective or to portray any one group or lifestyle in a rigid—and therefore stereotypical—way. If students see women pictured as mothers and as firefighters and as members of Congress, for example, they are less likely to form stereotypes.

Also, encourage children to use inclusive terms and to recognize stereotypes and biases as they arise. A great way to do this is to keep on hand materials that are biased or exclusive—don't throw them out. Use them for critical-thinking lessons, in which children compare and contrast the photographs, stories, etc., that are biased, with ones that are more inclusive and balanced, as in the activity "Look Again, Think Again" (11/26).

✦ **Avoid generalizing people and cultures.**

Be on the alert for materials and discussions in which entire groups are portrayed as "generic" or monolithic. Every group—even if it is simply the group of students in your classroom—is diverse. Think, for example, about the within-group diversity of Native Americans, who belong to more than 400 different Nations. It's difficult, if not impossible, to make a statement that would hold true for all 400 Nations, much less thousands of individuals!

✦ **Aim for authenticity.**

One of the most important things you can do is to provide children with materials and experiences that are authentic. How can you tell if something is authentic or not? First, ask yourself, "Whose perspective is the material presented from? Is it by someone from within the culture, someone who's very familiar with the culture, or a casual observer? What are the authors' (or artists' or speakers') credentials?"

If you're still not sure, check out your hunches with experts. Consult books (see pages 42 and 56 for resources) and make an effort to talk to people from within the culture. There are many ways to find experts: consult children's families, ask at a local university or social/civic organization, or call a nonprofit organization that represents the group you're researching. Most people are happy to share their knowledge!

Whose perspective is the material presented from? Is it by someone from within the culture, someone who is very familiar with the culture, or a casual observer?

✦ Create an atmosphere in which children feel safe to ask questions and explore difficult issues.

A common experience with implementing multiculturalism is that children often ask frank questions and voice prejudicial or discriminatory views. When they do, you have an excellent opportunity to address these issues head-on and model critical thinking for children. For example, a child might say, "I don't like those people. They're all bad." You could probe for reasons the child feels this way and ask, "Do you know all the people in that group? How would you feel if someone who didn't know you said that about you?"

Opening up discussions like this, without putting down the child who asks the question or makes the remark, creates a climate in which children will feel empowered to explore all of their feelings and thoughts—especially those that the poetry may give rise to.

Professional Resources

✦ *Anti-Bias Curriculum: Tools for Empowering Young Children*, Louise Derman-Sparks and The A.B.C. Task Force (National Association for the Education of Young Children, 1989). A guide to examining your own biases and for reducing, handling, and eliminating bias in the classroom.

✦ *The Book of Holidays Around the World*, Alice van Straalen (E. P. Dutton, 1986). Descriptions of local, regional, national, and religious holidays—one for every day of the year.

✦ *Cultural Awareness for Children*, Judy Allen, Earldene McNeill, and Velma Schmidt (Addison-Wesley, 1992). Activities, background, and resources for exploring foreign *and* U.S. cultures.

✦ *Roots and Wings: Affirming Culture in Early Childhood Programs*, Stacey York (Redleaf Press, 1991). Activities, strategies, staff-training recommendations, and helpful examples for infusing multiculturalism. Available from Hampton-Brown Books.

✦ *The Four Conditions of Self-Esteem: A New Approach for Elementary and Middle Schools*, Second Edition, Reynold Bean (ETR Associates, 1992). Rationale, techniques, and guidelines for promoting self-esteem in school.

✦ *Hands-On Heritage: An Experiential Approach to Multicultural Education*, Nancy Lee and Linda Oldham (Hands-On Publications, 1978). More than 200 activities for exploring heritage.

✦ *The Multicultural Caterpillar*, Ana Consuelo Matiella (ETR Associates, 1990). Promotes awareness of health, family life, and cultural diversity for children in kindergarten through third grade; reproducible activities. Available from Hampton-Brown Books.

✦ *Positively Different: Creating a Bias-Free Environment for Young Children*, Ana Consuelo Matiella (ETR Associates, 1991). Suggestions for teachers, parents, and other care providers for teaching children to celebrate diversity. Available from Hampton-Brown Books.

✦ *Teaching and Learning in a Diverse World: Multicultural Education for Young Children*, Patricia G. Ramsey (Teachers College Press, 1987). A blend of theory and practice, this book provides extensive examples and advice for implementing multicultural education.

✦ *The Whole Earth Holiday Book*, Linda Polon and Aileen Cantwell (Scott, Foresman, 1983). A treasure trove of holiday celebrations around the world. Available from Hampton-Brown Books.

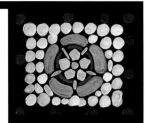

A Chorus of CULTURES™

Developing Literacy Through Multicultural Poetry

To America's voices, singing along,
Composing our verses,
Composing our song.
To our chorus of cultures
To our voices so strong
All part of the chorus, all part of the song.

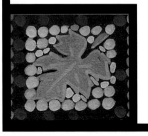
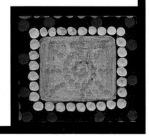

AUTUMN

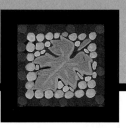

Fall is green leaves changing to rust—
Earth turning into a cold, hard crust.

—*Lee Bennett Hopkins*

MULTICULTURAL TRADE BOOKS

Anno, Mitsumasa. **Anno's U.S.A.** (Philomel, 1983). A traveler recounts his journey from the East to the West.

■

Caines, Jeannette. **I Need a Lunch Box** (HarperCollins, 1988). A boy wants a lunch box because his sister, who is entering first grade, gets one.

■

Delacre, Lulu. **Arroz Con Leche: Popular Songs and Rhymes from Latin America** (Scholastic, 1989). A resource of folk culture, in Spanish and English.

■

Haskins, Jim. **Count Your Way Through . . .** (Carolrhoda). A series of counting books. Titles include: **Africa** (Swahili), **Arabia, Canada** (French), **China, Germany, India, Israel, Japan, Korea, Mexico,** and **Russia**.

■

Dorros, Arthur. **Abuela** (Dutton, 1991). A girl and her grandmother take an amazing tour of New York City.

■

Greenfield, Eloise. **Grandpa's Face** (Philomel, 1988). A girl visits her grandfather at the theater and is surprised by the man she sees.

September

September brings together old and new, endings and beginnings. In September, vacation traditionally ends and school starts again (although many schools now operate year-round); summer ends and fall settles in. With the coming of the High Holy Days, the Jewish New Year begins.

September also brings celebrations of all sorts—for Hispanic heritage, Native American Day, good neighbors, grandparents, international peace, and even for the moon on the festival of Tet-Trung-Thu. With the arrival of the new school year comes a celebration of friendship and learning renewed.

So get ready, and get going! Here comes September.

Noteworthy Days

- ✦ Labor Day (first Monday)

8 International Literacy Day

- ✦ Grandparents' Day (Sunday after Labor Day)

- ✦ Tet-Trung-Thu (falls mid-September to early October*)

- ✦ Rosh Hashanah (falls mid-September to early October*)

- ✦ International Day of Peace (third Tuesday)

- ✦ National Good Neighbor Day (fourth Sunday)

22 or 23 Fall Equinox

- ✦ Native American Day (often last Thursday)

- ✦ Yom Kippur (nine days after Rosh Hashanah*)

- ✦ Hispanic Heritage Month (September 15–October 15)

* See page 265 for exact date.

1

YOUNG VOICES

TIME FOR SCHOOL

No more swimming,
No more pools,
Come on folks
It's back to school!
Time for desks, pencils, books and more
Get up, get dressed, get out the door!
Catch the bus
Don't be late
It's time for school
It will be great!

—Melissa Batulis, age 12
Marion Center, Pennsylvania

2

After hearing this poem, children can brainstorm answers to the questions at the end, giving reasons that may be academic or humorous.

SEPTEMBER

I already know where Africa is
and I already know how to
count to ten and
I went to school every day last year,
why do I have to go again?

—Lucille Clifton

3

After presenting this poem, encourage children to discuss some of the things they want to learn during the school year. You may record their suggestions on chart paper to help you plan your curriculum throughout the year.

MUCH TO LEARN

My child, there is much
for you to learn.
Wondrous things,
like how candles burn.

How tortillas puff up,
How the earth cools down,
How the sunset in the skies
changes colors all around.

How the chile turns red
When it's still on the bush.
How the hawk swoops down
to grab a field mouse with a swoosh!

How coyotes howl
In a voice that sounds like words.
How there's always food around
For even the smallest birds.

My child, there is much
For you to learn
And also much for you
To teach us in return.

Like how to make friends
With someone who is kind.
Like how to see the joy
In something old you find.

Like how to use a stick and string
As if it were a toy,
Or how to bring a smile
To another girl or boy.

Like how to dream the biggest dreams,
Or keep a tiny hope alive,
Or — when grownups say "Impossible!" —
To say, "We've never tried."

—Carmen Tafolla

DEVELOPING LITERACY
DRAMATIC INTERPRETATION — Choral Reading

Much Fun to Learn

You and the children can have fun with this poem by performing it as a choral reading. Organize the reading by copying on each of 12 index cards one of the "hows" of the poem, as follows:

Stanza 2, line 1	
Stanza 2, line 2	Stanza 6, lines 1–2
Stanza 2, lines 3–4	Stanza 6, lines 3–4
Stanza 3, lines 1–2	Stanza 7, lines 1–2
Stanza 3, lines 3–4	Stanza 7, lines 3–4
Stanza 4, lines 1–2	Stanza 8, lines 1–2
Stanza 4, lines 3–4	

Assign each card to partners or to an individual student. Then the reading proceeds as follows:

- ◆ You read the first stanza.
- ◆ Individual children or partners take turns reading the "hows" for stanzas 2–4.
- ◆ You read stanza 5.
- ◆ Individual children or partners take turns reading the "hows" for stanzas 6–7, and the first two lines of stanza 8.
- ◆ You read the last two lines of the poem, with the whole class joining in on "We've never tried."

On Labor Day we honor workers.

Labor Day (first Monday)

To keep younger children engaged during the presentation of this long poem, teach them to chant chorally the phrase "when the sun comes up," and hold up a picture of the sun as a signal to chant it as you read the poem.

CHANT OF THE WORKING PEOPLE

When the sun comes up
I set out
for the factory,
when the sun comes up,
for I am the laborer,
I am the worker,
when the sun comes up.

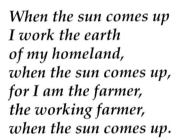

When the sun comes up
I work the earth
of my homeland,
when the sun comes up,
for I am the farmer,
the working farmer,
when the sun comes up.

When the sun comes up
I work the seas
of the whole world,
when the sun comes up,
for I am the seafarer
and I am the fisher,
when the sun comes up.

When the sun comes up
I bring out the heat
from inside the earth,
when the sun comes up,
for I am the miner,
the working miner,
when the sun comes up.

AS A MATTER OF FACT Labor Day was originally proposed by Peter J. McGuire, leader of the Knights of Labor, in 1882. Since 1894, the first Monday in September has been set aside in the United States to honor laborers. Special events such as parades, picnics, and concerts mark the day. In many other countries around the world, working people are honored on May 1.

When the sun comes up
I set out
to build our life,
when the sun comes up,
for I am the people,
the working people,
when the sun comes up,
when the sun
when the sun
when the sun comes up.

—*David Chericián (original in Spanish)*
English version by Juan Quintana

DEVELOPING LITERACY
COLLECTING AND RELATING WORDS & PATTERNED WRITING

World of Work
As you reread the poem, display photographs or sketches of people at work in each occupation, to provide comprehensible input for **students acquiring English**. Brainstorm other workers and their work places with children, recording their responses in two columns and using pantomime and other visual aids as often as possible.

Children can then use **Activity Sheet 1** to write their own versions of the poem, adding workers and work places from the chart. For example:

> *When the sun comes up*
> *I set out*
> *for the* __school__ *,*
> *when the sun comes up,*
> *for I am the* __teacher__ *,*
> *the working* __teacher__ *,*
> *when the sun comes up.*

ACROSS THE CURRICULUM
SOCIAL STUDIES

Career Connections
Children might use their class list of workers and work places from **World of Work** (see above) to create a class book.

Content-Area ESL
Pair less-fluent English speakers with more-fluent ones and ask partners to work together to choose a type of work to investigate. Suggest the library and interviews with people in the community and family members as sources of information on what the people who do that work wear, what tools or machines they use, and what their work place looks like.

Gather all the pages together into a book with the title *Working People*.

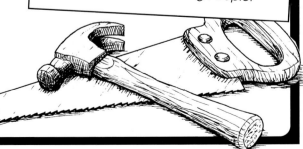

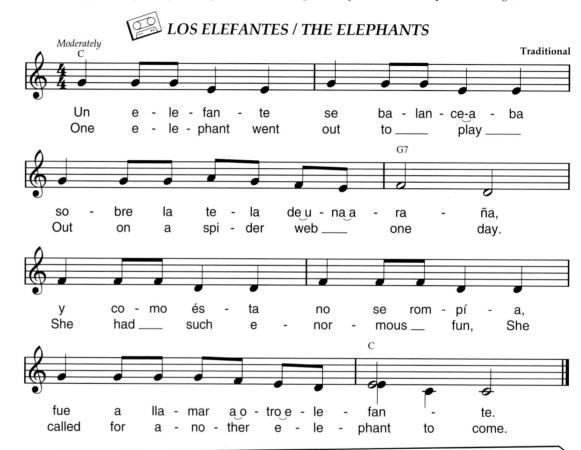

5

 ONE, TWO, THREE, FOUR, FIVE

One, two, three, four, five,
Once I caught a fish alive.
Six, seven, eight, nine, ten,
But I let it go again.
Why did you let it go?
Because it bit my finger so.
Which finger did it bite?
The little one upon the right.

—Mother Goose *counting rhyme*

6

This is a cumulative song, continuing with "two elephants," "three elephants," and so on. Explain to children that this was originally a Spanish game song. Use the **Music Tapes** to help them learn it in Spanish and English.

LOS ELEFANTES / THE ELEPHANTS

Moderately

Traditional

Un e - le - fan - te se ba - lan - ce-a - ba
One e - le - phant went out to _____ play _____

so - bre la te - la de_u - na_a - ra - ña,
Out on a spi - der web _____ one day.

y co - mo és - ta no se rom - pí - a,
She had _____ such e - nor - mous _____ fun, She

fue a lla - mar a_o - tro_e - le - fan - te.
called for a - no - ther e - le - phant to come.

ACROSS THE CURRICULUM
MATHEMATICS & SCIENCE

How Many Elephants Does It Take?
Using a damp paper towel to represent the spider web and gray rocks to represent the elephants, have children estimate the number of "elephants" it will take to break the "web." After estimates are recorded, children can sing the song, adding rocks, one at a time, until the web breaks. Children can compare the actual number with their estimates.

Older children might enjoy designing their own experiments, using such variables as different brands of paper towels, different amounts of moisture, and different types of rocks, and then making comparisons.

7

Tell children that almost every language has rhymes that teach counting, and that now they're going to learn one in Armenian. (Spelling is phonetic. Stressed syllables are underscored.)

MEG, YERGOO, YERGUNNAS/ ONE, TWO, GROW TALL

Meg, yergoo, yergunnas;
Yerec, chors, choranas;
Hinc, vets, vernas;
Yoten, ooten, orranas;
Innin, dacenin, jam yertas;
Dacen yergoo, hats geran.

—Armenian counting rhyme

One, two, grow tall.
Three, four, round as a ball.
Five, six, reach up high.
Seven, eight, don't scratch the sky.
Nine, ten, time for mass.
From ten till two, lunch at last.

dul/two (Korean)

set/three (Korean)

net/four (Korean)

four (Vietnamese)

five (Vietnamese)

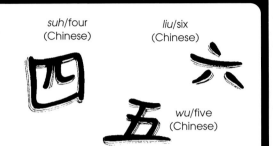

suh/four (Chinese)

liu/six (Chinese)

wu/five (Chinese)

ACROSS THE CURRICULUM
SOCIAL STUDIES

Everybody Counts

PROMOTING SELF-ESTEEM Language is an integral part of every person's identity. When teachers and administrators demonstrate their respect for children's native languages, they make use of a powerful tool for promoting self-esteem. Here are some ideas for turning children into language teachers, using numbers as the theme:

✦ Each week a different group of children might teach the principal to count from 1 to 10 in their native language. The principal can then use the PA system to help the rest of the school learn these numbers and to recognize the children who were his or her teachers.

✦ Children from various language groups can take turns teaching the rest of the class to count from 1 to 10 in their native language, perhaps using a counting book. Children whose native language uses characters other than Arabic numerals or Roman letters can teach the others how to make the characters.

✦ Choosing a different language each week, children can make signs in English and the featured language and attach them to any numbered objects around the room (the room number, the class clock), or make number cards in the two languages to post.

✦ Children might also learn the numbers from 1 to 10 in American Sign Language.

8

International Literacy Day

YOUNG VOICES

INSTRUCTIONS ON HOW TO READ

First
   take a piece of paper
   and write a word.
Then
   pronounce it
   bit by bit.
Then
   you say:
      —I read it, everybody!
      And it's my first word!

—Eloy Suárez, 4th grade
New York, New York

AS A MATTER OF FACT On International Literacy Day, the United Nations Educational, Scientific, and Cultural Organization (UNESCO) spotlights the need for literacy worldwide, helping to promote literacy as one of the basic human rights, especially for children. Different organizations around the world award prizes to literacy programs that have proved successful.

9

Grandparents' Day
(Sunday after Labor Day)

THERE IS A PLACE

on
the couch
　　　for
　　　　grandma

and
a place on
　　　　grandma

for
　me

　　in front
of
the
　　fire
　　and pop
　　　　ping
　　　　　corn

—Arnold Adoff

A WORD FROM THE POET "I grew up in a three-room apartment in the Bronx, a borough of New York City. Our heat came from floor-to-ceiling steam pipes, painted silver, that were usually too hot to touch. Popcorn was at the movies on Saturday mornings.

Now we live in a wood house at the edge of a big field, at the edge of this small town in Ohio. On winter evenings, when our two children were young, I would make a fire in the living-room fireplace, and invite grandma in for a cup of warm apple cider and a large bowl of freshly popped popcorn. We would all take turns shaking the popper, very carefully, over a low place at the side of the fire, until the corn would be all popped. Then we would sit on the low sofa in front of the fire, eating the corn and feeling warm, inside and out. And the children would always end up on grandma's lap. They always wanted more good stories, warm hugs, and popping corn."

10

ABUELITO*

Tell me something, Grandpa,
and please don't tell a lie—
When you were a little boy,
were you as good as I?

—Alma Flor Ada

*abuelito (ah-bweh-LEE-toh): Spanish
for "grandpa"

11

YOUNG VOICES

from
GRANDFATHER IS A CHINESE PINE

Grandfather is a Chinese pine
Standing firm on the sloping hillside.
From his bright, piercing eyes
All can see the evergreen spirit
That pushed its way up from poor,
*　　stony soil.*

I love, honor and revere him,
Our sturdy tree of shade and support.
From the tall height of his example
I can see my way straight and far.

—Zheng Xu, age 18
New York, New York

12

PIGGY-BACK

My daddy rides me piggy-back.
My mama rides me, too.
But grandma says her poor old back
Has had enough to do.

—Langston Hughes

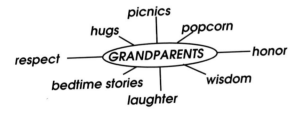

DEVELOPING LITERACY
COLLECTING AND RELATING WORDS & WRITING

For Someone Special
As you read the poems in this theme, compile a word bank for the theme, for example:

picnics
hugs
popcorn
respect — GRANDPARENTS — honor
bedtime stories
wisdom
laughter

Using the word bank for inspiration, children can make Grandparents' Day greeting cards. Younger children might draw and label a picture. Older children could try composing a poem or forming their greetings in an acrostic. For example:

Great
sto**R**ies
h**A**ppy
me**M**ories
Picnics
Tickle**S**

13

YOUNG VOICES

TOTA* MAN

My Tota Man,
An old Indian
His face wrinkled with wisdom
Tells of the old days
Before the reservation
When his family hunted
Like their ancestors.

His face fills with sorrow when
He thinks of the modern world,
*Stuck in Kanawake***
On the St. Lawrence near Montreal.
Once a free man in a free world,
Now a prisoner on a reservation.

My great-grandfather.

—Alex Imrie, 10th grade
Chico, California

* **Tota** (*DOE dah*): Mohawk for "grandfather"
* **Kanawake** (*kah nah WAH kee*): a reservation town on the St. Lawrence River near Montreal, Canada

CULTURESHARE To facilitate the westward expansion of the United States during the 1800s, the United States government compelled most Native American peoples to leave their ancestral lands and go into "reservations"—typically marginal lands considered useless for any other purpose. Many groups were forced to walk great distances under harsh conditions in order to get to their assigned reservations. As reflected in the poem, the reservation experience has been a bitter one for Native Americans.

ACROSS THE CURRICULUM
SOCIAL STUDIES

MULTICULTURAL FOCUS

The Wide World of Grandparents
VALUING DIVERSITY This activity explores the diversity of children's relationships with their grandparents. Draw a four-column chart on the chalkboard and label the columns *Where Do They Live?*, *How Many Can We Have?*, *When Do We See Them?*, *What Do We Do Together?* Talk about the possibilities for each column:

◆ In some families, grandparents live in the same home; in others, they live on the other side of the world.

◆ Children may have step-grandparents or "honorary" grandparents or no living grandparents.

◆ Children may see their grandparents every day, only on holidays, or not at all.

Record children's contributions, encouraging them to recall activities they have shared with their grandparents or to brainstorm ones they think would be fun.

Comment on how many different ways of being grandparents and grandchildren there are. For example: *Families come in lots of shapes and sizes, don't they? And even though they're different, every family is special and important.*

Or you might share a personal anecdote about your own grandparent(s) that took place when you were the age of your students, adding, *It's interesting to learn that some of you do similar kinds of things with your grandparents as I did—and some do very different things.*

A full-moon night, so bright and clear.

14

Tet-Trung-Thu (mid-September to early October)

The following folktale describes the origin of Tet-Trung-Thu (pronounced *tet-trung-too*) a mid-autumn festival traditionally celebrated by Vietnamese and other Southeast Asian peoples to honor the moon.

THE EMPEROR'S DREAM

One night, a long, long time ago, Emperor Minh-Mang fell asleep in his garden. While he slept, he dreamed that a fairy came to his garden and carried him to the bright full moon. On the moon, he saw beautiful dancers in silver and blue silks weaving a dance to a haunting melody. They were dancing for a queen who was more lovely than any woman the emperor had ever seen. The queen welcomed him and gave him a cushion to sit on at her side. Servants gave him delicious little cakes shaped like the moon. It was such a lovely dream—the kind of dream the dreamer hopes will never end. When the emperor did wake up, he felt very sad. He did not want to forget the beautiful queen and her magical court on the moon, so he taught his own servants to do the dance and asked them to make moon cakes. And every year since, people have celebrated the beauty of the moon with a holiday called Tet-Trung-Thu.

—*Vietnamese folktale*

CULTURESHARE Tet-Trung-Thu is celebrated this time of year—the eighth lunar month— because the moon is at its fullest and most beautiful now. Children traditionally make lanterns shaped like animals, moons, or boats and parade through the streets at night swinging their lanterns on a pretend journey to the moon. Sweet or meat-filled pastries called "moon cakes" are popular treats. Many of these traditions are observed by Vietnamese Americans today.

ACROSS THE CURRICULUM
ARTS AND CRAFTS

Journey to the Moon
EXPLORING CULTURE After hearing the folktale and learning about the customs associated with the holiday, children can make paper lanterns. (See the **How-To Directions** on page 240.) Children can carry the paper lanterns on a parade to another classroom, where they can tell the children there the story of the emperor's dream and share with them some moon-cake treats.

Moon cakes are usually available at Vietnamese markets in cities with large Vietnamese communities. If you like, substitute bread cut in circles (with a jar or cookie cutter) and spread with jam.

MULTICULTURAL FOCUS

A brand new person for a grand new year!

15

Rosh Hashanah (mid-September to early October)

ROSH HA-SHANAH* EVE

Stale moon, climb down.
Clear the sky.
Get out of town.
Good-bye.

Fresh moon, arise.
Throw a glow.
Shine a surprise.
Hello

New Year, amen.
Now we begin:
Teach me to be a new me.

—*Harry Philip*

*Rosh Ha-Shanah (*rosh hah-shah-NAH;* **also spelled** *Rosh Hashanah):* Hebrew for "the head (beginning) of the year"

CULTURESHARE Along with the new year come the High Holy Days—the period between Rosh Hashanah and Yom Kippur (see September 25). The most religious time of year for many Jews, the High Holy Days are a time both for reflecting upon the year passed and for celebrating the year ahead. Many families attend synagogue, praying for peace among nations, among peoples, and within themselves in the coming year. Many others simply exchange cards, greetings, and good wishes. And many children enjoy the sweet Rosh Hashanah treat of apple slices dipped in honey (the honey symbolizes hope for a sweet new year)!

Peace in the world and peace at home.

16

International Day of Peace (third Tuesday)

It is little children like you who will stop all war. This means that you never quarrel with other boys and girls or among yourselves. You cannot stop big wars if you carry on little wars yourselves.

—Mohandas K. Gandhi

As a Matter of Fact Mohandas Karamchand Gandhi led India to its independence from Britain in 1947. Remarkably, he did so without using violence. He urged his followers not to resist the British soldiers, which made the soldiers look cruel, and eventually rallied international support behind the Indian revolutionaries. The title *Mahatma,* or "Great Soul," was conferred upon Gandhi in recognition of his pacifism. Gandhi was assassinated in 1948.

17

Ask children to close their eyes and visualize the scene as you read the poem. Discuss what the children "saw," guiding them to understand that there are only two boys involved and that "the one who was hitting him" is the narrator. Then read the poem again.

EDUCATION

*one day I was dumb enough
to let somebody bet me
into a fight
and then I was mad with two
stupid boys
the one who was hitting me
and the one who was hitting
him*

—Eloise Greenfield

18

 WE SHALL OVERCOME

Musical and lyrical adaptation by Zilphia Horton, Frank Hamilton, Guy Carawan and Pete Seeger. Inspired by African American gospel singing, members of the Food and Tobacco Workers Union, Charleston, SC, and the Southern civil-rights movement.

1. We shall o-ver-come, _____ we shall o-ver-come, _____
We shall o-ver-come, some day; _____ Oh, _ deep in my
heart I do be-lieve We shall o-ver-come some-day. _____

2. We'll walk hand in hand, we'll walk hand in hand,
We'll walk hand in hand some day;
Oh, deep in my heart I do believe
We shall overcome some day.

3. We shall live in peace, we shall live in peace,
We shall live in peace some day;
Oh, deep in my heart I do believe
We shall overcome some day.

TRO–© 1960 (renewed) and 1963 (renewed) Ludlow Music, Inc., New York, NY. Reprinted by permission.

19

FANTASIA

*I dream
of
giving birth
to
a child
who will ask
"Mother,
what was war?"*

—Eve Merriam

Play a game with your neighbor and your neighbor becomes a friend.

20
National Good Neighbor Day
(fourth Sunday)

Read this poem in the rhythm of a jump-rope chant.

B *ROPE RHYME*

Get set, ready now, jump right in
Bounce and kick and giggle and spin
Listen to the rope when it hits the ground
Listen to that clappedy-slappedy sound
Jump right up when it tells you to
Come back down, whatever you do
Count to a hundred, count by ten
Start to count all over again
That's what jumping is all about
Get set, ready now,
                    jump
                        right
                            out!

—Eloise Greenfield

21

After children have learned this rhyme, partners can perform it as a handclapping rhyme, creating their own clapping patterns.

Y *OOO-AH, WANNA PIECE OF PIE*

Ooo-ah, wanna piece of pie,
Pie too sweet, wanna piece of meat,
Meat too tough, wanna ride a bus,
Bus too full, wanna ride a bull,
Bull too fat, want your money back,
Money too green, wanna jelly bean,
Jelly bean not cooked, wanna read a book,
Book not read, wanna go to bed.
So close your eyes and count to ten,
And if you miss, start all over again.

—Street rhyme

22

Encourage children to pantomime the actions in a game of hide-and-seek while they sing this Japanese song.

KAKURENBO / HIDE AND SEEK

Words by Ryuha Hayashi
Music by Kan'ichi Shimofusa

Ka - ku-ren - bo, su - ru mo-no yo - tto ii de, Jan - ken - pong, __ yo
Hide __ and __ seek, __ oh, __ join us __ here, Jan - ken - pong, __ yo

a - i-ko de-sho, Mo ii kai Ma-da da yo mo ii yo
a - i-ko de-sho,* All right now? Oh, not __ yet, Yes, all right!

* **Jan-ken-pong, aiko-de-sho** (*jahn-kehn-pong, IKE-oh-deh-shoh*): formula (like "eeny meeny miny moe") used in many Japanese children's games to decide who is "it" or who will be the leader

© 1960 Edward B. Marks Music Company. Copyright renewed. Reprinted by permission.

ACROSS THE CURRICULUM
SPORTS AND GAMES & WRITING

Rhymes 'Round the World
VALUING DIVERSITY Researchers have found that children all over the world use similar rhythmic chants, often nonsensical or full of nonsense words, to regulate their play—and just to have fun. This theme can be used as a springboard to small-group exchanges of chants and rhymes from different cultures.

Divide the class into several small groups. With some advance planning, members of the community from various cultural backgrounds might join the group. Give each group a type of chant to explore (clapping, rope-jumping, ball-bouncing, counting) and ask children to teach each other the rhymes they know, especially from their native cultures. Younger children might work in groups without assigned categories, trading any rhymes they know. Include **students acquiring English** in groups with more-fluent speakers who will help them share their ideas.

Then, groups can recite their rhymes for the rest of the class or make their collections into small books for the classroom reading center. At recess, remind children to try out some of the chants they have learned.

Help children see the similarities in the chants; though the languages are different, the rhythms, the ideas, and the fun with friends are much the same.

It's time to fall into a new season.

23 Fall Equinox

THE WIND IS COOL AND SWIFT

The wind is cool and swift.
The sea of colors is on the trees.
The mist of rain is soft and sweet.
The warmth of summer is gone.
Soon the land will be bare and gray.
I feel a warmth as the trees change color.

— Tanu Frank , 8th grade
Olympia, Washington

AS A MATTER OF FACT On this day, fall officially begins in the northern hemisphere. Day and night are of equal length today. From now until December, the nights will get progressively longer and the days will get progressively shorter. The shortened periods of sunlight will cause the northern hemisphere to grow cooler.

Native American Day honors the first Americans.

24 Native American Day (often last Thursday)

B LITTLE SISTER

I see her in the morning
Going down,
By the river,
In the mist.
She is brown
Like the honey,
Like the deer,
Like the ground
Of the Earth my Mother,
going round,
going round.

— Doris Seale

AS A MATTER OF FACT Native American Day, also called American Indian Day, is a day of celebration. It is a day to remember the histories of Native peoples, and to celebrate all the different ways tribal peoples live. It was first officially observed in New York state in 1916, after being sponsored by the Society of American Indians. In current practice, it is a "movable event," celebrated on many different days and in many different ways by various Native peoples. Many Indian groups celebrate it on the last Thursday of September. Some Native organizations are petitioning to have the day after Thanksgiving declared a federal holiday in honor of the first peoples of this land.

Yom Kippur brings the High Holy Days to a close.

25 Yom Kippur (nine days after Rosh Hashanah)

A NEW START

Praying together, we made a new start.
Now we feel fresh and bright,
and the future opens before us
like a flower in the sun.

In our prayers, we have said,
"I hope that I can be a better me."

L'shanah tovah!*
We look forward to a year of plenty—
for our people and for people
everywhere.

— Unknown

* L'shanah tovah *(luh-shah-NAH toh-VAH):* Hebrew for "a good year"

CULTURESHARE The holiest day of the year for many Jews, Yom Kippur *(yom kee-POOR)* brings to a close the High Holy Days and sets the stage for the year to come. Many spend the day in temple, acknowledging and asking forgiveness for the wrongdoings of the past year and pledging to make the new year a good one. Fasting is a traditional part of this "cleansing" process, and the day often ends with a festive and long-awaited meal.

Hurrah for Hispanic Heritage Month!

26

Hispanic Heritage Month (September 15–October 15)

ODE TO MY LIBRARY

It's small
with two rooms
Of books, a globe
That I once
Dropped, some maps
Of the United States and Mexico,
And a fish tank with
A blue fish that
Is always making jeta.*
There are tables and chairs,
And a pencil sharpener
On the wall: a crayon is stuck
In it, but I didn't do it.

It's funny, but the
Water fountain
Is cooled by a motor,
And the librarian reads
Books with her
Glasses hanging
From her neck. If she
Put them on
She would see me
Studying the Incas
Who lived two steps
From heaven, way in the mountains.

The place says, "Quiet, please,"
But three birds
Talk to us
Loudly from the window.
What's best is this:
A phonograph
That doesn't work.
When I put on the headphones,
I'm the captain of a jet,
And my passengers
Are mis abuelitos*
Coming from a dusty ranch
in Monterrey.* I want
To fly them to California,
But then walk
Them to my library.
I want to show them
The thirty books I devoured
In the summer read-a-thon.

I want to show them
The mural I helped paint.
In the mural,
An Aztec warrior
Is standing on a mountain
With a machete
And a band of feathers
On his noble head.
I made the cuts
Of muscle on
His stomach
And put a boulder
Of strength in each arm.

He could gather
Enough firewood
With one fist.
He could slice
Open a mountain
With that machete,
And with the wave of his arm
Send our enemies tumbling.

If I could fly,
I would bring
Mis abuelitos to California.
They would touch my hair
When I showed
Them my library:
The fish making jeta,
The globe that I dropped,
The birds fluttering
Their wings at the window.
They would stand me
Between them,
When I showed them
My thirty books,
And the cuts
On the warrior,
Our family of people.

—Gary Soto

*jeta (HEH-tah): Spanish for "lips," "snout," or "face."
 The phrase "making jeta" here means moving the
 mouth in typical fish-fashion
*mis abuelitos (mees ah-bweh-LEE-tohs): Spanish for
 "my grandparents"
*Monterrey: city located in northeastern Mexico

As a Matter of Fact In 1968, President Lyndon Johnson set aside a week to
honor Hispanic Americans. In a presidential proclamation in 1989, President Bush
extended the period to a month, proclaiming National Hispanic Heritage Month
from September 15 to October 15. During this time, people in the U.S. celebrate
the contributions of Hispanic culture and Hispanic Americans.

27

B *BORINQUEN**

Borinquen, my little island,
Like a seashell in the sun—
On the outside, like a flower;
On the inside, there's a song.

> —Isabel Freire de Matos (original in Spanish)
> English version by Juan Quintana

***Borinquen (boh REEN ken) or Boriquén (boh ree KEN; also
spelled Borikén):** name given to the island now known as
Puerto Rico by its original Taino inhabitants; currently used
as a poetic or endearing name, it means "land of courage"
in Taino

28

TWO IN ONE

Confusing, isn't it? This
Union of two languages and people.
But there are others like us,
A part of two cultures: not North, not South,
Not just one or the other. Cuba and
America wrap their arms around us,
Molding us so we stand strong.
Even though, it is said, we must choose: not
Remain wanting to live both,
I do not agree. Our place is to be
Cuban sometimes, some days;
American sometimes, some ways.
Native to both and to none.

> —Marisella Veiga

29

*THERE'S AN
ORANGE TREE OUT THERE*

There's an orange tree out there,
* behind that old,*
abandoned garden wall,
but it's not the same orange tree
* we planted,*
and it's a beautiful orange tree
so beautiful it makes us remember
that orange tree we planted
*   —in our land—*
before coming to this house
so distant and remote from that house
where we planted an orange tree
and even saw it—like this one—in flower.

> —Alfonso Quijada Urías (original in Spanish)
> English version by Darwin J. Flakoll

A WORD FROM THE POET Alfonso Quijada Urías is a
Salvadoran poet currently living in Canada. About this
poem he says: "I wrote it in 1981, while I was in Cuba. I
was away from my country and missing it. I think the
poem conveys my feelings pretty clearly."

Here's a rhyme to carry you through the rest of the year.

30

THIRTY DAYS HATH SEPTEMBER

Thirty days hath September,
April, June and November.
All the rest have thirty-one,
Except February alone,
Which has four and twenty-four
Till leap-year gives it one day more.

> —Traditional English rhyme

ACROSS THE CURRICULUM
SOCIAL STUDIES & READING

Remembering, Celebrating
EXPLORING CULTURE Throughout Hispanic Heritage Month,
remember the history and celebrate the contributions
of Hispanic Americans by reading aloud (or making
available for children to read) books by Hispanic
authors reflecting Hispanic perspectives. Some titles
are listed below.

As each book is read, display a classroom map of the
Americas and give each child a copy of the map on
Activity Sheet 2. Help children locate the geographical
setting of the author's culture of origin and/or the
book's setting on the large map and their small maps.
Children might keep track of their reading by labeling
their maps in the appropriate place with each book
title.

✦ *Baseball in April and Other Stories* by Gary Soto
   (Harcourt Brace, 1990).

✦ *Family Pictures* by Carmen Lomas Garza (Children's
   Book Press, 1990).

✦ *Felita* and *Going Home* by Nicholasa Mohr (Bantam,
   1990, 1989).

✦ *My Aunt Otilia's Spirits* by Richard Garcia (Children's
   Book Press, 1992).

✦ *My Name Is María Isabel* by Alma Flor Ada
   (Atheneum, 1993).

MULTICULTURAL FOCUS

OCTOBER

October is a month of change and promise, travel and discovery, beginnings and endings.

October brings apples, sweetened with a year's worth of patient cultivation. The leaves of October fall and make room for next spring's additions. The colder weather pushes us inside, only to invite us out again for Halloween.

Our thoughts turn worldly in October, with the sounds of World Poetry Day, the teamwork of the World Series, and the anniversary of Columbus's voyage to the "New World." We honor this nation's newest citizens in this month as well: the children and immigrants who are our future. So get ready for a month of surprises—who knows what you'll see before October is over!

Noteworthy Days

- ✦ National Apple Month
- **5** Universal Children's Day
- **12** Columbus Day (second Monday)/ Día de la Raza
- **15** World Poetry Day
- ✦ World Series (falls mid- to late October)
- **24** United Nations Day
- **31** Halloween

An apple a day!

1

from A. APPLE PIE

A
A was once
an apple-pie
Pidy,
Widy,
Tidy,
Pidy,
Nice-insidy
Apple-pie!

—Edward Lear

DEVELOPING LITERACY
PATTERNED WRITING

Take One Orange
To make the poem "Take One Apple" more comprehensible to **students acquiring English**, pantomime the actions as you read, using a whole apple and an apple core as props.

Children can then create innovations on the poem. Bring a variety of fruits to class and let pairs of children choose a favorite. One child in each pair can get the fruit ready to eat and eat it while the other notes the steps involved.

All children who chose the same fruit then get together, discuss their observations, and come up with a variation on the poem, focusing on the details of eating other fruit. For example:

TAKE ONE ORANGE

wash and dry
and strip the peel
in one long strip
and break it into wedges
and eat it up
then take one orange more

2

TAKE ONE APPLE

wash and
dry

and
eat

it up and down
and side
ways

to
the
core

then
take
one
apple
more

—Arnold Adoff

3

JOHNNY APPLESEED

Johnny, Johnny Appleseed
Wandered many miles,
Hung his sack upon his back
Spreading seeds and smiles.

Trees and orchards everywhere
In Johnny's honor stand:
Their fruits are gifts from Johnny's heart;
Their roots, from Johnny's hands.

—Josh Weinstein

CULTURESHARE Johnny Appleseed is a United States folk hero, said to have traveled the country barefoot, planting apple trees and giving apple seeds and saplings to everyone he met. Some tales praise his unassuming tin-pot hat and coffee-sack shirt; others detail his gentle, charming way with all creatures. However, few, if any, of these tales are true.

Johnny Appleseed was born John Chapman, in 1774. After moving to the Ohio–Indiana frontier, Chapman traveled and planted apple seeds, eventually owning and cultivating more than 1,100 acres of land. It is now thought that Chapman's orchards were not very productive because apple trees grown from seed are rarely good yielders.

The Johnny Appleseed legends may have been started by people who actually knew John Chapman. Their stories about this slightly eccentric, kind-hearted neighbor have created a folk hero as American as, well, apple pie.

4

A stone from the hand of a friend is an apple.

—Moroccan proverb

In children we see our past and our future.

5 Universal Children's Day

Children are the hope of the world because they are the ones who know how to love.

—José Martí

CultureShare Throughout Latin America, the name José Martí (1853–1895), a Cuban patriot and poet, is synonymous with respect for and devotion to children. Martí's writing often expresses his ardent belief that children are the hope for a better future because of their innate capacity for love and justice. In Spanish-speaking countries, his is often among the first poetry children read, because his style—sensitive, intense, simple, and direct—is so accessible. If you have Spanish-speaking children, ask one to read and translate the following poem so the class can experience the beauty of Martí's writing:

de VERSOS SENCILLOS	from SIMPLE VERSES
Tiene el señor presidente un jardín con una fuente, y un tesoro en oro y trigo: tengo más, tengo un amigo.	The President has a garden with a fountain, and a treasure in gold and wheat: I have more, I have a friend.

Of all the You's that you are, You are Yourself most often by far!

6

BEING NOBODY

Have you ever felt like nobody?
Just a tiny speck of air.
When everyone's around you,
And you are just not there.

—Karen Crawford, age 9

SUCCESS

I think I can succeed in anything I want to do. Myself -- I am a surprising human being.

—Unknown child
Dallas, Texas

7

BY MYSELF

When I'm by myself
And I close my eyes
I'm a twin
I'm a dimple in a chin
I'm a room full of toys
I'm a squeaky noise
I'm a gospel song

I'm a gong
I'm a leaf turning red
I'm a loaf of brown bread
I'm whatever I want to be

And when I open my eyes
What I care to be
Is me

—Eloise Greenfield

DEVELOPING LITERACY
GROUP TALK & WRITING

How to Be Somebody
PROMOTING SELF-ESTEEM Reread the poems aloud and, for **students acquiring English**, restate the central concepts. Restate the first entry as *Have you ever felt like a little grain of sand or a bit of dust—something that nobody cares about and nobody pays attention to?* Restate the second entry as *I can do anything I try to do; I am wonderful; I can do things that are hard to do.* Then discuss how differently the two **Young Voices** authors see themselves.

Partners can then share the things they do that make them feel like surprising human beings; each child can then record and illustrate several. **Students at early stages of acquiring English** who are not yet ready to write independently can point to their drawings or act out surprising things they can do, while their partners record for them.

Bind each child's papers into a book. Encourage children to read their books whenever they feel "like nobody," to remember how surprising they really are.

8

THE DRUM

daddy says the world is
a drum tight and hard
and i told him
i'm gonna beat
out my own rhythm

—Nikki Giovanni

9

I AM SUN SHINING

I am sun shining.
I am the warm sun that shines on
    the earth.
I am the hot warm sun shining in
    the sky.
I am the clouds moving in the sky.
I am the bright clouds that shine.
I am the sun setting.
I am the clouds moving away.
I am myself.

—Marla Want, age 11
Hayward, California

10

OKAY EVERYBODY

Okay everybody, listen to this:
I am tired of being smaller
than you
And them
And him
And trees and buildings.
So watch out
All you gorillas and adults
Beginning tomorrow morning
Boy
Am I going to be taller.

—Karla Kuskin

11

SILENT, BUT . . .

I may be silent, but
I'm thinking.
I may not talk, but
Don't mistake me for a wall.

—Tsuboi Shigeji

ACROSS THE CURRICULUM
ARTS AND CRAFTS

Self-Portraits

PROMOTING SELF-ESTEEM To celebrate their individuality, children can create life-sized self-portraits. Partners can trace each other's silhouette onto butcher paper. Then, as children fill in their silhouettes, encourage them to use colors and details to make their portrait unique, just as they are unique. (You might provide hand-held mirrors to help children focus on their features, hair, and skin tone. Also be sure to have varied colors of paint available so children can accurately portray their skin tones.) Children might enjoy signing their portraits, copying a favorite poem from this theme, or writing some of the reasons they are "surprising human beings" on their self-portraits. Children can use their self-portraits to "introduce" themselves to the class, explaining why they are unique.

VALUING DIVERSITY Here's a high-impact way to celebrate diversity. Cut around the outline of children's self-portraits and exhibit them in a hallway under the banner "Ourselves—We are surprising human beings!" Each time you pass the portraits with your students, notice something different and reinforce how special and beautiful they are in their diversity:

◆ Each one of these children amazes me—no one child is exactly like any other.

◆ Every time I see these beautiful portraits, I am happy that I know such special people.

The voyage that changed the world.

12

Columbus Day (second Monday)/
Día de la Raza

FRIDAY, 12 OCTOBER 1492

*At dawn . . . I went ashore in the ship's boat, armed, followed by Martín Alonso Pinzón, captain of the **Pinta**, and his brother, Vincente Yáñez Pinzón, captain of the **Niña**. I unfurled the royal banner and the captains brought the flags which displayed a large green cross with the letters F and Y*. . . . To this island I gave the name **San Salvador**. . . .*

—Christopher Columbus
From his log, 1492
English version by Robert H. Fuson

*F and Y: for Spain's King <u>F</u>erdinand and Queen <u>Y</u>sabella, who funded Columbus's voyage

AS A MATTER OF FACT Columbus Day has been observed in the United States since 1934 in commemoration of Christopher Columbus's October 12, 1492, landing in the Bahamas. In 1971, the holiday was moved to the second Monday in October.

Opposition to Columbus Day as a national observance has been growing in recent years, as more people join in the re-examination of Columbus's impact on the course of history in the Americas. For more information, you might consult *Rethinking Columbus*, available from Rethinking Schools, 1001 E. Keefe Avenue, Milwaukee, WI 53212, (414) 964-9646; or *The Columbus Controversy: Challenging How History Is Written*, available from American School Publishers, 155 North Wacker Drive, P.O. Box 4520, Chicago, IL 60680, (800) 843-8855.

13

B ORGULLO/PRIDE

*Orgullosa de mi familia
orgullosa de mi lengua
orgullosa de mi cultura
orgullosa de mi raza
orgullosa de ser quien soy.*

*Proud of my family
proud of my language
proud of my culture
proud of my race
proud to be who I am.*

—Alma Flor Ada

CULTURESHARE The mixing of Spanish and indigenous cultures eventually gave rise in the Americas to a new *raza*, or race, combining both backgrounds. The concept of *La Raza* is an important one for Hispanics of mixed Spanish and Native American ancestry, both in the U.S. and throughout the Americas. On *Día de la Raza*, this rich heritage is honored in Latin American countries and Hispanic areas of the U.S. with fiestas, speeches, and parades.

14

YOUNG VOICES

I LIVE FREE

*I feel inside
the need to live,
I feel I must
be free,
I must not let him
catch me.
I must not let that
be.
I represent my
people,
I represent their
lives.
If I live,
they will keep on living
to see me fly across the sky.*

—Laurie Y. Montoya, age 16
Minneapolis, Minnesota

CULTURESHARE Although Columbus has been called the "discoverer" of the "New World," Native Americans—whom Columbus called "Indians" because he believed he was in India—had lived in the Americas for tens of thousands of years before his landing. As Columbus and other colonists returned to settle in what they called the New World, they often enslaved the Native Americans they encountered, drove them from their lands, or killed them. As more of the continent was settled by European Americans, the number of Native Americans decreased due to war and disease. As a result, many people, including the poet, who is Chippewa, view Columbus as the symbol of the destruction of the Native Americans' civilization and way of life.

Poems are how words sing!

15

World Poetry Day

AN HISTORIC MOMENT

The man said,
after inventing poetry,
"WOW!"
and did a full somersault.

—William J. Harris

DEVELOPING LITERACY
PATTERNED WRITING

Who Said What, Why?
Children can create their own "historic moments" by writing a poem in the pattern of "An Historic Moment." Encourage children to think of an invention—it could be a real invention, such as a *can opener*, or a fanciful one, such as *sunshine*. Then, to finish their poems, children can think of who thought of the invention, and what that person might have said and done. For example:

The __firefighter__ said,
after inventing __water__,
"FINALLY!"
and __took a long shower.__

Children might like to read their poems to the class, or illustrate their ideas about inventors and inventions.

16

THINGS

Went to the corner
Walked in the store
Bought me some candy
Ain't got it no more
Ain't got it no more

Went to the beach
Played on the shore
Built me a sandhouse
Ain't got it no more
Ain't got it no more

Went to the kitchen
Lay down on the floor
Made me a poem
Still got it
Still got it

—Eloise Greenfield

17

YOUNG VOICES

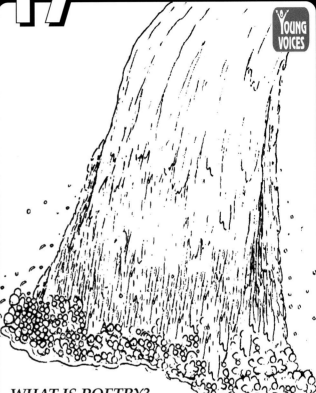

WHAT IS POETRY?

Poetry is like a cascade
It's everywhere
It falls from the sky
It mostly comes from the bottom of your
HEART
It's part of us
It's free
It surrounds us
Nobody owns poetry
Poems ask us to make them come to LIFE.

—Kien Po, 12th grade
San Francisco, California

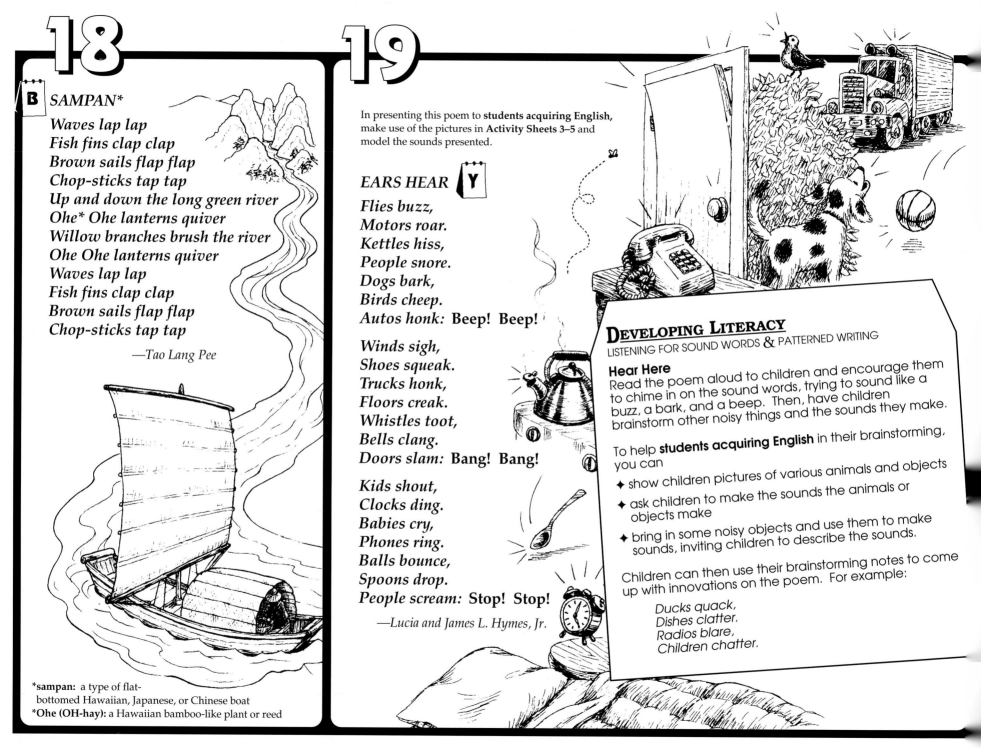

18

B SAMPAN*

Waves lap lap
Fish fins clap clap
Brown sails flap flap
Chop-sticks tap tap
Up and down the long green river
Ohe* Ohe lanterns quiver
Willow branches brush the river
Ohe Ohe lanterns quiver
Waves lap lap
Fish fins clap clap
Brown sails flap flap
Chop-sticks tap tap

—Tao Lang Pee

*sampan: a type of flat-
   bottomed Hawaiian, Japanese, or Chinese boat
*Ohe (OH-hay): a Hawaiian bamboo-like plant or reed

19

In presenting this poem to **students acquiring English**, make use of the pictures in **Activity Sheets 3–5** and model the sounds presented.

EARS HEAR **Y**

Flies buzz,
Motors roar.
Kettles hiss,
People snore.
Dogs bark,
Birds cheep.
Autos honk: Beep! Beep!

Winds sigh,
Shoes squeak.
Trucks honk,
Floors creak.
Whistles toot,
Bells clang.
Doors slam: Bang! Bang!

Kids shout,
Clocks ding.
Babies cry,
Phones ring.
Balls bounce,
Spoons drop.
People scream: Stop! Stop!

—Lucia and James L. Hymes, Jr.

DEVELOPING LITERACY
LISTENING FOR SOUND WORDS & PATTERNED WRITING

Hear Here
Read the poem aloud to children and encourage them to chime in on the sound words, trying to sound like a buzz, a bark, and a beep. Then, have children brainstorm other noisy things and the sounds they make.

To help **students acquiring English** in their brainstorming, you can

◆ show children pictures of various animals and objects

◆ ask children to make the sounds the animals or objects make

◆ bring in some noisy objects and use them to make sounds, inviting children to describe the sounds.

Children can then use their brainstorming notes to come up with innovations on the poem. For example:

Ducks quack,
Dishes clatter.
Radios blare,
Children chatter.

. . . when poetry's around!

20

Read this poem in a way that mimics the quickening tempo and increasing loudness of a steam locomotive getting under way. Be sure to pause after *click* in the first stanza, as indicated by the hyphen.

SONG OF THE TRAIN

Clickety-clack,
Wheels on the track,
This is the way
They begin the attack:
Click-ety-clack,
Click-ety-clack,
Click-ety, clack-ety,
Click-ety
Clack.

Clickety-clack,
Over the crack,
Faster and faster
The song of the track:
Clickety-clack,
Clickety-clack,
Clickety, clackety,
Clackety
Clack.

Riding in front,
Riding in back,
Everyone *hears*
The song of the track:
Clickety-clack,
Clickety-clack,
Clickety-clickety,
Clackety
Clack.

—*David McCord*

If the World Series is going on, October must be going, going, gone! . . .

21

World Series (falls mid- to late October)

PREDICTION: SCHOOL P. E.

Someday
when the baseball's
             hurtling
like some UFO,
       blazing
like some mad thing
             toward me
             in outfield
I won't gasp
and dodge. Oh, no!
Instead, I'll be
calmer than calm
             —so la-de-da!—
I'll just reach out
       like a **pro**
and catch it and—quick!—
             throw to second.
And everyone will say, "Hooray!
Natalie made a double-play!"
Some day.

—*Isabel Joshlin Glaser*

AS A MATTER OF FACT The World Series is the annual championship between the best teams in each of Major League Baseball's two leagues—the National League and the American League. The first team to win four games wins the best-of-seven game series, and is baseball's "World Champion" until next year's series. The World Series has been held every year since 1903 (except in 1904, when the National League champions refused to play) and is now one of the most popular sporting events in the U.S. and many other countries.

22

The following quotation comes from Peter Golenbock's book *Teammates* (Harcourt, Brace, Jovanovich, 1990). You may wish to read the book to children when discussing this entry.

WHAT COUNTS

I don't care if this man is black, blue, or striped. He can play and he can help us win. That's what counts.

—*Pee Wee Reese*

AS A MATTER OF FACT Pee Wee Reese was the shortstop for the Brooklyn Dodgers in 1947 when Jackie Robinson joined the team. The first African American player in the major leagues, Robinson was chosen as the Dodgers' first baseman by the team's owner, Branch Rickey. Reese made the above comment in response to a petition his teammates had circulated to get Robinson off the team—just one of the many indignities, including having to eat and sleep apart from the rest of the team, that Robinson suffered. Robinson's bravery, Reese's support, and Rickey's vision eventually ended segregation in professional baseball.

23

HUG O' WAR

I will not play at tug o' war.
I'd rather play at hug o' war,
Where everyone hugs
Instead of tugs,
Where everyone giggles
And rolls on the rug,
Where everyone kisses,
And everyone grins,
And everyone cuddles,
And everyone wins.

—*Shel Silverstein*

ACROSS THE CURRICULUM

SOCIAL STUDIES

What REALLY Counts

VALUING DIVERSITY Share the information in **As a Matter of Fact** with children and explain that *segregation* means keeping people apart. When there was segregation in professional baseball, African American players were not allowed to play in the major leagues. Then, ask children to discuss how Jackie Robinson might have felt. Help children understand the concept of *discrimination*—treating people unfairly because of their looks, their beliefs, their family background, or the fact that they are men or women—and that discrimination is wrong.

To help children learn ways of treating each other fairly, discuss discriminatory behaviors to avoid, such as name calling, making fun of people, or excluding people unfairly. Share a few of your own ideas, allowing children to add their ideas and reasons. Create a classroom poster with a series of questions that you and children can ask yourselves if these behaviors arise in the future.

ARE YOU FAIR TO PEOPLE?

Ask yourself
- Do I call anyone insulting or hurtful names?
- Do I make fun of people because of the way they act or look?
- Do I purposely leave people out of activities because of the way they act or look?

When nations work together, the whole world wins!

24

United Nations Day

You may want to adapt the nationalities/ethnic origins, mentioned in verse 5 of this song, to reflect the composition of your class.

UNDER ONE SKY

Words and music by Ruth Pelham

Medium

We're all a fa - mi - ly un-der one sky we're a fam - ily un - der one sky We're all a fa - mi - ly un-der one sky We're a fam - ily un - der one sky and we're

1. peo - ple __ and we're an - i-mals and we're flow - ers __ and we're
2. plum - bers _ and we're doc - tors _ and we're farm - ers __ and we're

birds in flight and we're peo - ple _ and we're an - i-mals and we're flow-ers _ and birds in flight _
teach-ers too and we're plum-bers _ and we're doc-tors _ and we're farm-ers _ and teach-ers too __

3. And we're sisters
And we're brothers
And we're friends
And we're neighbors too
And we're sisters
And we're brothers
And we're friends
And neighbors too

4. And we're happy
And we're angry
And we're frightened
And we're tender too
And we're happy
And we're angry
And we're frightened
And tender too

5. And we're Americans
And we're Russians
And we're Palestinians
And Israelis too
And we're Americans
And we're Russians
And we're Palestinians
And Israelis too

© 1982 Ruth Pelham Music ASCAP. Reprinted by permission.

AS A MATTER OF FACT The United Nations was founded in 1945, just after World War II. It is an organization working to ensure peace among countries and humane treatment of people throughout the world. Its original membership of 50 nations has since tripled, and the flags of all the member countries fly in front of the United Nations headquarters in New York City, where the nations' representatives meet.

25

SOMETHING NEW

Words and music by
Victor Cockburn and Judith Steinbergh

Bouncy, pop feel

1. We're proud we can sing our fam - ily's __ songs, __ in a lan - guage __ they un - der -
stand. It makes us feel __ like we __ be - long, __ like we're con - nect - ed to a - no - ther __ land. __
__ And we're learn-ing to sing __ to - ge - ther, __ our songs are a com-mon __ ground. We

Chorus

sing in so ma - ny __ lan - guag - es, __ How love-ly __ our voic - es sound. We love to learn __ from our
fam - i - lies, __ from neigh - bors and __ com - mu - ni - ties. __ We share what we know with a
new - found __ friend __ and learn some - thing new __ to take home a - gain. _____ 2. I'm

2. (I'm) proud I can cook my family's way,
with ginger root and noodles of rice.
It feels both close and faraway,
smelling lemon grass and spice.
I'll teach you to cook something new,
moussaka, brisket, fajita.
I'll teach you to make lasagna and stew,
Baba ganoush with pita.

3. I'm proud of this pot I can coil,
and the whistles I fire in clay.
Let me show you how to create a doll
or a lion in paper maché.
I'll cut out a shadow puppet,
Let me fold you a delicate swan.
I can weave you a shawl with a border of fringe,
Or show you how bamboo is drawn.

4. We know that we're all different,
our faces, voices, and names.
And we have so much to celebrate,
with our music, stories, and games.
A dance with a joyful rhythm
a story that's drawn in sand.
A playground chant or a special poem,
a song that's sung with our hands.

© 1993 Talking Stone Productions. Reprinted by permission.

26

The author of this poem is a classroom teacher in San Francisco, California. You may wish to personalize this poem to fit your background and that of the children in your class.

TO MY STUDENTS

When I look at you
I roam the globe
When I look at you
I sense I'm small
Western
so very white
When I look at you
I question
from where have you come
what have you seen
Have you been made
to live
beyond your years
When I look at you
I marvel
In one room
all our destinies
have found each other
When I look at you
I'm thankful.

—*Leslie Hughes*

27

CHINESE HOT POT

My dream of America
is like **dá bìn lòuh***
with people of all persuasions and
tastes
sitting down around a common pot
chopsticks and basket scoops here
and there
some cooking squid and others beef
some tofu or watercress
all in one broth
like a stew that really isn't
as each one chooses what he wishes
to eat
only that one pot and fire are shared
along with the good company
and the sweet soup
spooned out at the end of the meal.

—*Wing Tek Lum*

***dá bìn lòuh** (dah bin low)*: a large pot of hot water in which people dip and cook meat, vegetables, tofu, and other foods, popular in Chinese restaurants (especially in the winter). The food often leaves a tasty soup which is then also shared; the eating of dá bìn lòuh is as much a social as a culinary activity.

28

BROOMS

On stormy days
When the wind is high

Tall trees are brooms
Sweeping the sky.

They swish their branches

In buckets of rain,

And swash and sweep it
Blue again.

—*Dorothy Aldis*

29

WOULDN'T YOU?

If I
Could go
As high
And low
As the wind
As the wind
As the wind
Can blow—

I'd go!

—*John Ciardi*

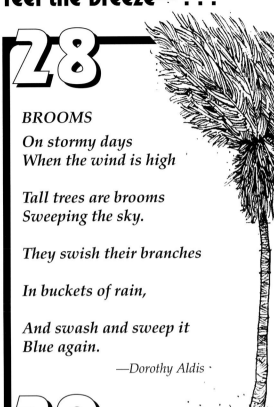

. . . leaves are falling from the trees.

AUTUMN

Autumn
Is when the ground puts on
A sweater of leaves
Until its winter coat is ready.

—Josh Weinstein

ACROSS THE CURRICULUM

SCIENCE

Leaf "Flight Patterns"
Children can stand on a chair and drop leaves of different shapes and sizes to the ground one by one. How do they fly? Do they glide a long way? Encourage students to record the results of the experiments.

Content-Area ESL
Do a directed-drawing exercise to introduce the parts of a leaf. Draw the parts one by one—stem, veins, pores—and have children draw after you.

Children can also sort leaves into categories. Hold up a leaf. Have children find other leaves that are similar in size and shape, and group the leaves in a display.

Halloween is here— the scariest night of the year!

Halloween

To make the poem more comprehensible for **students acquiring English,** use pantomime or sound effects for as many of the adjectives as possible.

HALLOWEEN

Hooting
　Howling
　　Hissing
　　　Witches,
Riding
　Rasping
　　Ragged
　　　Switches;
Fluttering
　Frightening
　　Fearsome
　　　Bats;
Arching
　Awesome
　　Awful
　　　Cats;
Long
　Lantern-
　　Lighted
　　　Streets;
Tricks!
　Tasty
　　Tempting
　　　Treats!

—Phyllis J. Perry

DEVELOPING LITERACY

ORAL COMPOSING & DRAMATIC INTERPRETATION—Choral Reading

Crazy, Clever, Creative Verses
Invite children to brainstorm topics to add to the poem, such as pumpkins, houses, ghosts, and skeletons. Then, encourage them to create additional verses by thinking of words (not necessarily alliterative) to describe each topic. Some examples are:

Orange
Glowing
Grinning
　Pumpkins

Spooky
Creaky
Haunted
　Houses

After children have added their verses to the poem, form three groups. The first group says the first word in each verse; the second group, the second word, and so on, with all three groups joining in to say the fourth word.

CULTURE SHARE Halloween is an excellent example of how a celebration or event spreads through cultures. The modern-day holiday of Halloween is probably based on a Celtic celebration. But, as often happens, the holiday's customs changed and developed as other cultures adapted them. November 1 marked the beginning of the year for the ancient Celts, who lived 2,000 years ago in what is now Ireland, Great Britain, and parts of France and northern Spain. The day honored the Celtic Lord of Death. Part of the celebration the evening before included dressing up in costumes. This celebration was later combined with two Roman holidays: one that honored the dead and one that honored Pomona, goddess of fruit and trees.

In the 800s the Christian church established All Saints' Day on November 1. The mass said on that day was the *Allhallowmas*. The night before was *All Hallow e'en,* or *Halloween.* In England, poor people went out *a-souling,* or begging, on All Souls' Day, November 2. In Ireland and England, carved-out beets, potatoes, and turnips were used as lanterns on Halloween. As people moved to the United States from traditional Celtic areas, they took with them their Halloween traditions: costumes, trick-or-treating, and jack-o-lanterns.

November

The winds of November bring memories of the past and promises of the future. November is a time to remember those who came before us and to think about growing up ourselves. It is a time to give thanks for what we have, and, on Veterans' Day, to thank those who have served in our Armed Forces during wartime.

On Election Day we choose our leaders; during National Children's Book Week we celebrate children's books and the wonders of reading. Toward the end of the month, in some parts of the country, the weather turns nippy and makes us bring out our winter gear.

So with breezes and shivers and thoughts to remember, here comes November!

Noteworthy Days

1–2 Day of the Dead/*Día de los Muertos*

✦ Election Day (Tuesday after the first Monday)

11 Veterans' Day

✦ National Children's Book Week (week before Thanksgiving week)

19 Puerto Rico Discovery Day

✦ Thanksgiving (fourth Thursday)

✦ Latin America Week (last full week)

1

Children can use this rhyme to see how many times they can hop on one foot, toss a bean bag with a partner, or clap hands with a partner, without missing. They might also use it as a choosing (or counting-out) rhyme, stopping at "three."

COLD NOVEMBER

Cold November dressed in brown,
Leaves are falling all around.
How many leaves do you see?
One, two, three . . .

—Unknown

ACROSS THE CURRICULUM

MULTICULTURAL FOCUS

ARTS AND CRAFTS

El Día de los Muertos

EXPLORING CULTURE For many children, celebrating a holiday in which death plays a prominent role will be a new experience, one that will require a festive classroom atmosphere and plenty of background information. A good source is *Indo-Hispanic Folk Art Traditions II* by Bobbi Salinas-Norman (Piñata Publications, 1988; available from Hampton-Brown). The humor in "*Estaba la muerte un día*" can set the stage for these activities:

◆ Children can make skulls (*calaveras*) out of modeling clay. For eyes and teeth, they can use buttons, beads, glitter, or bits of foil or yarn. A hole made at the top will accommodate a piece of string or yarn, so that the *calaveras* can be hung in the classroom. A traditional aspect of this activity is to name and label each skull with the name of its creator or the name of a friend or ancestor.

◆ Yellow marigolds are often part of Day of the Dead observances. Provide yellow crepe paper or tissue for children to make additional classroom decorations.

◆ Invite members of the Mexican American community to visit and teach children songs and how to make traditional foods.

◆ Read aloud *Pablo Remembers: The Fiesta of the Days of the Dead* by George Ancona (Lothrop, 1993).

Set an upbeat tone for the celebration, restating the positive aspects of valuing family ties and honoring one's ancestors.

2

Day of the Dead/*Día de los Muertos* (November 1–2)

ESTABA LA MUERTE UN DÍA / DEATH WENT AND SAT DOWN ONE DAY

Traditional
English version by Josh Weinstein

© 1980 Fondo de Cultura Económica (Mexico). Reprinted by permission.

Lively

Es - ta - ba la Muer - te un dí - a sen - ta -
Death went ___ and sat down one day, sat down

da en un a - re - nal, _____ co - mien - do tor - ti - lla
in a san - dy place, ___ and ate lots of cold tor -

frí - a pa' ver si po - dí - a en - gor - dar. _____
ti - llas just to try and gain some weight. ___

CULTURESHARE November 1 and 2 collectively make up the Mexican holiday known as *Día de los Muertos*, or Day of the Dead, with the first day devoted to the spirits of departed children and the second day set aside to honor all other deceased relatives. Descended from a two-month celebration that goes back as far as 1800 B.C.E., this commemoration marks a way both to honor ancestors and to view death in an irreverent, humorous manner.

The customs associated with *Día de los Muertos* deprive death of its "shock value" by making it seem familiar, casual, as much a part of life as being born, eating, or having a party.

The skeleton is the most common symbol of the holiday, and is seen in everything from toys and decorations to the bread and skull candies made as offerings to the dead. Altars to deceased relatives are set up in homes. A trip to the cemetery, where gravesites are cleaned and decorated and long, festive picnics are held, marks the finale of this two-day celebration.

Although the Christian holidays on which *Día de los Muertos* is partly based—All Saints' Day and All Souls' Day—are observed in other countries, it is essentially a Mexican celebration. Many of the customs associated with it remain intact in the traditionally Mexican western and southwestern United States.

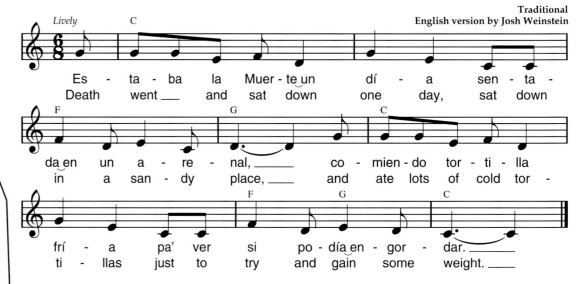

3

 HAIKU

i have looked into
     my father's eyes and seen an
         african sunset

—Sonia Sanchez

A Word from the Poet Sonia Sanchez remembers her inspiration for this poem: "My father and I were sitting in my house here in Philadelphia and the sun was filtering through the room. When it hit his face, I saw his history, his past, his beauty, and I wanted to share that. This haiku just popped into my head."

The author feels we owe a great debt to our elders and ancestors. "It's important for people to understand why we are on this Earth. We are here because people have come before us and done the work for us to be here. History is here whether we announce it or not. It's in our faces, our eyes, our lives. It's here in spite of ourselves and because of our ancestors, and it's important that we remember that. This poem was a way to capture some of that."

Developing Literacy
PATTERNED WRITING

Multicultural Focus

Simple Stories
Valuing Diversity After displaying "Haiku," talk about how the haiku form can express so much in only seventeen syllables. Then, cover parts of the original to create a frame:

     i have looked into
         my _____ eyes and seen
         _____

Next, invite children to write their own versions of the poem. Suggest that they begin by talking to a family member or friend, asking about that person's heritage and what is important to him or her.

Children can use the information they have gained to write their verses. Gather all the verses together to make a class book titled *Simple Stories*.

4

THE PATH

My ancestors can't see me
And I can't see them;
Although I do not see them,
I can see the path they trod.

If I see the path, is there
A reason not to follow it?

—Yi Hwang

As a Matter of Fact Sijo poetry, of which this poem is representative, originated in Korea in the twelfth century. Distinguished by its traditional three-line stanza (often rendered into English in the six-line pattern shown above), Sijo poetry originally was meant to be sung. Sijo often conveys Confucian values, among the most important of which is the honoring of ancestors.

5

STILL FINDING OUT
     Finding out that Grandpa Perry
was
born a slave   and died a free
                         farmer
here in Ohio:
               I am
                    free
here in Ohio
          on the Perry land planting tomatoes
                         on his same land.
I am part Perry
               and
          part still
               finding
                    out.

—Arnold Adoff

B from *FAMILY GIFTS*

Grandma stitched a special quilt,
She smoothed it on her bed,
And wore it 'round her shoulders.
Then one day my grandma said . . .
Here's a special present,
A quilt to bring you sleep,
I hope it makes you warm and safe,
A gift you'll always keep.

Chorus:
   Gifts of rings and patchwork,
   Coins and recipes,
   Pumpkin pies and lullabies,
   Will bind our families.

Aunt Rose has an armchair
With saggy saggy springs.
Its stuffing fluffs into the air
Like puffs of pigeon wings.
"Would you like this armchair?"
Our aunt Rose said one day,
"You will have a place to rest
When I have moved away."

Chorus

Grandpa came from Russia,
He brought a coin with him,
A coin his dad had given,
He sewed it in his hem.
He always rubbed it in his hand,
Until the picture blurred,
One day he slipped it in my palm
And didn't say a word.

Chorus

—*Victor Cockburn and Judith Steinbergh*

DEVELOPING LITERACY
GROUP TALK & WRITING

Legacies
VALUING DIVERSITY Families pass many things from generation to generation; some are tangible, some are not. Details vary from culture to culture, but legacies share the goal of keeping family heritage alive.

After reading the poems in this theme, discuss with children what objects or values may be passed down within families. Steer the conversation away from objects of inherent material value and towards objects of sentimental or cultural value. Validate all responses, using every opportunity to talk about the diversity of family life.

Then, younger children can work in pairs to talk about what keepsakes they might pass on when they are grandparents themselves. After they have shared ideas, ask them each to draw a picture of their keepsake. The drawings may be collected in a class album.

Older children can think about what they would like to be remembered for and what object might symbolize that. They can then write about or make their keepsakes. Their compositions or objects could be wrapped and labeled with tags that tell about the gift inside.

Students acquiring English might begin by working together in small native-language groups so that they can share their ideas more easily before they begin to work on their own.

While you cast your vote for today's leaders . . .

7 Election Day (Tuesday after the first Monday)

Dear Mr. president, I
Wish there Were peace
and lots of food for the
whole world to eat.

I'm only 6 yrs old and When
I grow up I Want to be
safe and enjoy my life.
every one Should try to
live together in peace
all ways

the ind

Christopher Vargas

—*Christopher Vargas, age 6*
Cathedral City, California

As a Matter of Fact Before 1845, states could hold presidential elections any time up to a month before the electors met in December. Seeking to standardize the electoral process, in 1845 Congress declared Election Day to be the Tuesday after the first Monday in November. Although this date officially applies only to presidential elections, many statewide and some local elections are held on this day as well, even in non-presidential election years.

Across the Curriculum
Social Studies & Writing

Power of the Pen
Ask children what they would like to tell or ask the president; remind them that their thoughts can be on any subject. Display topics children suggest. To expand on the theme of Election Day, you might hold a class-wide election to determine which topic to address in a class letter to the president. Prepare ballots and a ballot box, explaining the importance of casting secret ballots. Hold the election, count the votes, and announce the winning topic.

Then, younger children can dictate a class letter to the president; older children can write individual letters, addressed to:

The White House
1600 Pennsylvania Avenue
Washington, DC 20500

If the budget allows, the class could consider phoning the White House or sending a FAX to the president. The phone number of the White House office is (202) 456-1414; the phone number for the White House Comment Line is (202) 456-1111; and the FAX number is (202) 456-2461.

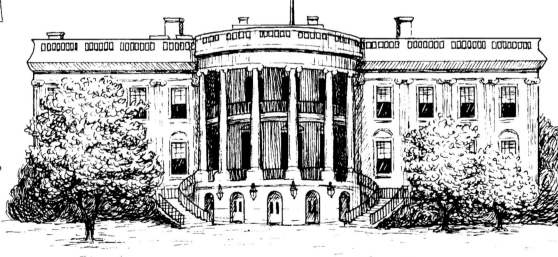

... tomorrow's leaders are growing right up!

8

POEM FOR RODNEY*

people always ask what
am i going to be
when i grow
up and i always
just think
i'd like to grow
up

—Nikki Giovanni

*Rodney: In the frontispiece of her book *Spin a Soft Black Song*, from which this poem comes, the author says, "Some of the poems and pictures are of children who talked to Nikki and Charles [the illustrator] and helped them remember what being a child is like." Rodney is the name of one of these children.

9

GOOD-BYE, SIX—HELLO, SEVEN

I'm getting a higher bunk bed.
And I'm getting a bigger bike.
And I'm getting to cross Connecticut Avenue
    all by myself, if I like.
And I'm getting to help do dishes.
And I'm getting to weed the yard.
And I'm getting to think that seven
    could be hard.

—Judith Viorst

10

WHEN I AM PRESIDENT . . .

I stood in front of the class
and read my essay on
"When I am President . . ."
The other kids just laughed
and said,
"You don't look like a President."
But my teacher smiled
at me and nodded.

—Lena Domyung Choe

DEVELOPING LITERACY
PATTERNED WRITING

MULTICULTURAL FOCUS

Look What I Can Do!
PROMOTING SELF-ESTEEM   "Goodbye, Six—Hello, Seven" provides an opportunity to help children value their developing abilities. Display *And I'm getting to* and record children's ideas about all the things they are starting to be able to do on their own.

Then, divide the class into groups by age and give each group a copy of **Activity Sheet 6.** Each group can brainstorm what they want to put in a book about their own privileges and responsibilities. Each child contributes a page or two, drawing a picture and pasting in a completed caption. The group writes their age in the last line and adds a cover, customizing the poem's title to their age.

Once children have assembled their books, read them aloud, focusing on the variety of abilities, skills, and accomplishments the pages reveal and commenting on how competent and capable the children are.

On Veterans' Day, we honor courage and service to one's country.

11

Veterans' Day

Before or immediately after the first reading of this poem, it may be necessary to discuss the terms *serve* and *return* as used in tennis, to make sure the students understand the play on words on which the poem is based.

DEAR UNCLE GREGG

The other day
I was watching the tennis match
on TV
and after it was over
they interviewed the winning player's
coach
and he said

"I'm proud of the way he served
And I'm even more pleased with his
return."

And I thought
If
after the war is over
they ever interview me
I'll be able to say the same thing
about
you.

—Josh Weinstein

AS A MATTER OF FACT Observed until 1954 as Armistice Day (in commemoration of the end of World War I in 1918), Veterans' Day honors all the men and women who have served in United States wars. While remaining true to its origins as a celebration of peace, the holiday is a way to officially recognize the courage, sacrifice, and contribution of all those who have risked their lives to serve their country.

Who knows where a week of reading may lead? . . .

12
National Children's Book Week
(week before Thanksgiving week)

A BOOK IS A PLACE

A book is a place
where you can go
whenever you wish:
just open it up
and step in!

For if you can read
you can sail seven seas,
explore lost kingdoms
with magic keys . . .

Climb snowy mountains,
Fly to the moon,
Speak with ghosts,
Hear mermaids croon . . .

Swim with whales
through sea-green depths,
Tame wild horses and . . .

When you come back
& close your book
& sit there with a dreamy,
faraway look . . .

It's because you
know you can go
anywhere you want
whenever you wish—
just open a book
and step in!

—Clyde Watson

13

THE REASON I LIKE CHOCOLATE

The reason I like chocolate
is I can lick my fingers
and nobody tells me I'm not polite

I especially like scary movies
'cause I can snuggle with Mommy
or my big sister and they don't laugh

I like to cry sometimes 'cause
everybody says "what's the matter
don't cry"

and I like books
for all those reasons
but mostly 'cause they just make me
happy

and I really like
to be happy

—Nikki Giovanni

14

BOOKS TO THE CEILING

Books to the ceiling, books to the sky.
My piles of books are a mile high.
How I love them!
How I need them!
I'll have a long beard by the time I
read them.

—Arnold Lobel

ACROSS THE CURRICULUM
MATHEMATICS

How Many Books Is That?
How many books would it take to reach the ceiling? Have children estimate how many feet high the classroom ceiling is, and record their estimates. Then, suggest that children collect several copies of the same book, such as a textbook, and stack them in a foot-high pile. Children can use the number of books in the pile and their estimates of the ceiling's height to calculate the number of books they think it will take to reach the ceiling.

Content-Area ESL
To help children with the units and terms for linear measurement used in the United States, tape a yardstick across the chalkboard and label appropriate segments with the words *inch*, *foot*, and *yard*.

15

GOOD BOOKS, GOOD TIMES!

Good books.
Good times.
Good stories.
Good rhymes.
Good beginnings.
Good ends.
Good people.
Good friends.
Good fiction.
Good facts.
Good adventures.
Good acts.
Good stories.
Good rhymes.
Good books.
Good times.

—Lee Bennett Hopkins

16

JAPAN POEM*

The
joy of
seeing
a
person
write

a
child
make
a
mark

the
joy
of
seeing

the
world
begin

—John Tagliabue

*Japan Poem: refers to the author's inspiration for the poem, which came during his extensive travels through Japan. Journals of these travels led to the poetry collected in the author's book *The Doorless Door: Japan Poems,* from which this poem is taken.

17

BEGINNING ON PAPER

on paper
I write it
on rain

I write it
on stones
on my boots

on trees
I write it
on the air

on the city
how pretty
I write my name

—Ruth Krauss

18

YOUNG VOICES

PENCIL

PENCIL
LONG   SKINNY
WRITING   ERASING   SHARPENING
RUNNING OUT OF LEAD
DEAD

—*James Loureiro, 8th grade*

Developing Literacy

PATTERNED WRITING

Delightful Diamantes

"Pencil" is an example of a *cinquain*, a patterned five-line poem. One commonly used pattern for a cinquain is that of the *diamante*—a poem whose subject gradually changes into its opposite. Here's a pattern children can follow to dictate or write their own diamante poems:

Line 1: a person, animal, place, or thing

Line 2: two adjectives (or a phrase) that describe Line 1

Line 3: a total of four verbs: two that describe the action of Line 1; two that describe the action of Line 5

Line 4: two adjectives (or a phrase) that describe Line 5

Line 5: the opposite of Line 1

Discover Puerto Rican heritage on Puerto Rico Discovery Day!

19

Puerto Rico Discovery Day

from *A PUERTO RICO/TO PUERTO RICO*

¡Patria!, jardín de la mar,
la perla de las Antillas,
¡tengo ganas de llorar!
¡tengo ganas de besar
la arena de tus orillas!

—*José Gautier Benítez*

My country! Mid-ocean garden,
of the Antilles* the jewel.
Tears well up in my eyes!
I long to kiss once again
the sand of your shores.

—*Translation by Juan Quintana*

*Antilles: a chain of islands in the Caribbean that includes Puerto Rico, Cuba, Jamaica, and Hispaniola

As a Matter of Fact Puerto Rico Discovery Day commemorates Columbus's landing on the island during his second voyage, in 1493. Discovery Day is celebrated in New York (and other cities with large Puerto Rican populations) with patriotic observances and school class projects that remember Puerto Rican history and affirm Puerto Rican heritage.

It's harvest time: think corn!

20

CHICOME-COATL*/SEVEN-SNAKE

corn stalks
are upright
snakes

corn ears
rattle
in the wind

—Francisco X. Alarcón

*Chicome-Coatl: pronounced *chee-KOH-meh COH-ah-tul*

A WORD FROM THE POET "'Chicome-Coatl/Seven-Snake' is just the tip of a cultural iceberg," says Francisco Alarcón, who explains that the title refers to the two wheels of time in Meso-American culture: *Seven* comes from the first wheel, which has 13 days; *Snake* is the fifth day of the second wheel, whose 20 days are each represented by a different animal. "Seven-Snake" is the day on which planting begins—March 21 (the beginning of spring) on the Gregorian calendar.

There is more, however. "Chicome-Coatl is the magical name of corn in the Meso-American tradition," explains Alarcón. "It is also the name of the goddess of corn. On March 21, people would ask the goddess for a good harvest. This is celebrated today with a play of shadows every year at noon in Chichen Itzá, in Yucatán." On the Spring Equinox (and also at the Fall Equinox), the arrangement of sculpture and architecture around the pyramid known as El Castillo causes the afternoon sunlight to project onto the pyramids an image of the goddess, who seems to descend the pyramid to bless the earth for a good harvest.

Why has corn been so important? "People survive because of corn," says Alarcón. "Where there is corn, there is life."

21

 LITTLE CORN PLANTS

Nicely, nicely, nicely, nicely,
there away in the east,
the rain clouds are caring for the
little corn plants
as a mother takes care of her baby.

—Acoma traditional song

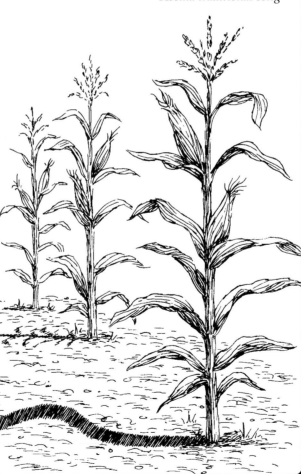

22

CORN

In early spring when Samuel plows
And then begins to sow,
I see the yellow seeds of corn,
And wish I were a crow.

But when the corn is tall as Sam,
And harvest time is near,
I'd rather be just what I am
And eat it off the ear.

—Esther Antin

AS A MATTER OF FACT North America is probably the first place corn ever grew—fossils of corn pollen found in Mexico are thought to date back 60,000 years. And corn has been sacred to the Native peoples of the Americas from time beyond memory. Native Americans grew all the main types of corn found today, and the numerous ceremonies in honor of the planting and harvesting of corn attest to its importance.

When the first Europeans came to what is now the U.S., they were taught to grow corn by the Native peoples. Corn became crucial to the survival of the European colonists as well.

Today, the United States produces about half of all the world's corn.

You might have children do the oral composing activity at right as a class *before* reading this poem. Then, children can compare and contrast their ideas with those in the poem.

OPENING CORN

sounds like pulling down a zipper

  a gray mouse squeaking

    scratching a chalkboard

washing windows

    tearing white paper

a metal violin playing music

    ripping rubber

Its silk looks like summer

    straw, thin gray string

    a witch's yellow white hair

Smells like onions

Feels like

    a little rock of diamonds—

  the road has bumps.

—*Group poem by Mr. Perucki's Fourth-Grade Class*
  Susan Terence, Poet-Teacher
  San Francisco, California

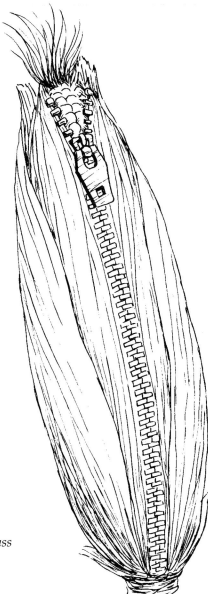

DEVELOPING LITERACY
ORAL COMPOSING

Perk Up Your Ears
Display these phrases:

OPENING CORN

Sounds like

Its silk looks like

Smells like

Feels like

If possible, bring an ear or two of fresh corn to class so that children can experience husking it. Ask them to look at the silk, smell the newly husked corn and touch the rows of kernels. This hands-on experience will be especially helpful to **students acquiring English**.

Then, ask children to suggest responses to each of the displayed phrases, based on their recent experience. Younger ones can dictate their responses for you to record, while older children can copy the phrases and write their responses, working with partners or in small groups. Finally, read the children's responses aloud as a poem. Children could go on to write other poems, based on this sensory-description pattern.

A Word from the Poet-Teacher "I bring in a dried ear of ornamental corn and ask children to close their eyes and listen to the sound of the corn husks scratching. What does it sound like? I write the students' responses on the board. Next, I hold up an ear of fresh corn, ask students to listen to the sound of the fresh corn husk being opened, and to, again, consider what the sound reminds them of. . . . I point to the cornsilk and ask what it reminds them of. . . . I write down all the student responses to compile a group poem.

"The inspiration for the exercise came from Richard Shelton's poem 'Wonders of the World.' In it he advises the reader to look for 'the star in the apple/the nest in the pomegranate/the maze in the onion.'"

It's Thanksgiving, today . . .

24

Thanksgiving (fourth Thursday)

Children may be surprised to know that "Over the River and Through the Wood" was originally a poem written in honor of Thanksgiving. Titled "The Boy's Thanksgiving Day," it first appeared in 1844.

OVER THE RIVER AND THROUGH THE WOOD

Brightly

Lydia Maria Child

1. O - ver the riv - er and through the wood, To grand-moth-er's house we go; _____ the horse knows the way to car - ry the sleigh Through the white _ and drift - ed snow. _
2. O - ver the riv - er and through the wood, Oh how __ the wind does blow _____ It stings __ the toes And bites _ the nose _____ As o - ver the ground we go. _
3. O - ver the riv - er and through the wood, To have __ a first - rate play _____ Hear the bells ring _____ "Ting - a - ling ding!" _____ Hur - rah for Thanks-giv - ing Day! _

As a Matter of Fact The United States holiday of Thanksgiving is said to commemorate a meal attended by English settlers and Native American Wampanoag in the fall of 1621. The Massachusetts winter had killed all but 55 of the 102 English colonists, and those who survived did so largely thanks to the Wampanoag, who had taught them to fish and hunt and to plant corn. To celebrate the summer corn harvest, the settlers are said to have invited the Wampanoag to join them for a feast of gratitude. After years of sporadic observance, Thanksgiving Day became an annual national holiday in 1863, under President Lincoln.

Today, many Native Americans think of Thanksgiving as a time of mourning, a time to remember with sadness the near-extermination of their peoples and cultures brought about by European colonization. Many activities common in schools at Thanksgiving time—for example, having children make and wear "Indian headdresses" and "act like Indians," and involving children in arts-and-crafts activities that trivialize Native clothes, dances, or ceremonies—have been insensitive and painful for Native people. To avoid the pervasive stereotypes and inaccuracies that have been promoted by Thanksgiving activities at schools, you might consult *How to Tell the Difference: A Checklist for Evaluating Children's Books for Anti-Indian Bias* by Beverly Slapin, Doris Seale, and Rosemary Gonzalez (New Society, 1992).

... and every day.

25

NOVEMBER

Thank you for the things we have,
thank you for Mama and turkey and fun,
thank you for Daddy wherever he is,
thank you for me, Everett Anderson.*

—Lucille Clifton

*Everett Anderson: the fictional main character in a series of poetry books by Lucille Clifton, including *Everett Anderson's Goodbye* (1978), *Everett Anderson's Nine Month Long* (1988), and *Everett Anderson's Christmas Coming* (1991), all published by Henry Holt.

26

YOUNG VOICES

AS I WALK THIS ROAD

As I walk this road I hear
the laughter of the new season
coming forth.
I see the green as it makes its way
through the white snowy blanket
as it greets the morning sun.
The sun is gone now
and soon will appear again
to see the new colors of a new season
when the sap will flow.
As the last of the rice is put away,
and as we give thanks for a good harvest
it is time to cover our mother
with a white blanket
so she may rest.

—Ricardo Rojas, age 14
Squaw Lake, Minnesota

DEVELOPING LITERACY

GROUP TALK

Look Again, Think Again

VALUING DIVERSITY Stereotypes, such as those mentioned in **As a Matter of Fact** (November 24), can sometimes be found in such classroom materials as greeting cards, advertisements, trade books, and textbooks.

To begin a discussion about **stereotypes**—false generalizations unfairly applied to groups of people or to individuals—invent a stereotype, such as: *My friend has blue eyes and doesn't like cats. All blue-eyed people hate cats. You have blue eyes and hate cats.* Once children understand the concept, you might show examples of stereotypes and corresponding examples of nonstereotypical material. Be sure to use diverse examples, dealing with gender, race, ability, etc. For example, you might show a series of pictures that portray boys and girls in caricaturish ways, and a series of photos that show each in a variety of authentic situations, while asking:

◆ *Which of these do you think shows a "real" boy/girl?*

◆ *Is this real? Or is this a false view of what a boy/girl looks like or does?*

◆ *What's wrong with this view? How would you feel if you were drawn like this?*

Use this activity as the basis for counteracting stereotypes as they arise in everyday classroom situations. Doing this consistently will help children learn to value the uniqueness of individuals and the diversity within *all* groups.

CULTURESHARE For Native people, thanksgiving comes not only once a year, but always, for all the gifts of life. While Native Americans do not have anything at all like the traditional U.S. Thanksgiving, there are various celebrations of the harvest that vary from Nation to Nation. These are very old traditions, originating in a world before supermarket foods, when a good harvest, a good hunt, were truly matters for which to be thankful.

27

Latin America Week (last full week)

Before presenting this poem, you may want to use a map to preview with the children the different countries that make up Latin America. You may also want to introduce the different words for "kite" used in the poem.

WHAT FLIES FREE

A kite is a kite, whatever its name.
A kite is a kite, is somehow the same:
A tail, two sticks, a painted face,
some string, a wind, a bit of grace.
Anyplace:

In Guatemala, in a breeze
a barrilete* glides with ease.

In a Haitian sky over Port au Prince*
Etienne's cerf volante* will dive and dance.

In Panama, where continents meet
a pandero's* flight is light and fleet.

Maruca's papalote* in a Mexico cloud
bobs butterfly bright and Azteca* proud.

In Nicaragua, a small lechuza* flies
with the wide sweep of owls that prowl windy skies.

In Colombia, a cometa* tugs on its string.
It's dreaming of meteors, we hear it sing.

A kite is a kite, whatever its name.
A kite is a kite, is somehow the same:
it's a way to feel joy
it's a way to fly free,
it's a way friends share fun,
it's a way you know me.

—Ina Cumpiano

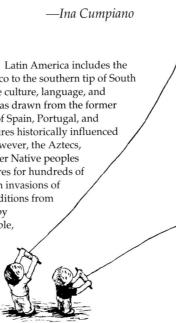

As a Matter of Fact Latin America includes the entire area from Mexico to the southern tip of South America. Much of the culture, language, and religion of this area was drawn from the former occupying countries of Spain, Portugal, and France—"Latin" cultures historically influenced by ancient Rome. However, the Aztecs, Mayas, Incas, and other Native peoples had established cultures for hundreds of years before European invasions of the area. Cultural traditions from Africa, brought over by enslaved African people, are also prominent in many Latin American countries. Today, many Latin Americans are of combined European, African, and Native American ancestry.

* **barrilete:** pronounced *bah-ree-LEH-teh*
* **Port au Prince:** the capital of Haiti; pronounced *port o prance*, to rhyme with *dance*
* **cerf volante:** pronounced *serf voh-LANT*
* **pandero:** pronounced *pahn-DEH-roh*

* **papalote:** pronounced *pah-pah-LOH-teh*; the word means "butterfly" in Nahuatl, the language of the Aztecs
* **Azteca (as-TEH-cah):** Spanish for "Aztec"
* **lechuza:** pronounced *leh-CHOO-sah*; literally, the word means "owl"
* **cometa:** pronounced *coh-MEH-tah*; a very similar Spanish word, with the same etymology, means "comet"

November brings the start of cold weather—and warm clothes!

28

Children can brainstorm names of animals and clothes that rhyme, and then create innovations on this humorous poem.

POLAR BEAR

The secret of the polar bear
Is that he wears long underwear.

—Gail Kredenser

29

Try wearing mittens when you present this poem!

THE MITTEN SONG

"Thumbs in the thumb-place
Fingers all together!"
This is the song
We sing in mitten-weather.
When it is cold,
It doesn't matter whether
Mittens are wool,
Or made of finest leather,
This is the song
We sing in mitten weather:
"Thumbs in the thumb-place,
Fingers all together!"

—Marie Louise Allen

30

ACROSS THE CURRICULUM
SCIENCE & SOCIAL STUDIES

Snowsuits or Swimsuits?
Not everybody has to bundle up when November comes; in some places, winter is warm. Use "The Mitten Song" and "Winter Clothes" to start a discussion about what fall and winter are like in different climates. As children talk about climates with which they are familiar, use a large map to point out (or have them point out) the places they are describing.

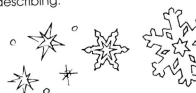

With older children, you might expand the discussion to countries in the Southern Hemisphere, where seasons are the opposite of those in the Northern Hemisphere, and talk about why this is so.

Then, ask children to draw a picture or write a poem about November weather. Younger children can draw a scene or dictate a few sentences about the November weather they know. Older children might compare different types of winter weather in their poems or imagine what it would be like to live in a place with a different November climate.

Content-Area ESL
To help build weather-related vocabulary, use the labeled pictures on **Activity Sheet 7** during the class discussion about different climates. Make copies so that children refer to them when writing their poems or drawing their pictures.

WINTER CLOTHES

Under my hood I have a hat
And under that
My hair is flat.
Under my coat
My sweater's blue.
My sweater's red.
I'm wearing two.
My muffler muffles to my chin
And round my neck
And then tucks in.
My gloves were knitted
By my aunts.
I've mittens too
And pants
And pants
And boots
And shoes
With socks inside.
The boots are rubber, red and wide.
And when I walk
I must not fall
Because I can't get up at all.

—Karla Kuskin

WINTER

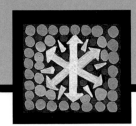

Winter is freezing—icicles, snow—
Bundling up from your head to your toe.

—*Lee Bennett Hopkins*

MULTICULTURAL TRADE BOOKS

Anno, Mitsumasa. **All in a Day** (Philomel, 1986). Renowned artists capture January 1st in nine places around the world.

■

Coutant, Helen & Vo-Dinh. **First Snow** (Knopf, 1974). A young Vietnamese girl experiences her first snow in the U.S. while coping with the death of her grandmother.

■

Ekoomiak, Normee. **Arctic Memories** (Holt, 1990). The author recalls his Inuit childhood with text and original artwork.

■

Johnson, Angela. **Do Like Kyla** (Orchard, 1990). A sister admires all that her big sister does, including the snow angels she makes.

■

Mora, Pat. **A Birthday Basket for Tía** (Macmillan, 1992). A young girl wants to create something special for her aunt's birthday.

■

Rylant, Cynthia. **Appalachia: The Voices of Sleeping Birds** (Harcourt Brace Jovanovich, 1991). Life in the mountains is shown through portraits of people and animals.

DECEMBER

December is a month of grand celebrations—Hanukkah, Christmas, Kwanzaa—with merriment, dancing, feasting, singing, and sharing. Winter arrives, and in the deep of dark, we cast our sights on the stars and keep hope alive. At home, we gather by candles and firelight as the year draws to an end, to celebrate life and our families.

Here comes December—the grand finale of the year!

Noteworthy Days

21 or 22 Winter Solstice

✦ Hanukkah (eight days, falls late November to late December*)

17–24 Posadas

25 Christmas Day

26 Kwanzaa begins (continues through January 1)

31 New Year's Eve

*See page 265 for exact date.

December makes one think of home . . .

1

 HOME

It's a place
Just to be me
Knowing it's all right
Being me.

—Chad Bulich, age 11
Monterey Peninsula, California

2

DUST IN THE CITY

Dust in the city
Reminds me of the prairie
I can only think of my family
It makes me think of my nation
It brings my heart home.

—Amanda Lyon and Jennifer Erickson, 7th grade
Omaha, Nebraska

3

THE PARK PEOPLE

A real old man
and a real old lady
stay out in the park.
They go into a little house
to sleep when it gets dark.
They burn newspapers
to keep them warm.
They wrap themselves in rags
and when it rains
they cover their heads
with old brown paper bags.

I am very sorry
that they have no place to stay
'cause they're real old
and very nice
and shouldn't live that way.

—Karama Fufuka

AS A MATTER OF FACT Homelessness is an increasing problem in American society. Studies based on the 1990 Census and other data place the homeless population in the U.S. at somewhere between a half a million and one million. The average homeless person is around 35 years old, just as likely to be female as male, and just as likely to be European American as not. Families make up about a third of the homeless population and constitute the fastest-growing group. The causes for the increase in the U.S. homeless population are complex; there is a great deal of controversy, both political and academic, about them. If you choose to discuss homelessness with your students, the point to emphasize is that homeless people deserve to be treated with compassion and respect for their human dignity.

If you and the children in your classroom want to do something about the problem of homelessness, contact a relief organization in your community. They will tell you how you can best help—through food drives, fund raising, or other activities.

The following books may help you in presenting the problem of homelessness to children:

- *A Rose for Abby* by Donna Guthrie (Abingdon, 1988)
- *An Angel for Solomon Singer* by Peter Catalanotto (Orchard, 1992)
- *Fly Away Home* by Eve Bunting (Clarion, 1991)
- *Sophie and the Sidewalk Man* by Stephanie Tolar (Four Winds, 1992)
- *Uncle Willie and the Soup Kitchen* by DyAnne DiSalvo-Ryan (Morrow, 1991)

A WORD FROM THE POET Sharon Morgan, who writes under the name Karama Fufuka, remembers her inspiration for this poem very clearly: "There were two people who lived in the park in Atlanta. They lived in this little 'house'—a kind of tin-roof shack where the rubbish was put. At night they would burn the rubbish to keep warm. It made me mad that anyone should have to live like that. It still does. No modern society should allow people to have to live the way these two people did. Our country has too much money for people to be homeless."

Ms. Morgan says there was something else about these two people that troubled her. "The idea that these were old people living this way bothered me, too. That's another issue in this poem. Seeing these people kind of cast away made me think that our society needs to take better care of its old people, as other cultures do. I hope that will change."

4

For an engaging presentation, turn off the classroom lights and have children sit in a circle as they pass around a lit flashlight.

JUST A FIRE

It's funny how a fire
In the fireplace
Can light up every
Friendly face
And warm us together
In the fiercest weather—
Just a fire
In the fireplace.

—Dee Lillegard

DEVELOPING LITERACY
GROUP TALK & WRITING

There's No Place Like Home
What makes any place feel like home? Ask children to contribute their own ideas about what home is. As you display their ideas, encourage children to think less in terms of what home looks like and more in terms of how they feel and what they do there.

Then, ask each child to write a short composition about home. Here are three ideas:

◆ Children write the title of the poem and its first line on their papers and compose new endings.

◆ Challenge older children or help younger ones work together to write an acrostic, using *home* as the key word. For example:

      Hugs
      Hot**d**Ogs
      Grand**M**a
      Bedtim**E** stories

◆ Children can describe their dream homes in words or pictures (collages or impressionistic sketches).

5

THE OUTSIDE/INSIDE POEM

Outside the night sneaks up with cat feet.
Inside my sisters listen to Chinese love songs
on the radio and sing along like movie stars.
Outside the snow rests on cars like thick rugs.
Inside my mother rubs circles in my brother's back
telling him stories of how she collected peanuts
from the riverbank after the spring floods in Lion Village.
Outside the stars climb into the cold winter sky.
Inside my father wraps our holiday presents,
newspaper and scotch tape crunching behind the door.
Outside the crescent moon hangs between the branches of a tree.
Inside I help my grandma make dumplings, pressing
my hands into the warm dough, shaping it into moon-smiles.
Outside the wind talks stories to the streets.
Inside my family stands at the window, holding hands,
listening to the whispers. The night rubs against the glass,
trying to get in.

—Sarah Chan

6

NOT ONE FROWN

Aunts and uncles, nieces and nephews;
Mothers and fathers, daughters and sons.
Flowers and gifts, hugs and kisses.
Grandma's birthday nobody misses.
A peck on the cheek wiped off by a hand.
"I saw you, Tito—you didn't like my kiss?"
"Grandma, I just rubbed it all up and down."
Roars of laughter, not one frown.

—Argentina Palacios

7

IN OUR ONE FAMILY

In our one family, around
> *this*
> *round*
> *table*
of our nights and days:
> *we are together*
> *in old ways,*
> *we are together*
> *in new ways.*

Pancakes and chicken. Pork chops and cream:
> *we*
> *are new people*
> *eating our way*
to a new time
> *of*
> *love*
> *We are trying for the*
> *dream.*

—Arnold Adoff

A WORD FROM THE POET I am Arnold, the poet. I am a man who is Jewish American. My wife is Virginia Hamilton, the novelist, who is an African American woman. Our children are a daughter, Leigh, and a son, Jaime. The children are biracial, or interracial, or mixed: different words for the same kind of "combination kid," as I like to say.

We have mixed our skin colors and facial features, and hair types. We have mixed our heritages and histories and backgrounds. We have mixed grandmothers and immigrant experiences, and slavery stories . . . all into this single family. We certainly mix our recipes and foods in the kitchen and dining room, as well. Our children, combining so many different pieces of their two past families, are really "new people" combinations. We hope we have "grown" them with enough love and respect and caring to go out into the wide world, trying to make the dream of equality and freedom and justice be a reality for them both . . . and for all their brothers and sisters of all the human races.

8

LOVE DON'T MEAN

Love don't mean all that kissing
Like on television
Love means Daddy
Saying keep your mama company
> *till I get back*
And me doing it

—Eloise Greenfield

ACROSS THE CURRICULUM
SOCIAL STUDIES & ARTS AND CRAFTS

Family Circles
VALUING DIVERSITY With children, discuss what makes a family a family—love, responsibility, respect, security, etc. Then, brainstorm a list of all the people who might be members of a family: father, daughter, uncle, grandmother, cousin, friend, godmother, and so on. Help them recognize the diversity in family life. The photo-essay *Families: A Celebration of Diversity, Commitment, and Love* by Aylette Jenness (Houghton Mifflin, 1990) is a good starting place.

Then, have small groups of children put one family member from the brainstorm list on each of several 3" x 5" cards. Ask groups to put together several family groupings using the cards.

Use photographs to create family trees with **students acquiring English,** to introduce English terms for extended-family relationships.

Finally, have each group choose one or two families to illustrate, from the groupings they have assembled. If you stretch a large piece of butcher paper across one or two walls of the classroom, children can work in their groups to create sections of a mural.

As opportunities arise, now and throughout the year, reinforce the diversity in real-life families and emphasize the idea that all family groupings have value. For example:

◆ *This family has a mother, a grandmother, and two children who are working together to do some chores. Working together is something a family does.*

◆ *All of these families have different numbers of members—and different members. What do you think they all have in common?*

9

BUBIE* ANNIE

Plump and golden
Bubie Annie walked through our door
every Friday night for Shabbos* dinner.
She'd climb the hallway steps,
groaning, her arms flapping,
her smile sprawling her face
and arrive in the kitchen to greet me
with those gigantic blue eyes.

Shelly, she'd shout
in my ear, **Ah you?**
I'm fine, Bubie Annie, I'd reply
shaking my head out.
Then she'd lift up my arm
and plant three giant kisses
suctioning a little more skin each time.

My mother sat her at the end
of the table, next to Papa Benny,
where she had plenty of room to sprawl
and wouldn't have room
to get up and help.
Once dinner started,
Bubie Annie spoke only Yiddish

with Papa Benny, Mom and Dad.
I'd strain the conversation
for words I knew, smiling to myself
when I understood.

After dinner, everyone would empty
into the den and I would be
assigned to the dishes.
One time Bubie Annie stayed
behind and asked if she could help.

I was supposed to say, **No,**
the respectable thing.
But I snuck to the doorway, peeked
into the empty hall, and smiling replied,
Sure, you can wipe.

Bubie Annie groaned
getting out of her chair,
caught me for a moment
in those gigantic blue eyes,
then smiled back
and grabbed a dish towel.

—Shelly Savren

*Bubie (BUH-bee): Yiddish for "grandmother" or other
respected older woman, from the Yiddish word *bubeleh*
(*BUH-beh-leh*) and Russian and Slavic *baba* (*BAH-buh*). Also
used as a general term of endearment.
*Shabbos (SHAH-biss): Yiddish for "Sabbath"; from the
Hebrew *Shabbat* (*shah-BAHT*). The Jewish sabbath begins
at sundown on Friday and is commonly observed with a
special dinner.

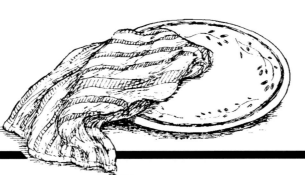

10

FAMILY

I can picture my
Mom singing with
her pretty voice.
It makes me
want to dance
harder every time
she sings.

Just thinking of
her singing makes
me want to get
up and dance
some more.

I wish we can dance
again so I can
dance to her pretty
voice.

—Daryl Nez, age 10
Oakland, California

Photo of the
poet

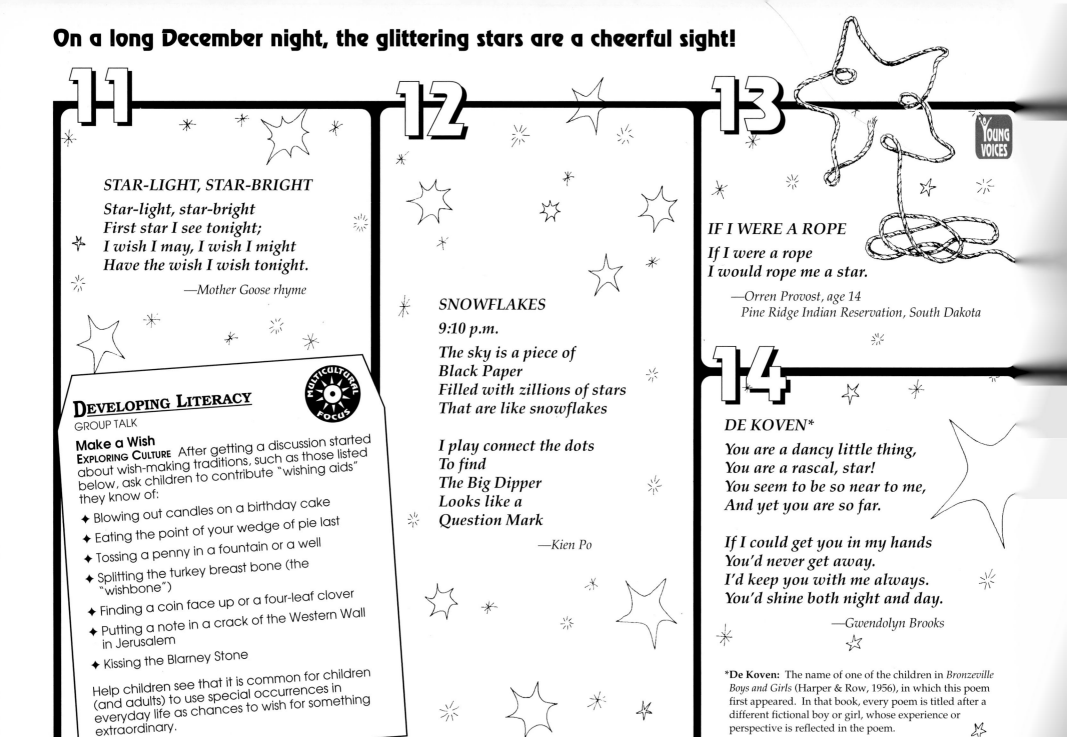

11

STAR-LIGHT, STAR-BRIGHT

Star-light, star-bright
First star I see tonight;
I wish I may, I wish I might
Have the wish I wish tonight.

—Mother Goose rhyme

DEVELOPING LITERACY

MULTICULTURAL FOCUS

GROUP TALK

Make a Wish
EXPLORING CULTURE After getting a discussion started about wish-making traditions, such as those listed below, ask children to contribute "wishing aids" they know of:

◆ Blowing out candles on a birthday cake

◆ Eating the point of your wedge of pie last

◆ Tossing a penny in a fountain or a well

◆ Splitting the turkey breast bone (the "wishbone")

◆ Finding a coin face up or a four-leaf clover

◆ Putting a note in a crack of the Western Wall in Jerusalem

◆ Kissing the Blarney Stone

Help children see that it is common for children (and adults) to use special occurrences in everyday life as chances to wish for something extraordinary.

12

SNOWFLAKES

9:10 p.m.

The sky is a piece of
Black Paper
Filled with zillions of stars
That are like snowflakes

I play connect the dots
To find
The Big Dipper
Looks like a
Question Mark

—Kien Po

13

YOUNG VOICES

IF I WERE A ROPE

If I were a rope
I would rope me a star.

—Orren Provost, age 14
Pine Ridge Indian Reservation, South Dakota

14

DE KOVEN*

You are a dancy little thing,
You are a rascal, star!
You seem to be so near to me,
And yet you are so far.

If I could get you in my hands
You'd never get away.
I'd keep you with me always.
You'd shine both night and day.

—Gwendolyn Brooks

*****De Koven:** The name of one of the children in *Bronzeville Boys and Girls* (Harper & Row, 1956), in which this poem first appeared. In that book, every poem is titled after a different fictional boy or girl, whose experience or perspective is reflected in the poem.

GREAT BIG STARS

Spiritual

Medium tempo

Great big stars 'way up ___ yon - der, Great big stars 'way up ___ yon - der, Great big stars 'way up ___ yon - der.

1. O my lit - tle soul's gon-na shine, shine! O my lit - tle soul's gon-na shine, shine!
2. All a-round the world gon-na shine, shine! All a-round the world gon-na shine, shine!

© 1991. Reprinted by permission of Atheneum Publishers, an imprint of Macmillan Publishing Company. All rights reserved.

ACROSS THE CURRICULUM
SOCIAL STUDIES & SCIENCE & READING

MULTICULTURAL FOCUS

Star Stories
EXPLORING CULTURE During this theme, make available nonfiction books about stars, and books of star legends and folktales from many cultures. Here are some suggestions:

Nonfiction:
- *The Constellations: How They Came To Be* by Roy A. Gallant (Four Winds, 1979)
- *The Sky Is Full of Stars* by Franklyn M. Branley (Thomas Y. Crowell, 1981)
- *Stars* by Seymour Simon (William Morrow, 1986)

Fiction:
- *The Heavenly Zoo* by Alison Lurie (Farrar Straus Giroux, 1979)
- *Her Seven Brothers* by Paul Goble (Bradbury, 1988)
- *The Star Husband* by J. Mobley (Doubleday, 1979)
- *Star Mother's Youngest Child* by Louise Moeri (Houghton Mifflin, 1975)
- *They Dance in the Sky: Native American Star Myths* by Jean Monroe and Ray Williamson (Houghton Mifflin, 1987)

Encourage children to find answers to their questions about the stars and help them see how people, for thousands of years and in all parts of the world, have been interested in the night sky. Invite children to share the information they have gained and find similarities and themes in the fiction they have read.

16

B *CELEBRATION*

I shall dance tonight.
When the dusk comes crawling,
There will be dancing
     and feasting.
I shall dance with the others
     in circles,
          in leaps,
               in stomps.
Laughter and talk
     will weave into the night,
Among the fires
     of my people.
Games will be played
And I shall be
     a part of it.

—*Alonzo Lopez*

CULTURESHARE Dance is probably one of the oldest forms of human expression. Native Americans dance for all the reasons people everywhere have always danced: in prayer, for healing, to tell a story, and for the pure fun of it. For Native Americans, dance has always been a source of tribal unity, spiritual strength, and renewal, and because of that, was outlawed for a long time by the federal government. Nevertheless, ceremonies such as the Kachina (Pueblo) and Sun Dances (Sioux) have survived and are still performed. There are dances in celebration of green corn, and of the harvest. There are social dances and powwows everywhere. Dance is still at the heart of Native peoples' relationship to the universe.

17

I'D LIKE TO HAVE A PARTY

I'd like to have a party
To mark this great occasion
A festival with friends and fun
A great big celebration!

I think we ought to have balloons
And dinner most delicious
Because today I have to say
I'm feeling celebricious!

Be sure to bring some songs to sing
Let's hear some harmonizing!
And if by chance you'd like to dance,
We'll dance while celebrizing.

There'll be stories told and secrets shared
And many speeches spoken
And later we'll be sure to see
That nothing's celebroken . . .

Yes I'd like to have a party
And I think we really ought to
A great big celebration for . . .
There's no celebreason not to!

—*Josh Weinstein*

ACROSS THE CURRICULUM

SOCIAL STUDIES & MUSIC &
SPORTS AND GAMES

MULTICULTURAL FOCUS

Congregate and Celebrate!
EXPLORING CULTURE By asking children to describe celebrations they know about and charting their responses, you can demonstrate similarities in the ways people get together to celebrate special occasions.

Display a seven-column chart, with the labels *Singing, Dancing, Feasting* (or *Eating), Laughing, Talking, Playing Games,* and *Being Together,* asking children to describe celebrations they have been part of. Help them consider ones beyond family celebrations—ones sponsored by religious groups, youth or school groups, community or ethnic organizations. Mark the appropriate columns as children describe the activities involved in each celebration. Once everyone has had a chance to contribute, ask children to study the chart and draw some conclusions about similarities and differences in celebrations, using the information they find there.

You might also have children or community members teach the songs and games that are a part of the celebrations listed.

18

PIÑATA

No quiero oro,
ni quiero plata.
Yo lo que quiero
es quebrar la piñata.

—*Spanish traditional rhyme*

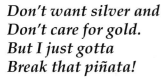

Don't want silver and
Don't care for gold.
But I just gotta
Break that piñata!

—*English version by Juan Quintana*

CultureShare The piñata *(pee-NYAH-tah)* is basically a hollow cardboard container filled with candies and other party favors and decorated with crepe paper. It is often in the shape of a toy or an animal. Its use in birthday parties and other festive occasions for children, traditional in Spain and Latin America, has spread to the U.S. The usual procedure is for the piñata to be suspended from a rope, and for someone to raise and lower it randomly while blindfolded children strike at it with a bat or club until one succeeds in breaking it. All the children then scramble to gather the goodies that spill from the broken piñata. Piñatas are a traditional part of the celebration for Posadas (see entry for December 24).

19

BURSTING

We've laughed until my cheeks are tight.
We've laughed until my stomach's sore.
If we could only stop we might
Remember what we're laughing for.

—*Dorothy Aldis*

20

I AM BESIDE MYSELF

I am beside myself
with glee.
I ho
and ho
and hee
and hee,
I hee
and hee
and ho
and ho.
I wonder why
I'm ho-ing so.

—*Karla Kuskin*

DEVELOPING LITERACY
PATTERNED WRITING & DRAMATIC INTERPRETATION—Poem for Two Voices

Gigglefest
Have children suggest other words for laughter, to use in writing their own versions of the poem. For example:

I am beside myself
with glee.
I _giggle_
and _giggle_
and _chuckle_
and _chuckle_ , etc.

Encourage **students acquiring English** to use words for laughter from their native languages.

Daffy Duets
Children can recite "I Am Beside Myself" as a poem for two voices (see page 34 for more information about this technique). Have partners practice, and when they are ready, recite the poem for the rest of the class, or tape-record their duets.

Get set for the shortest of days: winter arrives today.

21

Winter Solstice

YOUNG VOICES

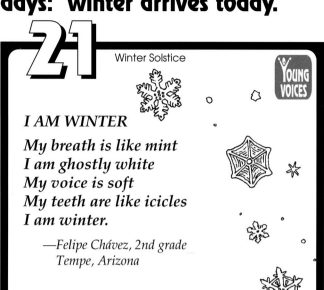

I AM WINTER

My breath is like mint
I am ghostly white
My voice is soft
My teeth are like icicles
I am winter.

> —Felipe Chávez, 2nd grade
> Tempe, Arizona

As a Matter of Fact On about December 21, winter officially begins in the northern hemisphere. The day of the Winter Solstice has the fewest hours of daylight of any day in the year; the sun rises and sets at its southernmost point on the horizon.

Many ancient cultures that lived in the extratropical areas of the northern hemisphere had joyous celebrations shortly after the Winter Solstice, to celebrate the return of the sun. Many of these celebrations involved the lighting of bonfires. Many of the cultural festivals associated with this season—Hanukkah, Christmas, Kwanzaa—are festivals of light, and the lighting of candles plays a prominent part in their observation. At the core of all of them is a celebration of the return of light, and with it, life.

December is the time for great festivals of light— Hanukkah . . .

22

Hanukkah (eight days, falls late November to late December)

Before presenting this poem, share with children the background information for Hanukkah in the **CultureShare**.

FIRST NIGHT OF HANUKKAH

I shouldn't tell you this, BUT
sometimes we fight! Why does Julie
get to light the shammash* candle
every time?

Josh grabs the shield we painted
blue and white—he says he's ALWAYS
Judah Maccabee* because
he's oldest. (We can be the brothers.)

NOT FAIR!
I'm the one who found the dreidls*
for our game. I'm the one who knows
the names on all four sides—
   NES GADOL HAYAH SHAM*

Sunset now. December's early
dark. No one remembers what we
quarreled about—or why. We love
each other in the shining light.

Mother's the one who looks around and says,
"A MIRACLE HAS HAPPENED HERE
TONIGHT."

> —Ruth Roston

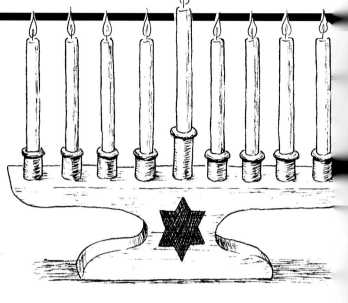

CultureShare Although the customs of Hanukkah (also spelled Hanukah, Chanukah, and other ways) are observed mostly by Jews, the events that the holiday commemorates have come to represent freedom from persecution for all peoples. In the second century B.C.E., Syrian King Antiochus forbade the Jews to practice their religion, eventually taking over the Temple of Jerusalem—the holiest site in Judaism. The Jews, led by the Maccabees (the priest Judah, his brothers, and others) fought the king's army for three years, and, in 165 B.C.E., succeeded in recovering the Temple.

The holiday's eight-day duration celebrates an occurrence during the Temple's rededication, or *hanukkah*. According to the biblical account, The Jews found that the Syrians had destroyed all but enough oil to light the synagogue's lamps for one day. Miraculously, the oil burned for eight days; it was decided then to commemorate the event as the Feast (or Festival) of Lights. Celebrations today include games, gifts, and the nightly lighting of candles on a special nine-branched *menorah*, or candelabrum (an additional candle is lit each night).

***shammash** (*SHAH-mash*): the candle used to light the other candles in a Hanukkah menorah
***Judah Maccabee:** the leader of the Jewish revolt which Hanukkah commemorates (see **CultureShare**)
***dreidls:** see entry for December 23
***NES GADOL HAYAH SHAM** (*ness gah-DOL hah-YAH sham*): see activity card for December 23

 *MY DREYDEL**

Words by S. Grossman
Music by S. Goldfarb

1. I have a lit-tle drey-del, I made it out of clay, And
2. My drey-del's al-ways play-ful, It loves to dance and spin, A

when it's dry and read-y, my drey-del I will play.
hap-py game of drey-del, come play now, let's be-gin.

Drey-del, drey-del, drey-del, I made it out of clay,

Drey-del drey-del, drey-del, my drey-del I will play.

***dreydel** (*DRAY-duhl*): (also spelled *dreidl* or *dreidel*) a four-sided toy
marked with a Hebrew letter on each side, traditional as a part of Hanukkah
celebrations. (For more information, see accompanying activity.)

© 1950. Reprinted by permission of the Board of Jewish Education of Greater New York. All rights reserved.

ACROSS THE CURRICULUM

MATHEMATICS & SPORTS AND GAMES

MULTICULTURAL FOCUS

The Dreidel Spins and Someone Wins

EXPLORING CULTURE Children can make dreidels using copies of **Activity Sheet 8** and pencils. As they work, explain that the Hebrew letters that appear on the sides of their dreidels (*nun, gimmel, heh,* and *shin*) are the first letters of the words *Nes gadol hayah sham*, which mean "A great miracle happened there." (Two thousand years ago, when Jewish children were forbidden to learn Jewish history, they disguised this lesson as a game of chance.)

Then, children can play the game, following these directions:

✦ Two to five players start with an equal number of tokens (e.g., dried chick peas, kidney beans, etc.). Players take turns spinning the dreidel. Before each spin, every player puts one token in the middle (the pot).

✦ If the dreidel lands on
Nun: the player does nothing
Gimmel: the player takes everything in the pot
Heh: the player takes half the pot (plus one extra if there is an uneven number of tokens in the pot)
Shin: the player puts one token in the pot

✦ The winner is the player who ends up with all the tokens.

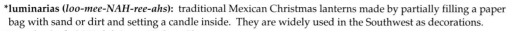

24
Posadas

NO ROOM! NO ROOM!

It's Christmas time here in my barrio
and I can hardly wait to see
the **luminarias,*** and taste tamales
that I know were made just for me!

But my favorite part of all is **Posadas***
when we go to each door and say,
like **Mary and Joseph*** on Christmas Eve,
"We need a place to stay."

But every door, wherever we go,
has someone who shakes his head
and says with a frown, "No Room! No Room!
Go someplace else instead!"

And even though Mom and Dad laugh
and know it's all pretend,
by the time we get to house Six or Seven,
I'm tired and want to go in!

And we sing, like Mary and Joseph did,
and say, "We're tired and cold,"
but they always say, "No Room! No Room!"
no matter what they're told!

Finally there's one special house
where they give you that second glance
and say, "Well, there's room around back . . ."
—and we all jump at the chance!

And we come to a candle-lit **manger scene***
where a little baby's laid
so softly and sweetly in the hay
with stars around his head.

Then we all go inside, smiling and happy,
singing songs of thanks and joy,
and they serve **chocolate***—Hot!—and treats
to every girl and boy.

And we're warm, and thankful for **Posadas.**
(**Posada** means room, you see—
a special place to stay a while,
a place for you and me.)

And we gladly say "Room for everyone!"
as we sing and laugh with glee,
and we get to taste those warm tamales
that I know were made just for me!

—Carmen Tafolla

*luminarias (loo-mee-NAH-ree-ahs): traditional Mexican Christmas lanterns made by partially filling a paper bag with sand or dirt and setting a candle inside. They are widely used in the Southwest as decorations.
*Posadas (poh-SAH-dahs): see **CultureShare**
*Mary and Joseph: in Christian tradition, Mary is the mother of Jesus. Joseph is her husband. For more information, see **CultureShare**.
*manger scene: an arrangement of figures depicting the baby Jesus laid down on a manger in a stable, surrounded by Mary, Joseph, and others
*chocolate: pronounce choh-coh-LAH-teh, as in Spanish

CultureShare In the Mexican celebration of Las posadas —which is also celebrated, with variations, in other Latin American countries—people reenact the traditional account of Mary and Joseph's search for lodgings in Bethlehem prior to the birth of Jesus. People go to various houses in the neighborhood, singing and asking for lodging. They are refused several times before being finally accepted and taken in. Then, all enjoy a party complete with refreshments and a piñata. Many of these customs are observed by Mexican Americans in the U.S., including citywide celebrations in many cities of the Southwest.

MUST BE SANTA

Who's got a beard that's long and white?
Santa's got a beard that's long and white.
Who comes around on a special night?
Santa comes around on a special night.
Special night, beard that's white,

> **Chorus:** *Must be Santa, must be Santa,*
> *Must be Santa, Santa Claus.*

Who's got boots and a suit of red?
Santa's got . . .
Who wears a long cap on his head?
Santa wears . . .
Cap on head, suit that's red,
Special night, beard that's white,

> **Chorus**

Who's got a great big cherry nose?
Santa's got . . .
Who laughs this way, "Ho, ho, ho"?
Santa laughs . . .
Ho, ho, ho, cherry nose,
Cap on head, suit that's red,
Special night, beard that's white,

> **Chorus**

Who very soon will come our way?
Santa very . . .
Eight little reindeer pull his sleigh,
Santa's little . . .
Reindeer sleigh, come our way,
Ho, ho, ho, cherry nose,
Cap on head, suit that's red,
Special night, beard that's white,

> **Chorus twice**

—Hal Moore and Bill Fredericks

CultureShare For Christians, Christmas is a joyous religious celebration of the birth of Jesus. With its long tradition of gift-giving—originating with New Testament accounts of the Three Wise Men bearing gifts to the newborn baby—it has also become a secular holiday, enjoyed by many non-Christians, as well. For many children, Christmas morning is the most exciting and magical time of the year. Children rise early to find that Santa Claus has filled their stockings with treats and toys. The day is also celebrated by exchanging gifts, singing, and visiting with family, some of whom have traveled great distances to celebrate this time together.

The tradition of Santa Claus took a long time to travel to America. The stories, which began in what is now Turkey and then spread all over Europe, were based on a real person—a bishop named Nicholas who gave gifts to children and poor people. The Dutch, who called Saint Nicholas "Sinter Klaas," brought the stories to America. The addition of Santa's sleigh pulled by eight reindeer is the creation of Clement C. Moore in his poem "A Visit from Saint Nicholas" (more popularly known as "Twas the Night Before Christmas"), written in 1822.

. . . Kwanzaa.

26

Kwanzaa begins (continues through January 1)

from KWANZAA IS . . .

One day after Christmas comes,
we listen to the Kwanzaa drums
and celebrate for seven days
our old customs and modern ways.

—Cedric McClester

CULTURESHARE Kwanzaa is a cultural observance created in 1966 to celebrate African-inspired traditional values and African American ancestry and heritage. Kwanzaa ("first fruits of the harvest" in Swahili) is being observed by increasing numbers of African American families.

Each day of the week during Kwanzaa a candle is lit in a seven-branched candelabrum called a kinara, to represent one of the seven principles celebrated during Kwanzaa: unity, self-determination, collective work and responsibility, cooperative economics, purpose, creativity, and faith. Children receive educational and cultural gifts, such as books or African clothes, and the week ends with a great feast—the Kwanzaa Karamu—followed by dance, music, and readings.

27

MY PEOPLE **B**

The night is beautiful,
So the faces of my people.

The stars are beautiful,
So the eyes of my people.

Beautiful, also, is the sun.
Beautiful, also, are the souls of my
people.

—Langston Hughes

28

BLACK IS BEAUTIFUL

Black is beautiful
Black is fine
Black is wonderful
Black is mine.

—Unknown

29

ENVOLVIENDO REGALOS/ WRAPPING PRESENTS

¡Qué divertido
envolver un regalo
y guardar el secreto
de lo encerrado!

—Alma Flor Ada

Once a present's wrapped
and the ribbon tied,
only you know the secret
of what's inside.

—English version by Juan Quintana

MULTICULTURAL FOCUS

DEVELOPING LITERACY
COLLECTING AND RELATING WORDS & PATTERNED WRITING

All Peoples Are Beautiful
PROMOTING SELF-ESTEEM As you emphasize that every child can take pride in who he or she is, that every skin color is one to be proud of, have children look at and compare skin colors. Make a list of color words on the chalkboard, encouraging children to go beyond the words often used to talk about skin color, and to use terms that describe more accurately the various shades of real skin.

Then, have children write variations on the poem, using their own skin colors. For instance:

Golden-brown is beautiful
Golden-brown is fine
Golden-brown is wonderful
Golden-brown is mine

A color chart with blends of tempera paint (or skin-color crayon swatches) can help **students acquiring English** learn the specific colors that are being named.

As volunteers share their poems with the class, comment on the feeling the words express. For example: *What a beautiful color word you've created—it's as unique as you are!*

.. brings the greatest warmth.

30

B *GIVING*

> *A person gives double who gives unasked.*
>
> —*Arab proverb*

> *Hands that give also receive.*
>
> —*Ecuadoran proverb*

> *A good heart always gives a little extra.*
>
> —*Chinese proverb*

> *A thing is bigger for being shared.*
>
> —*Gaelic proverb*

DEVELOPING LITERACY
MULTICULTURAL FOCUS

WRITING

Little Sentences; Large Messages
VALUING DIVERSITY After presenting the proverbs about giving, talk with children about what proverbs are— short, memorable sayings that give rules to live by or that tell a profound truth.

Invite children to contribute proverbs they know and to ask their families for proverbs to add to the collection (in English and/or other languages). Explain that proverbs are often passed down from generation to generation, sometimes without being written down; they are part of a family's heritage.

Then, each child can write and illustrate a proverb for classroom display or for a class book. Help children appreciate the similar themes (and the unique ones) in proverbs from many cultures.

Quite suddenly it's here—the very last day of the year!

31

New Year's Eve

This is a "concrete" poem, depending for its effect on the typographical arrangement. To give children the full visual effect, display this poem before reading it.

Y THE YEAR
goes
skid-
ding
down
to
the
bot-
tom
of
the
cal-
en-
dar
slip-
ping
out   *HAPPY NEW YEAR!*
the
end.   top.
Then   the
Z O O M . . . . . . UP   to

—*Felice Holman*

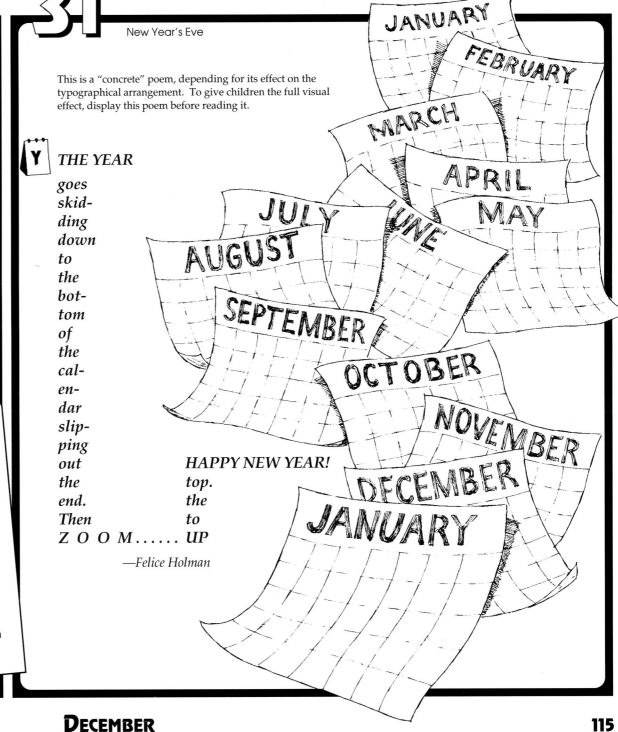

JANUARY

January is a time to look at ourselves as one year ends and another begins. It's a time to think of others, too, as we remember the dream of Martin Luther King, Jr.

In some areas, snowflakes fall; each one different, but with much in common with the others—what better time of year to recognize our own diversity, and our own unity?

The colder weather outside makes for warm stories inside, where folktales show us unseen lands. The Superbowl, a January classic, adds a finishing touch to the month.

So, reach out—next year is here.

Noteworthy Days

1   New Year's Day

✦   Martin Luther King, Jr., Day (third Monday)

20   Inauguration Day (in presidential-election years)

✦   Superbowl Sunday (most often the last Sunday in January)

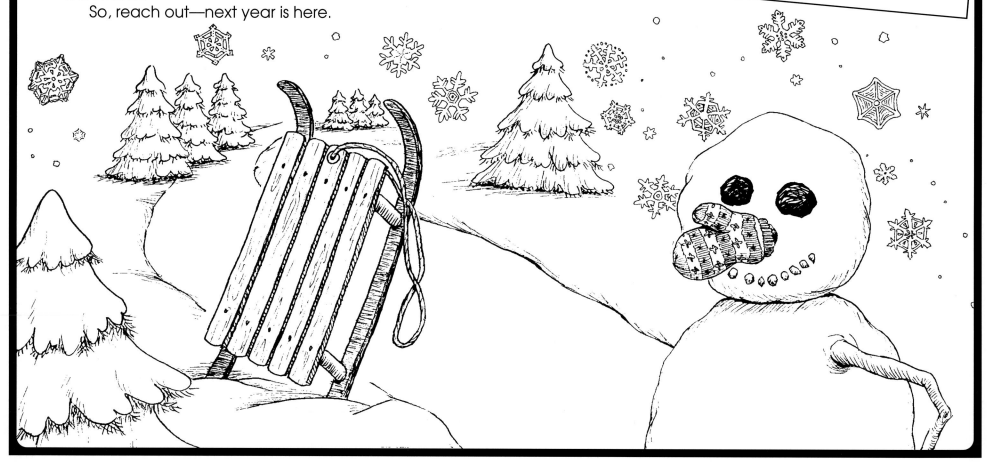

A happy New Year . . .

New Year's Day

This poem was written originally in both English and Spanish. You may choose to present both versions or the English version only, depending on the composition of your class and your knowledge of Spanish.

B EL AÑO NUEVO*/THE NEW YEAR

Si los niños fuéramos
el año nuevo
seríamos un pájaro
cantando canciones de paz
a los pobres
o una flor
para llenar el mundo
con el respiro de amor.

If children were
the new year
we'd be a bird
singing songs of peace
to the poor
or a flower
so we could fill the world
with love's breath.

Si los niños fuéramos
el año nuevo
seríamos un arco iris
lloviendo dulces
de mil colores
o una nube
para llevar a la gente
a lugares que no hayan visto.

If children were
the new year
we'd be a rainbow
raining candy
of a thousand colors
or a cloud
so we could take people
to places they haven't seen.

Si los niños fuéramos
el año nuevo
seríamos el sol
o una estrella
para brillar con amor
y calentar
el corazón.

If children were
the new year
we'd be the sun
or a star
so we could shine with love
and warm
the heart.

Si los niños fuéramos
el año nuevo
seríamos un atardecer
para regalarle al mundo
abrazos
de pájaros
y de colores.

If children were
the new year
we'd be a sunset
so we could give the world
hugs
of birds
and of colors.

Si los niños fuéramos
el año nuevo
seríamos un corazón con alas
volaríamos a México
a África
y por todo el mundo
y estaríamos felices
de estar ¡vivos!

If children were
the new year
we'd be a heart with wings
we'd fly to Mexico
to Africa
and all over the world
and we'd be happy
to be alive!

—Margot Pepper's First-Grade Class
San Francisco, California

A Word from the Poet-Teacher Ms. Pepper says she "worked with groups of six children for twenty minutes while the rest of the class rotated through four other centers (math, language arts, art, and science)." Each group wrote one stanza, "saying what they would be if they were the new year and what they could do and why." Ms. Pepper's students had been collecting strong poetic images on cards, and she had them use these cards as they wrote their stanzas, so they would learn "to reject weaker images and keep stronger ones."

*el año nuevo: pronounced *el AN-yo NWEH-voh*

. . . and you can make it your best year yet!

2

YOU WHOSE DAY IT IS

You whose day it is
make it beautiful.
Get out your rainbow,
make it beautiful.

—*Nootka traditional song*

ACROSS THE CURRICULUM
ARTS AND CRAFTS & WRITING

Rainbows and Resolutions
This poem can be a springboard for discussing new-year traditions, such as making resolutions or setting goals. Children can then write their resolutions or goals and save their plans in a class book, illustrated with rainbows.

To make colorful rainbows, children can use crayons to cover a sheet of paper with bright colors and then cover *that* completely with black (or dark blue) crayon. A paper clip or penny can be used to scratch out a rainbow's arc. Place their written resolutions face down on their rainbow pictures, stapling the two along the left side, and compile all of the two-page spreads into a class book.

3

I HAVE A FUTURE

I have a future in the bottom of my heart.
I will have a bigger future
when I am bigger.

—*Aaron Boland, kindergarten*
Santa Cruz, California

4

BEGINNING A NEW YEAR MEANS

taking off
clothes spattered with
chocolate milk
and mud
throwing away
scribbled pages
full of crossed out words
and mistakes
watching
old snow
melting away

putting on
clean clothes
without spots or wrinkles
opening
white pages
with nothing written
on them yet
watching
fresh snow
falling
without tiremarks
or footprints

—*Ruth Whitman*

What can warm a winter's chill? A good book will.
You'll meet characters of the cagy kind . . .

5

 *ANANSI*

Music by Raffi
Words by Bert Simpson

© 1979 Homeland Publishing, a division of Troubadour Records Ltd. All rights reserved. Reprinted by permission.

Calypso

A - nan - si, he is a spi - der.   A - nan - si, he is a man.   A-

nan - si,   he is a   la - zy one,   do   lit - tle   as   he
(last time:) clev - er one,   he   al - ways have   a

can,   yeah, _   do   lit - tle   as   he   can.
plan,   yeah, _   he   al - ways have   a   plan.

1. A - nan - si has a   man - go tree,   He   loves the fruit   so   ripe.
2. A - nan - si tells his   friend the crow,   "You're beau - ti - ful   to   me."
3. The crows fly   to   the   man - go tree,   they   bend the branch - es   down.

He can - not reach the   man - goes but   he   longs to have a   bite.
Old __ crow calls her   friends so they can   hear his flat - ter -   y.
A - nan - si watch them   swing and sway and   man - goes hit the   ground.

DEVELOPING LITERACY
GROUP TALK & WRITING

The Same . . . but Different
VALUING DIVERSITY Help children discover that common themes appear in folktales from many cultures, making the stories universal. For example, read aloud several stories with "Cinderella-like" plot patterns, asking children to compare and contrast the settings, attributes of the characters, difficulties encountered, and endings:

◆ *Yeh-Shen: A Cinderella Story from China,* retold by Ai-Ling Louie, illustrated by Ed Young (Philomel Books, 1982)

◆ *Mufaro's Beautiful Daughters: An African Tale* written and illustrated by John Steptoe (Lothrop, Lee & Shepard Books, 1987)

◆ *Cinderella,* translated from the French of Charles Perrault by Marcia Brown, illustrated by Marcia Brown (Charles Scribner's Sons, 1954)

Older children might work in small groups to read and discuss one version, summarizing and perhaps reenacting it for the class. Younger children can work cooperatively to dictate a class version of the story set in a new time and place.

Children might discover that the difference in details makes each story relevant to its culture.

AS A MATTER OF FACT Anansi is one of the most common characters in West African folklore. Enslaved Africans brought his stories to the Americas, and now he is a common character in the folklore of much of the West Indies, the Caribbean, and some parts of the American South.

Anansi is a "trickster" figure, who embodies both the best and the worst of ourselves. Sometimes he displays more-than-human ingenuity; at other times, greed and sneakiness. Sometimes, he ends up outsmarting himself. No matter what happens, he lives to play another day, and that is part of the great appeal of Anansi and other trickster figures.

6

OLD MAN COYOTE AND THE ROCK

Old Man Coyote was going along. It was quite a while since he had eaten and he was feeling cut in half by hunger. He came to the top of a hill and there he saw a big rock. Old Man Coyote took out his flint knife.

"Grandfather," Old Man Coyote said to the rock, "I give you this fine knife. Now help me in some way, because I am hungry."

Then Old Man Coyote went along further. He went over the top of the hill and there at the bottom was a buffalo that had just been killed.

"How lucky I am," Old Man Coyote said. "But how can I butcher this buffalo without a knife? Now where did I leave my knife?"

Then Old Man Coyote walked back up the hill until he came to the big rock where his knife still lay on the ground.

"You don't need this knife," he said to the big rock.

Then he picked his flint knife up and ran back to where he had left the buffalo. Now, though, where there had been a freshly killed buffalo, there were only buffalo bones and the bones were very old and gray. Then, from behind him, Old Man Coyote heard a rumbling noise. He turned around and looked up. The big rock was rolling down the hill after him. GA-DA-RUM, GA-DA-RUM.

Old Man Coyote began to run. He ran and ran, but the stone still rumbled after him. GA-DA-RUM, GA-DA-RUM. Old Man Coyote ran until he came to a bear den.

"Help me," he called in to the bears.

The bears looked out and saw what was chasing Old Man Coyote. "We can't help you against Grandfather Rock," they said.

GA-DA-RUM, GA-DA-RUM. The big rock kept coming and Old Man Coyote kept running. Now he came to a cave where the mountain lions lived and he called out again.

"Help me," Old Man Coyote said. "I am about to be killed!" The mountain lions looked out and saw what was after Old Man Coyote. "No," they said, "we can't help you if you have angered Grandfather Rock."

GA-DA-RUM, GA-DA-RUM. The big rock kept rumbling after Old Man Coyote and he kept running. Now he came to the place where a bull buffalo was grazing.

"Help me," Old Man Coyote yelled. "That big rock said it was going to kill all the buffalo. When I tried to stop it, it began to chase me."

The bull buffalo braced his legs and thrust his head out to stop the big rock. But the rock just brushed the bull buffalo aside and left him standing there dazed, with his horns bent and his head pushed back into his shoulders. To this day all buffalo are still like that.

GA-DA-RUM, GA-DA-RUM. The big rock kept rolling and Old Man Coyote kept running. But Old Man Coyote was getting tired now and the rock was getting closer. Then Old Man Coyote looked up and saw a nighthawk flying overhead.

"My friend," Old Man Coyote yelled up to the nighthawk, "this big rock that is chasing me said you are ugly. It said you have a wide mouth and your eyes are too big and your beak is all pinched up. I told it not to say that and it began to chase me."

The nighthawk heard what Old Man Coyote said and grew very angry. He called the other nighthawks. They began to swoop down and strike at the big rock with their beaks. Each time they struck the big rock a piece broke off and stopped rolling. GA-DA-RUM, GA-DA-RUM. The rock kept rolling and Old Man Coyote kept running, but now the rock was much smaller. The nighthawks continued to swoop down and break off pieces. Finally the big rock was nothing but small pebbles.

Old Man Coyote came up and looked at the little stones. "My, my," he said to the nighthawks, "Why did you wide-mouthed, big-eyed, pinch-beaked birds do that to my old friend?" Then Old Man Coyote laughed and started on his way again.

Now the nighthawks were very angry at Old Man Coyote. They gathered all the pieces of the big rock and fanned them together with their wings. The next thing Old Man Coyote knew, he heard a familiar sound behind him again. GA-DA-RUM, GA-DA-RUM. He tried to run, but he was so tired now he could not get away. The big rock rolled right over him and flattened him out.

—Retold by Joseph Bruchac

CULTURESHARE Coyote is the trickster common to the folklore of many Native Nations. In many stories, he appears to be somewhat more of a supernatural figure than is Anansi, but he shares much of the same conceited foolishness. For many peoples, he shares a role in creation stories. Many things, both good and bad, have come about through his interference. Another somewhat similar character is Raven, who appears in Northern and Northwestern stories.

Stories are of vital importance to Native societies. The stories carry history, traditions, and spiritual beliefs. They are an important way of teaching the young. They are part of one's cultural identity. Stories are as important today as they have ever been.

7

AUNT SUE'S STORIES

Aunt Sue has a head full of stories.
Aunt Sue has a whole heart full of stories.
Summer nights on the front porch
Aunt Sue cuddles a brown-faced child to her bosom
And tells him stories.

Black slaves
Working in the hot sun,
And black slaves
Walking in the dewy night,
And black slaves
Singing sorrow songs on the banks of a mighty river
Mingle themselves softly
In the dark shadows that cross and recross
Aunt Sue's stories.

And the dark-faced child, listening,
Knows that Aunt Sue's stories are real stories.
He knows that Aunt Sue never got her stories
Out of any book at all,
But that they came
Right out of her own life.

The dark-faced child is quiet
Of a summer night
Listening to Aunt Sue's stories.

—Langston Hughes

8

AS WE SIT AROUND GRANDPA'S CHAIR

As we sit around grandpa's chair
We wait for the stories we're about to
 hear
Of war, depression, love and joy.
It touches the heart of the girl and the
 boy.

He tells his adventures of flying a
 plane,
And searching for enemies in the
 outpour of rain.

As we sit and listen to stories so fine,
I wonder what grandpa will tell us
 next time.

—Jamie Fleming, age 11
Cherry Tree, Pennsylvania

9

 LISTEN

every
landscape

a wondrous
story

—Francisco X. Alarcón

Across the Curriculum
SOCIAL STUDIES & ARTS AND CRAFTS

So Many Ways To Tell Stories
EXPLORING CULTURE Songs, poetry and prose in spoken and written form, dances, plays, paintings, drawings, needlework—people have found many ways to tell stories. The Hmong people of Southeast Asia have created story cloths—appliqued or embroidered panels called *pa ndau* (pan-DOW)—to tell stories. These cloths are like history books, preserving folktales and contemporary stories for a culture that has not needed or used written language. *Pa ndau* have been brought to the U.S. by Hmong refugees from Laos in recent years.

Children can make their own story cloths from squares of felt and felt scraps or paper in different colors. Show students an actual story cloth and point out how the events in the story are told in sequence as the "reader's" eye travels along a path. You might also consult *Creating Pa ndau Applique: A New Approach to an Ancient Art Form* by Carla Hassel (Wallace-Homestead, 1984). Set up an Author-Artist Chair in which individuals can share their story cloths.

10

"FAIRILY WORRIED"?

Last night at bedtime
I just stayed awake
Because of this question I had in my head:

Do fairy-tale people
tell their kids about **us**
When it's time for **them** *to go to bed?*

—Josh Weinstein

11

A FAIRY TALE

Bedtime. I tell stories, tales
of Robert Rattlesnake, Bennie Beaver,
Yolanda Panda Bear, Jerry Giraffe
and Danny the Dog.
And then it's Elisa's turn. She begins
"Once upanza time . . . . . ."
"¡Panza!" I say. "It's not upanza,
it's **once upon** *a time. This is a panza,"**
and grab her stomach, tickle her
until she can laugh no more.
"Once upanza time . . . . . ."
"No No No No No!" I scream,
"It's once upon a time, not **upanza** *time."*
This is a panza," and I grab her stomach,
tickle her again until she's weak from
     laughter.
"Please tell me a real story," I plead,
"and please don't say panza."
"Once upanza time . . ." she begins.
"O.K.," I say, resigned. "You can say
     panza."
"Once upanza time
there lived a panza
and it lived happily ever after.
Good night, Daddy."

—Leroy V. Quintana

***panza (PAHN-sah):** Spanish for "paunch, belly, stomach"*

12

*When spider webs unite,
they can tie up a lion.*

—*Ethiopian proverb*

ACROSS THE CURRICULUM
SOCIAL STUDIES

Connections
PROMOTING SELF-ESTEEM When children can see that they are connected to, and important to, a group, self-esteem can soar. Use this proverb to demonstrate how each student is an important part of the class.

Have students sit on the floor in a circle and give one child a large ball of yarn (or string). Have that child hold on to one end of the yarn and roll the ball to a child who has helped him or her or who has made a positive contribution to the class, telling about what happened. The second child then relates another story and rolls the ball of yarn on to a third, and so on, until everyone is connected by the "spider web" of yarn.

To ensure that all children are included, you may need to recall special deeds or moments: *Remember the time when Jaime shared the good news about his brother? That made us all feel good that day.* Then, point out how each member is important to the whole class, as shown by the web.

13

CLOUD BROTHERS

*Four directions
cloud brothers
share one sky.*
    Each has its own path.
    Each has its own mood.
    Each has its own face.
*The cloud brothers are many
But they are one family.*

*The cloud brothers are scattered
but they are one in spirit.*

*They mingle
within themselves
changing with every moment.*

*They tell us
that we too
are brothers
on this land.*

*And
like our cloud brothers*

we are all yellow
    as are the sunrise clouds
we are all white
    as are the noonday clouds
we are all black
    as are the thunder clouds
we are all red
    as are the sunset clouds.

*So let us look up to our cloud brothers
as one family
and one spirit.*

*For we are truly different
and yet*
    we are truly the same.

—*Ramson Lomatewama*

A WORD FROM THE POET "'Cloud Brothers' is really a summation of my philosophy of dealing with people," says Ramson Lomatewama. "It was a way of expressing the connection that we people have with one another. I wanted to convey that although we have cultural differences, we have many similarities on a human level."

The poet explains the significance of the cloud brothers: "In our culture (Hopi), we believe that when people die, their breath goes to the clouds. I see the clouds as a metaphor for people here on Earth"—all different, yet all the same.

CULTURESHARE For Native peoples of the Americas, four is the significant number, as opposed to three, the significant number in European cultures. In European folk stories and folklore, things tend to happen in threes. There are three little pigs and three blind mice. Things happen three times and "third time's the charm." Even such phrases as "Get ready, get set, go" testify to the ingrained nature of the number three in European culture.

For Native peoples, for whom the natural world was and is of supreme importance, the four cardinal directions—North, South, East, West—assume sacred aspects, and the number four is the culturally ingrained number. One way to tell just how much a traditional story or song has been edited out of its original form is to note whether the things in it happen in threes or fours. If you are Native, you might say "What I tell you four times is true."

JANUARY

14

This song works particularly well as a round. The "2" shows where the "second" group starts the song from the beginning.

HINEH MA TOV / OH, HOW GOOD

① Hi - neh ma tov u - ma na - yim. She-vet a - chim gam
Bro-thers and si-sters to - ge - ther li - ving in u - ni -

ya - chad. ② Hi - neh ma _____ tov
ty. _____ Oh, how _____ good it is

she - vet a - chim gam ya - chad. Hi - neh
li - ving in u - ni - ty. _____ Oh, how _____

ma _____ tov she - vet a - chim gam ya - chad.
good it is li - ving in u - ni - ty. _____

*Hineh ma tov u'mana'yim, shevet achim gam yachad: literally, Hebrew for "Behold how good it is and how pleasant when brothers live together in unity" (the translation above has been keyed to the notes of the song). The word *achim* (brothers) in this context is often translated as "brothers and sisters," denoting "all people." However, to avoid this potentially exclusive term, you may wish to replace *achim* with *amim* (AH-meem), a shortened form of *amamim* (ah-MAH-meem), which means "nations" or "peoples."

15

YOUNG VOICES

PEACE STARTS AT HOME

At home with family is where love starts
Mom and Dad feel deeply in their hearts
Love is for me and love is for you
Love is for the world and people too
You can love your clothes and you can
* love your things*
But there's nothing like love for
* human beings*
Don't be mad don't be sad
Just open up your heart and be very glad
You have family on who you depend
You have your buddies you have your friends
When you talk about love
You feel it in your bones
If you want world peace
It starts at home.

—*Tianah Awezi Maji, age 9*
San Francisco, California

. . . That was the dream of Martin Luther King, Jr.

Martin Luther King, Jr., Day (third Monday)

Martin Luther King, Jr.'s most famous speech, known now as the "I Have a Dream" speech, was delivered August 28, 1963, to a crowd of more than 200,000 people after a march from the Washington Monument to the Lincoln Memorial in Washington, D.C. You may wish to play an audiocassette of the speech before presenting the following song. Audiocassettes of King's speeches are available through Lushena Books, 3732 W. Century Blvd., Bldg. 1, Units 4 & 5, Englewood, CA 90303. Telephone: (310) 671-9630.

MARTIN LUTHER KING, JR.

Dr. King was a man
Who saw the mountain top
Who saw the mountain top
Dr. King was a man
Who saw the mountain top
And he did not stop

Glory Hallelujah
Glory Hallelujah

Dr. King was a man
Who climbed the mountain top
Who climbed the mountain top
Dr. King was a man
Who climbed the mountain top
Because he could not stop

Glory Hallelujah
Glory Hallelujah

Dr. King was a man
Who reached the mountain top
Who reached the mountain top
Dr. King was a man
Who reached the mountain top
Because he would not stop

Glory Hallelujah
Glory Hallelujah

Dr. King was a man
Who stood on the mountain top
Who stood on the mountain top
Dr. King was a man
Who stood on the mountain top
Because he would not stop

Free at last
Free at last

—Useni Eugene Perkins

AS A MATTER OF FACT Since 1986, the third Monday in January has been observed as Martin Luther King, Jr., Day, a federal holiday in commemoration of the minister who, in the 1950s and 1960s, was one of the leaders of the African American civil-rights movement in the drive for racial equality. King took part in the 1955 boycott of buses in Montgomery, Alabama, where, as in most other Southern cities, African Americans were forced to sit in the rear of the bus. The boycott showed the effectiveness of nonviolent protest, and set the tone for much of King's career. King's eloquent speeches and his message of nonviolence and unity won him widespread support and made him the symbol of the civil-rights movement. In 1964, King won the Nobel Peace Prize. From the beginning, he made it clear that his efforts were not just "for the children and grandchildren of slaves," but for all disenfranchised and poor people in the U.S. Martin Luther King, Jr., was assassinated in 1968.

Dreams are something we all have in common.

DREAMS ARE

Dreams are lights
that go on at night
so our hopes won't get scared of the dark.

—Josh Weinstein

YOUNG VOICES

IN DREAMS

*It's bedtime and I dream
I'm falling into a
strange hole like
Alice . . .*

*flying like a bird
with Mary Poppins . . .*

*being a hero better
than Robin Hood . . .*

*It's like being stronger
than Superman . . .*

*growing bigger
than Hercules . . .*

*having the wisdom
to be as smart as an
owl . . .*

*Just then, I wake
up an ordinary kid
in my pajamas.*

—Justin Gall, 4th grade
Moorhead, Minnesota

DREAMS

*Hold fast to dreams
For if dreams die
Life is a broken-winged bird
That cannot fly.*

*Hold fast to dreams
For when dreams go
Life is a barren field
Frozen with snow.*

—Langston Hughes

DEVELOPING LITERACY
ORAL COMPOSING

Hold On Tight
"Dreams" lends itself to a poetic dialogue. See page 40 for specific techniques. First, transfer "Dreams" onto a transparency, leaving space after the first, second and fourth lines of each stanza. Then, mask the title and reveal the poem one line (or thought) at a time, asking volunteers to contribute new lines. After you have written these in the spaces between the lines, read the poem aloud with the lines children have contributed.

Older children can respond to an oral presentation of the poem. Read only one line at a time, giving children time to write a line of their own. Then, invite a volunteer to join you in a duet: you read the original lines of the poem while the child reads the lines he or she has written. Or, two or three children can take turns sharing their lines after you read each original line.

An inauguration to lead the nation.

20

Inauguration Day (in presidential-election years)

The following is an excerpt from the poem read by the author at the inauguration of President William Clinton on January 20, 1993.

from ON THE PULSE OF MORNING

Here on the pulse of this new day
You may have the grace to look up and
*   out*
And into your sister's eyes, into
Your brother's face, your country
And say simply
Very simply
With hope
"Good morning."

—Maya Angelou

AS A MATTER OF FACT The inauguration officially begins a President's term. The ceremony marking the inauguration is held on January 20 at noon in Washington, D.C., when the President recites the oath of office that is called for in the Constitution: "I do solemnly swear (or affirm) that I will faithfully execute the office of President of the United States, and will to the best of my ability, preserve, protect and defend the Constitution of the United States." Prior to 1933, March 4th served as inauguration day. However, in 1933, Congress passed the 20th Amendment, moving the inauguration to its current date to shorten the "lame duck" period of leadership by departing presidents.

In some places, at this time of year the cold gets colder and the ice is not so nice!

21

A WINTER SONG

If I
were the
cold weather
and people
talked about me
the way they talk
about it,
I'd just
pack up
and leave town.

—William J. Harris

DEVELOPING LITERACY
DRAMATIC INTERPRETATION—Choral Reading & Pantomime

Snow Song
As you reread the poem, invite children to chime in on the words SNOW! SNOW! SNOW! The rhythm and predictability of the words will encourage **students acquiring English** to join in. And you can aid their comprehension by setting the stage with pictures of snowy winter scenes.

After hearing the poem, children might work in small groups to invent pantomime actions for each of the verses. Assign each group a verse, allowing time to brainstorm and rehearse. Then, read the poem with animation, giving each group a signal when their verse is about to be read, and everybody will enjoy the silliness that results.

22

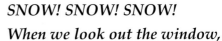

Chant this poem rhythmically and musically —like a rap—for an effective presentation.

SNOW! SNOW! SNOW!

When we look out the window,
What do we see?
SNOW! SNOW! SNOW!
Lovely, white, cold and deep.
SNOW! SNOW! SNOW!

The snow is falling in the night.
SNOW! SNOW! SNOW!
Whoooooooooooooooooooooo,
*   Whoooooooooooooooooooooo!*
The cold wind blows,
SNOW! SNOW! SNOW!

We prefer to stay inside.
SNOW! SNOW! SNOW!
Shiver, shiver,
Brrrrrrrrrr. I'm cold!
SNOW! SNOW! SNOW!

The sun comes out to warm the world.
SNOW! SNOW! SNOW!
Build a snowman, sled and run.
Winter, winter, so much fun!
SNOW! SNOW! SNOW!

—Kori Frazier, age 7
Kent, Ohio, and
April Philabaum, age 7
Akron, Ohio

23

JANUARY

In January
it's so nice
while slipping
on the sliding ice
to sip hot chicken soup
with rice.
Sipping once
sipping twice
sipping chicken soup
with rice.

—Maurice Sendak

24

SNOW, SNOW

Snow, snow, fly away
Over the hills and far away.

—Unknown

25

LONELINESS

No sky at all;
no earth at all—and still
the snowflakes fall . . . .

—*Hashin*
English version by Harold G. Henderson

天も地もなしに雪の降りしきり。

芭臣

ACROSS THE CURRICULUM

SCIENCE

A Cupful of Weather

Here are some ways to measure precipitation, whether your winter weather means rain or snow.

✦ After a snowfall, challenge children to predict how much water is in a cup of snow. After recording their guesses, children can fill dry-measure cups with snow, leveling off the top. To measure the moisture, have them melt the snow and pour the water into liquid-measure cups, to compare the actual amounts with their estimates. They might also compare the amount of water in different types of snow—newly fallen, packed, powdery, slushy, etc. To further explore types of snow, see *The Secret Language of Snow* by Terry Tempest Williams and Ted Major (Sierra Club/Pantheon, 1984), which describes different types of snow in Alaska, and related Inuit terms.

✦ A simple rain gauge can be made from a clear, wide-mouth jar or coffee can. Put the rain-catcher out in an open area, away from buildings or trees; if winds are gusty, anchor it in a box of sand. After a rainstorm, children can hold a ruler to the outside of the jar or put it down inside the can to measure the amount of rainfall.

No matter what the weather, and no matter what the date, there's nothing as chilling as hate.

THE WAY I SEE ANY HOPE FOR LATER

The way I see any hope for later,
we will have to get
               over this color
                    thing,
and stop looking
          at how much brown
          or tan there is
          in
          or on   this
                woman
          or that   man.
And stop looking
          at who is a woman
          and
          who is a man.

Stop looking
Start loving.

                    —*Arnold Adoff*

WHY DO THEY STARE?

Why do they stare at me?
Is it because my clothes
Are torn and ragged?
Or is it because
My skin is dark and beautiful?
And they envy my beauty?
Why do they stare?

          —*Wendy Rountree, junior high school*
               East Orange, New Jersey

DEVELOPING LITERACY
GROUP TALK & ROLE PLAY

Taking Care of Ourselves—and Each Other

PROMOTING SELF-ESTEEM The poems in this theme deal with hatred based on stereotypes and prejudices. Use this opportunity to help children learn how to avoid perpetuating this kind of hatred and how to protect themselves from it. After reading the poems, discuss children's feelings, experiences, and reactions:

◆ *What do you think all of these poems are about?*

◆ *Why do you think the poets chose to write about this topic?*

◆ *What are some reasons that people might do hateful things like teasing or staring?*

Then, help children think of specific responses they (or the poets) could make to handle such difficult situations. Some possibilities include telling the person how you feel, asking the person not to talk to or treat you that way again, talking to a trusted adult about the situation, or expressing feelings in writing (a journal or a poem) when it is too hard or unsafe to talk to the person directly.

Encourage small groups or partners to role-play a situation they've been in, or one described in the poetry, using the responses they brainstormed. Be sure that children trade roles, so they experience all sides of a situation; this will help build empathy. Throughout the activity, let children speak freely, but respond to stereotypes and prejudice directly and promptly. Remind children of the classroom rules they have all agreed to abide by (or create some now; see entry for October 22).

28

SLIT EYES

Mommy,
today Jason called me "slit eyes"
so I pushed him
and he punched me
and the teacher sent us both
to the principal
who only said,
"No fighting on the playground."

It's hard to play when
someone else
calls you names.
And I thought Jason
was my friend.

Son,
pushing Jason didn't help,
but it's good to be proud
of who you are.
We may have smaller eyes
but we can see quite well.

—Amy Ling

A Word from the Poet "'Slit Eyes' was my need to get a recent incident off my chest. The subject I find most persistent for me as an Asian American is racism and the pain of being the target of discrimination and racist slurs. Between the ages of 8 and 10 I lived in a small town—we were the only Asian family. Racial prejudice marked my early years, and I'm deeply sorry that my son is having to go through the same experience."

29

TEASING

Teasing is being laughed at.
It feels like a needle.

Teasing is being told your clothes are ugly.
It looks like tears in your eyes.

Teasing is being told your mom is ugly.
It sounds like a scream from a hurt puppy.

Teasing is being laughed at for locking
*   yourself in a room.*
It smells like dead fish.

Teasing is being told you're stupid.
It tastes like chewing rocks.

—José Jiménez, 5th grade
Santa Ana, California

30

IT'S ALL AROUND

It's all around us
you can't see it
you can't touch it
You can't hear it
But it affects you
It's hate

—Joanie King, 4th grade
Brooklyn, New York

31

Superbowl Sunday (most often the last Sunday in January)

AFTERNOONS: TWO*

No one owns
a   foot   ball
on   this
*   street.*
We   roll   the
morning
*   paper*
and
tie   it   with
*   old*
*   rope*
and
hope it
*   holds*
through   the
tough
passing
game.

When you catch my pass you tuck this paper
in your gut and make your feet deliver the
*   winning news.*

—Arnold Adoff

*****Afternoons: Two:** This is the second of a series of poems describing afternoon sports activities, in *Sports Pages* (HarperCollins, 1986), a collection of poetry by Mr. Adoff.

FEBRUARY

Weather-wise, February is a month of transition in many parts of the U.S. The weather can make us feel that we're still in the midst of winter—or it can signal the approaching spring. And the joy of a new season, a new beginning, pervades the exuberant celebrations of Lunar New Year.

While we look to the future, there are also opportunities this month to commemorate the past: in the celebration of Black History Month, in the solemn observance of Ramadan (parts of which fall in February from 1993 to 1998), or in the honoring, on Presidents' Day, of two figures—Washington and Lincoln—who helped shape U.S. history.

And what better time to express appreciation for friends and loved ones than Valentine's Day? In leap years, there's even a special February surprise—an extra day.

So leap right in. It's February!

Noteworthy Days

- ◆ Black History Month

- ◆ Lunar New Year (falls between January 21 and February 20*)

- **14** Valentine's Day

- ◆ Ramadan (may fall any time of year, following the Muslim calendar, which is strictly lunar*)

- ◆ Presidents' Day (third Monday)

- **29** Leap Year Day (every four years)

* See page 265 for exact date.

Great stories of great women and great men! . . .

Black History Month

from WHO I AM IS WHO THEY WERE

Who I am is who they were
My African brothers and sisters
were a proud people.
Great Nubian* warriors
brave and filled with courage
A strong people, determined to survive.
I, too, am proud, brave and determined to survive.
Who I am is who they were.

> —Tony Campbell, 11th grade
> Woodside, California

***Nubian (NOO-bee-ahn):** from Nubia, a region of ancient Africa, part of what is now Sudan. The Nubian civilization of Kush flourished for thousands of years and became a center of learning, technology, and trade.

CULTURESHARE What eventually became Black History Month started out in 1926 as a week-long observance celebrating the achievements and assessing the current status of African Americans. It was proposed by Carter G. Woodson, an African American historian who founded the Association for the Study of Afro-American Life and History (ASALH). In 1976, the observance was extended to the entire month of February. Each year the ASALH chooses a different theme as the focus of Black History Month.

The month of February was chosen because it contains the birthdays of two prominent figures in African American history: Abraham Lincoln and Frederick Douglass (1818?–1895), activist for racial justice and equality.

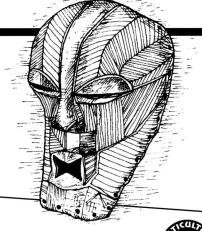

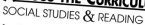

ACROSS THE CURRICULUM
SOCIAL STUDIES & READING

Let's Find Out More
EXPLORING CULTURE During this theme, make available to children books to celebrate Black History Month, for example:

✦ *Afro-Bets Book of Black Heroes from A to Z: An Introduction to Important Black Achievers* by Wade Hudson and Valerie Wilson Wesley (Just Us Books, 1988)

✦ *Book of Black Heroes, Volume Two: Great Women in the Struggle,* edited by Toyomi Igus (Just Us Books, 1991)

✦ *Malcolm X* by Arnold Adoff (Harper Collins, 1985)

✦ *A Picture Book of Harriet Tubman* by David Adler (Holiday House, 1992)

✦ *A Picture Book of Martin Luther King, Jr.* by David Adler (Holiday House, 1989)

✦ *Rosa Parks* by Eloise Greenfield (HarperCollins, 1973)

Children can share what they have learned by:

✦ constructing a time line of major plot or historical events

✦ writing and presenting television or radio commercials to promote books they enjoyed

When you present this poem, pause after the fifth line. Read the rest of the poem as a wistful remembering of the attributes of the grandmother's place.

WHERE MY GRANDMOTHER LIVED

Where my grandmother lived
there was always sweet potato pie
and thirds on green beans and
songs and words of how we'd
survived it all.
Blackness.
And the wind
a soft lull
in the pecan tree
whispered
Ethiopia*
* Ethiopia, Ethiopia*
E-th-io-piaaaaa!

> —Doughtry Long

* **Ethiopia:** a country in northeastern Africa; once called Abyssinia, Ethiopia is one of the few African countries that never became a European colony; it has remained independent for two thousand years

A WORD FROM THE POET Doughtry Long says he wrote this poem when he was very young. "It took few rewrites to make this poem work," he says. He describes it as a "searching for cultural roots, a definition of roots, and an insight into roots."

3

BLACK HISTORY

There were so many people
who helped us
Rosa Parks,* King,* Malcolm X*
and Tubman*
Rosa Parks got arrested for
sitting in the front of the city bus
Martin Luther King
spoke against what he thought was wrong
Because of what he did he no longer
lives on
Harriet Tubman rescued
300 slaves
Imagine how many lives they saved.

—Formikia Jeffrey, 6th grade
New York, New York

---

*Rosa Parks: African American whose commitment to attain
justice for her people led her, in 1955, to refuse to give up her
seat in a Montgomery, Alabama, bus to a European American
man, in violation of a city law. The ensuing bus boycott by
African Americans was one of the early successes of the Civil-
Rights Movement.

*King: Martin Luther King, Jr.; for more information on King,
see entry for January 16

*Malcolm X: African American who led a movement that
sought to unite Black people throughout the world. His
affirmation of Black pride and self-respect deeply influenced
the generation of African Americans coming of age during the
1960s.

*Tubman: Harriet Tubman, who had herself escaped from
slavery, risked her own freedom time and again to lead more
than 300 others to freedom on the "Underground Railroad," a
clandestine network of people dedicated to helping escaped
slaves reach freedom in the north. Though there was a $40,000
reward posted for Tubman, she was never captured.

4

HARRIET TUBMAN*

Harriet Tubman didn't take no stuff
Wasn't scared of nothing neither
Didn't come in this world to be no slave
And wasn't going to stay one either

"Farewell!" she sang to her friends one night
She was mighty sad to leave 'em
But she ran away that dark, hot night
Ran looking for her freedom

She ran to the woods and she ran through
* the woods*
With the slave catchers right behind her
And she kept on going till she got to the North
Where those mean men couldn't find her

Nineteen times she went back South

Have
Children
Read About
These People

Across the Curriculum
ARTS AND CRAFTS & SOCIAL STUDIES

Hail the Heroes

VALUING DIVERSITY Every culture has its
heroes—and here's an opportunity to
recognize and celebrate them throughout
the year. Using the pattern on **Activity
Sheet 9,** children can create bookmarks for
the Reading Center and use a new
bookmark each week to learn about a
variety of heroes, past and present.

To ensure diversity, you might suggest types
of heroes, with several names for each
category, allowing children to choose. For
example, you might suggest:

◆contemporary political figures, such as
March Fong-Eu or Henry Cisneros

◆astronauts and other explorers, such as
Christa McAuliffe, Mae Jamison, or
Jacques Cousteau

◆historical figures, such as Malcolm X, Anne
Frank, Crazy Horse, or Queen Liliuokalani

◆children's authors and poets, such as
Lawrence Yep, Virginia Hamilton, Yoshiko
Uchida, Tomie DePaola, Gary Soto, or
John Steptoe

Older children might contribute names of
people they (or their family) consider
heroes—a great home-school connection!

5

LISTEN CHILDREN

listen children
keep this in the place
you have for keeping
always
keep it all ways

we have never hated black

listen
we have been ashamed
hopeless   tired   mad
but always
all ways
we loved us

we have always loved each other
children   all ways

pass it on

—Lucille Clifton

6

DRAGON SMOKE

Breathe and blow
white clouds
      with every puff.
It's cold today,
      cold enough
to see your breath.
Huff!
   Breathe dragon smoke
      today!

—Lilian Moore

DEVELOPING LITERACY
COLLECTING WORDS

Weather Webs
Word banks can be lively and dynamic classroom tools. Give them plenty of time to grow; they can pique interest, activate research, and build a love of language. For this theme, you might draw a series of clouds at the top of a long piece of butcher paper. Collect weather words from the poems and all the sound words children can think of, and group them under the clouds, adapting the clouds to suit the different types of weather.

Content-Area ESL
Add pictures to the words in the web to promote the acquisition of weather vocabulary by **students acquiring English.**

7

ICY

I slip and I slide
On the slippery ice;
I skid and I glide—
Oh, isn't it nice
To lie on your tummy
And slither and skim
On the slick crust of snow
Where you skid as you swim?

—Rhoda W. Bacmeister

8

WINTER POEM

once a snowflake fell
on my brow and i loved
it so much and i kissed
it and it was happy and called its cousins
and brothers and a web
of snow engulfed me then
i reached to love them all
and i squeezed them and they became
a spring rain and i stood perfectly
still and was a flower

—Nikki Giovanni

9

Take advantage of the mention of the word *lodge* in this song to discuss the diversity of Native American dwellings—lodges, long houses, cliff dwellings, and others, as well as the portable teepees.

WHEN THE DAY IS CLOUDY

When the day is cloudy,
The thunder makes a low rumble
And the rain patters against the lodge,
Then it's fine and nice to sleep,
   isn't it?

—Crow traditional song

DEVELOPING LITERACY

DRAMATIC INTERPRETATION—Sound Effects

Here Comes the Rain!
Recreate the sound of a rainstorm in your classroom. Just ask children to follow your lead:

1. Rub hands together in a circular motion (the rustling of the leaves as the wind picks up).

2. Snap fingers—one hand at a time—slowly and lightly at first, then faster and harder (the patter of the first tiny raindrops).

3. Clap hands (the rain pours down).

4. Slap hands on desk or table (the rain pounds on the roof).

5. Stamp feet (thunder!).

6. Reverse the order of these movements so that the final sound is the whish of hands rubbing together in a circular motion (the storm blows over).

10

WEATHER

Whether the weather be fine
Or whether the weather be not,
Whether the weather be cold
Or whether the weather be hot,
We'll weather the weather
Whatever the weather,
Whether we like it or not.

—Unknown

11

Wake the dragon! It's Lunar New Year!

Lunar New Year (falls between January 21 and February 20)

DRAGON DANCE

A Chinese dragon's in the street
And dancing on its Chinese feet
With fearsome head and golden scale
And twisting its ferocious tail.
Its bulging eyes are blazing red
While smoke is puffing from its head
And well you nervously might ask
What lies behind that fearful mask.
It twists and twirls across the road
While BANG the cracker strings explode.
Don't yell or run or shout or squeal
Or make a Chinese dragon's meal
For, where its heated breath is fired
They say it likes to be admired.
With slippered joy and prancing shoe
Why, you can join the dragon too.
There's fun with beating gongs and din
When dragons dance the New Year in.

—Max Fatchen

12

This poem is meant to be performed by two voices. You can create your own script: a simple pattern is for two voices to read alternating lines until the sixth line from the end, and then finish reading the poem in unison. This is the pattern used for the reading featured on the **Music Tapes**.

LION DANCE*

Drum drum gong drum
gong gong cymbal gong
*gong she fah chai**
cymbal clang drum clash
gong she fah chai
lion saunter lion strut
gong-she gong-she
yellow body bright eye
gong she fah chai
eye wink eye flash
cymbal clang drum clash
lion coy lion cute
she-she she-she
lion lie lion sleep
fah chai fah chai
fah chai fah chai
gong she fah chai

man walk man creep
gong she fah chai
lion wake! lion leap!
gong she fah chai!
lion angry lion cross
gong-gong she-she fah-fah chai-chai
lion leap lion high
chai! chai! chai! chai!
people cower people fly
gong chai! gong chai!
lion pounce lion prance!
gong gong gong gong gong gong gong gong
gong she fah chai!
gong gong gong gong gong gong gong gong
GONG SHE LION DANCE!!
GONG SHE LION DANCE!!

—*Trevor Millum*

* **Lion Dance:** part of the celebration for Chinese New Year, the lion dance is performed by two dancers inside a lion costume, to an exciting rhythm marked by drums and cymbals.

* **gong she fah chai (***gong shee fah chy***— rhymes with *my*):** Mandarin for "Happy New Year!" (literally, "good fortune, congratulations")

CultureShare The Lunar New Year is traditionally observed by many Asian peoples beginning on the second new moon following the Winter Solstice (see entry for December 21). This tradition is carried on by some Asian Americans today. Although the details of the celebration vary from culture to culture, it is generally a time to make a new beginning. Houses, and especially kitchens, are thoroughly cleaned in preparation for the New Year. Debts are settled. New clothes—particularly, new shoes—are considered important to start out the New Year right.

Among Chinese Americans, the celebrations that follow the New Year traditionally last two weeks. Families visit each other during this time. There are special holiday foods, such as candied melon, boiled dumplings (some with a surprise message inside), and *jiazoi (JOW-zuh)* (meat dumplings). Children receive good-luck money wrapped in red paper. Friends exchange large red greeting cards and gifts of oranges, tangerines, and new clothes. Seasonal decorations include flags, banners inscribed with good-luck slogans, lanterns and hand-made paper chariots, and pyramids of fruit. Many families attend performances of traditional Chinese opera.

The celebrations culminate with the Lantern Festival, with its grand parade led by the Golden Dragon (symbol of strength and goodness) weaving and dancing through popping firecrackers set off to keep him awake. San Francisco has the largest Chinese New Year parade outside of Mainland China. Its Dragon Dance features a 120-foot-long Golden Dragon operated by more than twenty dancers.

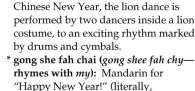

Tet is a special New Year's celebration!

13

TET

Lotus seed candy
and yellow flowers everywhere—
Firecrackers rip the air.
For me, a red envelope
with money within—
While grown-ups stroll
in their favorite clothes
there are lots of games to win.

—*Emily Nguyen*

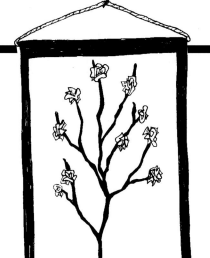

CULTURESHARE The Vietnamese observance of the Lunar New Year (which coincides with the Chinese New Year) is known as Tet. It shares with the Chinese New Year the concept of a new beginning. It also has its own special characteristics. A special, very serious ceremony is performed at midnight on the last night of the year to express honor and respect for ancestors. The details of the ceremony vary according to the religious orientation of the family. Tet is a time of happiness and celebration. Banners are hung on house doors, some with the greeting "CUNG CHÚC TÂN XUÂN" *(koong chook tahn shwahn)*, meaning "compliments of the season." This time of the year is also considered an auspicious season to get married, and so there are many weddings during Tet.

ACROSS THE CURRICULUM

ARTS AND CRAFTS & SOCIAL STUDIES

Welcoming the New Year

VALUING DIVERSITY All cultures celebrate the new year as a symbol of a new beginning. The celebrations take different forms in different cultures. Explore the diversity of new-year's customs, while emphasizing the universality of the celebration. Here are some ideas:

◆ Read aloud all the new-year poems and background information in this anthology: Rosh Hashanah (9/15), New Year's Day (1/1), and the Lunar New Year (2/11–13).

◆ Encourage children to research new-year celebrations. You might make available *Happy New Year Round the World* by Lois S. Johnson (Rand McNally, 1966), *Happy New Year* by Emily Kelly (Carolrhoda, 1984), and *Joy Through the World* by the U.S. Committee for UNICEF (Allen Bragdon Publishers, 1985).

◆ Invite community members from various cultures to teach children more about holiday foods, songs, decorations, apparel, greetings, games, and other traditional activities.

◆ Help children synthesize all the information they've found. Using **Activity Sheets 10** and **11**, children can make "culture wheels" to compare and contrast the names, greetings, and customs of different new-year traditions.

What can grow in any weather Love . . .

14

Valentine's Day

I LOVE YOU LITTLE

I love you little,
I love you lots,
My love for you would fill ten pots,
Fifteen buckets,
Sixteen cans,
Three teacups
and four dishpans.

—*Unknown*

AS A MATTER OF FACT The association of February 14 with love is uncertain and obscure. It may have something to do with the two saints named Valentine whom Christian tradition has honored on this day since the fifth century C.E. Legends about the lives of both saints associate them with romantic love. Cementing the focus of the day as a day for sweethearts is an ancient belief that birds and small animals choose their mates at this time of year. The modern observances of Valentine's Day—the giving of cards, flowers, and gifts to friends and, especially, sweethearts—are probably a combination of many old traditions and customs.

15

MY LOVE

*My love is
for my mother.
It is in my heart
And I don't care
if there are
millions of hearts.
Mine,
belongs to my Mom.*

—Daniel Henríquez, 2nd grade
New York, New York

© 1989. Reprinted by permission of We Shall Overcome Fund.

16

I LOVE EVERYBODY

Fast blues feel

Spiritual

I love ev - ery-bo - dy, __ I love ev - ery-bo - dy, __

I love ev - ery - bo - dy, in my heart. _____

I love ev - ery - bo - dy, I love ev - ery - bo - dy,

I love ev - ery - bo - dy in my heart. _____

17

PATCHWORK

*It takes more than saying
to make love so.
It takes being and doing
as stitch by stitch
Love makes a pattern
that endures.*

—Marilou Awiakta

... and friendship.

18

B

THE NEW GIRL

*I can feel
we're much the same,
though I don't
know your name.*

*What friends
we're going to be
when I know you
and you know me!*

—*Charlotte Zolotow*

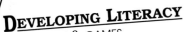

DEVELOPING LITERACY
GROUP TALK & GAMES

Getting To Know You
PROMOTING SELF-ESTEEM The confidence that comes from making new friends—and sharing personal information—is a powerful self-esteem booster. Here are some non-threatening ways for children to share parts of themselves with their peers and, of course, find new friends!

◆ **Make-a-New-Friend Bingo:** With a copy of the game card that appears on **Activity Sheet 12**, each child circulates around the room, finding children who have the likes, dislikes, experiences, or talents indicated on the squares of the card. The object of the game is to get each square signed by a different person. (With a small group, you might allow the same person to sign two squares.) The pictures on the cards will help **students acquiring English** participate in the game.

◆ **Shoe and Tell:** Each child takes off one shoe and uses it as a puppet or a prop to tell a personal story. They (or, really, the shoe!) can tell about where the shoe has been or the circumstances surrounding its acquisition or where it "sleeps" at night—the possibilities are almost endless. **Students acquiring English** may need some time to watch others before telling their own stories, but the use of a prop often helps children gain confidence in speaking.

19

YOUNG VOICES

FRIENDS

*beautiful
long black hair
  skinny
brown skin
  Mexican
playing together
loving each
  other
  never
  fighting
helping each
  other
sharing things and secrets
  sometimes
  staying
over her
  house
  special
  friend
staying together
  for
a long, long,
long time*

—*María Rendón, 4th grade
New York, New York*

20

POEM

*I loved my friend.
He went away from me.
There's nothing more to say.
The poem ends,
Soft as it began—
I loved my friend.*

—*Langston Hughes*

21

A LOT OF KIDS

There are a lot of kids
Living in my apartment building
And a lot of apartment buildings on my street
And a lot of streets in this city
And cities in this country
And a lot of countries in the world.
So I wonder if somewhere there's a kid I've never met
Living in some building on some street
In some city and country I'll never know—
And I wonder if that kid and I might be best friends
If we ever met.

—*Jeff Moss*

DEVELOPING LITERACY
GROUP TALK

Golden Friendship
This theme can become a starting place for a discussion about the importance of friends. Though the content of the discussion will be determined by the age of the participants, appropriate questions or observations can result in a clearer understanding of the value of a true friend. With younger children, talk about specific examples of friendship, such as helping or sharing:

◆ What would a friend do if you fell down and skinned your knee?

◆ What would a friend do if he or she had something special that you didn't have?

Invite older children to discuss the criteria for being a good friend and the value of friendships with people of different cultures and ages.

22

As you present these proverbs, share their origin with students, so that they can discuss the value of friends in all cultures.

FRIENDSHIP

A friend—one soul, two bodies.

—Chinese proverb

Wealthy the man who has true friends.

—Spanish proverb

Who is mighty? One who makes
an enemy into a friend.

—Jewish proverb

Real friends will share even
a strawberry.

—Slovakian proverb

As for clothes, the newer the better;
as for friends, the older the better.

—Korean proverb

DEVELOPING LITERACY
WRITING

Kindred Spirits
After reading these proverbs, challenge children to write their own proverb, using *A friend is* as a beginning. Younger children can illustrate an act of friendship, while **students acquiring English** might start with a drawing and then work with a more-fluent partner to put their proverbs into words.

With Ramadan comes a time for fasting and contemplation.

23

Ramadan (may fall any time of year, following the Muslim calendar, which is strictly lunar)

OUR FIRST FAST

Days of Ramadan begin before sunrise, when we eat heaping plates and drink sugary tea.

Stomachs grumble and energy is low—our eyes are hungry in the late afternoon.

But the sun sets as it always does. We look for the crescent moon in the sky. Our mom has made our favorite dishes, the smells from the kitchen make our stomachs talk.

We bite into our Medina dates* and sip the Zamzam water.* We think of those who don't have what we have, and we whisper, in God's Ear, our thanks.

We fasted our first fast and we laugh and kid because we are proud.

"Happy Ramadan," our parents smile.

—Sophia Mir

*Medina dates: dates from the surroundings of Medina, a city in Saudi Arabia associated with Muhammed; Medina dates are considered sacred food by Muslims

*Zamzam water: water from a well in Mecca, site of the holiest shrine of Islam; the water is considered holy by Muslims

CultureShare Ramadan (*RAM-uh-dan*) is a religious observance prescribed in the Koran (also spelled Quran; pronounced *kuh-RAHN*), the holy scripture of Muslims. Held during the ninth month of the Muslim year, Ramadan is an austere time, a time for introspection, for self-evaluation, and for spiritual contemplation. Muslims fast from sunrise to sunset every day during this month. At the end of the month, a joyous three-day celebration called *Eid al-Fitr* (*eed ul-FIT-ur*) ends the fast. The festivities that accompany *Eid al-Fitr* emphasize family togetherness and a sense of community. Families feast together at midday, go to fairs, shop for new clothes, and watch fireworks displays. Children often receive coins and other gifts from their parents.

It's Presidents' Day! Happy birthday, George and Abe!

24

Presidents' Day (third Monday)

DREAM AMERICA

George Washington
helped get the Dream started—
praise and honor to him—
But he couldn't finish dreaming it for us.
No one can finish dreaming the Dream.

Abraham Lincoln
helped shape the Dream—
praise and honor to him—
But he couldn't finish dreaming it for us.
No one can finish dreaming the Dream.

Great men and women
can help us to dream—
praise and honor to them—
But they can't dream it all up for us.
The Dream of America must be our Dream.

—Juan Quintana

As a Matter of Fact Presidents' Day is a combined remembrance of two presidents whose birthdays fall in February—George Washington (born February 22, 1732) and Abraham Lincoln (born February 12, 1809).

George Washington, the first president of the United States, is best remembered as the commander of the colonial army during the Revolutionary War, the person most responsible for making American independence a reality. Lincoln is remembered for keeping the nation together during the Civil War, which encompassed his entire presidency (1861–1865). Lincoln's Emancipation Proclamation (1862) freed all slaves in the states which had seceded from the Union. The 13th Amendment (1865) continued the work of the Proclamation by constitutionally outlawing slavery in the U.S.

And it's not only George and Abe who have birthdays, you know!

 25

BIRTHDAY CANDLES

Grandma's baked a cake for me.
See the candles, one, two, three.
Put them out with one big blow.
Ready, set, now here we go.

—Unknown

26

 THE WISH

Each birthday wish
I've ever made
Really does come true,
Each year I wish
I'll grow some more
And every year

    I

       DO!

—Ann Friday

ACROSS THE CURRICULUM
SOCIAL STUDIES

Birthday Timeline
A good way to keep track of everyone's birthday is with a birthday timeline. Cut large stars out of colored construction paper and paste a photo (or a photocopy of a photo) of each child on one side of the star. On the other side, write the date of the child's birthday. Help children arrange the stars in chronological order and attach them with clothespins to a clothesline.

27

MY FIRST BIRTHDAY GIFT

They didn't give me
a doll, or book,
a stuffed giraffe
or game.
On the day I was born
my present
was my name!

—Sandra Liatsos

SANDY

28

YOUR BIRTHDAY CAKE

Your birthday cake is made of mud
Because I cannot cook.
I cannot read a recipe or follow in a book.
I'm not allowed to use the stove
To simmer, roast, or bake.
I have no money of my own to buy a
*   birthday cake.*
I'm sure to get in trouble if I mess around
*   with dough.*
But I've made your birthday cake of mud
Because I love you so.

—Rosemary Wells

February 29—it's hardly ever here. It turns up every now and then, but then it disappears.

29 Leap Year Day
(every four years)

RIDDLE

Q. Why are 1996, 2000, and 2004 good years for kangaroos?

A. They are all leap years.

SPRING

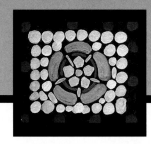

Spring is as magic as powerful rhyme—
Spring is a bird worm-ing overtime.

—*Lee Bennett Hopkins*

MULTICULTURAL TRADE BOOKS

Burstein, Chaya M. **The Jewish Kids' Catalog** (The Jewish Publication Society of America, 1983). A resource of customs, history, language, holidays, crafts, recipes, and music.

■

Cowen-Fletcher, Jane. **Mama Zooms** (Scholastic, 1993). A boy and his mother have adventures, zipping around in her wheelchair.

■

Hamilton, Virginia. **Drylongso** (Harcourt Brace Jovanovich, 1992). A farm family faces drought, until a mysterious stranger arrives.

■

McLain, Gary. **The Indian Way: Learning to Communicate with Mother Earth** (John Muir, 1990). Through Grandpa Iron's stories, two Arapaho children learn how to live in harmony with the environment.

■

Moss, Marisa. **Regina's Big Mistake** (Houghton Mifflin, 1990). Each student in Mrs. Li's class is supposed to draw a rainforest, but Regina is too worried about making a mistake.

MARCH

It's time to journey into the sights and sounds of a brand new season—a season of hope, renewal, and celebration.

Hope is the keynote as we observe the United Nations' International Day for the Elimination of Racial Discrimination—hope that someday no one will know the withering power of prejudice.

Renewal comes with the beginning of spring, when gardeners in many parts of the country eagerly return to the earth to add to the rebirth of the green. And the month honors other sorts of renewal as well: the renewal and growth that children experience through art and music.

March is also a time for celebration. We honor the joy of knowing more than one language. Children take delight in the celebrations for the festival of Purim and for St. Patrick's Day. And celebration is also the mood during National Women's History Month, as we remember and appreciate the aspirations and achievements of women in U.S. history.

So look out, look up—and March into the new season!

Noteworthy Days

- ✦ National Foreign Language Week (first full week)
- ✦ Youth Art Month
- ✦ Purim (falls mid-February to mid-March*)
- ✦ National Women's History Month
- **17** St. Patrick's Day
- **20 or 21** Spring Equinox
- **21** International Day for the Elimination of Racial Discrimination
- ✦ Music in Our Schools Month

* See page 265 for exact date.

It seems like you know more when you know it in two languages.

1

National Foreign Language Week
(first full week)

BEING BILINGUAL

I say it and feel it's true:
Being bilingual is a gift
That lasts you the whole year through.

—Alma Flor Ada

ACROSS THE CURRICULUM

SOCIAL STUDIES

On Being Bilingual
To help students understand the value of knowing a second language—especially in today's interconnected world—use a web like this one to begin a brainstorming session.

teacher   translator   newcomer   traveler   student

give and get information   BEING BILINGUAL HELPS PEOPLE   make new friends

traveler   worker   hospital worker

student   communicate in an emergency

fire fighter

telephone operator   police officer

PROMOTING SELF-ESTEEM Invite bilingual community members to visit the classroom, and encourage them to tell children about the advantages their ability to speak two languages has in their jobs and in other parts of their lives. Pair **students acquiring English** with visitors who speak the same first language and encourage the pair to work together to tell a story, sing a song, or recite a poem in their first language. Encourage performers to use dramatization, props, or other visual aids to communicate with the audience. Valuing each student's first language boosts self-esteem for all children and allows **students acquiring English** to "shine" in their first language. It also helps children who speak only English empathize with the difficulties students acquiring English can have in understanding a second language.

2

YOUNG VOICES

THE LOSS OF SOMETHING VERY SPECIAL

The summer started, I played. Soon came August, Hebrew school started. I forgot how to speak Hebrew, the first day it was petrifying. I knew everyone. Except for my teachers. They went around the room. We had to tell them our English name and Hebrew name. They came to me. I said my name in English. I forgot my Hebrew name. I felt funny. Then I said my name was

*מניה

It took me ten minutes.

—Melissa Frieden, 4th grade
San Jose, California

*מניה : Manya (MON-yuh), a Hebrew name

During Youth Art Month, every picture tells a story . . .

3

Youth Art Month

CRAYONS

I've colored a picture with crayons.
I'm not very pleased with the sun.
I'd like it much stronger and brighter
And more like the actual one.
I've tried with the crayon that's yellow,
I've tried with the crayon that's red.
But none of it looks like the sunlight
I carry around in my head.

—Marchette Chute

4

YOUNG VOICES

WHY THE SUN IS YELLOW

Long ago everything in the world was yellow, like the sun, the grass, the trees. One day Coyote* said, "The world should have some color to it." So Coyote took some paint and started to paint things. He painted the grass green. He painted the trees green and brown. Then everything was different colors. But when he was going to the sun there was no more paint. So that's why the sun is yellow.

—Christine LaRock, age 9
San Leandro, California

* Coyote: figure of cultural importance for many Native American peoples. For more information on Coyote, see January 8.

5

YELLOW

Green is go,
and red is stop,
and yellow is peaches
with cream on top.

Earth is brown,
and blue is sky;
yellow looks well
on a butterfly.

Clouds are white,
black, pink, or mocha;
yellow's a dish of
tapioca.

—David McCord

DEVELOPING LITERACY
COLLECTING AND RELATING WORDS

Color Quiz
Here is a simple game the class can play during the Colors theme. Show one child a color card without letting other children see it. Ask him or her to give several examples of things that are the mystery color while the rest of the class guesses what the color is. Children might record and use their guesses for each color in the activity **Colorful Compositions** (see entry for March 5).

ACROSS THE CURRICULUM
ARTS AND CRAFTS & WRITING

And Now . . . Lavendorange!
With water colors, tempera paint, finger paint, or food coloring, children can experiment with creating unusual colors. Challenge children to name the "new" colors they create and to decide what things should be this new color. Older children might enjoy writing an innovation on the poem "Rhinos Purple, Hippos Green" (March 6), to explain their choices.

DEVELOPING LITERACY
PATTERNED WRITING

Colorful Compositions
Invite children to compose their own versions of the poem "Yellow" using **Activity Sheet 13**, reminding them that poems don't have to rhyme. To help **students acquiring English**, display color cards as you read the poem. Read slowly and hold up each card only when you are saying the color word; then, immediately put it down so children make a clear connection between the color they are seeing and the word they are hearing, without being confused by other words in the sentence. Make available as many pictures as possible that show objects of the colors mentioned in the poem, to give children ideas for their own poems.

RHINOS PURPLE, HIPPOS GREEN

My sister says
I shouldn't color
Rhinos purple,
Hippos green.
She says
I shouldn't be so stupid;
Those are things
She's never seen.
But I don't care
What my sister says,
I don't care
What my sister's seen.
I will color
What I want to—
Rhinos purple,
Hippos green.

—*Michael Patrick Hearn*

DEVELOPING LITERACY
DRAMATIC INTERPRETATION—Poem for Two Voices

Fun for Two
Create a script, and then have children perform "Rhinos Purple, Hippos Green" as a poem for two voices. (See page 34 for more information about this technique.)

Have children work in pairs to rehearse, and, when they are feeling confident, suggest they tape-record their duets. Making recordings will allow for multiple tries and result in less "performance stress" (and more fun). When pairs are ready, they can play their recordings for the class.

Purim (falls mid-February to mid-March)

THE FOURTEENTH DAY OF ADAR*

See the spring sky
full of kites and small birds!

Our kitchen
fragrant
with honey and poppyseed
fills up with fat little
*three-cornered pies—***Hamantaschen!***

Tonight
in my long dress I will be
Esther the Queen.*
Tonight
on a small stage I will save
my people. I will remember
my lines.

"There he crawls!" I will say
to the King.
"There he crawls—in his
*three-cornered hat—the serpent, Haman!"**

Come into our Purim kitchen*
and nibble the three-cornered
hats—sweet to recall
a sweet queen, a sweet victory,
a wicked man   gone!

—*Barbara Juster Esbensen*

CultureShare Purim is a joyous holiday marked by costumes, plays, and parties. The holiday celebrates the Jews' escape from the death plotted for them by Haman, an advisor to King Ahasuerus of Persia in the sixth century B.C.E. Haman had convinced the king to draw lots, or *purim*, to determine the day on which the Jews were to be killed. When King Ahasuerus found out that his wife, Esther, was Jewish, he instead had Haman put to death, on the very day the Jews were to have been killed.

In addition to the eating of *hamantaschen*—which are said to be three-cornered in imitation of the kind of hat Haman wore—Purim celebrations today often include raucous plays or retellings of the Purim story, complete with costumes. Whenever Haman's name is mentioned, children try to drown it out by yelling, stamping their feet, or using noisemakers called *groggers* or *gregers*.

*Adar (*uh-DAHR*): sixth month of the Jewish year; Purim falls on the 14th of Adar (or of Adar II, which comes after Adar in leap years)
*Hamantaschen (*HAY-muhn-TAH-shen*): German for "Haman's pockets" (for Haman, see **CultureShare**); triangular pastries filled with fruit, cheese, or poppy seeds, traditional for Purim
*Esther: see **CultureShare**
*Haman: pronounced *HAY-muhn*
*Purim: the Hebrew pronunciation is *poo-REEM*, commonly pronounced in English as *PUHR-im*

Women's history . . .

8

National Women's History Month

SO THAT'S WHAT GIRLS ARE MADE OF

denim and sneakers
books and bikes
mothers and grandmothers
stories and heroes
and

I suppose

sugar and spice
(but only sometimes)

—Julie Cason

AS A MATTER OF FACT National Women's History Month was established in 1981 by the Women's History Project, a nonprofit organization that works year-round to "promote the celebration and appreciation of multicultural women's history in every area—school, work, home and community." The month-long commemoration was founded to publicize women's influence on the history of the United States. Appropriately, this month contains International Woman's Day, which, since 1910, has honored working women annually on March 8.

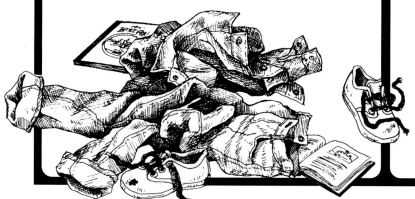

9

This is part of a song written in 1912, at the height of the women's suffrage movement. You may wish to discuss with students that many people today consider the suffix *-ette* insulting, trivializing, or condescending when applied to women. The suffix *-ist*, as in *suffragist*, is a respectful and gender-neutral alternative.

I AM A SUFFRAGETTE

I met a little country girl, eighteen years old, she said.
Her eyes were black, her hair was jet, and she sadly to me said,
"Yes, Papa votes, but Mama can't, Oh no, not yet, not yet.
No matter what the others think, I am a suffragette."

—M. Olive Drennen

AS A MATTER OF FACT The women's suffrage movement—the drive by women to obtain the right to vote—was a direct result of the anti-slavery campaign of the 19th century. Two of the most active abolitionists, Elizabeth Cady Stanton and Lucretia Mott, met at an antislavery convention and agreed that, along with equality of the races, they should also work for equality of the sexes. From this meeting grew first one and then several organizations devoted to women's suffrage. In 1890, the two most prominent organizations combined to form the National American Woman Suffrage Association, led by Carrie Chapman Catt. The efforts of this organization and of the many great women who led the fight for women's rights—women such as Jane Addams, Mary Church Terrell, Ida B. Wells, and Susan B. Anthony—finally led to the passing of the 19th Amendment in 1920, establishing women's right to vote.

ACROSS THE CURRICULUM
SOCIAL STUDIES & WRITING

MULTICULTURAL FOCUS

The Past, the Present, and the Future
VALUING DIVERSITY The poems in this theme explore the changing roles and rights of women over time. Children can explore this idea by interviewing women of different generations in their own families and neighborhoods.

First, children can brainstorm a list of the possible interviewees: grandmother, mother, aunt, older sister, baby-sitter, friend, neighbor. Then encourage each child to talk to two women of different ages about the hopes and goals these women had when they were children. **Activity Sheet 14** can be used to record the information.

When interviews are completed, chart the goals on a timeline by decade and help children look for patterns. Add a column for the present decade, and have all children contribute their own goals for the future.

As you review the chart, help children draw conclusions about the acceptability of all choices for everyone—women and men, girls and boys.

◆ *People have many different goals in their lives, don't they?*

◆ *Each person has the right to dream his or her own dreams and to decide what's best for him or her.*

10

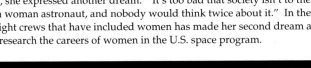

LAST LAUGH

They all laughed when I told them
I wanted to be

A woman in space
Floating so free.

But they won't laugh at me
When they finally see
My feet up on Mars
And my face on TV.

—*Lee Bennett Hopkins*

A Word from the Poet "'Last Laugh' was first published in 1974, before women were considered to become part of space travel in the United States. I have always believed that women should and could be part of space exploration. When it finally happened, Ride's ride made the verse very popular throughout the country. Although no woman—or man—has yet to set foot upon Mars, I am sure this event will happen. 'Last Laugh' was, and still is, a promise of *beginning*."

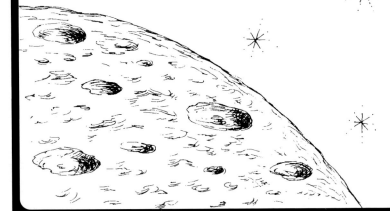

RIDE, SALLY RIDE

Chorus:
  Ride, Sally Ride
  Ride that big bird to the sky
  Ride, Sally Ride
  It's your turn to fly among the stars
  We'll rendezvous on Mars

I have ridden rocket ships since I was only ten
With my science fiction fantasies
  I could only dream back then
But you have pushed all the buttons that made my wish come true
Oh, Ride, Sally Ride, I'll ride along with you

Chorus

Mother Earth above you, and your space boots to the Sun
The freedom of pure weightlessness your determination won
You have got the right stuff to be an astronaut
Oh ride, Sally Ride, I'm riding on this shot

Chorus

Challenge your tomorrows and who knows what will come
I'm betting on prosperity and a chance for everyone
Each walk in space will show us our frontiers never end
Oh ride, Sally Ride, the future is our friend.

—*Casse Culver*

As a Matter of Fact On June 18, 1983, Sally Ride joined the crew of the space shuttle *Challenger*. It was a dream come true for the astrophysicist. At the time, she expressed another dream: "It's too bad that society isn't to the point where the country could just send up a woman astronaut, and nobody would think twice about it." In the years since then, the number of U.S. space-flight crews that have included women has made her second dream a reality as well. Older students may want to research the careers of women in the U.S. space program.

RICE AND ROSE BOWL BLUES

I remember the day
Mama called me in from
the football game with brothers
and neighbor boys
in our front yard

said it was time
I learned to
wash rice for dinner

glancing out the window
I watched a pass interception
setting the other team up
on our 20

Pour some water
into the pot,
she said pleasantly,
turning on the tap
Rub the rice
between your hands,
pour out the clouds,
fill it again
(I secretly traced
an end run through
the grains in
between pourings)

with the rice
settled into a simmer
I started out the door
but was called back

the next day
Roland from across the street
sneeringly said he heard
I couldn't play football
anymore

I laughed loudly,
asking him
where
he'd heard
such a thing

—Diane Mei Lin Mark

12 **13**

TOMMY*

I put a seed into the ground
And said, "I'll watch it grow."
I watered it and cared for it
As well as I could know.

One day I walked in my back yard,
And oh, what did I see!
My seed had popped itself right out,
Without consulting me.

—*Gwendolyn Brooks*

*Tommy: the name of one of the children in the author's book *Bronzeville Girls and Boys* (Harper and Row, 1956), in which the poems are written from various children's perspectives

ACROSS THE CURRICULUM

SCIENCE

Sprout a Garden
This theme might spark an interest in having a classroom mini-garden. Bean sprouts are an ideal crop, since they require few supplies, grow quickly, and are easy for small gardeners to care for.

Punch holes with a hammer and nail in the screw-on lids of several quart-size jars. Rinse mung beans (1/2 cup for each jar) and soak in water overnight. Drain the water, screw on the lids, and put the jars in a dark place. Rinse beans two or three times a day. Sprouts will be ready to harvest in about five days and can be used in salads or sandwiches. *Your First Garden Book* by Marc Brown (Little, Brown, 1981) shows how to grow other easy things.

Content-Area ESL
Use an illustrated chart to track the growth of classroom crops. Keep a word bank beside it as children build a vocabulary of garden words: *beans, shoots, sprouts, seeds, seedlings, leaves,* etc. (For slower-growing plants, keep track of weeks rather than days.)

ARTZA ALINU / WE'VE COME TO THE LAND

With spirit

Traditional

Ar - tza a - li - nu   ar - tza a - li - nu   ar - tza a - li -
We've come to the land, __ we've come to the land, __ we've come __ to the __

nu   a - li - nu   nu   kevar   ha - rash - nu   ve - gam za - ra - nu
land the   land __   land   We've plowed al - read - y   we've al - so plant - ed

kevar   ha - rash - nu   ve - gam   za - ra - nu   a - val   od   lo   ka -
we've plowed al - read - y   we've al - so   plant - ed   but we   have not   yet

tzar - nu   a - val   od   lo   ka -   tzar - nu   a - val   od   lo   ka -
harvest - ed   but we   have not   yet   harvest - ed   but we   have not   yet

tzar - nu   a - val   od   lo   ka -   tzar - nu
harvest - ed   but we   have not   yet   harvest - ed

14

MY NIPA* HUT

My nipa hut is very small,
But the garden is full, there is food for us all.
Singkamas* *and* **talong,***
Sigarillas*, mani*
Sitao,* batao,* patani.*

All kinds of good things are found everywhere,
Of cabbage and squash there is plenty to spare.
Cucumbers and peas
So tender and sweet,
And everything else good to eat.

—*Filipino folk song*

*nipa *(NEE-puh):* thatch made from the East Indian palm
*singkamas *(SING-kmuss):* Tagalog for "beans"
*talong *(tuh-LONG):* Tagalog for "eggplant"
*sigarillas *(ZIG-uh-REEL-yus):* Tagalog for "spinach"
*mani *(muh-NEE):* Tagalog for "peanuts"
*sitao *(SEE-tow—*rhymes with *cow):* Tagalog for "string beans"
*batao *(BAH-tow):* Tagalog for "lima beans"
*patani *(puh-TAH-nee):* Tagalog for "turnips"

15

AFTER ALL THE DIGGING

　　　　　　　　and the planting
　　　　　　　　and the　pulling
of weeds
　　　　　on hot summer afternoons

there are cool mornings
we can
　　　　walk between
the rows
　　　and bite a bean　　or chew a lettuce
　　　　　　　　　　　　　　leaf
　　　and taste the ripe tomatoes

the
way
the rabbits
　　take
breakfast

—*Arnold Adoff*

16

ODE TO TOMATOES

they make
friends
anywhere

red
smiles
in salads

tender
young
generous

hot
salsa
dancers

round
cardinals
of the kitchen

hard
to
imagine
cooking

without
first asking
their blessings!

—Francisco X. Alarcón

DEVELOPING LITERACY
LISTENING TO VISUALIZE

Tom-art-o
"Ode to Tomatoes" is full of delightful images. After reading it once, read it again while children listen with closed eyes. Pause for at least one minute after each stanza, while children visualize each image and make a quick sketch of their mental pictures. After reading, children can finish and color their drawings. You might create a bulletin-board display, with each stanza illustrated by children's drawings.

ACROSS THE CURRICULUM
MATHEMATICS

The Tasty Tomato
Is salsa or ketchup the favorite tomato product in your classroom? Take a poll to find out. Ask children to brainstorm as many uses for tomatoes as they can think of, while you chart the suggestions. Each child can vote by writing his or her name in the appropriate column of the chart. After volunteers total the number of votes for each column, discuss the number relationships—most popular, least popular, how many votes separate most from least popular, etc. To extend this activity for older students, you might make ingredients available so that children can prepare and/or taste all or some of the tomato dishes on the chart.

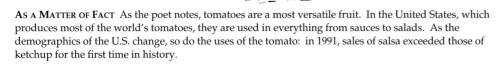

AS A MATTER OF FACT As the poet notes, tomatoes are a most versatile fruit. In the United States, which produces most of the world's tomatoes, they are used in everything from sauces to salads. As the demographics of the U.S. change, so do the uses of the tomato: in 1991, sales of salsa exceeded those of ketchup for the first time in history.

17

St. Patrick's Day

WEARING OF THE GREEN

It ought to come in April,
or, better yet in May
when everything is green as green—
I mean St. Patrick's Day.

With still a week of winter
this wearing of the green
seems rather out of season—
it's rushing things, I mean.

But maybe March is better
when all is done and said:
St. Patrick brings a promise,
a four-leaf-clover promise,
a green-all-over promise
of springtime just ahead!

—Aileen Fisher

AS A MATTER OF FACT Originally a religious holiday in Ireland, St. Patrick's Day came to the United States with Irish immigrants and has become part of the national culture. Marked by parades and the sharing of Irish music and food, St. Patrick's Day celebrations in the U.S. have crossed cultural boundaries to the point that, on this day, it's not unusual to see just about anyone wearing the green.

18

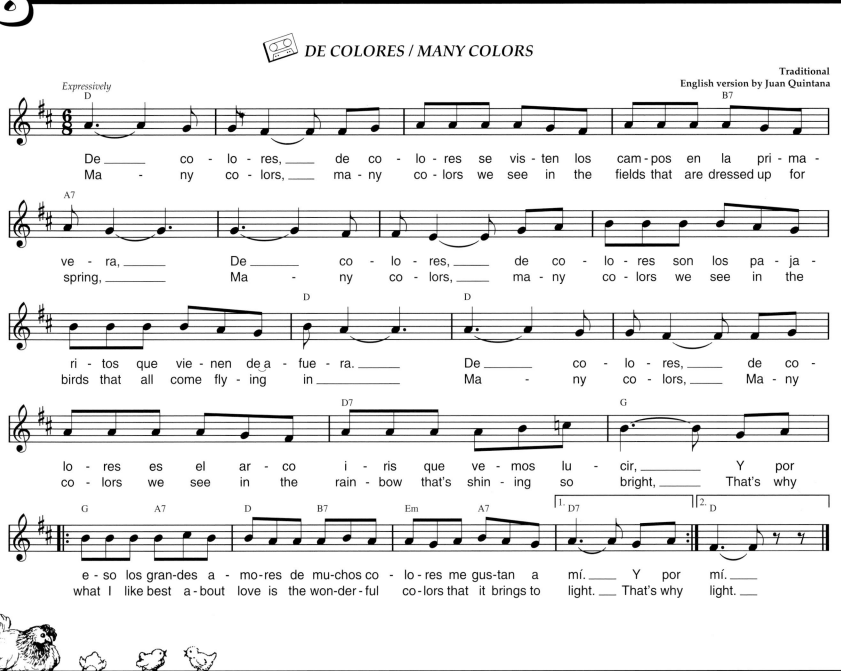

DE COLORES / MANY COLORS

Traditional
English version by Juan Quintana

Expressively

De _____ co - lo - res, _____ de co - lo - res se vis - ten los cam - pos en la pri - ma -
Ma - ny co - lors, _____ ma - ny co - lors we see in the fields that are dressed up for

ve - ra, _____ De _____ co - lo - res, _____ de co - lo - res son los pa - ja -
spring, _____ Ma - ny co - lors, _____ ma - ny co - lors we see in the

ri - tos que vie - nen de a - fue - ra. _____ De _____ co - lo - res, _____ de co -
birds that all come fly - ing in _____ Ma - ny co - lors, _____ Ma - ny

lo - res es el ar - co i - ris que ve - mos lu - cir, _____ Y por
co - lors we see in the rain - bow that's shin - ing so bright, _____ That's why

e - so los gran - des a - mo - res de mu - chos co - lo - res me gus - tan a mí. ___ Y por mí. ___
what I like best a - bout love is the won - der - ful co - lors that it brings to light. ___ That's why light. ___

19

SPRING SONG

As my eyes
Search the prairie,
I feel the summer in the spring.

—*Chippewa traditional song*

20

Spring Equinox (20 or 21)

When you read this poem, pause after line 8 ("my extra graham crackers") to indicate that a new thought follows. Read the last four lines more quickly and joyfully.

SPRINGTIME

in springtime the violets
grow in the sidewalk cracks
and the ants play furiously
at my gym-shoed toes
carrying off a half-eaten peanut
butter sandwich i had at lunch
and sometimes i crumble
my extra graham crackers
and on the rainy days i take off
my yellow space hat and splash
all the puddles on Pendry Street and not one
cold can catch me

—*Nikki Giovanni*

AS A MATTER OF FACT The Spring (or Vernal) Equinox signals the beginning of Spring in the Northern Hemisphere. The sun is directly over the equator on this day, and rises due east almost everywhere on Earth. The length of the daylight period on this day is identical everywhere—just over 12 hours.

On this date let's vow . . .

21

International Day for the Elimination of Racial Discrimination

COLOR

Wear it
Like a banner
For the proud—
Not like a shroud.
Wear it
Like a song
Soaring high—
Not moan or cry.

—*Langston Hughes*

AS A MATTER OF FACT The International Day for the Elimination of Racial Discrimination was proclaimed by the United Nations in 1966. The date was chosen to commemorate the killing of 69 Black demonstrators in Sharpeville, South Africa, in 1960, but the day also honors "those countless others in different parts of the world who have fallen victim to racial injustice." Throughout the 1990s, as part of the U.N.'s Decade for Action to Combat Racism, March 21 also marks the beginning of the Week of Solidarity with the Peoples Struggling Against Racism and Racial Discrimination, ending March 27.

22

Before presenting this poem, share with children the **Word from the Poet** that appears below and discuss with them the meaning of *minority*. After presenting the poem, make sure children understand, first of all, that the speaker in the poem is a member of a "minority" who doesn't see himself or herself as such. Then, you might engage older children in a discussion of ethnic identity. Is it important to think of yourself as part of an ethnic group? Is this more, or less important if you are in the "majority" than if you are in the "minority"?

LOOKING OUT

It must be odd
to be a minority
he was saying.
I looked around
and didn't see any.
So I said
Yeah
it must be.

—*Mitsuye Yamada*

A WORD FROM THE POET "This poem was inspired by a comment that was made by a friend, a Japanese American woman. She was brought up in white suburbia and had forgotten, for a moment, that she was a member of a 'minority.'"

. . . no more hate!

23

SHAME

I washed
my arms
scrubbed
my face

powdered
soap
fell from
my hands

but
my skin
only got
redder

I was
just
another
itching

brown
boy
getting
ready

for school

—*Francisco X. Alarcón*

Photo of the poet

DEVELOPING LITERACY
GROUP TALK & MEMORIZING AND RECITING

The Secret Inside
PROMOTING SELF-ESTEEM A strong sense of self-worth can make the hurts of the world less painful. Discussing each poem in this theme will arm children with strategies for dealing with unkind words or actions, and help them develop confidence in their ability to handle difficult situations.

✦ "Image": Help children see that the person who *makes* discriminatory remarks, not the person who receives them, is the one who has the problem.

✦ "If They Hate Me": Ask children to discuss who the speaker is, what the situation might be, and what the speaker means by "right here." Point out that the poem offers one strategy for turning arrows into boomerangs.

Remind children of the strategies discussed in **Taking Care of Ourselves—and Each Other** (January 26). Work with them to memorize "Image" or "If They Hate Me"; suggest that reciting the words to themselves is one strategy they might use if they are hurt by an insensitive or disrespectful remark or action.

A WORD FROM THE POET "This poem has to do with my experience here in the United States when I was a child," says Francisco Alarcón. "Many brown children never saw reflections of themselves in the curriculum; every face was white. We seemed to be totally ashamed of our indigenous roots. I was the darkest in my family and they seemed to hold it against me. So, when I was a little boy, I actually used soap to try to get the color off of me."

Mr. Alarcón remembers what changed this shame to pride: "Meeting my grandmother really gave me a sense of self. She was an Indian, living in Mexico. She was beautiful! I feel I was rescued by meeting the rest of my family." (See "Matriarch" on May 25 for the poet's description of his grandmother.)

24

Before reading this poem, discuss with children the literal difference between an arrow—which shoots straight at its target—and a boomerang, which returns to the person who threw it. Then, after children are familiar with the poem, help them understand how words might sometimes be like arrows or boomerangs, and how the "I" of the poem avoids being hurt by turning what people say into boomerangs.

IMAGE

I cannot be hurt anymore.
I see that their arrows
are really boomerangs.

—*Henry Dumas*

25

IF THEY HATE ME

If they hate me
*   they*
are
*   sick*
and
*   hurt*
and
*   need*
*   some*
*   kind*
of
*   help.*

I will
*   stay*
right
*   here.*

—*Arnold Adoff*

When it's Music In Our Schools Month . . .

26

Music in Our Schools Month

Let's start at the very beginning
A very good place to start
When you read you begin with A, B, C
When you sing you begin with do re mi
do re mi, do re mi
The first 3 notes just happen to be
Do re mi, do re mi
Do re mi fa so la ti*—

DO RE MI

Words by Oscar Hammerstein II
Music by Richard Rodgers

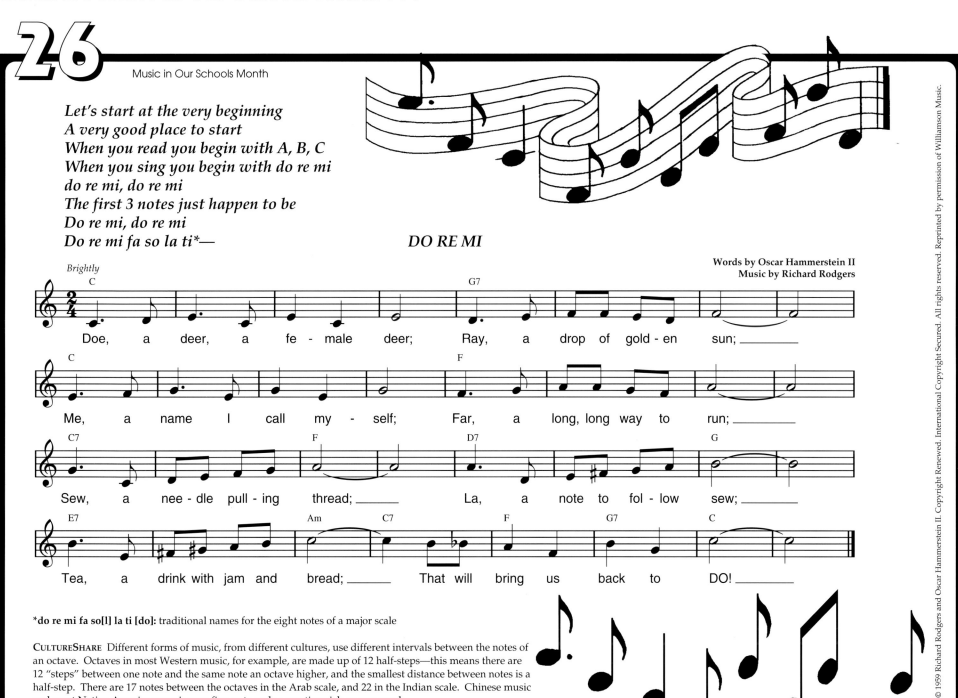

Brightly

Doe, a deer, a fe - male deer; Ray, a drop of gold - en sun; _____

Me, a name I call my - self; Far, a long, long way to run; _____

Sew, a nee - dle pull - ing thread; _____ La, a note to fol - low sew; _____

Tea, a drink with jam and bread; _____ That will bring us back to DO! _____

*do re mi fa so[l] la ti [do]: traditional names for the eight notes of a major scale

CultureShare Different forms of music, from different cultures, use different intervals between the notes of an octave. Octaves in most Western music, for example, are made up of 12 half-steps—this means there are 12 "steps" between one note and the same note an octave higher, and the smallest distance between notes is a half-step. There are 17 notes between the octaves in the Arab scale, and 22 in the Indian scale. Chinese music and most Native American music uses five-note scales, creating rich, open sounds.

© 1959 Richard Rodgers and Oscar Hammerstein II. Copyright Renewed. International Copyright Secured. All rights reserved. Reprinted by permission of Williamson Music.

27

OURCHESTRA

So you haven't got a drum, just beat your belly.
So I haven't got a horn—I'll play my nose.
So we haven't any cymbals—
We'll just slap our hands together,
And though there may be orchestras
That sound a little better
With their fancy shiny instruments
That cost an awful lot—
Hey, we're making music twice as good
By playing what we've got!

—*Shel Silverstein*

ACROSS THE CURRICULUM
MUSIC

Sounding Your Best
Help children explore the concept that people often develop musical instruments from materials at hand. For example, because Trinidad produces a lot of oil, empty steel oil drums are abundant; steel-drum music is popular there (see March 29).

There's one instrument that's always available and everyone can play: the body! There are all kinds of "body percussion" sounds. Here are just a few. Children can clap hands, alone or with a partner; rub palms in a circular motion; snap fingers; tap two fingers of one hand in palm of the other; pat knees; brush knees in a side-to-side motion; slap thighs; slide hands down sides; stamp feet; cluck with tongue to roof of mouth while making different shapes with lips.

What others can you think of?

28

DRUMS

I stand in the woods
hearing nature's drums
water from the waterfall pounding
the woodpecker pecking on a hollow tree
the wolf's heart thumping
as he goes in for the kill

—*Adam O'Dea, 8th grade*
Potter Valley, California

29

To accompany the reading of this poem, you may wish to play children a tape of steel-drum music, such as *Down the Road* by Andy Harrell (Windham Hill, 1992)

STEEL DRUM

Music always playin'
on my own island.
Reggae, rockers, calypso
the steelband panorama.
Long into the evening
after sun done gone
I keep on hearing the pan man
pom da de de de dom pom
sweet on that steel drum!

—*Lynn Joseph*

AS A MATTER OF FACT Steel bands are the most common form of musical ensemble in Trinidad, an island in the Caribbean of which the author is a native. Steel drums are actual empty oil drums (barrels), one end of which is hammered in until it is concave. Striking the surface of the drum in different places creates different notes, higher around the rim of the drum, and progressively lower toward the middle.

ACROSS THE CURRICULUM
MUSIC

Making Music
Make available craft supplies and as many of the following materials as you can for children to make and play their own musical instruments: rubber bands of all sizes; containers, such as shoe boxes, cans, egg and oatmeal cartons, plastic bottles; dried corn and beans, rice, gravel or stones; paper towel rolls and paper plates; wooden sticks and drinking straws

EXPLORING CULTURE You might invite family members and members of the community to demonstrate musical instruments from their own cultures.

BLOWING COLD

What did the musician do when someone put his trumpet in the freezer?

He played it cool!

—Roy Doty

To accompany the reading of this poem, you may wish to play children a tape of shakuhachi music, such as "Music for Two Shakuhachi," available from Audio-Forum, 96 Broad Street, Guilford, CT 06437; (800) 243-1234.

Before reading this poem, tell children briefly who John Coltrane was: one of the most influential jazz saxophonists of the 1960s. (He died in 1967.) You may wish to play children a tape of John Coltrane, such as "John Coltrane Retrospective" (Impulse, 1992). Children may be interested to hear the musician's jazz version of the song "My Favorite Things."

SHAKUHACHI*

*When his son-in-law
asked for lessons,
he nodded.
Slipped the bamboo
out of its silk case.
Played one note.
Played it till it hung
clear as the moon.
Handed over the instrument.
Said, "Practice this note.
Come back in a year
for the second."*

—Jim Mitsui

JOHN COLTRANE DITTY

*John be playin'
I be swayin'
help me git dat jazz*

*He be tootin'
I be hootin'
help me git dat jazz*

*I be crowin'
while he blowin'
funky razamataz*

*John be screechin'
I be r e a c h i n'
reachin' out for jazz!*

—Dakari Kamau Hru

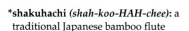
*shakuhachi (shah-koo-HAH-chee): a traditional Japanese bamboo flute

CULTURESHARE Jazz has been called the only truly American art form—and like the United States, it draws its influences from many places. A mixture of European classical music, West African rhythms, and African American work songs and spirituals, jazz is marked by its incorporation of improvisation and of complex, richly textured chords. Among the many scales that have been used by jazz musicians is the five-note scale characteristic of some Asian and Native American music. Jazz today continues to grow and evolve as it incorporates an ever wider diversity of influences.

APRIL

April is a joyous month. It bursts forth with laughter on April Fools' Day and happily celebrates new life and renewal throughout the month with holidays, such as Passover, Easter, and the Cherry Blossom Festival, and with celebrations, such as the Week of the Young Child. While April showers are busily bringing forth beautiful blossoming gardens, the animal world shows off its own array of new life with a parade of newly-born or newly-hatched creatures. Nature is at its very best, and so, what better time for Earth Day—a time to commit ourselves to protecting Nature.

Jewish Heritage Week offers its own special observance of remembrance and renewal. And, speaking of renewal, . . . don't forget that library book! Like April, books, too, have the power to enliven, to nurture, and to provide new growth. National Library Week is here to remind us of that.

So . . . here's to April. Here's to life!

Noteworthy Days

1   April Fools' Day

◆   Passover (falls between March 27 and April 24*)

◆   Week of the Young Child (third full week)

◆   Easter (falls between March 22 and April 25*)

◆   Cherry Blossom Festival (last two weekends)

◆   National Library Week (Sunday through Saturday of third week)

22   Earth Day

◆   Jewish Heritage Week (falls between April 16 and May 14)

* See page 265 for exact date.

Feel giddy and silly and happy as can be.
Get ready, get set for some April fooleree— . . .

1

April Fools' Day

APRIL FOOLS' DAY

Look out! Look out! You've spilt the ink.
You're sitting in a purple puddle.
Your pants are ripped and I should think
You'd hate to have a nose so pink
And hair in such a dreadful muddle.

Look out! Behind you there's a rat.
He's hiding now behind the stool.
He's going to jump up on your hat.
Look out! Watch out! Oh dear,
 what's THAT!
It's only you, you April fool!

—Marnie Pomeroy

CULTURESHARE The custom of playing tricks on the first day of April probably originated in France in 1564, when the date of the New Year was changed from April 1 (as it had traditionally been celebrated) to January 1. Communications being what they were at the time, many people did not know that a new calendar had been adopted and continued to celebrate the New Year on April 1, which led not only to much confusion, but to an inevitable jest or two. The custom of playing tricks and sending folks on fool's errands on April 1 spread to other countries. Today, in English-speaking countries April 1 is an opportunity for frivolity, foolishness, and good-natured pranks. Similar customs are observed in Spanish-speaking countries on December 28, popularly known as *Día de los Inocentes* (Holy Innocents Day).

Note: Humor is notoriously idiosyncratic and conditioned by culture. Beware of forcing a certain sense of humor on students, or of making students feel strange or deficient for not fully "appreciating" the humor enjoyed by other classmates.

2

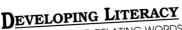 *WAY DOWN SOUTH*

Way down south where bananas grow,
A cricket stepped on an elephant's toe.
The elephant said, with tears in his eyes,
"Pick on somebody your own size."

—Unknown

DEVELOPING LITERACY
COLLECTING AND RELATING WORDS

A Pear Game—Oops, A *Pair* Game
Here's a game partners can play with homophones. Brainstorm a list of homophones—words that sound alike but are spelled differently and have different meanings. Start with *way/whey* and *pear/pair*. Here are some more to keep the ball rolling: *kernel/colonel, board/bored, peak/peek, heard/herd, won/one, cheap/cheep, meet/meat, beat/beet, wail/whale.*

Have each child choose one pair of homophones and construct a puzzle like the one below, using one letter that the two words have in common as the intersection for the puzzle squares. To make the puzzle easier, children can put that letter in the square and also fill in letters for the beginning or ending squares.

P	A	I	R
E			
A			
R			

After writing clues for their puzzles, children can work in pairs to solve each other's puzzles.

Students acquiring English may need some extra time to sort out the differences in meaning between the words in homophone pairs. Work with them using pantomime and manipulatives before they construct their puzzles.

3

THREE SILLY POEMS

There is no milk
in the Milky Way.
There isn't even
any whey.

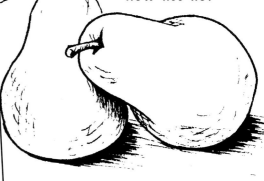

A pear is one
and a pair is two.
What a confusing
how-dee-do.

I ran a race
with a tiny bird.
He came in first
and I came in third.

—Ernesto Galarza

4

Before presenting this poem, discuss with children what a revolving door is. Then read the poem at a fast pace.

 Y

I AM RUNNING IN A CIRCLE

I am running in a circle
and my feet are getting sore,
and my head is
spinning
spinning
as it's never spun before,
I am
dizzy
dizzy
dizzy.
Oh! I cannot bear much more,
I am trapped in a
revolving
. . . volving
. . . volving
. . . volving door!

—*Jack Prelutsky*

5 Passover (falls between March 27 and April 24)

PASSOVER

Out of a land
that held us slaves,

Under the wings
of the angel of death,

Over hot sands,
across cold seas,

We sing again
with freedom's breath.

—*Myra Cohn Livingston*

CULTURESHARE A celebration of the Israelites' flight to safety from Egyptian slavery in the thirteenth century B.C.E., Passover has come to symbolize the very ideal of freedom and perseverance. The observance of Passover has another aspect to it as well. Passover is celebrated by more Jews than any other holiday on the Jewish calendar—perhaps because it is so essentially and uniquely a *family* holiday. The *seder (SAY-der)*—the traditional meal held on the first night of this eight-day holiday—is often attended by complete extended families, many of whom have not seen one another since the previous Passover. Also, because charity and community are such important elements of the holiday, it is common for families to invite to their seder people who, for whatever reason, are not able to have one of their own.

Everyone is involved in the activities of the seder, which is a unique combination of religious symbolism and individual family tradition. Generally presided over by the oldest male, the meal is guided by the reading of the *Haggadah (hah-GAH-dah)*, which tells of the Jews' exodus to Israel. The reading is often divided among all the attendees, with the youngest child (or children) reading the "Four Questions"—the part of the Haggadah that explains many of the traditions of Passover. Songs are often sung at the seder, and *motzoh (MAHT-suh)* and other special foods, with symbolic significance, are eaten during Passover week.

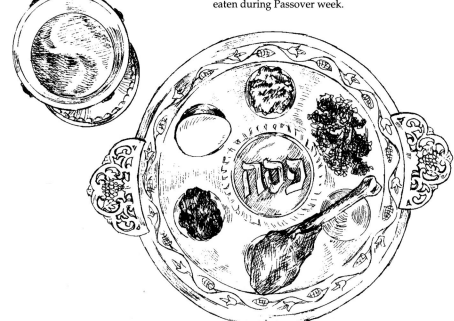

6

APRIL

Rain is good
for washing leaves
and stones and bricks and
even eyes,
and if you hold
your head just so
you can almost see
the tops of skies.

—Lucille Clifton

7

SPRING RAIN

The storm came up so very quick
It couldn't have been quicker.
I should have brought my hat along,
I should have brought my slicker.

My hair is wet, my feet are wet,
I couldn't be much wetter.
I fell into a river once
But this is even better.

—Marchette Chute

8

APRIL RAIN SONG

Let the rain kiss you.
Let the rain beat upon your head
with silver liquid drops.
Let the rain sing you a lullaby.

The rain makes still pools
on the sidewalk.
The rain makes running pools
in the gutter.
The rain plays a little sleep-song
on our roof at night—

And I love the rain.

—Langston Hughes

DEVELOPING LITERACY
ORAL COMPOSING & WRITING

Making Magic with Poetry
The poem "April Rain Song" has just the right structure for a poetic dialogue. (See page 40 for more information about this technique.)

Have children respond to all the lines of the poem but the last one by writing or dictating lines of their own. When the new versions are read, pause before the last line and read it quietly but with emphasis.

9

After reading the poem to the children, discuss with them the image in the third stanza. Ask them to close their eyes and visualize the movement of the flower as it fills with water and then bends and empties.

I ASK MY MOTHER TO SING

She begins, and my grandmother joins her.
Mother and daughter sing like young girls.
If my father were alive, he would play
his accordion and sway like a boat.

I've never been in Peking,* or the Summer Palace,*
nor stood on the great Stone Boat* to watch
the rain begin on Kuen Ming Lake,* the picnickers
running away in the grass.

But I love to hear it sung;
how the waterlilies fill with rain until
they overturn, spilling water into water,
then rock back, and fill with more.

Both women have begun to cry.
But neither stops her song.

—Li-Young Lee

*Peking *(pee-KING)* : the capital of mainland China; the name is now more commonly transliterated into English as *Beijing (bay-JING)*
*Summer Palace: one of many summer residences of China's emperors and empresses; this one, built by order of the Empress Tz'u-hsi, is just outside of Beijing
*Stone Boat: a huge marble pavilion rising out of Kuen Ming Lake; the pavilion was created as a replica of a Mississippi paddle-steamer at the Empress's request.
*Kuen Ming *(kwen-ming)* **Lake:** the lake created for the grounds of the Empress Tz'u-hsi's Summer Palace

A WORD FROM THE POET Li-Young Lee says that when he wrote this poem he was trying to capture something about how his mother sings, and that, as frequently happens in poetry, that "something" is hard to define. He describes writing this poem the way he describes his feeling about poetry in general—"Poetry is about something you suggest. You create a space with the words, and that space fills up with a feeling."

DEVELOPING LITERACY
GROUP TALK
MULTICULTURAL FOCUS

Telling Stories, Singing Songs
PROMOTING SELF-ESTEEM After reading "I Ask My Mother to Sing," lead a guided discussion of the story it tells.

✦ Who is singing?

✦ What is the song about?

✦ How do the singers feel? How does the listener feel?

Help children see that stories and songs are an important part of a family's heritage. Children gain self-esteem as they begin to see themselves as part of the continuing history of a family.

Ask children if there are any stories or songs in their families that are told over and over again (you might share one of your own). Encourage them to pay attention to the feelings they experience as they talk and listen.

✦ These stories and songs give us special feelings. That's why we like to hear them again and again.

✦ They help us remember important people in our lives and connect us with our family.

Suggest that children work with their parents, grandparents, or caregivers to record—in writing, with a tape recorder, or with pictures—stories and songs from their own families.

10

A SPIKE OF GREEN

When I went out
The sun was hot,
It shone upon
My flower pot.

And there I saw
A spike of green
That no one else
Had ever seen!

On other days
The things I see
Are mostly old
Except for me.

But this green spike
So new and small
Had never yet
Been seen at all!

—Barbara Baker

11

YOUNG VOICES

THE FLOWERS

*The flowers
are pretty
and soft.
Every morning
when I wake up,
the flowers
grow, grow and grow;
and I grow with
them too.*

—Paola Sánchez, 2nd grade
New York, New York

12

Week of the Young Child (third full week)

This song is often sung on birthdays in Mexico and other Spanish-speaking countries.

B

EL DÍA EN QUE TÚ NACISTE / THE DAY YOU WERE BORN

Traditional
English version by Suzanne Crain

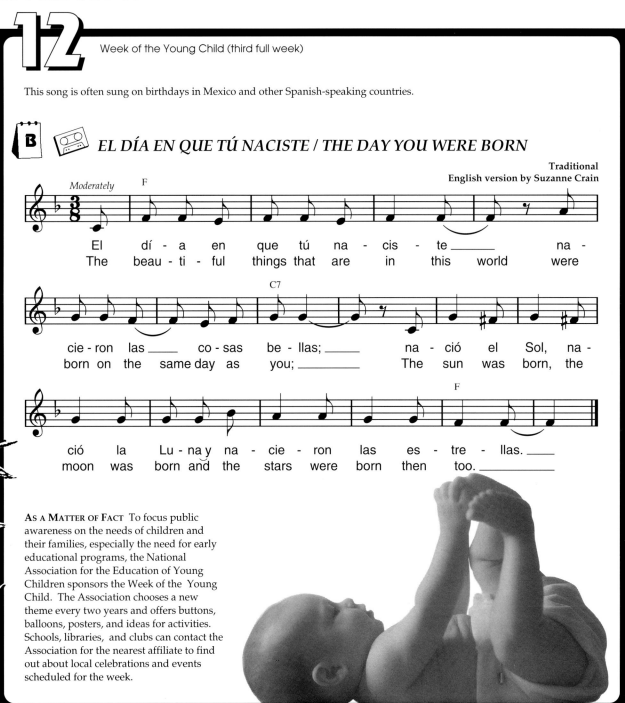

Moderately   F

El   dí - a   en   que tú   na - cis - te _____   na -
The   beau - ti - ful   things that   are   in   this   world   were

C7

cie - ron   las _____ co - sas   be - llas; _____   na - ció   el   Sol,   na -
born on   the   same day as   you; _____   The   sun   was   born,   the

F

ció   la   Lu - na y   na - cie - ron   las   es - tre - llas. _____
moon   was   born and   the   stars   were   born   then   too. _____

As a Matter of Fact To focus public awareness on the needs of children and their families, especially the need for early educational programs, the National Association for the Education of Young Children sponsors the Week of the Young Child. The Association chooses a new theme every two years and offers buttons, balloons, posters, and ideas for activities. Schools, libraries, and clubs can contact the Association for the nearest affiliate to find out about local celebrations and events scheduled for the week.

Easter is a season of renewal.

13

Easter (falls between March 22 and April 25)

EASTER BASKET

Extra chores and no T.V.
 and cutting down on money spent—
Sacrifice was gladly made
 *during the time of Lent.**

There've been ashes, palms and prayers
 all for special reasons.
But now, it's time for pink and purple,
 the colors of the season.

A brand new dress with matching hat,
 an end to all the fasts—
It's off to church our family goes
 for Easter Day at last.

—*Julie Cason*

Lent: in Christian tradition, a period of forty days just prior to
Easter, marked by fasts and penances to remember the crucifixion
of Jesus

CULTURESHARE The Christian commemoration, on Easter Sunday,
of the New Testament account of the resurrection of Jesus, makes
this the holiest day of the year for Christians, and also fits in with
ancient folk celebrations of new life and renewal in the spring. The
word *Easter* itself comes from Osters or Eostre, the name of a
goddess of spring worshipped by the ancient peoples of the
British Isles. The symbols that are associated with the holiday in
the U.S. are also taken from ancient roots. Rabbits became
associated with Easter because, in England, rabbits were among
the first animals to be born in spring. The custom of dyeing eggs,
symbols of new life, goes back even farther—to the ancient
Egyptians, Persians, and Romans. Wearing new clothes (for a
season of a new beginning) was considered good luck even
then. These popular customs and symbols, however, are by
no means common to all Christian peoples. On the other
hand, many of these customs and symbols have counterparts
in non-Christian celebrations of spring.

ACROSS THE CURRICULUM
SOCIAL STUDIES &
ARTS AND CRAFTS & READING

MULTICULTURAL FOCUS

Glorious Eggs
EXPLORING CULTURE Over the centuries, in
many cultures, eggs have been
decorated and given as gifts to celebrate
the arrival of spring. Ukrainian Easter
eggs, known for their vivid colors and
traditional motifs, are among the most
beautiful decorated eggs.

Ukrainian eggs are decorated using a
wax-resist technique: wax is used to keep
colors away from certain parts of the
design while the egg is dyed with several
different colors. Children can get an idea
of how the technique works by drawing a
design with a birthday-cake candle or a
white crayon on a large egg shape (see
Activity Sheet 15) outlined on heavy
typing paper, before coloring the shape
with colored pencils (using the side of the
lead) or broad-tipped highlighting pens.
The wax will keep the color from adhering
to the paper. Then, they can cut around
their eggs and paste them to clean
pieces of paper.

Books on Ukrainian Easter eggs include:

✦ *Eggs Beautiful: How To Make Ukrainian
Easter Eggs* by Johanna Luciow, Ann
Kmit, and Loretta Luciow (Ukrainian Gift
Shop, Minneapolis, Minnesota)

✦ *Rechenka's Eggs* by Patricia Polacco
(Philomel, 1988).

From every farmyard, nest and den . . .

14

You may want to prepare young children for this
poem by telling them it is a letter from one animal to
another. Ask them to listen carefully to tell who is
writing the letter to whom.

BEE! I'M EXPECTING YOU!

Bee! I'm expecting you!
Was saying Yesterday
To Somebody you know
That you were due—

The Frogs got Home last Week—
Are settled, and at work—
Birds, mostly back—
The Clover warm and thick—

You'll get my Letter by
The seventeenth; Reply
Or better, be with me—
Yours, Fly.

—*Emily Dickinson*

DEVELOPING LITERACY
WRITING

Bee's Reply
What might Bee write back to Fly? After
reviewing with children the form for a friendly
letter, ask them to compose letters from Bee to
Fly. *Where is Bee now? When will Bee arrive?
Whom is Bee looking forward to seeing?* Post
children's letters on a bulletin board with
construction-paper bees and flies buzzing
around the edges.

15

THE SECRET

We have a secret, just we three,
The robin, and I, and the sweet
cherry-tree;
The bird told the tree, and the tree
told me,
And nobody knows it but just us three.
But of course the robin knows it best,
Because he built the—I shan't tell the
rest;
And laid the four little—somethings
in it
I'm afraid I shall tell it every minute.
But if the tree and the robin don't peep,
I'll try my best the secret to keep;
Though I know when the little birds
fly about
Then the whole secret will be out.

—Mary Mapes Dodge

16

ONG DAL SAM / LITTLE SPRING

Suk-Joong Yoon
Adapted from English translation
by Francis Taewon Yoon and David L. Lapham

Lightly

1. Gip un san __ sok ong dal sam Nu ga wa so mong na yo
   In the moun-tain there's a lit - tle spring Who will come here for a drink?

Sae byo geh to ggi ga nun bi bi go ih ro na
Rab - bits at break of day come here __ when they a - wake

Seh su ha __ ro wat da ga mul man mok go ga ji yo.
Use the wa-ter to wash their face take a drink and hop a - way.

2. Malggo mal guen ong dal sam
   Nu ga wa so mong na yo
   Dal ba meh no ru ga
   soom ba ggo kjil ha da ga
   Mong ma reu myon dal lyo wa
   Eolleun mok go ga ji yo.

In the mountains there's a little spring
Who will come here for a drink?
Deer when the night has come
Come here to play and run
Use the water for their nighttime fun
Take a drink and then they're gone.

© 1978. Reprinted by permission of F.T. Yoon Co.

. . . and again.

17

Spelling for this poem is phonetic. Stressed syllables are underscored.

ARNAB /THE RABBIT

Arnab bil maghara,
Arnab ma'yeraf yimshe.
Arnab miskeen imshawesh.
Arnab nutt, wa nutt, wa nutt.

—Arabic nursery rhyme

Rabbit in your little hole
Rabbit eyes peek over the top.
Rabbit looks so very hot.
"Rabbit, hop and hop and hop!"

—English version by Suzanne Crain

أرنب بالمغارة
أرنب ما يعرف يمشى
أرنب مسكين مشوش
أرنب نط ونط ونط

When the cherry trees blossom, spring is in full swing.

18

Cherry Blossom Festival (last two weekends)

SAKURA/CHERRY TREES

Sakura! sakura! Yayo-i no sora wa
Miwatasu kaghiri, Kasumi ka? kumo ka?
Ni-o-i zo izuru
Iza ya! Iza ya! Mini yuka-n.*

Cherry trees, cherry trees, bloom so bright in April breeze
Like a mist or floating cloud
Fragrance fills the air around, shadows flit along the ground
Come, o come! Come, o come! Come, see cherry trees!

—Japanese traditional song
English version by Katherine F. Rohrbough

* **Pronunciation is as follows:**
  sah-koo-RAH sah-koo-RAH yah-yoh-ee noh soh-RAH wah
  mee-wah-tah-SOO kah-GHEE-ree kah-SOO-mee kah KOO-moh kah
  nee-oh-ee soh ee-SOO-roo
  ee-sah yah ee-sah ya mee-nee yoo-KAHN

CULTURESHARE The cherry blossom holds particular significance in Japan. It is Japan's national flower, and celebrations honoring the blossoms' return in the spring are held at various times throughout the country depending on the local blooming seasons. Commemorations range from dances and songs to quiet, reflective viewing of the delicate flowers, which are traditionally thought to be a symbol of life in their brief beauty.

The cherry blossom season is also a time for many Japanese Americans to celebrate their heritage. In San Francisco, the Japanese American community has been hosting the Cherry Blossom Festival—most often the middle or last two weekends of April—since 1967. The festival includes traditional Japanese food, dances, art, music, martial arts, and crafts, and is thought to be a larger collection of traditional Japanese cultural events in one place— even than in Japan. The festival also includes a parade through Japantown.

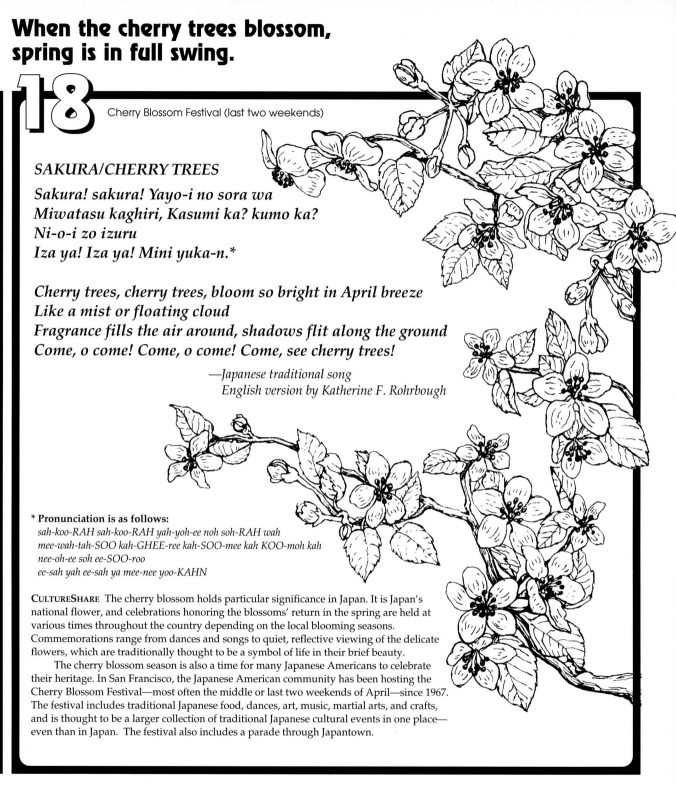

What could be better on a bright April day than a walk to the library?

 19

National Library Week (Sunday through Saturday of third week)

THE LIBRARY

It looks like any building
When you pass it on the street,
Made of stone and glass and marble,
Made of iron and concrete.

But once inside you can ride
A camel or a train,
Visit Rome, Siam, or Nome,*
Feel a hurricane,
Meet a king, learn to sing,
How to bake a pie,
Go to sea, plant a tree,
Find how airplanes fly,
Train a horse, and of course
Have all the dogs you'd like,
See the moon, a sandy dune,
Or catch a whopping pike.
Everything that books can bring
You'll find inside those walls.
A world is there for you to share
When adventure calls.

You cannot tell its magic
By the way the building looks,
But there's wonderment within it,
The wonderment of books.

—*Barbara A. Huff*

*Rome, Siam, or Nome: Rome is the capital of Italy; Siam is the ancient name of Thailand; Nome is a city in Alaska

20

The mouth tastes food;
The heart tastes words.

—*Hmong proverb*

Across the Curriculum
ARTS AND CRAFTS

Surprise!
Shoe-box dioramas are one way children can illustrate the poem "The Library"—and tell about their favorite books as well.

✦ Cover the lids of shoe boxes with gray or brown construction paper, butcher paper, or grocery-sack paper, or with sheets of white paper on which bricks or stones have been drawn. (The entire box can be covered, but the lid and bottom must be covered separately.)

✦ Cut doors in the box lids and draw details (door knobs, windows, signs, etc.).

✦ Remove the lids and build three-dimensional scenes depicting the characters and events from favorite stories inside the boxes. Remember to label dioramas with title and author.

✦ Put the lids back on the boxes and close the doors.

✦ Display the boxes and invite everyone to explore the "treasures" each small "library" holds inside.

21

Ask children to close their eyes and try to visualize what is happening in this poem as you read it.

ELEVATOR

down
in the corner
my book and i
traveling
over the project
walls
so the world
is more than this
elevator
stuck between
floors again
and home
is a corner
where i crouch
safe
reading   waiting
to start moving
up

—*Lucille Clifton*

Treat the Earth well—
it was not given to you by your parents . . .

22

Earth Day

B | THE BEAUTIFUL

Above, above,
The birds flying.
Below, below,
The flowers on the earth.

In the mountains, the mountains,
The trees growing.
In the ocean, the ocean,
The fish of the sea.

Here ends my song,
The beautiful world.

—Hawaiian traditional song

AS A MATTER OF FACT Earth Day was first celebrated in 1970 to promote awareness of global environmental issues and respect and appreciation for all of nature. Individuals, businesses, and industries are urged to try to reverse the damage that has been done to the environment—to protect wildlife; to stop harmful industrial practices; to stop pollution of air, water, and soil; to practice conservation; and to explore alternative resources.

23

YOUNG VOICES

THE PRICE

All over the world,
Trees disappear.
People cut forests,
Too quickly, I fear.
Animals suffer.
So let's stop this vice,
Or else in the end,
We'll pay the price.

—Laura Greeson, age 13
Knoxville, Tennessee

AS A MATTER OF FACT Tropical rain forests act as the Earth's lungs, absorbing carbon dioxide (one of the principal contributors to global warming) from the air and processing it into oxygen. In addition, about half of the Earth's plant and animal species are found only in rain forests. Among the thousands of plant species that grow there, are ones such as the rosy periwinkle, which can cure some kinds of cancer. Past successes lead scientists to hope that other tropical-rain-forest plants may also provide cures in the future. However, burning (to clear the land for farming) and logging result in the destruction of 40 million acres of rain forest a year—a trend that might quickly threaten the health of the Earth itself and all of its inhabitants.

24

BIRDFOOT'S GRAMPA

The old man
must have stopped our car
two dozen times to climb out
and gather into his hands
the small toads blinded
by our lights and leaping,
live drops of rain.

The rain was falling,
a mist about his white hair
and I kept saying
you can't save them all
accept it, get back in
we've got places to go.

But, leathery hands full
of wet brown life
knee deep in the summer
roadside grass,
he just smiled and said
they have places to go
too

—Joseph Bruchac

. . . it was lent to you by your children.
—Kenyan proverb

25

B *I LOVE THE WORLD*

I love you, Big World.
I wish I could call you
And tell you a secret:
That I love you, World.

—Paul Wollner, age 7
San Francisco, California

ACROSS THE CURRICULUM
ARTS AND CRAFTS & SCIENCE & READING

Every Little Bit Helps
Here's a classroom recycling project that's easy and fun. Help children collect small empty boxes and turn them into holders for notepaper they make from scrap paper that still has one clean side. They can decorate their boxes with found objects: confetti made with a hole-punch and small scraps of colored paper, the perforated edges of computer paper. Challenge children to think of as many other uses as they can for discarded items.

Finding Out More
Here are some books that will enrich children's appreciation for the abundance—and the fragility—of the earth's resources and give them some ideas on ways they can share in the big job of protecting this small planet.

♦ *Kids' Guide to Social Action* by Barbara A. Lewis (Free Spirit, 1991)

♦ *Loving the Earth* by Frederic Lehrman (Celestial Arts, 1990)

♦ *Trash* by Charlotte Wilcox (Carolrhoda, 1988)

♦ *Under Your Feet* by Joanne Ryder (Four Winds, 1990)

26

THE EARTH IS MY MOTHER

Words and music by CAROL A. JOHNSON

The earth is my mo-ther __ (The earth is my mo-ther) __ She's
Food on the ta-ble ____ (Food on the ta-ble) __ The

good to me (She's good to me) She gives me ev-ery-thing that I
clothes I wear (The clothes I wear) The sun and the wa-ter and the

ev - er __ need (She gives me ev-ery-thing that I ev-er __
cool fresh _ air (The sun and the wa-ter and the cool fresh _

need) air) The earth is my mo-ther and my best friend,

too The great pro - vi-der for me and __ you. The you.

2. Her ways are gentle, her life is strong
Living in tune like a beautiful song
There's only one thing she asks of me
I treat her as kindly as she treats me

© 1981 Carol A. Johnson, Noeldner Music (BMI), All rights reserved. Reprinted by permission of Carol A. Johnson.

A week to celebrate Jewish heritage!

Jewish Heritage Week (falls between April 16 and May 14)

 BEING JEWISH

*feels like having
the whole team
on your side
whether you
strike out
or not*

—Josh Weinstein

AS A MATTER OF FACT Observed since 1977, Jewish Heritage Week is celebrated in the spring to coincide with several important Jewish celebrations—Passover, Yom Hashoah (Holocaust Day), and the anniversary of the Warsaw Ghetto Uprising. Each year a different theme is chosen by the Jewish Community Relations Center of New York for the week-long celebration, which recognizes the history, religion, culture, traditions, and achievements of the Jewish people. Public events, art and essay contests, and the distribution of resources to teachers are some of the ways in which the week is observed.

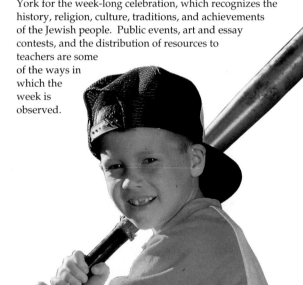

Introduce this entry by talking to children about the historical facts surrounding Anne Frank's diary: In 1940, Anne was an 11-year-old Jewish girl living with her family in Holland. That year the German army occupied Holland and began persecuting Jews. By 1942, the persecution had intensified, and the Germans began rounding up Jews and sending them off to extermination camps. Anne and her family went into hiding in a secret set of rooms above a warehouse, where they lived for two years. Like millions of other Jews, they lived in terror of discovery. They could move around only at night. Anne ate poorly—whatever trusted friends could spare and smuggle in. She never went outside. She was lonely, bored, and impatient for the war to end. Her diary was a friend, someone to talk to in the midst of her misery. Anne's hiding place was discovered by the Nazis in August of 1944. She died in a concentration camp in 1945.

from *THE DIARY OF ANNE FRANK*

It is the silence that frightens me so in the evenings and at night. I wish like anything that one of our protectors could sleep here at night. I can't tell you how oppressive it is **never** *to be able to go outdoors, also I'm very afraid that we shall be discovered and be shot. That is not exactly a pleasant prospect. We have to whisper and tread lightly during the day, otherwise the people in the warehouse might hear us. Someone is calling me.*

—From the entry for Saturday, 11 July 1942

AS A MATTER OF FACT The Holocaust was only the most recent large-scale, government-sponsored attack on the Jewish people, who have been victims of persecution throughout history. However, the sheer scale of the organized murders carried out by the Third Reich during World War II has given the Holocaust a preeminent place in the Jewish consciousness. More than six million Jews were systematically killed by Hitler's forces, along with others of "undesirable" ethnicity—mostly Slavs and Gypsies. The National Holocaust Museum, which opened in Washington, D.C. in April 1993, both commemorates the loss of these people and serves as a monument to the endurance and continued strength of the Jewish people.

You may wish to explore the Holocaust with older children through such books as:

- *The Children We Remember* by Chana Byers Abells (Greenwillow, 1986)
- *The Devil in Vienna* by Doris Orgel (Dial, 1978)
- *A Frost in the Night: A Girlhood on the Eve of the Third Reich* by Edith Baer (Pantheon, 1980)
- *Make Me a Hero* by Jerome Brooks (Dutton, 1980)
- *Remember Not to Forget* by Norman Finkelstein (Watts, 1985)

29

THE GRANDMA SONG

If there's one woman who I've loved in
my life
It's my grandma Minnie, my mother's
mom
From Rumania she came, Goldberg is her
name
She's my grandma, my mother's mom.

On Friday night she'd light the **Shabbas***
candles
And she'd say a prayer
She'd say **Baruch atoi adonoi***
Her hands moving in the air
I can see her in the kitchen where she
stood
Blessing the bread that smelled so good
My grandma, my mother's mom.

Grandma, grandma won't you tell me
What it was like when you were a girl
Did you have to run, did you have to flee
Living in a dangerous world?
Oh, I left Europe before the war
I married David and we opened a store
Said my grandma, my mother's mom.

—Ruth Pelham

*__Shabbas__ __(SHAH-bahs)__: the Jewish Sabbath, which starts at
sundown on Friday and lasts until after sunset on Saturday
*__Baruch atoi adonoi__ __(buh-ROOKH ah-TOY ah-doh-NOY)__:
Yiddish (ultimately from Hebrew) for "Blessed are You, the
Lord," words that begin many Jewish prayers

30

SOCIAL SERVICES

When we used to go to synagogue,
before we found a seat,
We'd stand around and "schmooze"* a while
with the people that we'd meet.
The grown-ups all would smile, and hug,
and talk about their week,
And introduce their children,
who always seemed too shy to speak.
And we'd drift that way from friend to friend,
and each reached warmly for us,
Our movements like some sacred dance,
the voices like a chorus.
And although we'd go to temple for the
services held in it,
I learned all I know about living life
from those fine first twenty minutes.

—Josh Weinstein

*__schmooze:__ from Yiddish; "to talk informally, to chat"

ACROSS THE CURRICULUM
SOCIAL STUDIES & READING

Commemorate and Celebrate
EXPLORING CULTURE Make arrangements for
Jewish members of your community to
visit your class during this week to talk
about their heritage, traditions, and
contemporary life. Read aloud (or make
available for children to read) books that
tell about the history and culture of the
Jewish people, for example:

◆ *Poems for Jewish Holidays,* selected by
Myra Cohn Livingston (Holiday, 1986)

◆ *Stories for Children* by Isaac Bashevis
Singer (Farrar, Straus & Giroux, 1984)

◆ *The Carp in the Bathtub* by Barbara
Cohen (Dell, 1975)

For other books on Jewish history and
culture, consult *The Jewish Kids Catalog*
by Chaya Burstein (Jewish Publication
Society of America, 1983) or contact the
Jewish Book Council, 15 East 26th Street,
New York, New York 10010.

MULTICULTURAL FOCUS

MAY

May opens like a spring flower, inviting us in to appreciate all its colors and textures and varieties. And, like a flower, it changes almost every day, giving us something new to see each time we look.

A tour of May's garden reveals many diverse annual bloomers: National Transportation Week pops up every May, as do Mother's Day, Memorial Day, and National Pet Week. Part of May's variety is cultural, with celebrations such as Cinco de Mayo and Asian and Pacific American Heritage Month. In 1994 and 1995, May also contains the Islamic observance of Eid al-Adha. And, of course, there is always room in the garden for the perennials: May is Older Americans Month.

So in this month of open flowers, open up to the variety of May!

Noteworthy Days

- ✦ National Pet Week (first full week)

- **5** Cinco de Mayo

- ✦ Mother's Day (second Sunday)

- ✦ National Transportation Week (the week containing the third Friday)

- ✦ Eid al-Adha (may fall any time of year, following the Muslim calendar, which is strictly lunar *)

- ✦ Older Americans Month

- ✦ Asian and Pacific American Heritage Month

- ✦ Memorial Day (last Monday)

* See page 265 for exact date.

There's no day like a day in May!

1

 *MAYTIME MAGIC*

A little seed
For me to sow . . .

A little earth
To make it grow . . .
A little hole,
A little pat . . .
A little wish,
And that is that.

A little sun,
A little shower . . .
A little while,
And then—a flower!

—Mabel Watts

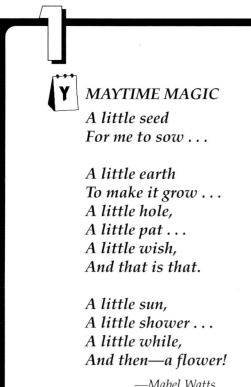

It's National Pet Week . . .

2

National Pet Week (first full week)

For a special presentation, bring in photos of cats in playful
poses to display as you read this poem.

ODE TO MY KITTEN

Three stripes
Of good luck
Saddle her back,
Four stripes crown
Her tail.
And two run
Down her throat
Like milk
Coughed up from drinking
Too quickly.

My kitten has nine stripes,
Nine lives of good luck,
And at ten after twelve
She may use one:
She's on the roof
Crying, "Meooooooooow,"
While I'm eating
Lunch, a flap
Of baloney in my sandwich
And salty rafts of potato
 chips
On a paper towel.

I gulp my milk
And hurry outside.
I shade my brow
With a salute,
Squint and eye her eyeing me,
Beads of water
On her whiskers.

"Come down," I plead,
And stomp my foot.
But she cries
The cry of millions
Of other cats,
Cries, "meooooooooow."
I call again
And again she cries,
 "meooooooooow,"
Shaking the watery beads
From her whiskers.
I have no choice.
I prop my father's ladder
Against the roof
And climb eight wooden
 rungs,
My lucky number.

I snap my fingers,
Throw a kiss,
And promise
A plate of milk.
Her ears perk up,
And just like that,
She walks into my arms,
Me the big brother
Of kittens in trouble.
I bring her down
And live up to my
 promise—
A puddle of milk.
And because she pumps
Her paws and meows,
I toss her a corner of my
 sandwich.
I love my kitten,
This spring gift with nine,
Make it eight, furry lives.

—Gary Soto

3

DID I TELL YOU?

Did I tell you
I have a poodle?
He jumps like a baby lamb,
He eats like
    a little horse,
he drinks like
a skinny whale
and he runs
    and
plays with me . . .

—Gladys Weeks

DEVELOPING LITERACY
COLLECTING AND RELATING WORDS & PATTERNED WRITING

Pet Poetics
After reading this poem once or twice, encourage children to write their own versions, using pets they have or would like to have. First, help children brainstorm different pets and their characteristics, recording children's ideas on a word web.

Then, encourage children to use the ideas on the word web to write poems of their own, using the frame of "Did I Tell You?"

Younger children might work together to choose one pet and dictate a class poem about it. **Students acquiring English** can work together to produce a group poem with your help.

Here is an example to get things started:

> Did I tell you
> I have a ___cat___?
> ___She stalks___ like a ___little lion___,
> ___She arches her back___ like
> a ___tiny bridge___,
> ___she sleeps___ like
> a ___fuzzy rock___
> and ___she runs___
> and
> ___plays___ with me . . .

4

After you have read this poem, encourage children to make the water sounds indicated—or others they make up—as you read it again.

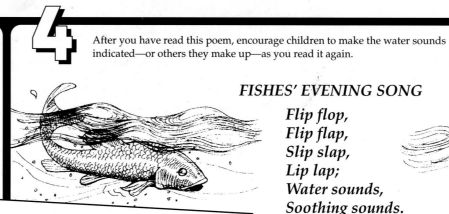

FISHES' EVENING SONG

Flip flop,
Flip flap,
Slip slap,
Lip lap;
Water sounds,
Soothing sounds.
We fan our fins
As we lie
Resting here
Eye to eye.
Water falls
Drop by drop,
Plip plop,
Drip drop,
Plink plunk,
Splash splish;
Fish fins fan,
Fish tails swish,
Swush, swash, swish.
This we wish . . .
Water cold,
Water clear,
Water smooth,
Just to soothe
Sleepy fish.

—Dahlov Ipcar

¡Viva la fiesta del Cinco de Mayo!

Cinco de Mayo

YOU DON'T HAVE TO BE BIGGER TO BE IMPORTANT
A Cinco de Mayo Victory Poem

You don't have to be bigger to be important.
You don't have to be stronger to win.
You have to be who you are and think what you think
And follow that voice from within.

More than one hundred years ago
A nation was fighting to stay
Free from the rule of a stronger land
Who wanted to take its freedom away.

On the Cinco de Mayo (the fifth of May)
Two armies met face to face.
One fought for power and money and fame.
One fought to defend their own place.

The enemy army was richly dressed.
Its guns were the newest and best.
They called it the finest army in the world
and stronger than all the rest.

But the Mexican army said, "Let's be who we are
and think what we think, 'cause we know
We're fighting for our own freedom.
We're fighting for our own home."

The Mexican army was just made of people
Who wanted to do the right thing.
They didn't have fancy uniforms.
Their courage was all they could bring.

ACROSS THE CURRICULUM
SOCIAL STUDIES & ARTS AND CRAFTS

A Tradition Meant to Be Broken
EXPLORING CULTURE For many children, the highlight of Cinco de Mayo festivities is breaking a piñata. **How to Make a Simple Piñata,** page 241, shows an easy way to make piñatas for the classroom.

As children decorate their piñatas, talk about the traditions of Cinco de Mayo. The book *Fiesta! Mexico's Great Celebrations* by Elizabeth Silverthorne (Millbrook Press, 1992) is a helpful source of information.

VALUING DIVERSITY After the festivities, ask children to talk about celebrations similar to Cinco de Mayo. For instance, Fourth of July celebrations and Kamehameha Day (in Hawaii) share some of the same traditions: parades, speeches, and fireworks. What parts of these festivities do children most look forward to? Help them see that the traditional celebrations of many cultures have elements in common.

The rest of the world said "Impossible!
Not a chance in the world you could win!"
The Mexican army said, "Let us try
To fight for what we believe in!

"Our country, our family, and our own lives
Our right to be Mexican and proud.
These are the things that our freedom means.
And we'll shout it clear and loud!"

So they went into battle the fifth of May.
And when all the fighting was done,
They thought what they thought and were who they were
And surprised the whole world—'cause they won.

—Carmen Tafolla

AS A MATTER OF FACT On May 5, 1862, Mexican troops—outnumbered three to one—defeated invading French forces in what became known as the Battle of Puebla. The anniversary of this victory is celebrated with festive Cinco de Mayo parades, dances, and speeches. The holiday provides a key link to Mexican history and culture for many Mexican Americans; fiestas honoring the holiday in parts of the United States are often more elaborate than those in Mexico. And, without losing its Mexican roots, this celebration is serving as a bridge for unity among all Hispanic Americans; in many areas of the country, schools frequently observe a Hispanic week around the Cinco de Mayo celebration.

Let sunshine stream in with May's warmth behind it, and you'll see that beauty is right where you find it . . .

6

BEAUTY

Beauty is seen
In the sunlight,
The trees, the birds,
Corn growing and people working
Or dancing for their harvest.

Beauty is heard
In the night,
Wind sighing, rain falling,
Or a singer chanting
Anything in earnest.

Beauty is in yourself.
Good deeds, happy thoughts
That repeat themselves
In your dreams,
In your work,
And even in your rest.

—E-Yeh-Shure

7

B DIRT ROAD

A shiny stone by a dirt road
So small, yet so beautiful
I picked it up. So beautiful it was
I put it down
And walked on.

—Calvin O'John

DEVELOPING LITERACY

GROUP TALK

Beauty Shared
Lead a guided discussion after reading "Dirt Road" to children. Asking open-ended questions will help children give their own reactions to the poet's words, rather than trying to give "correct" answers. For example:

✦ What do you think this poem is about?

✦ What do you think the stone in the poem looks like?

✦ How did the stone make the poet feel?

✦ Why did he do what he did with the stone?

Help children draw some conclusions about the special beauty that objects have in their natural surroundings: a stone, a seashell, a wild flower, a butterfly, a shiny beetle; each is most beautiful in its natural setting.

Extend the activity for older children by asking them if they can see the parallel between the words of the poem and the signs in parks, wildlife refuges and other natural areas that ask visitors to enjoy but not remove plant and animal life. Children can appreciate that leaving these objects in their natural surroundings not only protects them but also means others will be able to enjoy them.

. . . especially when rainbows paint the springtime sky.

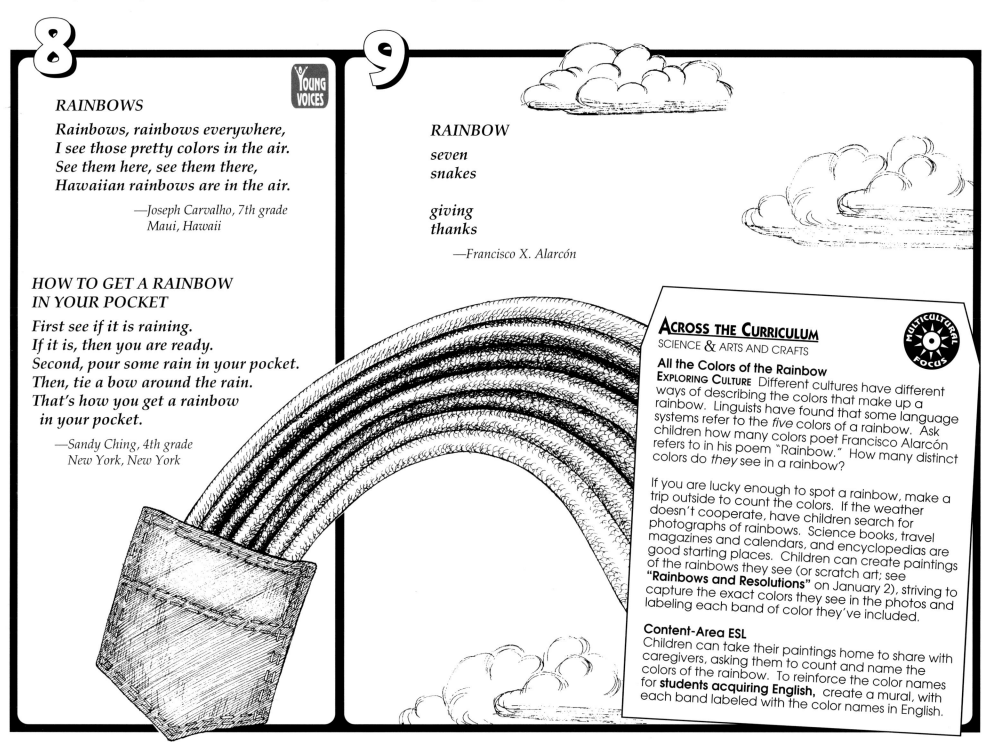

8

YOUNG VOICES

RAINBOWS

Rainbows, rainbows everywhere,
I see those pretty colors in the air.
See them here, see them there,
Hawaiian rainbows are in the air.

—Joseph Carvalho, 7th grade
Maui, Hawaii

HOW TO GET A RAINBOW
IN YOUR POCKET

First see if it is raining.
If it is, then you are ready.
Second, pour some rain in your pocket.
Then, tie a bow around the rain.
That's how you get a rainbow
in your pocket.

—Sandy Ching, 4th grade
New York, New York

9

RAINBOW

seven
snakes

giving
thanks

—Francisco X. Alarcón

ACROSS THE CURRICULUM
SCIENCE & ARTS AND CRAFTS

MULTICULTURAL FOCUS

All the Colors of the Rainbow
EXPLORING CULTURE Different cultures have different ways of describing the colors that make up a rainbow. Linguists have found that some language systems refer to the *five* colors of a rainbow. Ask children how many colors poet Francisco Alarcón refers to in his poem "Rainbow." How many distinct colors do *they* see in a rainbow?

If you are lucky enough to spot a rainbow, make a trip outside to count the colors. If the weather doesn't cooperate, have children search for photographs of rainbows. Science books, travel magazines and calendars, and encyclopedias are good starting places. Children can create paintings of the rainbows they see (or scratch art; see **"Rainbows and Resolutions"** on January 2), striving to capture the exact colors they see in the photos and labeling each band of color they've included.

Content-Area ESL
Children can take their paintings home to share with caregivers, asking them to count and name the colors of the rainbow. To reinforce the color names for **students acquiring English,** create a mural, with each band labeled with the color names in English.

10

Mother's Day (second Sunday)

TOMMY'S MOMMY

Mommy did you bring my flippers
Tommy asked his Mommy

Is that all you have to say
Mommy asked her Tommy

Did you bring my diving mask
Tommy asked his Mommy

Is that all you have to say
Mommy asked her Tommy

Did you bring my snorkel
Tommy asked his Mommy

Is that all you have to say
Mommy asked her Tommy

I love you Mommy
Tommy said Did you bring them Did you

I love you Tommy Mommy said
Yes I brought them to you

—Nikki Giovanni

AS A MATTER OF FACT Many countries and many cultures have holidays devoted to honoring parents. The celebration of Mother's Day in the United States probably comes from England, where "Mothering Sunday" was observed every year during the Christian period of Lent. The first known suggestion for a national Mother's Day was made by Julia Ward Howe, a New England writer and suffrage activist who is perhaps best known for writing the words to *The Battle Hymn of the Republic*. The idea spread and eventually led to the 1914 federal designation of Mother's Day as an annual national observance.

DEVELOPING LITERACY
DRAMATIC INTERPRETATION—Readers' Theater

Performance Fun
Often children who might be uncomfortable reciting poetry alone will enjoy the cooperative fun of participating in a Readers' Theater presentation. And the humor in "Tommy's Mommy" will defuse the performance jitters even more. Create a script for the performance and remind children to:

✦ decide who will play each part

✦ practice until they are comfortable and can keep a pace they think suits the poem

✦ speak clearly when they perform, watch the pace, and have fun!

11

MOMMY, WHEN I'M BIG AND TALL

Mommy, when I'm big and tall
I will build myself a ladder
So high I can climb the sky
And that's not all—

I will fill my pockets full
With bright-shining stars and comets
To bring down and share around
With the kids at school.

I'll bring something better still
For you, Mommy—the full moon,
So we can light our house at night
And save on the electric bill.

—Álvaro Yunque (original in Spanish)
English version by Juan Quintana

12

NEW MOTHER

She came to take
my mother's
place.

I like her smile.

I like her face.

I like the way
*   she talks to me*
*   although it's seldom*
*   we agree*
*   on bedtime*
*   or some places where*
*   I go.*
*   But then*
*   she seems to care.*

And often, when
we both get mad
and have to settle things
with Dad

at least
we learn about each other.

I'm sort of getting used to—
Mother.

—R. H. Marks

13

 MAMA

Mama was funny
was full of jokes
was pretty
dark brown-skinned
laughter
was hard hugs
and kisses
a mad mama
sometimes
but always
always
was love

—Eloise Greenfield

14

WHAT YOUR MOTHER TELLS YOU

haha ga ima yu-koto
sono uchi ni
wakatte kuru*

What your mother tells you now
in time
you will come to know.

—Mitsuye Yamada

*Pronunciation of the Japanese is as follows:
HAH-hah gah EE-mah YOO-koh-toh
SOH-NOH OO-chee NEE
wah-KAH-teh KOO-roo

A WORD FROM THE POET Mitsuye Yamada says: "This is, verbatim, a phrase that I used to hear all the time from my mother."

ACROSS THE CURRICULUM

WRITING

Honoring Someone Special
VALUING DIVERSITY "New Mother" and "Mama" can provide a springboard for writing about those who fill the role of mother for children. Begin by reading the poems and talking about their meaning. Ask children to work together to create a word web that talks about the characteristics of their own mothers or mother figures, in preparation for writing. This step of the process is helpful to **students acquiring English** if words and phrases are accompanied by definitions, synonyms, pantomime, or sketches.

Then, encourage children to write their own compositions. Suggest that they use the poem "Mama" as a frame for their writing or write in any form they like.

When discussing material that honors family members, it is important that every child should feel included. Be sure discussions take into account diversity in family relationships, and reinforce the importance of respecting everyone's family:

✦ *Each one of us has qualities that make us special, and so do our families.*

✦ *Every family is different, but in all families people care for and love each other.*

Whether you travel by highway or subway, you'll find something here to take you away.

15

National Transportation Week (the week containing the third Friday)

With some photos or drawings, (such as those on **Activity Sheets 16–17**) this poem works well to introduce the names of different modes of transportation to **students acquiring English.**

PREFERRED VEHICLES

A bicycle's fine for a little trip
Up the street or down;
An automobile for a longer trip,
Off to another town;
An airplane's fine for around the world,
To many a far-put place;
And a rocket, oh, for the longest trip
Away into outer space.

—Leland B. Jacobs

16

MY HORSE, FLY LIKE A BIRD

My horse, fly like a bird
To carry me far
From the arrows of my enemies,
And I will tie red ribbons
To your streaming hair.

—Virginia Driving Hawk Sneve
adapted from a Lakota warrior's
song to his horse

17

YOUNG VOICES

SKATEBOARDING

I believe in skateboarding
I believe in slamming my back foot
down on the tail
And sliding my front foot forward
to level out the board
I believe
in picking up as much speed as possible
while going down a deserted sidewalk
I
Believe
In
not stopping until you have made the goal
you set for yourself
I believe in trying and trying
until you finally do
Ollie* up onto the curb

—Sean Fuller, 8th grade,
Mendocino, California

*ollie: skateboarding term meaning "to jump up in such a way that the skateboard rises as well"

ACROSS THE CURRICULUM
SOCIAL STUDIES & WRITING

From Airplane to Zoo Train
Explore this theme from A to Z! First, work with children to brainstorm a web of transportation words like this:

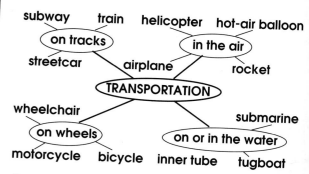

subway   train   helicopter   hot-air balloon
on tracks   in the air
streetcar   airplane   rocket
TRANSPORTATION
wheelchair   submarine
on wheels   on or in the water
motorcycle   bicycle   inner tube   tugboat

Content-Area ESL
Draw sketches or put photographs or pictures beside each vehicle on the web. (See **Activity Sheets 16–17**.) Provide picture books on transportation and picture dictionaries.

Then, invite children to make a class ABC book of transportation. Assign a small group of letters to partners, who can work together to write as many forms of transportation as they can think of beginning with each letter. For example:

A airplane, automobile
B bullet train, bus, bike, biplane
C camel, city bus, cart, car
D dog sled, dhow
E elevated train

When the list is complete, partners can illustrate their letters, one to a page, and all the pages can go into a class book.

18

You may want to discuss subways before reading this poem.

SUBWAYS ARE PEOPLE

Subways are people—

People standing
People sitting
People swaying to and fro
Some in suits
Some in tatters
People I will never know.

Some with glasses
Some without
Boy with smile
Girl with frown

People dashing
Steel flashing
Up and down and round the town.

Subways are people—

People old
People new
People always on the go
Racing, running, rushing people
People I will never know.

—Lee Bennett Hopkins

19

WINDOW

Night from a railroad car window
Is a great, dark, soft thing
broken across with slashes of light.

—Carl Sandburg

TRAIN IS A-COMIN'

Slowly and expressively

Spiritual

1. Train is a-com-in', oh yes. Train is a-com-in', ___ oh yes.
2. Better get your tic-ket, oh yes. Better get your tic-ket, ___ oh yes.
3. Train is a-leav-in', oh yes. Train is a-leav-in', ___ oh yes.

Train is a-com-in', Train is a-com-in', Train is a-com-in', oh yes.
Better get your tic-ket, Better get your tic-ket, Better get your tic-ket, oh yes.
Train is a-leav-in', Train is a-leav-in', Train is a-leav-in', oh yes.

Eid al-Adha—a feast in honor of a faraway journey.

With age comes wisdom; . . .

20

Eid al-Adha (may fall any time of year, following the Muslim calendar, which is strictly lunar)

EID*

Once after Ramadan,*
the month of fast.
Once after the Hajj,*
we remember the sacrifice.

Two celebrations,
two times a year,
we celebrate Allah,
we rejoice and cheer.

—*Riyad Shamma*

*Eid (*eed;* also spelled *Id*): either of the two major Islamic feast days: one takes place at the end of Ramadan; the other at the end of Hajj

*Ramadan (*RAM - uh - dan*): a month of fasting and reflection culminating in the Eid al-Fitr (see entry for February 23)

*Hajj: pronounced *hadge;* for more information, see CultureShare

CultureShare Eid al-Adha (*eed ul-AD-dah*), or "feast of sacrifice," is the ceremonial meal that marks the end of the Muslim month of Hajj. Hajj is the pilgrimage to Mecca, Saudi Arabia, the holiest city in the Muslim religion. The Quran (*kuh-RAN;* also spelled *Koran*) requires that every Muslim make this pilgrimage at least once if he or she is able, and Muslims travel from all over the world during *Dhu al-Hijjah,* (*dool HIDJ-ah*) the twelfth month on the Muslim calendar, to do so. Even those who are not able to travel to Mecca mark the Eid al-Adha with large gatherings for prayer and unity. During the Eid, which begins on the tenth day of the month of Hajj, many Muslims kill a sheep or a goat or sometimes a smaller animal, cook it, eat some of the meat, and give the rest to the poor. Otherwise, the holiday is celebrated much like Eid al-Fitr, with food, gifts for children, and general merrymaking.

21

Older Americans Month

THE WISDOM OF THE AGES

Only those that have traveled the road know where the holes are deep.

—*Chinese proverb*

A house without an elderly person is like an orchard without a well.

—*Arab proverb*

Tangled hair, use a comb to unsnarl it. Complicated dispute, use an elder to solve it.

—*Hmong proverb*

22

GROWING OLD

When I grow old I hope to be
As beautiful as Grandma Lee.
Her hair is soft and fluffy white.
Her eyes are blue and candle bright.
And down her cheeks are cunning piles
Of little ripples when she smiles.

—*Rose Henderson*

23

OLD FRIENDS

My class sang at the retirement home
Last winter. It was hot.
I was sorry I wore my sweater,
But they liked our visit a lot.

There's an old woman on our street
I always like to see.
She listens to every word I say.
She's interested in me.

When Mom was in the hospital,
Grandpa came to stay
He taught me how to play checkers
And made pancakes every day.

So I'm thinking that this being old
Could be a lot of fun
With lots of time to sing and talk
And play with everyone.

—Suzanne Crain

24

YOUNG VOICES

MY GREAT AUNT

My great aunt Marcella
Is a woman of celebration.
She is a special addition
To our tradition.
To see her smile
Is sometimes a mile away.
It is a great time to
Spend with my own
Great aunt so
Still and silent.

—Jenny Ferderber, age 8
Indiana, Pennsylvania

25

MATRIARCH

my dark
grandmother

would brush
her long hair

seated out
on her patio

even ferns
would bow

to her splendor
and her power

—Francisco X. Alarcón

DEVELOPING LITERACY
INTERVIEWING & WRITING

Book of Life
Elders are a rich resource of experience and stories, but many children seldom have the chance to interact with them. Provide that opportunity by inviting a group of elders to visit; ideally, one for every two children in your classroom.

Before the visit, work with children to come up with an important topic or question for the visitors: perhaps, "What one thing you learned in school has helped you most throughout your life?" Encourage visitors to bring photos, letters, or other memorabilia to address the topic your class selects.

During the visit, assign pairs of children to each visitor. Partners might take notes, draw pictures, and/or tape-record the conversation. After the visit, partners can work together to make a book about "their" elder. See the **How-To Directions** on page 242 for hardback-bookmaking instructions. Children might even invite the subjects of their books back to the classroom for a reading and an in-person "thank you." The resulting books will be a welcome addition to your classroom library.

26

Asian and Pacific American Heritage Month

To be sure children understand the two distinct voices in the poem, pause between the two stanzas, changing your voice, your inflection, and/or your physical position in the classroom.

SISTER

"So what if our parents and you came from China?
What's China to me?
I'm American, always have been,
born in Brooklyn—can't get more American than that.
Never felt any prejudice,
always had friends,
Don't even know any Chinese,
but you,
Why dredge up the past?
Forget it.
Move on."

But can't you see, sister,
you're building a brick wall,
sealing yourself out,
cutting off a past
ever present
on your
face.

—*Amy Ling*

AS A MATTER OF FACT "Asian and Pacific American" refers to a broad range of cultures, nationalities, and backgrounds found in the United States—among them, Chinese, Japanese, Korean, Vietnamese, Laotian, Hmong, Filipino, Thai, Cambodian, and Hawaiian. Within these broad cultural distinctions are many smaller ones and within those, of course, individuals. So, while this is a month in honor of "Asian and Pacific Americans," we encourage you to explore the tremendous diversity found within this umbrella term.

27

I WASN'T BORN IN MY COUNTRY

I wasn't born in my country.
I was born in New Mexico.
I don't want to go to Laos because
I wasn't born there.
I am used to America.
I feel like I am an American.
I am an American.

—*Kaykham Southivongnorath, age 11*
Philadelphia, Pennsylvania

ACROSS THE CURRICULUM
SOCIAL STUDIES & READING

Salute to Asian and Pacific Americans
EXPLORING CULTURE Make arrangements for Asian American and Pacific American members of your community to visit your class. Invite them to bring photographs and artifacts, if possible, and to tell stories, reminisce about the traditions of their own families, and talk about how they celebrate their heritage.

Make available books that will help children share in the history and culture of Asian Americans and Pacific Americans. For example:

Angel Child, Dragon Child by Michele Maria Surat (Scholastic, 1989)

♦ *Elaine, Mary Lewis and the Frogs* by Heidi Chang (Crown, 1988)

♦ *How My Parents Learned To Eat* by Ina R. Friedman (Houghton Mifflin, 1984)

♦ *Nine-in-One Grr! Grr!: A Folktale from the Hmong People of Laos*, retold by Blia Xiong, adapted by Cathy Spagnoli (Children's Book Press, 1989)

♦ *Soon-Hee in America* by Schi-Zhin Rhie (Hollym, 1977)

28

I AM SANSEI*

I am Sansei.
I am the fruit of my parent's suffering.
I reflect the strength by which they endured.
They were humiliated and relocated.
Torn between two cultures, they reassured
Themselves, silently, of their identity.

—*Susan Matoba Adler*

***Sansei** *(san-say)*: Japanese for "third generation"; a U.S.-born American citizen whose grandparents were Japanese immigrants to the United States. Sansei are the children of Nisei (*nee-say,* "second generation") parents.

AS A MATTER OF FACT Shortly after the bombing of Pearl Harbor by the Japanese air force in 1941, the United States government relocated most Japanese Americans to internment camps in Arkansas, California, Colorado, Utah, and other states. The entire Japanese population of the Pacific Coast states of California, Oregon, and Washington—more than 110,000 in all—was moved into these prison-like camps and forced to give up their homes, jobs, businesses, belongings, and friends. The government ignored the fact that these were loyal United States citizens, many of whom had served (or would soon serve) with distinction in the war; the 442nd Regimental Combat Team, made up almost entirely of Japanese American soldiers, won more awards in the war than any other unit its size.

In 1988, recognizing the "grave injustice" motivated by "racial prejudice and war hysteria," Congress passed a law granting $20,000 to each of 75,000 internment-camp survivors. A presidential letter handed to each survivor acknowledged that "words alone cannot restore lost years or erase painful memories."

29

YOUNG VOICES

Tell children the boy who wrote this poem was born in Vietnam, and help them locate Vietnam on a map.

MY BELOVED COUNTRY

Native country like a branch of starfruit.
Let the sun climb up to pick it every day.
Native country small like a
* bamboo bridge.*
Native country like a child that
* understands.*
Let the child grow up to be
* a gentle person.*

—*Trung Nguyen, 9th grade*
Philadelphia, Pennsylvania

30

O KA LEO / OH, THE VOICES

Traditional
English version by Josh Weinstein

*Nanakuli: a city on the west coast of Honolulu. This popular Hawaiian folk song is often adapted to include the name of the singers' hometown; the "Nanakuli" version is the best known. You might substitute your city or town in this spot when your class sings this song.

MAY

This day is a Memorial to those whose memories we hold dear.

31

Memorial Day (last Monday)

SUNDAY MORNING LONELY

Daddy's back
is broad and black
and Everett Anderson* loves to ride it.

Daddy's side
is black and wide
and Everett Anderson sits beside it.

Daddy's cheek
is black and sleek
and Everett Anderson kisses it.

Daddy's space
is a black empty place
and Everett Anderson misses it.

—Lucille Clifton

*Everett Anderson: character in a series of books by Ms. Clifton
(see entry for November 25)

AS A MATTER OF FACT Most countries and cultures have holidays like Memorial Day,
on which people visit and decorate graves. It is thought that the United States' Memorial Day
(or "Decoration" Day) commemorations began in Waterloo, NY, where, on May 5, 1866, people closed
businesses, flew flags at half-mast, and decorated Civil War soldiers' graves with flowers and flags. Like
Veterans' Day, which started as a commemoration for soldiers of one war and was later applied to all wars,
Memorial Day grew from this local celebration (and others like it) into a federal holiday honoring all those whose
memories we cherish, especially those who have died in the country's wars. In some parts of the country, the
holiday has retained its original practices, with people visiting graves of loved ones and cleaning and decorating
the gravesites.

Most Northern states and many Southern states observe Memorial Day on the last Monday in May. In
the South, however, holidays in honor of Confederate soldiers who died in the Civil War are often celebrated
in addition to, or instead of, the federal Memorial Day. These holidays are celebrated in various Southern states
any time from January (in Texas) to June (Louisiana and Tennessee).

SUMMER

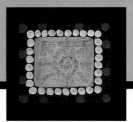

Summer is lazy—giving us time—
To sit under a tree, read a book, write a rhyme.

—*Lee Bennett Hopkins*

MULTICULTURAL TRADE BOOKS

Ada, Alma Flor. **My Name Is María Isabel** (Atheneum, 1993). A girl struggles to keep her full given name, while others try to shorten it.

◼

Ancona, George. **Helping Out** (Houghton Mifflin, 1984). A photo essay of diverse children performing many kinds of jobs.

◼

Goble, Paul. **The Girl Who Loved Wild Horses** (Aladdin, 1986). A young girl possesses a love for horses that does not abate until she becomes one with them.

◼

Martel, Cruz. **Yagua Days** (Dial, 1987). A boy visits Puerto Rico for the first time and experiences the joy of meeting new relatives.

◼

Pinkney, Gloria J. **Back Home** (Dial, 1992). A young girl leaves the city to visit relatives in North Carolina.

◼

Say, Allen. **The Lost Lake** (Houghton Mifflin, 1989). A father attempts to recapture the joys of his childhood and share them with his son as they search for the lake of his youth.

JUNE

As every s-t-u-d-e-n-t knows, June brings the Spelling Bee Finals, the end of the traditional school year, and the beginning of summer. It is a good time to thank teachers for all they do, and to get ready for all the warm-weather fun that summer brings.

June holidays are as warm as the weather. Hug Holiday brings hugs from family and friends—and right on its heels comes Father's Day. For outdoor fun that's as bright and colorful as June itself, what could be better than catching the Puerto Rican Day Parade or watching dragons race upon a lake during the Dragon Boat Festival!

So, open your arms to summer. There's plenty of fun to hold in June.

Noteworthy Days

- ✦ National Spelling Bee Finals (Wednesday and Thursday of Memorial Day week)

- ✦ Teacher "Thank You" Week (first full week)

- **15** Hug Holiday

- ✦ Father's Day (third Sunday)

- ✦ Puerto Rican Day

- **21 or 22** Summer Solstice

- ✦ Dragon Boat Festival (late June)

O U can C how good I can B at S-P-E-L-L-I-N-G.

1

National Spelling Bee Finals (Wednesday and Thursday of Memorial Day week)

M-I-S-S-I-S-S-I-P-P-I

M-i-s-s-i-s-s-i-p-p-i,
That used to be so hard to spell,
It used to make me cry.
But since I studied spelling,
It's just like pumpkin pie,
M-i-s-s-i-s-s-i-p-p-i.

—*Bert Hanlon and Benny Ryan*

AS A MATTER OF FACT More than 200 students, sponsored by newspapers throughout the U.S., compete every year in the National Spelling Bee Finals, held in Washington, D.C.

2

Accompany the presentation of these two silly "spelling" poems with a mini geography lesson, pointing out on a map the cities of Chicago, Illinois, and Istanbul, Turkey, formerly known as Constantinople.

CHICAGO

Chicken in the car,
The car won't go,
And that's the way to spell
Chi-ca-go.

—*Unknown*

CONSTANTINOPLE

Can you Con,
Can you Stan,
Can you Constanti?
Can you Steeple,
Can you Stople,
Can you Constantinople?

—*Unknown*

DEVELOPING LITERACY

WRITING

Just Between You and Me

PROMOTING SELF-ESTEEM Use a journal exchange to help children see that, throughout the school year, you have been learning from them just as they have been learning from you. Ask each child to write a journal entry telling about one thing he or she has learned from you this year; then, write a response to each child, telling what you have learned from him or her.

In this personal exchange lies a wonderful opportunity to validate something special each child brings to the classroom: a sense of humor, a special talent, knowledge of a language other than English, knowledge of a particular culture. Make your reply as specific as possible, recalling details and circumstances that will make clear that you value each child's contribution.

Teachers deserve a big gold star! . . .

3

Teacher "Thank You" Week (first full week)

E.S.O.L.

Today
As I sat in my 4th Period class
I started to wonder
About how amazing it is
To know how to speak English.
I have no idea
How I started
To know English.
Did I learn it from all my teachers
Or from my friends?
I believe everybody has helped me learn
To talk
And to know
How to speak
The way I do today.

—*Nhung Bui, age 14*
Philadelphia, Pennsylvania

AS A MATTER OF FACT The end of the school year is a natural time for students to show their appreciation for their teachers. Teacher "Thank You" Week reminds adults, as well, to send a card or make a phone call to a teacher or professor who made a difference in their lives.

4

MISS TEACHER

I hear the school bell ringin'
all the way over here.
I know the teacher waitin'
for me to appear.
"Miss, I sorry I late ag'in.
I had to feed the fowls."
Miss look me up and down
in my blue and white uniform.
"Class start at half eight sharp,"
she says.
And she try to look stern.
But Miss black eyes be smilin'
and I smile in return.

—*Lynn Joseph*

A WORD FROM THE POET Lynn Joseph says that this poem captures a very true-to-life experience for many small children in Trinidad. "Often children living near the school would hear the bell ringing and rush to finish feeding the chickens before hurrying into the classroom. The teacher knew they weren't just fooling around, that they had a good reason for being late."

5

TEACHERS

Better than a thousand days of diligent study
is one day with a great teacher.

—*Japanese proverb*

To become a teacher one must first respect one's teacher.

—*Vietnamese proverb*

Your teacher can lead you to learning;
the actual learning you have to do yourself.

—*Chinese proverb*

6

WHY I TEACH

Each year in September, I make a little speech
To welcome back my students and tell them why I teach.
The first day in my classroom they seem a little shy
Until the magic moment when someone asks me, "Why?"

Why does rain fall hardest when we plan to go outside?
Why do trees keep living after all the leaves have died?
Why do we have numbers and how can you explain
Why there are no dinosaurs to walk the earth again?
Why do stars come out at night and when did Egypt start?
Why do we have sciences and what makes people smart?

And every year I feel a great excitement as I try
To find out all the answers to all their questions, "why?"
And every year I tell them as I give my little speech,
That what I learn from them each day is really why I teach.

—*Susan L. Reichin*

A child might become a teacher one day— there are so many choices along the way.

7

After children are familiar with the melody, they can play a ring game, following the directions below.

JUMP SHAMADOR*

Jamaican game song

Good morn-ing to you Jo-seph. / Mari-a Good morn-ing to you too.

What is your in-ten-tion? I want to be a doc-tor. / an art-ist You

can't be a doc-tor. / an art-ist I will be a doc-tor! / an art-ist! Well,

Chorus
Jump sha-ma-dor my dar-ling, Jump sha-ma-dor my dear.

Jump sha-ma-dor __ Jump sha-ma-dor __ Jump sha-ma-dor, my dar-ling.

Jump sha-ma-dor __ Jump sha-ma-dor __ Jump sha-ma-dor, my dear.

Reprinted by permission of Cheryl Mattox.

ACROSS THE CURRICULUM
SOCIAL STUDIES & READING

Vocation Vocabulary

VALUING DIVERSITY Use this theme to initiate a discussion of the diversity of occupations and the value of each one. Ask children to work in small groups to name as many jobs as they can think of within a two- or three-minute time limit. After you list their ideas, help children see that every job has value. Add careers, as necessary, to encompass a wide variety of jobs—from doctor and mechanic to nurse and factory worker. Children's responses may present a "teachable moment" when you can introduce nonsexist job titles, such as *fire fighter*, *police officer*, and *postal carrier*.

Invite a variety of community members to speak about their jobs. To find speakers, try your local chamber of commerce, Rotary Club, or Toastmasters Club.

Or, you might use these books to explore diverse occupations:

◆ *All in a Day's Work: Twelve Americans Talk About Their Jobs* by Neil Johnson (Little, Brown, 1989)

◆ *And What Do You Do?: A Book About People and Their Work* by George Ancona (E. P. Dutton, 1976)

◆ *Careers to Explore* (Girl Scouts of the U.S.A., 1979)

*__Shamador:__ a nonsensical word

GAME DIRECTIONS Children form a circle and take turns going to the middle, naming their choice of a career, and showing their determination to achieve this goal by how forcefully they respond with "I **WILL** be a _____!"

8

I SEE MY FUTURE

I see my future
clear as I don't know what
not all the things around me
not furniture or houses
or sidewalks and stuff
I just see me
my serious man face
thinking
my laughing man face
my big Nathaniel* me
moving through the world
doing good and unusual
things

—Eloise Greenfield

* **Nathaniel:** the main character in *Nathaniel Talking* (Writer and Readers Publishing, 1988), a collection of poetry by Eloise Greenfield

ACROSS THE CURRICULUM
SOCIAL STUDIES & WRITING

Real-Life Learning
Make arrangements for children to spend time *on the job* with a secretary, custodian, cafeteria worker, playground supervisor, librarian, principal, school nurse. Tell children their task is to act as a shadow, silently observing what each person's day involves and taking notes (or making mental notes).

Before children "go to work," help them put together a list of questions they might ask at the end of the experience to learn more about the backgrounds and choices of the people they have chosen to shadow. Children can share their experiences orally or as a written report.

9

WHAT I'LL BE WHEN I GROW UP

Tommy sits behind me
In Miss Abernathy's class.
When he grows up he wants to be
The man who mows the grass.

Lisa wants to write big books.
Andy wants to sing.
Paula says she'll sleep all day
And not do anything!

And as for me, I think I'll be
The captain of a ship.
I'll sail it to the moon and back—
Oh, what a lovely trip!

—Unknown

In June, more time in the sun means more time for fun!

10

Adding pantomimed actions will add to everyone's enjoyment of this poem and will also be especially helpful for **students acquiring English.**

I LIKE TO . . .

This is the way I like to swim,
Over at the pool.
This the way I roller skate,
When I'm not in school.
This is the way I fly my kite,
When the wind begins to blow.
This is the way I play jump rope,
See how fast I can go.

—Unknown

11

WONDERFUL DAY

What a wonderful day! No one in the village doing anything.

—Shiki

12

B ### TWO LITTLE SISTERS

Two little sisters went walking one day,
Partly for exercise, partly for play.
They took with them kites
    which they wanted to fly,
One a big centipede, one a great butterfly.
Then up in a moment the kites
    floated high,
Like dragons that seemed to be touching
    the sky!

—Chinese traditional rhyme

ACROSS THE CURRICULUM
ARTS AND CRAFTS & SOCIAL STUDIES & READING

Art in the Air
Kites are not only for flying; they can also be works of art. Provide children with construction paper, tissue paper, markers, streamers, ribbons, stickers, glitter, and glue to make small decorative kites. Finish each kite with a tail of string tied with bits of fabric. Then, let children "fly" their finished kites on a bulletin-board "sky."

For inspiration on shapes and design, children can look at books, such as *Chinese Artistic Kites* by Ha Kuiming and Ha Yiqi (China Books and Periodicals, 1990). Older children can write bits of kite lore on their kites or on small pieces of paper to add to the bulletin board.

EXPLORING CULTURE Asian cultures—especially those of China, Japan, Korea, Thailand, Indonesia, and India—have a long tradition of making and flying kites, viewing them as links to the heavens, able to bring good luck and carry off misfortune. You might read aloud books about kites, such as:

◆ *Dragon Kite of the Autumn Moon* by Valerie Reddix, illustrated by Jean and Mou-Sien Tseng (Lothrop, Lee & Shepard, 1991)

◆ *The Emperor and the Kite* by Jane Yolen (Philomel, 1988)

◆ *Catch the Wind! All About Kites* by Gail Gibbons (Little, Brown, 1989)

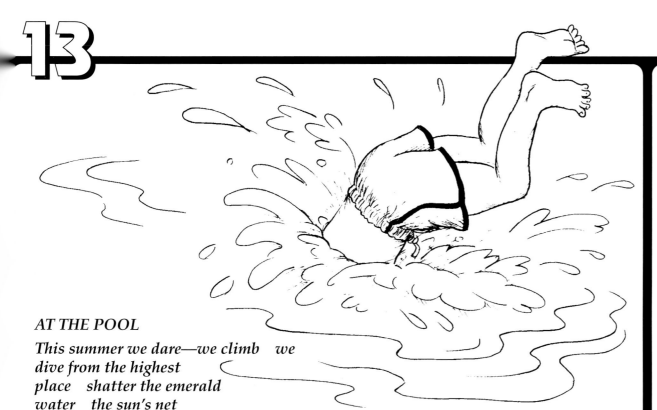

AT THE POOL

*This summer we dare—we climb   we
dive from the highest
place   shatter the emerald
water   the sun's net
flickers on our bodies
catches our shouts.*

*We are seals! Porpoises!
Silver bubbles form
in our tumbling wake
cling
to our seal-whiskers   our
porpoise-tails.*

*The clear green water
is our world
until lungs explode us
into air.*

—*Barbara Juster Esbensen*

PICNICS

*Sunshine and weiners and pickles and ham,
Not enough salt for the eggs,
Marshmallows cooked on the end of a stick,
Ants crawling over our legs.*

*Candy and cookies and peanuts and cake,
Finding the frosting has run,
All of us knowing we've eaten too much—
Picnics are certainly fun!*

—*Marchette Chute*

DEVELOPING LITERACY
GROUP TALK

Summer Buzzin'
Divide the class into buzz groups of five or six children. Ask them to take two minutes to think of as many ways to have fun in the summer as they can. Then, have them categorize their random lists.

Have groups volunteer their category headings as the first step to compiling a whole-class list. Representatives of each group can write specific activities under the appropriate headings. Suggest that each child make his or her own private list to use as a summertime jump-start when it seems like "there's nothing to do."

Since **students acquiring English** may have difficulty participating in the timed buzz groups, make sure they have individual help when compiling their private lists. You can suggest that they draw sketches or pictures if they are not yet comfortable with writing.

It's Hug Holiday. Have you hugged a loved one today?

Whether it's Pops, Dad, or Papa, we love him!

15

Hug Holiday

GOODNIGHT, JUMA

Go to bed, Juma.
>Just one more game?
Go to bed, Juma.
>Just one more show?
Go to bed, Juma.
>Just one more minute?
Juma, go to bed,
I said.
>Just—
No.
>—a hug?
Oh, You bet.
>Goodnight, Daddy.
Goodnight, Juma.

—Eloise Greenfield

AS A MATTER OF FACT Hug Holiday, which reminds us to express appreciation of others with some simple form of recognition, such as a hug, has been warmly celebrated since 1983.

Note: Different cultures express affection and appreciation differently. Hugging is not a universal idiom. Be sensitive to cultural differences as you explore this theme in your class.

DEVELOPING LITERACY
DRAMATIC INTERPRETATION—Choral Reading

Bedtime Script
Many children will hear a familiar cadence in Juma and Daddy's time-for-bed routine. Turn "Goodnight, Juma" into a choral reading with one partner taking the role of Juma and the other that of his father.

16

Father's Day (third Sunday)

ME AND MY DAD

Me and my Dad
sitting in a tavern eating
liverwurst sandwiches
We laugh and have
a good time
Me and my Dad

—James O'Connor, 5th grade
Bronx, New York

AS A MATTER OF FACT Father's Day has been celebrated nationally since 1966. The holiday traces its origins to a proclamation issued by the city of Spokane, Washington, in 1910, at the urging of Sonora Louise Smart Dodd. Dodd, whose own father had raised her and her five brothers after the death of their mother, was inspired by a Mother's Day sermon to establish a similar holiday to honor fathers.

Note: As on Mother's Day, be sensitive. Not all children will have a father present in the home.

17

MY DADDY IS A COOL DUDE

When my daddy comes in from work
at night
he always say
"Hey man, gimme five"
and I lay it on him
and he smiles.

My daddy sure is a cool dude.

—Karama Fufuka

DEVELOPING LITERACY

PATTERNED WRITING

Happy Times
VALUING DIVERSITY Have children work in pairs to talk about special times they have had with their fathers or those who are like a father to them. As with all family-centered holidays, it is important that the diversity of families be addressed so that all children feel a part of the celebration. (See **Honoring Someone Special,** May 12.)

Then, have a whole-class discussion and help children see both the variety and the similarities in the ways families have fun together. Suggest that children use "Me and My Dad" as a frame for writing poems about their own fathers or father figures. Encourage **students acquiring English** to write in their native language. Children can enclose their poems in decorative cards made of construction paper and present them on Father's Day.

18

A pause before the last line of each stanza makes for a very effective presentation of this poem, stressing the child's sadness and sense of longing.

B *MY FATHER*

My father doesn't live with us.
It doesn't help to make a fuss;
But still I feel unhappy, plus
    I miss him.

My father doesn't live with me.
He's got another family;
He moved away when I was three.
    I miss him.

I'm always happy on the day
He visits and we talk and play;
But after he has gone away
    I miss him.

—Mary Ann Hoberman

19

Y *DADDY*

Daddy, help me up the tree,
Daddy, help me make a kite,
Daddy, fix my doll for me,
Daddy, tell me a story,
Daddy, I'm so tired,
Daddy, can you carry me?
Daddy, I sleep so well in your arms.

—Alma Flor Ada

20
Puerto Rican Day (second Sunday)

PUERTO RICAN DAY PARADE

Come sing and dance in our parade,
come celebrate our history,
one of the beauties of America
is its rich diversity.

Puerto Rico means Port of Riches—
jewel of the Caribbean Sea,
Borinquen to the Taínos,* natives
who lived there for centuries.

Sing the many songs of our island,
move your feet in time to the beat,
hear the tick tick tick of maracas,
as you rhumba down the street.

Wear the costume of the jíbaros,*
white clothes from head to toe,
a red sash around your waist and
on your hat a bright red bow.

*In your hand wave **la bandera***—*
the flag—red, white, and blue
wave to all the people watching
as you march up the avenue.

Come march with us in our parade,
come celebrate our history:
one of the beauties of this country
is its rich diversity.

—Gloria Vando

Borinquen** *(boh-REEN-ken)/Taínos** *(tah-EE-nohs):* See entry for September 27.
***jíbaros** *(HEE-bah-rohs):* farmers of the mountainous regions of Puerto Rico
***la bandera** *(lah bahn-DEH-rah):* Spanish for "the flag"

AS A MATTER OF FACT The Puerto Rican Day Parade in New York City has been an annual event since 1958. The parade of floats, marching bands, folk musicians, and costumed flag-wavers that proceeds up Fifth Avenue draws more than a million people together to celebrate pride in Puerto Rican culture. Media coverage allows people all over the U.S. to witness and enjoy this display of Puerto Rican culture, talent, and pride.

What a world of happiness in one word . . . summer!

21

Summer Solstice (June 21 or 22)

A reading of this poem in both the original Hebrew and in English appears on the **Music Tapes**.

SHIR KAYTZI/SUMMER SONG

Summer, summer and a shell,
white sand and parasol,
cold red watermelon,
one orange peach.
Coffee house, vanilla sundae,
cherry peeking from the drips,
whipped cream mountain,
  all these almonds,
apricots and grapes.

Summer, summer and a shell,
white sand and parasol,
cold red watermelon,
and a deep blue sea.

—*Ilana Israeli (original in Hebrew)*
English version by Mazal Jaret
and Judith Steinbergh

AS A MATTER OF FACT The Summer Solstice marks the beginning of summer for the Northern Hemisphere as the sun reaches its northernmost point. The period of daylight is the longest today and is followed by the shortest night of the year.

22

KNOXVILLE, TENNESSEE

I always like summer
best
you can eat fresh corn
from daddy's garden
and okra
and greens
and cabbage
and lots of
barbecue
and buttermilk
and homemade ice cream
at the church picnic
and listen to
gospel music
outside
at the church
homecoming
and go to the mountains with
your grandmother
and go barefooted
and be warm
all the time
not only when you go to bed
and sleep

—*Nikki Giovanni*

23

SANDÍA/WATERMELON

¡Del verano, roja y fría
carcajada
rebanada
de sandía!

—*José Juan Tablada*

Summer's laughter, red and cool
on the ice—
watermelon
slice.

—*English version by Juan Quintana*

24

JUNE SUNSET

The day is wrapping
            itself up.
—In the sky
            lie pink
and orange ribbons.

—Emily Nguyen

DEVELOPING LITERACY
LISTENING TO VISUALIZE

Wonder of Words
"Ode to the Sprinkler" showcases the power of words to paint pictures. After you have read it once, have children close their eyes while you read it again. Pause between each "scene" to make a comment or ask a question to sharpen children's mind's-eye pictures of the words they are hearing. Children might draw a quick sketch or jot a few words in response to your questions.

✦ I can just see the street where the children are playing, can't you? What do you suppose the houses and yards look like?

✦ Bee stings hurt, don't they? I can imagine what that child's face—and toe—looked like. What do you imagine?

✦ I wonder what happened after the toe got better. Did the child run in the sprinkler again, or stay on the porch and watch the bees from a safe distance? What do you think?

Each child can share his or her mind-pictures with a partner. Finally, bring the whole class together to share their ideas as you read the poem once more.

25

ODE TO THE SPRINKLER

There is no swimming
Pool on
Our street,
Only sprinklers
On lawns,
The helicopter
Of water
Slicing our legs.
We run through
The sprinkler,
Water on our
Lips, water
Dripping
From eyelashes,
Water like
Fat raindrops
That fall from
Skinny trees when
You're not looking.
I run **como**
Un chango,*
In my orange
Swimming trunks,
Jumping up and
Down, pounding
The mushy grass
With my feet.

One time a bee
Stung my toe,
The next-to-the-biggest
Toe. Then that toe
Got bigger
Than my real
Big toe,
Like a balloon
On its way up.
I cried and
Sat on the porch.
The water on
My face was not
Water from the sprinkler,
But water from
Inside my body,
Way down where
Pain says, ¡Híjole!*
That hurts!
Mom brought me
A glass of Kool-Aid.
I drank some
And then pressed
The icy glass
Against my throbbing toe.

The toe
Shrank back
Into place,
And on that day
I began to think
Of Kool-Aid not
As sugar on
The tongue
But as medicine.
And as for the bees,
You have to watch
For them. They buzz
The lawn for
Their own sugar
And wet play.

—Gary Soto

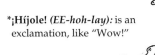

***como un chango** *(KOH-moh oon CHANG-goh):* Spanish for "like a monkey"

***¡Híjole!** *(EE-hoh-lay):* is an exclamation, like "Wow!"

26 Dragon Boat Festival (late June)

THE DRAGON BOATS

*The dragon boats! There they go!
Beat the drums! Row and row!
The swiftest dragon in the race
Will be the dragon in first place!*

—Chinese nursery rhyme

CultureShare The Dragon Boat festival commemorates the death of a hero of ancient China—Qu Yuan *(choo ywahn)*, a 4th century B.C.E. poet and statesman. Punished with banishment for openly criticizing the government, Qu Yuan jumped into a river and drowned himself. Today, the dragon boat races are held to reenact the efforts of his friends to save him. Customs associated with this holiday include eating of *zhong zi (jahng zuh)* (rice dumplings filled with meat and wrapped in bamboo leaves), and throwing rice into the river to keep Qu Yuan's spirit alive.

27

DRAGON

*A Dragon named Ernest Belflour,
Who lived in a dark palace tower,
　　Played an old violin
　　Of dried-out sharkskin
Hour after hour after hour.*

*An Indian Princess one day,
Who happened to wander that way,
　　Said: "The sound of that thin
　　Dried-out violin
Has stolen my heart away."*

*So she climbed the steps of the tower
And there beheld Ernest Belflour,
　　Who was changed by her glance
　　To a handsome young Prince:
She had broken the Old Witch's power.*

*They were married the very next minute
By a neighbor, Sir Larchmont of Linnet,
　　And they danced to a thin
　　Dried-out violin
Accompanied by a very shrill spinet.*

*And Ernest said: "Princess, my dear,
I will never blow smoke in your ear,
　　No Dragon am I
　　But a Prince till I die;
You have nothing whatever to fear.*

*"Let me buy you some angelfood cake
That we'll munch while we walk by the lake,
　　Enjoying the smile
　　Of the sweet Crocodile,
And the music the Bullfrogs make.*

*"When a dragon roars down from the hill,
Having come to do us both ill,
　　Belching up flames
　　And calling us names,
I will say, 'GO AWAY!' And he will."*

—William Jay Smith

28

LET ME TELL YOU ALL ABOUT ME

Let me tell you all about me.
Children love me.
You're a child.
All my heads are green and handsome.
All my eyes are red and wild.
All my toes have claws upon them.
All the claws have hooks.
I blow smoke through all my noses.
It is hotter than it looks.
All my tails have points upon them.
All my teeth are sharp and blue.
I won't bite you very badly.
I am fond of you.
All my scales are shaped like arrows.
They will hurt you if you touch.
So, although I know you'll love me,
Do not pet me very much.

—*Karla Kuskin*

29

A MODERN DRAGON

A train is a dragon that roars
   through the dark.
He wriggles his tail as he
   sends up a spark.
He pierces the night with his
   one yellow eye,
And all the earth trembles
   when he rushes by.

—*Rowena Bastin Bennett*

30

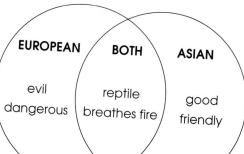

SONG OF THE DRAGON

See the dragon come on a hundred legs!
He brings us all good cheer;
   him we do not fear!
Long life and peace and joy
   in the bright New Year!
New Year, New Year, New Year is here!

—*Chinese traditional folk song*

DEVELOPING LITERACY
GROUP TALK & READING

Dragon Lore

EXPLORING CULTURE Dragons appear in the folklore of many different cultures around the world. Although dragons often look similar from one culture to another, they are viewed in very different ways. In Europe and the Middle East, dragons usually represent danger or evil; however, sometimes they symbolized power and were incorporated into the motifs of armor and flags. In Asian cultures, the dragon is seen as a beneficent creature, representing well-being, good fortune, and the wonders of nature. In China, it also symbolized power as the emblem of the Imperial family. A Venn diagram will help children compare the features of dragons in different cultures.

To extend this theme, try these new and old stories about dragons:

◆ *How Droofus the Dragon Lost His Head* by Bill Peet (Houghton Mifflin, 1971)

◆ *The Knight and the Dragon* by Tomie de Paola (G. P. Putnam's Sons, 1980)

◆ *St. George and the Dragon: A Golden Legend* adapted by Margaret Hodges from Edmund Spenser's *Faerie Queene* (Little, Brown, 1984)

◆ *Tatsu the Dragon* by Helen Van Aken (Charles E. Tuttle, 1966).

EUROPEAN   **BOTH**   **ASIAN**

evil
dangerous

reptile
breathes fire

good
friendly

JULY

Oh, the days and nights, the sounds and sights of July are here at last. This most summery of months is also in many ways the most "American"—what better time to celebrate all the ingredients that make up our national "climate"?

July brings summery things—clear night skies that stir our dreams, scoops and scoops of cool ice cream, trips to the zoo to make the most of the July weather outside. And a celebration of the first moon walk, which brought this nation so much pride.

Pride in the U.S. is as natural as the weather for July. Independence Day—the nation's birthday—brings millions of people outside. And it is our independence that makes us explore the most basic elements of this country. We celebrate freedom; we search for the meaning of America; we honor the first Americans—Native Americans; and we explore the cities and suburbs, farms and fields, where life in the States takes place.

So, get ready for a month of warm celebrations—outside or in, there's nothing like July and the fun it brings!

Noteworthy Days

4 Independence Day

✦ National Ice Cream Month

20 Anniversary of First Moon Walk

For summer adventure and fun in July, a trip to the zoo is a "roaring" good time . . .

1

🎵 THE ANIMAL SONG

Moderately

Folk song from Michigan

1. Al - li - ga - tor, hedge - hog, ant - eat - er, bear,
2. Bull - frog, wood - chuck, wol - ver - ine, goose,

Rat - tle - snake, buf - fa - lo, an - a - con - da, hare.
Whip - poor - will, chip - munk, jack - al, and moose.

3. Mud turtle, whale, glowworm, bat,
   Salamander, snail, and Maltese cat.

4. Polecat, dog, wild otter, rat,
   Pelican, hog, dodo, and bat.

5. House rat, toe rat, white deer, doe,
   Chickadee, peacock, bobolink, and crow.

Across the Curriculum
ARTS AND CRAFTS

Mixed-Up Critters
With all the animals in this theme, children may mix them up—here's a way to make the most of the mix-up! Children can contribute pages to a mixed-up animal book (see **How-To Directions** on page 243). You might ask children to make up names for the new creatures that appear. The class might make several books, using a different animal category for each one: farm animals, pets, wild animals.

2

📓 TAILS

A dog's tail
          is short
And a cat's tail
          is long,
And a horse has a tail
          that he
          swishes along,
And a fish has a tail
          that can
          help him
          to swim,
And a pig has a tail
          that looks
          curly on him.
All monkeys have tails
And the elephants too.
There are
hundreds of
tails
if
     you
          look
               in
                    the
                         zoo!

—Myra Cohn Livingston

. . . so you better pack your trunk!

3

THE ELEPHANT

If you had a trunk instead of a nose
you could swish it around
  like a garden hose.
If you had a trunk where your nose
  should be
you could pick up a log or even a tree.
If you had a trunk
  attached to your jaw
you could sip a soda without a straw.
If you want to know the reason
  you can't
*it's because you are **not** an elephant.*

—*Ernesto Galarza*

You've seen July 4th picnics and fireworks, too . . .

4

Independence Day

FOURTH OF JULY NIGHT

Pin wheels whirling round
Spit sparks upon the ground,
And rockets shoot up high
And blossom in the sky—
Blue and yellow, green and red
Flowers falling on my head,
And I don't ever have to go
To bed, to bed, to bed!

—*Dorothy Aldis*

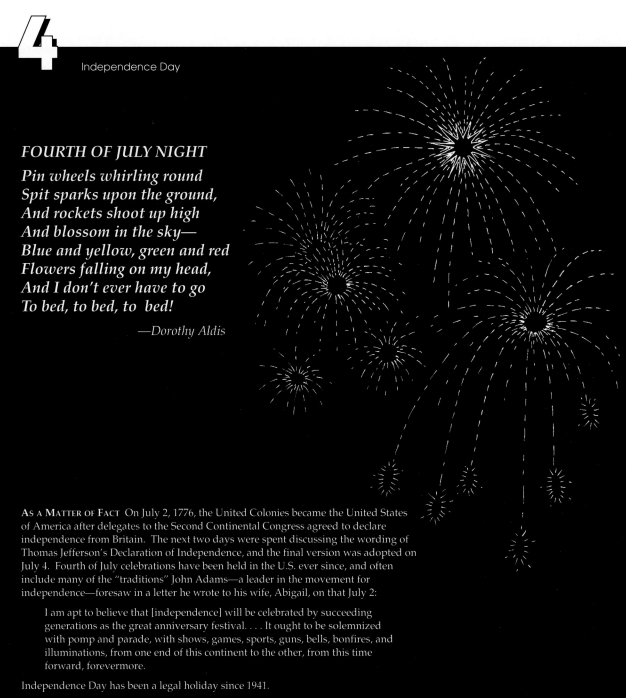

AS A MATTER OF FACT On July 2, 1776, the United Colonies became the United States of America after delegates to the Second Continental Congress agreed to declare independence from Britain. The next two days were spent discussing the wording of Thomas Jefferson's Declaration of Independence, and the final version was adopted on July 4. Fourth of July celebrations have been held in the U.S. ever since, and often include many of the "traditions" John Adams—a leader in the movement for independence—foresaw in a letter he wrote to his wife, Abigail, on that July 2:

> I am apt to believe that [independence] will be celebrated by succeeding generations as the great anniversary festival. . . . It ought to be solemnized with pomp and parade, with shows, games, sports, guns, bells, bonfires, and illuminations, from one end of this continent to the other, from this time forward, forevermore.

Independence Day has been a legal holiday since 1941.

... but what does freedom really mean to you?

5

I AM FREEDOM'S CHILD

I like me,
*   No doubt about it,*
I like me,
*   Can't live without it,*
I like me,
*   Let's shout about it,*
I am Freedom's Child.

You like me,
*   No doubt about it,*
You like you,
*   Can't live without it,*
You like you,
*   Let's shout about it,*
You are Freedom's Child.

We need all the different kinds of people we can find
To make Freedom's dream come true,
So as I learn to like all the differences in me,
I learn to like the differences in you.

I like you,
*   No doubt about it,*
You like me,
*   Can't live without it,*
We are free,
*   Let's shout about it.*
Hooray for Freedom's Child.

—Bill Martin Jr

6

BLACK CHILD

I am hewn from
*   the solid ledge of rock*
*   the soaring songs of birds*
*   the rocking motions of the ocean*
*   the uplifted branches of the tree*

I am a root
*   that will be free*

—Joyce Carol Thomas

A Word from the Poet "I was looking at a child's portrait—a black child—trying to see what was behind the expression, when I began to imagine what the child would say if that young mouth could speak in poetry. So I put myself—the poet—in the child's place until my mouth became the child's mouth, until my eyes turned into the child's eyes. I saw all this hope, this heritage, this *promise*, all mixed up into one being, one self, for that's where true freedom begins, with the self. I like to think that this young child's words remind us that we are inherently free; that we're born free and that we have a right to live free."

DEVELOPING LITERACY
DRAMATIC INTERPRETATION—Choral Reading

Let Freedom Ring
Divide the class into two groups for a choral reading of "I Am Freedom's Child." One group says lines 1, 3, 5, and 7 of the first two verses; the other group, lines 2, 4, and 6 of these verses. Both groups (or a narrator) can say the third verse. For the fourth verse, the first group says lines 1 and 3, and the second group, lines 2 and 4. Everyone joins in on the last three lines.

7

YOUNG VOICES

POEM

The first day I came to America,
I met my Sponsor mom in an airport.
She is a very nice mom.
She took me home
A few days later
She taught me,
Here is America.
It doesn't look like your Country
Everything is different
She taught me how to speak English
How to get buses
How to learn a map of the City
How to talk to the people
How to behave in school
How to stay free in America.

—*Bay Vo, 12th grade*
Philadelphia, Pennsylvania

DEVELOPING LITERACY
GROUP TALK & WRITING

Thinking About Freedom
Each of the poems in this theme has a very different tone: one is joyous, one strong, one grateful, one brave. Ask children to write about what each poem says to them about freedom:

✦ As I read this poem, I feel happy. How does it make you feel? Freedom gives us the chance to learn about and appreciate the differences in people. Why is that important? ("I Am Freedom's Child")

✦ What does the author of this poem think being free means? I think being free asks us to be strong sometimes. Why does it take strength to believe in the value of who we are? ("Black Child")

✦ It must be hard adjusting to a new country. What are some of the things that a newcomer to the United States might find most difficult about life here? How do you think the author felt? ("Poem")

✦ Being free takes courage. Some of us left countries we loved and experienced danger to live where we could be free. What are some of the emotions people must feel when they decide to start a whole new life? ("Drifting on the Ocean")

Conclude the discussion by asking children to write about what freedom means to them. They might share with their family what they've written and ask family members to talk about their own thoughts about freedom.

YOUNG VOICES

DRIFTING ON THE OCEAN

Drifting on the ocean for almost seven days
away far from the shore, hungry, thirsty, tired and sick.

A wild storm comes.
It shakes and tries to drown the boat.
Heavy winds blow; sails are broken.
The boat shakes; water leaks inside.
Heavy waves batter the boat.
Unbalanced, the boat struggles;
it goes to an unknown direction.
All pale and scared, faces look
at each other with hopelessness.

Half an hour passes. Storm goes away
leaving everything in ruins.
Children, women and men lay motionless
on the boat floor.
Fright is gone. Happiness comes.
The angel of death disappears;
the angel of life comes.
Smiles are on everyone's faces.

Scared, I wake up.
I'm glad that I'm still alive.
It is just a dream of the terrible escaping
my people had to face
for finding freedom.

—*Tuyen Pham, 9th grade*
Castro Valley, California

AS A MATTER OF FACT In the 1980s alone, more than 6,000,000 people immigrated legally to the United States and many more did so illegally. The bulk of these immigrants are from Southeast Asia, Mexico, and Central America.

The means of travel to the U.S. are as varied and often as dangerous as the conditions these refugees are escaping. Southeast Asian refugees are often referred to as "boat people" because of the overcrowded crafts that make the dangerous journey across the Pacific Ocean, as the poet describes. Haitian and Cuban refugees, too, often must crowd into boats to travel to the U.S. Some Central Americans travel to the U.S. through Mexico, then often risk their lives by crossing the Rio Grande. One Mexican American immigrant describes this river crossing as follows:

Crossing the river can be very dangerous, especially if you cross alone. There are fast water currents, and sometimes the water is quite high. If you don't know how to swim, the undercurrents can pull you right down. And in places the bottom of the river is like quicksand that can trap you. The water turns into kind of a tunnel that can drag you down. Some friends of mine have died.

9

MIRROR MIRROR

*People keep asking where I come from
says my son.
Trouble is   I'm american on the inside
and oriental on the outside*

No Kai*
Turn that outside in
THIS is what American looks like.

—*Mitsuye Yamada*

*Kai: the name of the poet's son; pronounced to rhyme
with *my*

ACROSS THE CURRICULUM
ARTS AND CRAFTS & SOCIAL STUDIES

The Face of the U.S.A.
VALUING DIVERSITY Here's a way to bring home the diversity that characterizes life in this country. Draw a large outline map of the United States on butcher paper and post it on a wall. Provide children with drawing paper and magazines and ask them to draw and cut out pictures to represent the rich diversity of life in the U.S. They can use their drawings and pictures to fill in the map with a "diversity collage." They can include pictures of different ethnic groups and celebrations, a variety of foods, rural and urban scenes, people of all ages at work and play.

To help children get ideas and to be sure the map is inclusive, you might read poems from the themes on Hispanic heritage (September), Native American culture (September and later this month), multicultural United States (October), African American history (February), women's history (March), Jewish heritage (April), older Americans (May), and Asian and Pacific American heritage (May).

PROMOTING SELF-ESTEEM To help children sense that they have a place in the diversity the collage celebrates, have them attach pictures or photos of themselves, or circles of foil (about 6" across) at random spots on the map so they will see their own faces reflected there.

10

FIRST DAY OF SCHOOL

*standing before
the teacher*

*I squeezed
my grandma's*

*hand
harder*

*the teacher
smiled*

*and said something
odd in English*

*then my grandma
gave me*

*her blessing
and left*

*I stayed behind:
a chair*

*in a very strange
world*

—*Francisco X. Alarcón*

AS A MATTER OF FACT Almost 15% of the United States population speaks a language other than English at home. In some states, such as Arizona, California, Hawaii, New Mexico, New York, and Texas, that number   is more than 20%, and can be as high as 35%. Among the languages spoken, Spanish is most common by far, accounting for more than half of all non-English-speaking households.

Your students might be the best resource for discovering the various languages spoken in U.S. schools, but some of these languages include: Arabic, Chinese, French, German, Greek, Hawaiian, Hebrew, Hmong, Hungarian, Indic languages, Italian, Japanese, Korean, Mon-Khmer, Native American languages, Polish, Portuguese, Russian, Scandinavian languages, Slavic languages, Tagalog, Vietnamese, and Yiddish.

11

12

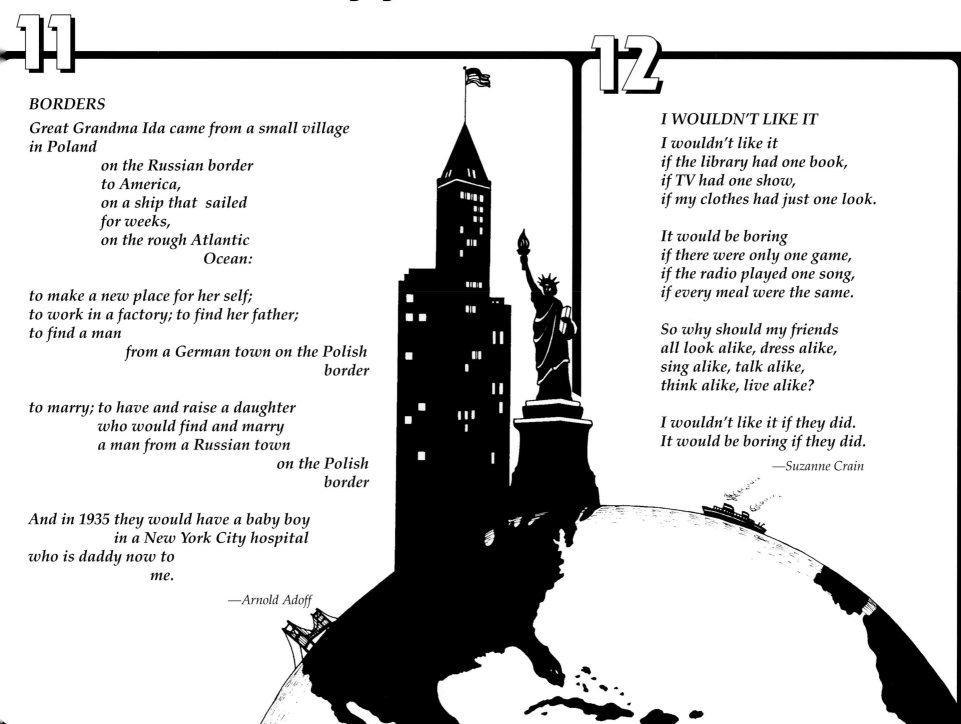

BORDERS

*Great Grandma Ida came from a small village
in Poland*

        *on the Russian border
        to America,
        on a ship that sailed
        for weeks,
        on the rough Atlantic
            Ocean:*

*to make a new place for her self;
to work in a factory; to find her father;
to find a man*
        *from a German town on the Polish
            border*

*to marry; to have and raise a daughter
        who would find and marry
        a man from a Russian town
            on the Polish
            border*

*And in 1935 they would have a baby boy
        in a New York City hospital
who is daddy now to
        me.*

        —Arnold Adoff

I WOULDN'T LIKE IT

*I wouldn't like it
if the library had one book,
if TV had one show,
if my clothes had just one look.*

*It would be boring
if there were only one game,
if the radio played one song,
if every meal were the same.*

*So why should my friends
all look alike, dress alike,
sing alike, talk alike,
think alike, live alike?*

*I wouldn't like it if they did.
It would be boring if they did.*

        —Suzanne Crain

13

14

YOUNG VOICES

POW WOW

It is only with this dancing,
It keeps,
It is only
With this dancing,
It keeps
Us alive.

—*Doris Seale*

MY HAIR IS LONG

My hair is as long as a pony's tail
and as shiny as a river.
My skin is as brown as a bear
getting up in the sunlight.
My eyes are as big as berries
but as dark as buffalo hide.
My ears are like pears cut in half
ready to eat.
My heart is like the drum beat as
I dance in the arbor.
My hands are soft as a rabbit's fur
in the forest.
My legs are as long as a baby deer's legs
as they run along the edge of the river.
My stomach is as big as a buffalo's
as it grazes through the land.
My voice is like the scream of an eagle
but can be as quiet as a mouse.
When I laugh, it sounds like
a woodpecker getting some food.
And my smile is as big as a lake.

—*Loyen Redhawk Gali, age 11*
Oakland, California

DEVELOPING LITERACY
GROUP TALK & WRITING

MULTICULTURAL FOCUS

Self-Portrait
PROMOTING SELF-ESTEEM Running throughout the self-portrait in "My Hair Is Long" are many strong images of nature, each chosen to support the poem's theme. Discuss this characteristic of the poem with children.

◆ How does the poet tell you that nature is a very important part of her life?

◆ What are some of the images she uses to describe herself?

◆ How does she succeed in giving you such a clear picture of who she is?

Then, ask children to think of something they identify strongly with and encourage them to use the general pattern of the poem to write their own personal versions. For example, a swimmer might write about hair like seaweed, skin as wet and shiny as fish scales, eyes as sparkling as ocean waves, ears like seashells, and so on. Or, a baseball player might write about hair as short as infield grass, skin the color of a catcher's mitt, eyes as big as the zeros on the scoreboard, a smile as big as the ball field, and so on.

15

ROUND HOUSE DANCING

The dancers come in the round house.
As the singing begins, the dancers
*   go around.*
But before the people come in the
*   round house*
They must turn two times.
The people say that we do this
*   because it lets the badness out.*
I am happy about who I am,
*   and proud of it.*

—*Albert Townsend, 5th grade*
Oakland, California

ACROSS THE CURRICULUM
SOCIAL STUDIES

Learning About the First Americans

EXPLORING CULTURE Here are some resources for a classroom library that contains accurate information about the diversity of culture, history, and contemporary life within the more than 400 tribes of North America's indigenous peoples.

✦ *Daybreak Star Indian Reader* (United Indians of All Tribes Foundation, 1945 Yale Place East, Seattle, WA 98102, 206-325-0070, ext. 46). Published ten times a year, this magazine focuses on the peoples of a different geographical region in each issue. Back issues are available.

✦ *Dancing Teepees: Poems of American Indian Youth,* edited by Virginia Driving Hawk Sneve (Holiday House, 1989)

✦ *Keepers of the Earth: Native American Stories and Environmental Activities for Children* by Michael Caduto and Joseph Bruchac (Fulcrum, 1988)

✦ *The People Shall Continue* by Simon Ortiz (Children's Book Press, 1988)

✦ *Two Pairs of Shoes* by Esther Sanderson (Pemmican, 1990)

As always, one of the best sources of information about people's lives is the people themselves. Inviting Native Americans to the classroom to talk about their heritage, customs, and everyday lives will help children learn about these cultures in a most meaningful and memorable way.

16

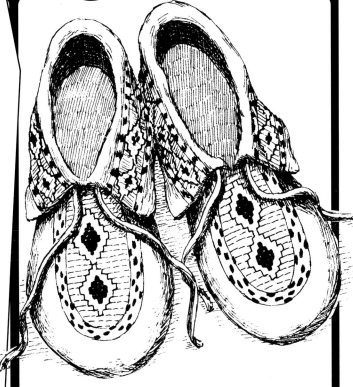

ANOTHER KID

I was just another kid
in T-shirt and blue jeans
until Grandmother gave me
new beaded moccasins.

—*Virginia Driving Hawk Sneve*

A WORD FROM THE POET "This poem is one in a series of poems I've been doing about children and their experiences, trying to find some way of representing their uniqueness. Indian children, in particular, often don't realize they are Indian until something happens to remind them of it. They are just 'another kid,' unaware of their heritage or background."

I scream, you scream, we all scream for ice cream!

17

National Ice Cream Month

THE PALET* MAN

"Soursop, coconut, mango, lime!"*
Neville, Arjune, Jasmine and I
run down the street
to the palet man.
Count out our change
as we get in line.
Wait our turn
*and **then** decide:*
soursop, coconut, mango, or lime?

—*Lynn Joseph*

*palet: name for a popsicle in the poet's native Trinidad
*soursop: a tart tropical fruit

AS A MATTER OF FACT Ice cream, like most things "American," has its roots elsewhere, changing and developing to reflect the United States' own character. A form of frozen dairy dessert was brought to Europe from China and other parts of Asia by Marco Polo in the 13th century. This treat grew increasingly popular in Italy and probably came to resemble modern ice cream sometime in the 16th century. It quickly spread through Europe, and was found in what became the United States by the 1700s.

By the 1850s the United States had produced the world's first full-fledged ice cream manufacturer and wholesaler, and—although its exact origins are not certain—the first ice cream cone is said to have been introduced at the 1904 St. Louis World's Fair. Chocolate-covered ice cream bars, ice-cream-on-a-stick, and ice cream sodas are just some of the many other ice cream innovations the United States claims—perhaps that's why National Ice Cream Month was established in honor of "America's favorite dessert."

DEVELOPING LITERACY
DRAMATIC INTERPRETATION

Delicious Dramas
Turn "The Palet Man" into a mini-play with simple props: real popsicle sticks; coins; popsicles made out of construction paper in bright colors, cut in rectangles (for flat popsicles) or wrapped around three-dimensional cardboard "frames." Children can turn the lines of the poem into a script and present as many performances as it takes to let everyone perform who wants to.

Or try a story-theater presentation. A narrator can read the poem while actors pantomime the action. Divide the class into small groups to plan and rehearse. Then, each group presents its rendition for the class.

Students acquiring English can work with you in one group. Demonstrate the poem's meaning with props and pantomime and, when children understand, turn the pantomime and props over to them as you recite the words.

18

THE ICE CREAM PAIN

Where the back of my throat meets the
  bottom of my brain
Comes the incredible ice cream pain.
When I swallow wrong with a
  bite of ice cream,
It hurts so bad that I almost scream.
It freezes so bad that I want to howl
Or drink boiling water or eat a towel.
Beware of ice cream! It could
  drive you insane—
With that (Oooh! Owww!) incredible
  ice cream pain!

—*Jeff Moss*

19

Show children a photo or illustration of a slide trombone before reading this poem, and pantomime for them how it's played.

SLIDE TROMBONE

Into Mother's slide trombone
Liz let fall her ice cream cone.
Now when marching, Mother drips
Melting notes and chocolate chips.

—*X. J. Kennedy*

One GIANT leap!

20

MARI AND THE MOON

Mari and the moon
are the best of friends.
One reaches up and stretches,
one reaches down and bends.

One points and calls her name out,
the other sends her light
One rides her Daddy's shoulders,
the other rides the night.

One sings and laughs and giggles,
one dances with a cloud.
One learns a new word every day,
one is so old, she's proud.

One sits upon a horsie,
toes dangling, dreaming meadows.
One sits perched on a rooftop,
toes playing with the shadows.

One peeks out through the window
to see her friend in sky.
One sneaks her fingers through curtains
    and cracks,
her touch—a lullaby.

Mari and the moon
are the best of friends.
They play together every night:
one sleeps, and one pretends.

—Carmen Tafolla

AS A MATTER OF FACT On July 20, 1969, astronauts Eugene "Buzz" Aldrin and Neil Armstrong landed the lunar module *Eagle* on the surface of the moon, the first people ever to accomplish such a feat. The next day they added another first, spending more than two hours walking on the moon, collecting soil samples and exploring this new frontier. The words Neil Armstrong spoke when he stepped from the module have become nearly as famous as the feat itself: "That's one small step for a man, one giant leap for mankind."

Oh, those summer nights of July!

21

 **USAGI / RABBIT**

Traditional

Slowly and expressively

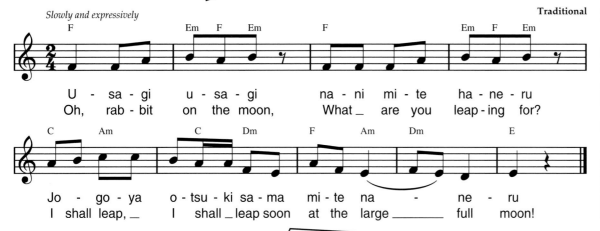

| U - sa - gi | u - sa - gi | na - ni mi - te | ha - ne - ru |
| Oh, | rab - bit on the moon, | What _ are you | leap - ing for? |

| Jo - go - ya | o - tsu - ki sa - ma | mi - te na - | ne - ru |
| I shall leap, _ | I shall _ leap soon | at the large ___ | full moon! |

© 1983 & 1991 The Japan Times, Ltd. Reprinted by permission.

CultureShare The shadows created on the moon by its rugged terrain have inspired various interpretations. United States folklore often refers to the Man in the Moon. In Scandinavian countries, the dark shapes are interpreted as a boy and a girl—the two children we came to know as Jack and Jill. In some South American cultures, people see a fox in the moon. In Mexico, people see a rabbit. People in Japan, where this song is from, also see a rabbit which, according to legend, was taken there to live as a reward for its kindness to a beggar.

DEVELOPING LITERACY
READING & WRITING

MULTICULTURAL FOCUS

Lunar Legends
EXPLORING CULTURE The moon's shadows have stirred the imaginations of peoples all over the world for centuries (see **CultureShare**) and some have created legends about them. Here are some sources for children to use in exploring the many variations on this universal theme:

✦ *How the People Sang the Mountains Up: How and Why Stories* by Maria Leach (Viking, 1967)

✦ *The Man in the Moon: Sky Tales from Many Lands* by Alta Jablow and Carl Withers (Holt, Rinehart, and Winston, 1969)

✦ "The Rabbit in the Moon" from *Japanese Children's Favorite Stories*, edited by Florence Sakade (Tuttle, 1958)

The next time the moon is full (or nearly so), remind children of the legends. Ask them to spend some time studying the moon's surface and to write their own stories about what they see there.

22

CAT IN MOONLIGHT

Through moonlight's milk
She slowly passes
As soft as silk
Between tall grasses.
I watch her go
So sleek and white,
As white as snow,
The moon so bright
I hardly know
White moon, white fur,
Which is the light
And which is her.

—*Douglas Gibson*

23

SLEEPING OUTDOORS

Under the dark is a star,
Under the star is a tree,
Under the tree is a blanket,
And under the blanket is me.

—*Marchette Chute*

24

THE PRAIRIE

Prairie
is a
place
where the moon shines down
on the little maroon house with a
silver door.

—Monique Mitchell, 3rd grade
Oakland, California

DEVELOPING LITERACY
LISTENING TO VISUALIZE & PATTERNED WRITING

A Sense of Place
After reading "The Prairie" once, have children close their eyes while you read it again. Ask them to picture in their minds the scene it describes. Now, ask each child to choose a place he or she knows well—a forest, a park, a pond, a vacant lot, a neighborhood, a city street—and use the basic frame of the poem to describe it. For example:

   THE NEIGHBORHOOD
   Neighborhood
   is a
   place
   where kids play kick the can
   until Mom calls out it's time to come home
   for dinner.

Children can illustrate their poems, read them, or have them read while the other children close their eyes again and listen.

25

I LIVE IN A CITY

Words and music by Malvina Reynolds

With spirit

I live in a ci-ty, _ yes I do _ I live in a ci-ty, _ yes _ I _ do _ I live in a ci-ty, _ yes _ I _ do _ Made by hu-man _ hands. ___

1. Black hands, white hands, tan and _ brown, _ All to-ge - ther _ built this town. _ Black hands, white hands, tan and _ brown, _
2. Brown hands, tan hands white and _ black, _ Mined the coal _ and _ built the stack. _ Brown hands, tan hands, white and _ black, _

All to - ge - ther make the wheels go round. And I
Built the en - gine and ___ laid the track.

3. Black hands, brown hands, tan and white,
   Built the buildings tall and bright.
   Black hands, brown hands, tan and white,
   Filled them all with shining light.

4. Black hands, white hands, brown and tan,
   Milled the flour and cleaned the pan.
   Black hands, white hands, brown and tan,
   The working woman and the working man.

© 1960 Schroder Music Co., Renewed 1988. Reprinted by permission. All rights reserved.

26

27

YOUNG VOICES

Read this poem quickly and with spirit to convey the poem's energy and excitement.

Y SUNRISE

The city YAWNS
And rubs its eyes,
Like baking bread
Begins to rise.

—Frank Asch

CITY

In the morning the city
Spreads it wings
Making a song
In stone that sings.

In the evening the city
Goes to bed
Hanging lights
About its head.

—Langston Hughes

GOING TO SCHOOL ON THE SUBWAY

Go downstairs,
Show your pass to the man.
Here comes a train
Catch it if you can.
You miss that train,
And then you see
That was an F*
And you want a GG.*
You go on, then stop
To rest your back.
A GG comes rumbling
Down the track.
The door slides open,
You hop inside
You sit down and wait
For the end of the ride

There are all sorts of people
You never saw before
Hoyt Schermerhorn* now
And you see the open door.
People get on, people get off,
The train starts moving
With a bang and a cough.
Fulton* is the next stop
Doors open and shut,
Yours is the next stop
You might as well get up.
Clinton Washington* next,
You get off here.
One ride less out of the
Whole school year.

—Sarah Underhill, 4th grade
Brooklyn, New York

*F, GG: subway lines in New York City
*Hoyt Schermerhorn, Fulton, Clinton Washington: subway stations in New York City

ACROSS THE CURRICULUM

MATHEMATICS

The Scope of the City
To help children comprehend the size, density, and complexity of large cities, discuss some of the characteristics of metropolitan areas: population, numbers of schools and parks, various modes of transportation. Then, try one or more of these activities.

◆ Younger children can do mental math estimations, such as counting the number of floors in a tall building and, given a standard height for each floor (10 feet, for instance), estimating the height of the building. Children can use blocks or other manipulatives as estimation aids.

◆ Older children can figure out the population density (the number of people divided by the number of square miles) of their own cities or the nearest large city. The local chamber of commerce or a city map will supply the figures they need.

◆ Older children might plot routes on a simple city map; choosing a starting point and a destination, they can figure the number of miles they would cover if they walked, took a bus, or rode a subway.

PUNCHBALL

Sometimes in the cool summer dusk
I can smell a punchball game: the burn
of sneaker rubber against bare feet, the slap
of ball and palm, screams flying from mouth
to open mouth, skinned knees drying hard.
I can hear Eugene's serious voice giving the calls
in the losing light: "Strike One." "Strike Two."
The heat of the Brooklyn streets rises
to meet the coming darkness, pricking my nose
with smell and memory. My hands, black
with caked sweat, search under parked cars
for a lost ball; my cheek is grimy from putting my face
to the hot black streets; my bare legs bruised and scraped
from climbing in and out of backyards. My little brother screams
"Foul ball! Foul ball!" as the ball thumps
off a windshield. It is quiet for a second
as Eugene runs over to check the glass.
Then we are screaming again as he returns, smiling.
Grandma sits on the stoop in slippers, her shirt
unbuttoned from the heat of cooking. Her hair
flies out from under the clip; she smiles as she watches us
play out the World Series on 60th Street and 7th Avenue
in Bay Ridge, Brooklyn.

—Sarah Chan

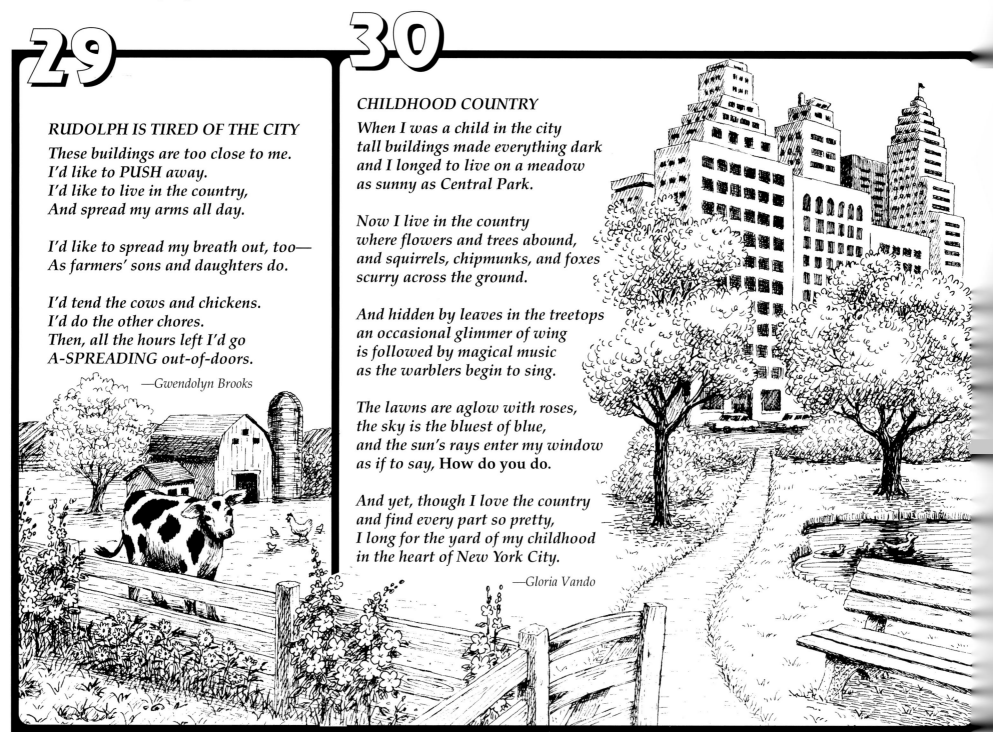

29

RUDOLPH IS TIRED OF THE CITY

These buildings are too close to me.
I'd like to PUSH away.
I'd like to live in the country,
And spread my arms all day.

I'd like to spread my breath out, too—
As farmers' sons and daughters do.

I'd tend the cows and chickens.
I'd do the other chores.
Then, all the hours left I'd go
A-SPREADING out-of-doors.

—Gwendolyn Brooks

30

CHILDHOOD COUNTRY

When I was a child in the city
tall buildings made everything dark
and I longed to live on a meadow
as sunny as Central Park.

Now I live in the country
where flowers and trees abound,
and squirrels, chipmunks, and foxes
scurry across the ground.

And hidden by leaves in the treetops
an occasional glimmer of wing
is followed by magical music
as the warblers begin to sing.

The lawns are aglow with roses,
the sky is the bluest of blue,
and the sun's rays enter my window
as if to say, **How do you do.**

And yet, though I love the country
and find every part so pretty,
I long for the yard of my childhood
in the heart of New York City.

—Gloria Vando

. . and always feels like home.

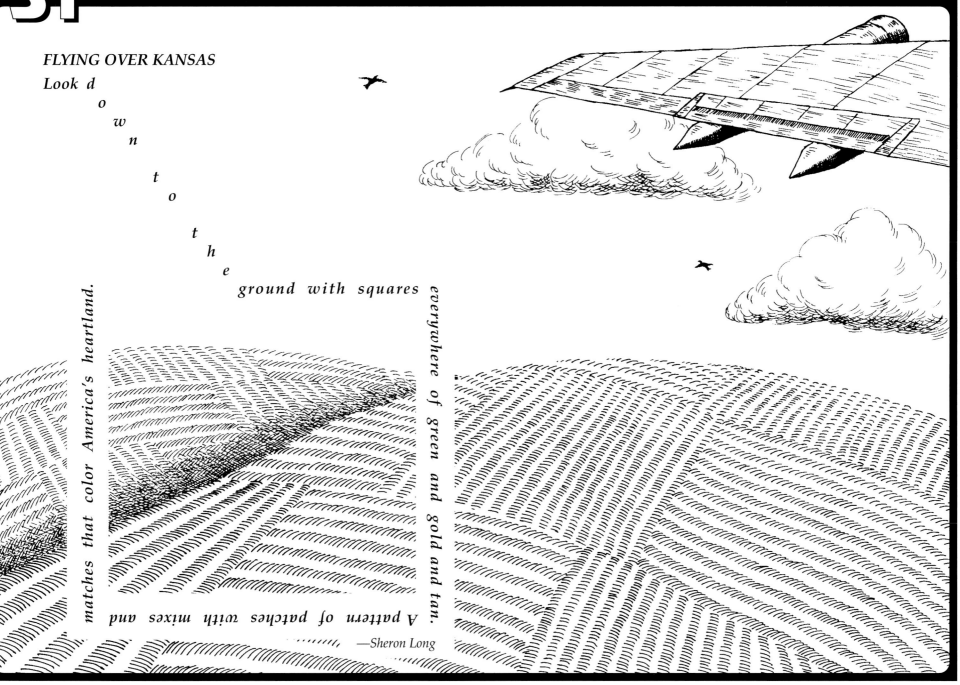

31

FLYING OVER KANSAS

Look d
    o
      w
        n
          t
            o
              t
                h
                  e
                    ground with squares everywhere of green and gold and tan. A pattern of patches with mixes and matches that color America's heartland.

—Sheron Long

AUGUST

Smile! August is here—that hot lazy month when everyone just tries to cool off. The beaches swarm with bathers seeking cool waves. Local parks are bursting with picnickers. Any place with some shade can be a haven in August.

Although we sometimes complain that it's **too** hot, August is a wonderful time to take advantage of the warm weather and long days enjoying outdoor summer activities and festivals with family and friends.

Quickly now, before the summer is over and fall is upon us, get the family together, pack your favorite foods, brave the bugs, and go out and soak up some August!

Noteworthy Days

✦ National Smile Week (begins first Monday)

✦ Family Day (first or second Sunday)

✦ O-Bon (varies)

✦ Mawlid al-Nabi (may fall any time of year, following the Muslim calendar, which is strictly lunar*)

*See page 265 for exact date.

A smile makes every day sunny.

National Smile Week (begins first Monday)

 PUT ON A HAPPY FACE

Words by Lee Adams
Music by Charles Strouse

1. Gray skies are gon - na   clear up, ___   Put on a hap - py   face;
2. Pick out a pleas-ant   out - look, _   Stick out that no - ble   chin;

Brush off   the clouds and   cheer up, ___   Put on a hap - py   face.
Wipe off that "full   of   doubt" look, _   Slap on a hap - py   grin!

Take off   the gloom-y   mask of trag - e - dy,   It's not your style;

You'll look so good that   you'll be   glad _ ya' de - cid - ed to smile! _

Coda

Spread   sun - shine   all   o - ver   the   place,   Just

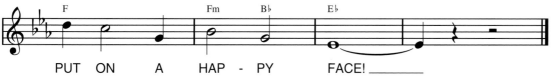

PUT   ON   A   HAP - PY   FACE! _____

© 1960. Reprinted by permission of C.P.P. Belwin.

*Everyone in the world
smiles in the same language.*

—Mexican American proverb

SIX SALAMANDERS

*Six sad salamanders
Set off in single file,
Searching for adventure
Beside the River Nile.*

*Second salamander
Sighed softly to the rest,
"I want to find the secret
To simple happiness."*

*Six salamanders stumbled
Six salamander miles
Until at last they found
Six sunning crocodiles.*

*Six sad salamanders
Couldn't help but stare
At lovely crocodile smiles
Looming everywhere.*

*Suddenly salamanders
Smiled and smiled with pleasure,
Caught the grins upon their chins,
And sped home with their treasure.*

—Suzanne Crain

On Family Day—and almost any day— brothers and sisters can bring many reasons to smile.

4 Family Day (first or second Sunday)

 WHERE DID THE BABY GO?

I cannot remember—
And neither can my mother—
Just when it was our baby
Turned into my brother.

—Julie Holder

AS A MATTER OF FACT If you travel during the summer, you may find yourself celebrating Family Day more than once. Some states, such as Arizona and Michigan, officially celebrate it on the first Sunday in August whereas, in other parts of the country, Family Day is observed on the second Sunday.

5

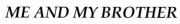

ME AND MY BROTHER

me and my brother
are like
little squirrels
racing up
a tree
competing over
everything
and I always win

—Tara Skidders, 5th grade
Rooseveltown, New York

6 WHEN ANNIE WAS ADOPTED

When Annie was adopted,
Her brand-new brother smiled;
He thought they were so lucky
To have a brand-new child.

He gave her tiny tickles,
Some kisses and a hug;
He tucked her in her basket
And wrapped her nice and snug;

And just before she fell asleep,
She looked at him and smiled
As though she knew already
She was their brand-new child.

—Mary Ann Hoberman

DEVELOPING LITERACY
GROUP TALK & WRITING & READING

Our Families
VALUING DIVERSITY To remind children of the wide diversity in today's families, look back with them at the themes that feature family poems: Grandparents' Day (September), Family (December), Mother's Day (May), Father's Day (June).

Talk about the feelings family members share, such as love, respect, pride, trust, and caring. Then, use the poems in this theme to center the discussion on relationships between brothers and sisters.

◆ *Though brothers and sisters can have disagreements, they "stick up" for each other, too. Can you tell about a time when you helped a brother or sister? Or, a time when your brother or sister helped you?*

◆ *Are you the oldest or youngest child in your family? Or, are you in the middle? What do you like best about your place in your family?*

To encourage further discussion, you might read *Brothers and Sisters* by Maxine B. Rosenberg (Houghton Mifflin, 1991) and *Poems for Brothers, Poems for Sisters*, selected by Myra Cohn Livingston (Holiday House, 1991).

Children might respond to the ideas they've talked about by:

◆ making a book about their own families to take home and share

◆ thinking back on all the poems and writing a response to the prompt "A family is . . ."

7

HALF-WHOLE-STEP

I have *a half-sister*
I have *a whole-sister*
I have *a step-sister*
　　That adds up to three.

I am *a half-brother*
I am *a whole-brother*
I am *a step-brother*
　　There's just one of me!

—*Mary Ann Hoberman*

8

MY SISTER'S JUST LIKE ME

My sister and I are almost the same
when she gets angry
she wants to throw something
just like me
she loves my dad
she's always there when my dad needs her
just like me
she likes to wear jeans and shirts
just like me
she likes to read Vietnamese
just like me
she likes computers
just like me
but when she writes
it's about her private life
she has secrets
just like me

—*Phuc Huynh, 5th grade*
Santa Ana, California

My name is part of who I am . . .

9

NAME POEM

My name sounds like a
dragon
munching
my face.

My name sounds like a
dinosaur
yelling
at someone.

My name sounds like a
car
crashing
into a building.

I hate it when someone
makes fun of my name!

—Norberto Fernández, 2nd grade
Tempe, Arizona

10

Before reading this poem to the children, you can sketch a family tree beginning with boxes for "Mother" and "Father" of the four brothers. As you read the poem to the children, fill in the names of the brothers, their wives, and their children on the family tree.

THE FOUR BROTHERS

Fito* is a farmer and he lives in Aguadilla.*
Chito* is a teacher and he lives in Guayanilla.*
Tito* is a poet and he lives in a tree.
But Lalito* is a baby and he lives with me.

Fito married Fita* and they had a son Fitito.*
Chito married Chita* and they had a son Chitito.*
Tito still writes poetry and lives in a tree.
But Lalito is a little boy and lives with me.

When Fitito grew up, he got married to Fitita.*
When Chitito grew up, he got married to Chitita.*
When Tito got old, he came down from the tree.
And Lalito, my Lalito, no longer lives with me.

Now Lalito is a plumber and he lives in Aibonito,*
With Lalita,* who's an engineer and works in Naranjito,*
And they have a little son, very little, muy chiquito,*
And they named him—did you guess it?—Willy.

—Charlotte Pomerantz

***Fito:** *FEE-toh*
***Aguadilla:** *ah-gwah-DEE-yah*
***Chito:** *CHEE-toh*
***Guayanilla:** *gwah-yah-NEE-yah*
***Tito:** *TEE-toh*
***Lalito:** *lah-LEE-toh*
***Fita:** *FEE-tah*
***Fitito:** *fee-TEE-toh*

***Chita:** *CHEE-tah*
***Chitito:** *chee-TEE-toh*
***Fitita:** *fee-TEE-tah*
***Chitita:** *chee-TEE-tah*
***Aibonito:** *ie(rhymes with pie)-boh-NEE-toh*
***Lalita:** *lah-LEE-tah*
***Naranjito:** *nah-rahn-HEE-toh*
***muy chiquito (mwee chee-KEE-toh):**
Spanish for "very little"

YOUNG VOICES

from
WHEN I HEAR THE MUSIC
IN MY NAME

My name is like a music breeze
flying through the earth's sky,
going places all over the world
even the galaxy.

—*Johnny Chou, 6th grade*
Oakland, California

HOW A GIRL GOT HER CHINESE NAME

On the first day of school the teacher
  asked me:
What do your parents call you at home?

I answered: Nellie.

Nellie? Nellie?
The teacher stressed the l's, whinnying
  like a horse.
No such name in Chinese for a name like
  Nellie.
We shall call you **Nah Lei***
which means **Where** *or* **Which Place.**

The teacher brushed my new name,
black on beige paper.
I practiced writing **Nah Lei**
holding the brush straight, dipping
the ink over and over.

After school I ran home.
Papa, Mama, the teacher says my name
  is **Nah Lei.**
I did not look my parents in the eye.

Nah Lei? Where? Which Place?
No, that will not do, my parents
  answered.
We shall give you a Chinese name,
we shall call you **Lai Oy.***

So back to school I ran,
announcing to my teacher and friends
that my name was no longer **Nah Lei,**
not **Where,** *not* **Which Place,**
but **Lai Oy, Beautiful Love,**
my own Chinese name.
I giggled as I thought:
Lai Oy *could also mean* **lost pocket**
depending on the heart
of a conversation.

But now in Chinese school
I was **Lai Oy,** *to pull out of my pocket*
every day, after American school,
even Saturday mornings,
from **Nellie,** *from* **Where,** *from* **Which**
  Place
to **Lai Oy,** *to* **Beautiful Love.**

Between these names
I never knew I would ever get lost.

—*Nellie Wong*

*****Nah Lei:** pronounced *nah lay*
*****Lai Oy:** pronounced *lie oy*

. . . my name is important to me.

MY TRIBE IS CHOCTAW

*My tribe is Choctaw and the name
reminds me of chocolate!
I don't have an Indian name but I wish
I did.
One that means the glorious sunrise and the
heavenly sunset.
One that means the dazzling wild flowers
with their sensuous scent of perfume.
One with extraordinary waterfalls crashing
over rocks sending colorful rainbows
into the blue peaceful sky.
One that means the beautiful gifts
of earth.*

—*Victoria Wilson, 6th grade
Oakland, California*

AS A MATTER OF FACT Names are important to everyone and new students will feel much more welcomed if teachers and classmates know how to pronounce their names correctly. Consult other students from the same culture for help with pronunciations if you cannot reach parents or guardians. In order to be respectful, it helps to know the naming traditions of a culture. Here are a few examples:

- Hispanic children are sometimes named for one of the saints honored on their date of birth. Children born outside of the U.S. are given the surnames of both the father and the mother, for example, Luis Fernández López has both his father's (Fernández) and his mother's (López) surnames.

- Most Asian cultures traditionally place the family name first and then the given name. However, Nguyên Thu is never called Mr. Nguyên, but rather Mr. Thu or Mr. Nguyên Thu. Once in the U.S., the American pattern is usually followed.

- Laotians are an exception to the rule above, in that naming parallels the American style: given name followed by the family name.

- Native American names often refer to animals or other elements from nature. Native Americans may have different names at different stages of their lives.

- People concerned about retaining their ethnicity or demonstrating pride in their heritage may change their own names or give their children names that reflect their culture.

ACROSS THE CURRICULUM
ARTS AND CRAFTS & WRITING

What's in a Name?
PROMOTING SELF-ESTEEM In learning the stories behind their names, children gain a sense of their own personal history.

Here are some ways children might learn more about their names:

◆ Have them find out how their own names were chosen. Are there family stories about the day they were born and the names they were given? Are they named for a family member, a friend, or a famous person?

◆ Make available books that tell about the origins and meanings of names, such as *A Book About Names* by Milton Meltzer (Crowell, 1984) and *Dictionary of First Names* by Alfred J. Kolatch (Putnam, 1990). Call on students' families and community members from various cultures to supply information about names from their culture. Invite children to find out whether their names have a special meaning.

Children can celebrate their names by:

◆ making yarn paintings—each child writes his or her first name on a piece of oaktag, spreading glue all around it and outlining it with pieces of yarn, pressing the yarn down into the glue.

◆ writing acrostics using their first names (or last names, or both). Have them think about their characteristics, favorite things, talents, and strengths.

◆ creating collages using pictures from magazines, their own drawings, and mementos pasted around cut-out letters from newspapers or magazines.

African Americans may choose Muslim, Swahili, or Yoruban names. People of Celtic background may choose Gaelic spellings.

- "New Age" themes may work their way into children's names—Forest, Rainbow, Condor.

Be sensitive to children's feelings about their names. Do not Americanize a child's name as a matter of course, but do not refuse a student's request to be addressed differently if he or she so chooses. In this personal matter that so affects a child's self-image and self-esteem, it is best simply to follow the child's lead.

14

NATHANIEL'S RAP

It's Nathaniel talking
and Nathaniel's me
I'm talking about
My philosophy
About the things I do
And the people I see
All told in the words
of Nathaniel B. Free
That's me
And I can rap
I can rap
I can rap, rap, rap
Till your earflaps flap
I can talk that talk
Till you go for a walk
I can run it on down
Till you get out of town
I can rap
I can rap
Rested, dressed and feeling fine
I've got something on my mind
Friends and kin and neighborhood
Listen now and listen good
Nathaniel's talking
Nathaniel B. Free
Talking about
My philosophy
Been thinking all day
I got a lot to say
Gotta run it on down
Nathaniel's way
Okay!

I gotta rap
Gotta rap
Gotta rap, rap, rap
Till your earflaps flap
Gotta talk that talk
Till you go for a walk
Gotta run it on down
Till you get out of town
Gotta rap
Gotta rap
Rested, dressed and feeling fine
I've got something on my mind
Friends and kin and neighborhood
Listen now and listen good
I'm gonna rap, hey!
Gonna rap, hey!
Gonna rap, hey!
I'm gonna rap!

—Eloise Greenfield

DEVELOPING LITERACY
GROUP TALK & ORAL COMPOSING

What's On Your Mind?
After children have listened to "Nathaniel's Rap" several times and have internalized the rhythm and rhyme scheme, invite them to create raps celebrating their own "philosophies." Try the "Think-Pair-Share" technique. First, children spend several minutes **thinking**—on their own—about what's on their mind. Then, **pairs** of children can discuss their ideas and try putting their ideas into a rhyme. After partners have helped and encouraged each other, children can **share** their raps with the whole group.

15

The summer season brings the O-Bon festival.

O-Bon (varies)

YOUNG VOICES

THE FEAST OF LANTERNS

Tonight
my father is going back by boat
to the stars
in heaven.
I am lonely.

—Yoshimura Jinto, age 6
Japan (original in Japanese)
English version by Haruna Kimura

CULTURESHARE The traditional Japanese O-Bon festival celebrates a three-day period in mid-July or mid-August when the spirits of the dead are believed to visit relatives. Food is traditionally placed at the graves of relatives, and lanterns are lit to show the spirits the way home. It is a solemn but welcomed time. In Japan, the celebration ends with the festive *bon-odori (bohn oh-DOR-ee)*—an all-night celebration of folk dance and folk music where dancers compete for prizes for best dancing and best costumes. In the United States, the conclusion of O-Bon is celebrated with games in addition to the dancing and music, and frequently culminates with the launching of paper lanterns on a pond or lake. In some places, the lanterns are floated out to sea. Similar festivals honoring the dead are the Chinese Hungry Ghosts Festival and the Christian All Souls' Day, celebrated as *Día de los muertos* in Mexico and the U.S. Southwest. (See November 2.)

16

AUGUST HEAT

In August, when the days are hot,
I like to find a shady spot,
And hardly move a single bit—
And sit—
  And sit—
    And sit—
      And sit!

—Unknown

17

 ### I'LL TELL YOU SOMETHING

I'll tell you something
I really know.
A butterfly
is a pretty bow.

—Ernesto Galarza

BEES

Bees won't bother you.
Relax.
They are busy
making wax.

—Ernesto Galarza

18

HOW FIREFLIES GOT THEIR LIGHT

Once upon a time there was a fly that was very mischievous. Every time he went out to play at night his mother told him never to go near the campfires. He wondered why. So one night he and his friends flew toward the fire and went in it. The blaze was so hot that their behinds lit up with heat. They flew out of the fire so fast that the blaze blew in the opposite direction. As they flew into their fly village they bumped into a couple of other flies. Every fly they touched, the fly's behind lit up. All the flies came to see what the noise was about and noticed the glowing behinds. Every fly wanted a glowing behind. As soon as everyone got one they started a new breed of flies. That's why they are called fireflies because they got their light from the fire.

—Victoria Wilson, 6th grade
Oakland, California

19

Ask another teacher, a parent, or an aide to join you in presenting this poem for two voices to your class.

FIREFLIES

Light	*Light* *is the ink we use*
Night *is our parchment*	*Night*
fireflies *flitting*	*We're* *fireflies* *flickering*
fireflies *glimmering*	*flashing*
	fireflies *gleaming*
glowing *Insect calligraphers* *practicing penmanship*	*Insect calligraphers*
Six-legged scribblers *of vanishing messages,*	*copying sentences* *Six-legged scribblers*
Fine artists in flight *adding dabs of light*	*fleeting graffiti* *Fine artists in flight*
Signing the June nights *as if they were paintings*	*bright brush strokes* *Signing the June nights* *as if they were paintings* *We're*
flickering *fireflies* *fireflies*	*fireflies* *flickering* *fireflies.*

—Paul Fleischman

ACROSS THE CURRICULUM
SCIENCE & WRITING

Bug Observation
Children can take paper and pencil and go outdoors to discover insects "in the wild" above and below ground. Have them use **Activity Sheet 18** to make drawings and notes that contain as much detail as possible so they can later share their findings with the class.

Content-Area ESL
Children's drawings can be used to extend their vocabularies. Help them label body parts and use their drawings to fill in the details on the **Activity Sheet.**

20

ANCESTRY

I splash in the ocean
My big brother watches me
We sing,
   "Wade in the water
   Wade in the water, children."

Mom and Dad
Teaching us spirituals
Reading us African tales
Singing songs
Telling stories
Reminding us
Of our ancestry

On the beach
Other children
Dig to China
I dig
To Africa

—Ashley Bryan

21

Before reading this poem to the class, let children know that on the island of Trinidad, where the author of this poem grew up, *pullin' seine* means "hauling in the fishing nets." Anyone may join in to help pull in the nets, and children are allowed to take small fish. For an enjoyable choral reading of this poem, list words in left column on chalkboard. Children can say each word with feeling when you point to it as you read the poem.

PULLIN' SEINE

Splash!	Afternoon tide roll in.
Heave!	Fishermen pullin' seine.
Come on!	Jasmine pulls me along.
Grab!	de nets like we big and strong.
Sink!	our feet deep down in de sand.
Hold!	on tight with both we hands.
Pull!	and tug and pull some more.
Show!	de fish who go win this war.
Crash!	We fall and de fish laughin'.
Grunt!	We up and pullin' again.
Wet!	and sandy through and through.
Oh no!	I wonder what Mama go do.
Look!	A big wave rollin' in.
Hurray!	Is now we bound to win!

—Lynn Joseph

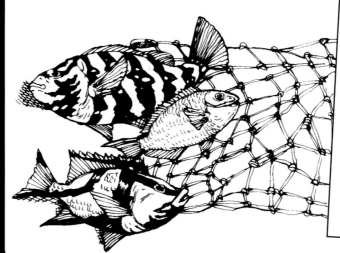

DEVELOPING LITERACY
GROUP TALK & WRITING

MULTICULTURAL FOCUS

Building Language Pride
PROMOTING SELF-ESTEEM Just as teachers build self-esteem by respecting the home languages of the children in their classrooms, so they promote a sense of self-worth by recognizing and validating the variations of English that are spoken by their students. Hearing dialects in the classroom gives children pride in themselves and their cultural backgrounds.

Use "Pullin' Seine" to begin an exploration of dialects. Discuss why the poet spelled certain words the way she did. Compare the sounds of "pullin' seine" to "pulling seine" and "deep down in de sand" to "deep down in the sand." Talk about features of dialects: changes in the beginnings and endings of words (*pullin'*, *de*), differences in pronunciation (*park, pahk; wash, warsh*), the use of different words to name the same thing (*soda, pop; sack, bag*). Encourage children to provide examples from their own speech.

Now, ask each child to write a sentence or phrase phonetically in his or her own dialect. Help children listen carefully to their own speech, and they will begin to see that everyone speaks in a dialect. Then, ask each child to trade sentences with a partner. Each partner reads aloud what the other has written while the author decides whether he or she succeeded in getting down the exact sounds of the words.

22

I AM A SHELL DANCER

I am a shell dancer
I am good at what I do
and beautiful

I am a beautiful
shell dancer
I dance until the tide comes in
for I live by the sea
The rain comes down and blesses
my feet as I dance

The rain spirit is happy
I dance in his honor and the sea's
for the shells are my friends
and the rain
and the sea

—*Beverly WhiteBear, 4th grade*
Big Pine, California

DEVELOPING LITERACY
DRAMATIC INTERPRETATION—Choral Reading

Serenade of the Sea
For a choral reading of "Sea Timeless Song," divide
the class into four groups. A narrator reads the first
three lines of each verse; then, all four groups say
the first "sea timeless," with one group dropping out
each time the phrase is repeated. (The last four lines
of each verse become softer and softer as fewer
children say them.)

23

SEA TIMELESS SONG

Hurricane come
and hurricane go
but sea—sea timeless
sea timeless
sea timeless
sea timeless
sea timeless

Hibiscus bloom
then dry-wither so
but sea—sea timeless
sea timeless
sea timeless
sea timeless
sea timeless

Tourist come
and tourist go
but sea—sea timeless
sea timeless
sea timeless
sea timeless
sea timeless

—*Grace Nichols*

24

Mawlid al-Nabi (may fall any
time of year, following the
Muslim calendar, which is
strictly lunar)

MAWLID AL-NABI*

Mawlid is a very happy day.
We dress up the house
With the names of the Prophet.
We eat special food,
We pray
And we remember.
We light candles
And light up the night.
We sing the praises
Of the Prophet Muhammad
Because it's his birthday.

—*Karam Sperling, age 8*
Santa Cruz, California

***Mawlid al-Nabi:** pronounced *MOW-* (rhymes
with *how*) *lid ahl-NAH-bee*; for more information
see **CultureShare**

CULTURESHARE Mawlid al-Nabi, the celebration of
the Prophet Muhammed's (also spelled *Muhammad,
Mohammed*) birthday, takes place on the twelfth day of
the month of Rabi I in the Islamic calendar. Unlike the
two great Eids (see entries for February 23 and May 20),
it is not an observance mandated by the Quran (*kuh-
RAHN*; also spelled *Koran*); it has more of the feeling
of a popular festival. Speeches about Muhammed's
life are given at gatherings and special dinners. The
festivities and gift-giving surrounding this celebration
are particularly appealing to children.

25

GRANDMA AND THE THUNDER [B]

I hear Ah-Pau* in the kitchen
cooking thunder in her wok.
I hear it rolling and clattering
    over the fire
like some live animal. Ah-Pau
pushes the hair from her eyes,
stands away as it hisses
garlic and scallion, bok-toy
    and "black cloud,"
breathing black mushroom, choong-toy
"snow cloud" and snowpea,*
    snorting and rocking
like some heavenly dragon. Gently
she soothes it to a simmer, talking
to it softly, asking it to behave.
Steam rises beneath her spatula.
Storm-scent clings to her hair.

—Sarah Chan

*Ah-Pau *(ah-pow):* Mandarin for "grandmother"
*bok-toy . . . snow pea: various vegetables used in Chinese
  cooking

A WORD FROM THE POET "When I wrote this poem," says
Sarah Chan, "I was playing with a lot of sounds. Those sounds
were not just the sounds of cooking, but also the sounds of
being Chinese and growing up Chinese." The poem is based
on Chan's many recollections of her grandmother cooking for
the family.

26

The lyrics below can be sung to the tune of "Alouette" or read as a choral reading,
with everyone reading the "ravioli" lines and individuals reading other lines.

[Y] RAVIOLI*

Ravioli, ravioli—
Ravioli, that's the stuff for me.
Do you have it on your sleeve?
Yes, I have it on my sleeve.
On your sleeve?
On my sleeve.
Ravioli, ravioli—
Ravioli, that's the stuff for me.

Do you have it on your pants?
Yes, I have it on my pants.
On your pants?
On my pants.
On your sleeve?
On my sleeve.
Ravioli, ravioli—
Ravioli, that's the stuff for me.

Do you have it on your shoe?
Yes, I have it on my shoe.
On your shoe?
On my shoe.
On your pants?
On my pants.
On your sleeve?
On my sleeve.
Ravioli, ravioli—
Ravioli, that's the stuff for me.

—Unknown

*ravioli *(rah-vee-O-lee):* a traditional Italian dish made
  from squares of spicy meat- or cheese-filled dough

DEVELOPING LITERACY
ORAL COMPOSING

Tasty Tunes
When children are familiar with the cumulative pattern
of "Ravioli," challenge them to add new articles of
clothing, or other places the ravioli might be, as they
sing the song. For other renditions, children can
change *ravioli* to a dish from their own cultures.

For **students acquiring English**, build a list from the
bottom up (since the song adds each new place at
the beginning of the list, not the end); as each word
on the list is sung, point to the word and pantomime
the locale it names. This combination of accumulation
and repetition is a great vocabulary builder.

Finally, children might explore the whole idea of
"piggyback songs." People often put original lyrics to
familiar melodies from their own and other cultures (for
example, "On Top of Spaghetti," sung to the tune of
"On Top of Old Smoky"). Choose a melody like "Row,
Row, Row Your Boat" or "Twinkle, Twinkle, Little Star"
and invite children to write their own lyrics. They might
create a piggyback song to sing as they tackle a
classroom chore or form lines to go out for recess. For
more information about, and ideas for, piggyback
songs, see *Piggyback Songs for School* by Jean Warren
and Gayle Bittinger (Warren, 1991).

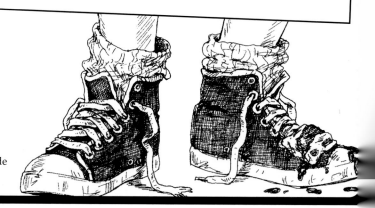

27

COOKING FOR SHABBAS*
WITH MY FAMILY

*Mom is simmering brisket on the stove
in a heavy pan, and the silver onions
and dark paprika drip down into gravy
I will sop up with* **challah***
on **bubbe's*** *old china plate.
I toss the raisins into the glass
casserole of rice* **kugel*** *that will bake
firm and sweet, freckled
with cinnamon on top.
Grandma is nearby,
drawn down from heaven
by familiar smells from the oven,
and Mom mutters to her,
the table cloth flutters a little,
I lift a spoon of honey into the air
to share with Grandma who loves
to cook with us, who still likes
to supervise the soup.*

—Judith W. Steinbergh

*__Shabbas (SHAH-bahs):__ Yiddish for "sabbath"; the Jewish sabbath, which starts at sundown Friday and lasts until sunset on Saturday, is often celebrated with a special meal

*__challah (KHAH-lah):__ braided bread traditionally served on the Sabbath

*__bubbe (BUH-bee):__ Yiddish for "grandmother" or other respected older woman, from the Yiddish word *bubeleh* (BUH-beh-leh) and Russian and Slavic *baba* (BAH-buh). Also used as a general term of endearment

*__kugel (KOO-gel):__ a pudding-like side dish which can be made from potatoes, onions, and spices; or from noodles or rice with raisins and cinnamon

28

Before presenting this poem, discuss with children the traditional Mexican way of making hot chocolate by mixing it vigorously with a *molinillo (moh-lee-NEE-yoh)*, held between the palms of the hands and made to twirl very fast by rubbing the hands together. Then present the rhyme, accompanying it with rhythmic handrubbing that becomes frenzied at the end. Even in the English version, pronounce *chocolate* the Spanish way: *choh-coh-LAH-teh.*

RIMA DE CHOCOLATE/
CHOCOLATE RHYME

*Uno, dos, tres, cho-
Uno, dos, tres, -co-
Uno, dos, tres, -la-
Uno dos, tres, -te
Bate, bate chocolate.*

—Traditional Mexican rhyme

*One, two three, cho-
One, two, three, -co-
One, two, three, -la-
One two, three, -te
Churn the* **chocolate.**

29

A RIDDLE TO CHEW ON

*Not just a food—
It can also be a
plate or a spoon.
It's a ___?___.*

(tortilla)

—Based on a Nahuatl
traditional riddle

ACROSS THE CURRICULUM
SOCIAL STUDIES & SCIENCE & READING

Pancakes Everywhere!
EXPLORING CULTURE Tortillas, crepes, focaccia bread. Poori, blintzes, blini. Flapjacks, lefse, langos. Lavash, pita, pancakes. People all over the world eat flat, round breads in many variations. When children learn about such similarities, they discover common threads in the daily lives of people everywhere and begin to put their own cultures in a wider perspective.

Make a list of all the types of pancakes the class can think of; include the country (or countries) where each version is made. Groups of children can then work with adult leaders to prepare various kinds of pancakes, sharing the results in a tasting session. Encourage children to compile copies of the recipes into cookbooks, with additional information about traditions or history.

Content-Area ESL
Students acquiring English can demonstrate a recipe and cooking techniques with which they are familiar, while more-fluent speakers narrate the demonstration.

To learn more about how people cook the same types of staple foods in many different ways, read aloud or have children read *Bread, Bread, Bread* by Ann Morris (Lothrop, Lee & Shepard, 1989) and *Everybody Cooks Rice* by Norah Dooley (Carolrhoda, 1991).

30

31

WHAT SHALL I PACK IN THE BOX MARKED "SUMMER"?

A handful of wind that I caught with a kite
A firefly's flame in the dark of the night
The green grass of June that I tasted with toes
The flowers I knew from the tip of my nose
The clink of the ice cubes in pink lemonade
The fourth of July Independence parade!
The sizzle of hot dogs, the fizzle of coke
Some pickles and mustard and barbecue smoke
The print of my fist in the palm of my mitt,
As I watched for the batter to strike out or hit
The splash of the water, the top-to-toe cool
Of a stretch-and-kick trip through a blue swimming pool
The tangle of night songs that slipped through my screen
Of crickets and insects too small to be seen
The seed pods that formed on the flowers to say
That summer was packing her treasures away.

—*Bobbi Katz*

CRICKETS

Crickets
Talk
In the tall
Grass
All
Late summer
Long.
When
Summer
Is gone,
The dry
Grass
Whispers
Alone.

—*Valerie Worth*

DEVELOPING LITERACY
LISTENING TO VISUALIZE & WRITING

MULTICULTURAL FOCUS

Memory Box
To capitalize on the wonderful word pictures in this poem, divide the class into groups, with each group creating a big book. Give each child one or more lines from the poem to copy and illustrate. Assemble the pages into big books that can be shared with other classes.

PROMOTING SELF-ESTEEM Children can use the frame of the poem to hold on to their memories of a season ("What Shall I Pack in the Box Marked 'Winter'?"), address a difficult emotion ("What Shall I Pack in the Box Marked 'Sad'?"), or organize their thoughts on a certain theme ("What Shall I Pack in the Box Marked 'Heritage'?").

Introducing children to the idea of taking stock of their thoughts or emotions in private writing gives them a tool for recognizing and valuing these personal parts of their lives.

RESOURCES AND INDEXES

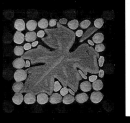

HOW-TO DIRECTIONS

HOW TO MAKE PAPER LANTERNS

Use the following instructions to help children make paper lanterns.
(See **Journey to the Moon,** September 14). You will need a 9" x 12" piece of colored construction paper, a pencil, a ruler, glue or a stapler, and red or yellow tissue paper.

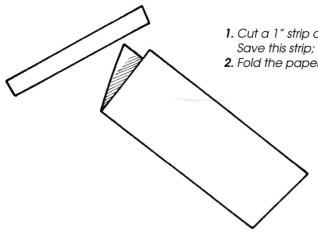

1. Cut a 1" strip off the 9" end of the construction paper. Save this strip; it will be the handle of the lantern.
2. Fold the paper in half lengthwise.

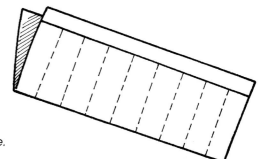

3. Draw a dark line along the length of the folded piece, about 1" from the "open" end.
4. Use a ruler and pencil to make cutting lines (about 1" apart) from the fold to the dark line.

5. Cut along these lines just to the dark line.

6. Unfold the paper and glue or staple together the two 9" ends to form a cylinder.

7. Place a slightly crushed piece of tissue paper inside the lantern for make-believe light.
8. Staple the strip of paper (from step 1) onto the lantern as a handle.

Taller lanterns can be made by folding the 9" sides of the paper together before cutting, rather than folding it lengthwise. 12" x 18" pieces of construction paper can be used for larger lanterns.

HOW TO MAKE A SIMPLE PIÑATA

Here's a way children can make a simple type of piñata that they can use for Cinco de Mayo festivities. (See **A Tradition Meant to Be Broken,** May 5). You'll need lightweight paper bags, craft items (such as magic markers, stickers, glitter, crepe-paper streamers), and a long piece of yarn. You will also need a collection of small treats—edible or inedible—to put in the piñatas, and rulers or long sticks.

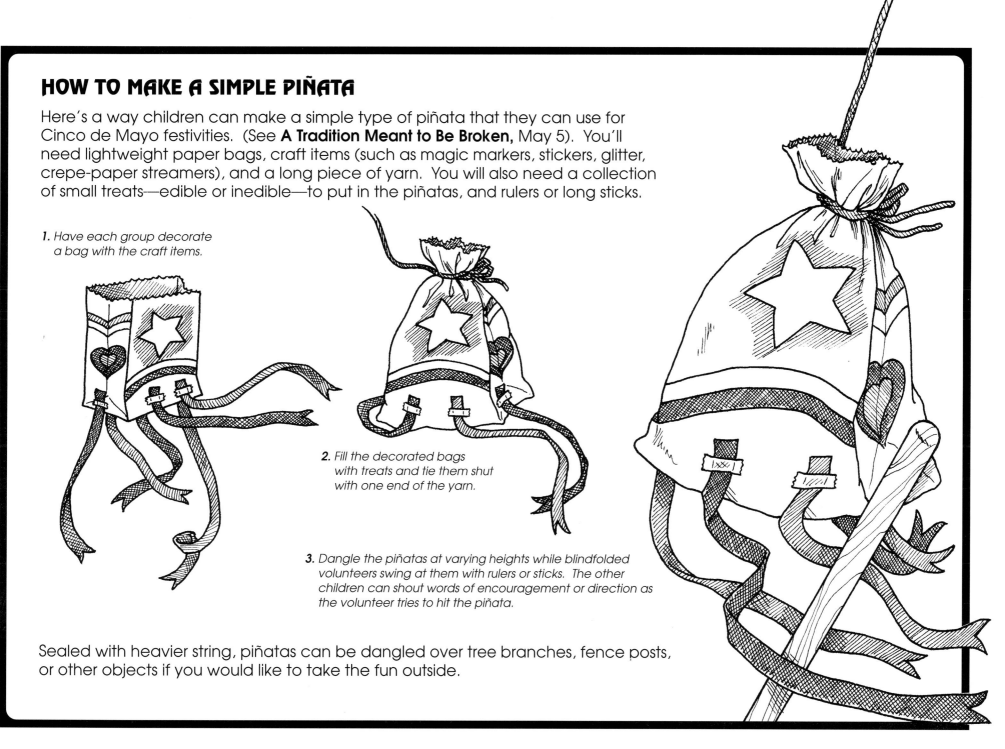

1. *Have each group decorate a bag with the craft items.*

2. *Fill the decorated bags with treats and tie them shut with one end of the yarn.*

3. *Dangle the piñatas at varying heights while blindfolded volunteers swing at them with rulers or sticks. The other children can shout words of encouragement or direction as the volunteer tries to hit the piñata.*

Sealed with heavier string, piñatas can be dangled over tree branches, fence posts, or other objects if you would like to take the fun outside.

HOW TO MAKE A HARDBACK BOOK

The following directions will help children make a durable book that will last through many readings. (See **Book of Life,** May 21–25). You'll need scissors, oaktag or cardboard, vinyl contact paper, typing paper, a long-arm stapler, and 2" wide cloth tape (optional).

1. For the book covers, cut a 9" x 12" piece of oaktag or cardboard in half to create two 6" x 9" pieces.

2. Cut two 9" x 11" pieces of contact paper, peel the backing off the vinyl, and carefully center the oaktag on the sticky side. Fold the corners of the vinyl in and the sides over.

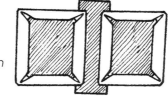

3. Lay both covers on the sticky side of an 11" strip of vinyl (or an 11" piece of cloth tape). Leave a 1/2" space between the covers and equal lengths of the strip at top and bottom. Then, fold the strip over at top and bottom.

4. To make a 16-page book (counting endpapers), fold four pieces of 8 1/2" x 11" typing paper in half. Unfold the paper and use a long-arm stapler to staple the pages together in three places along the fold line.

5. Center the folded pages on the strip of vinyl or cloth tape. Press firmly. Close the covers and smooth.

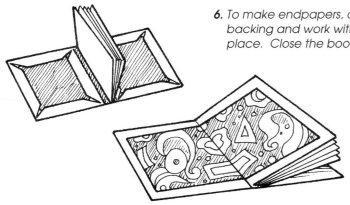

6. To make endpapers, cut two 8 1/2" x 11" pieces of vinyl. Peel off the backing and work with a partner to position each piece and press it into place. Close the book and firmly smooth down the covers.

7. Write the book's title on a self-adhesive label or small piece of paper and glue it to the front cover. Add a picture if you like.

8. When children write stories, copy them onto small pieces of paper that can be glued to the pages of the book. Remember to leave room for any pictures you want to add, and don't forget the title, copyright, and dedication pages.

HOW TO MAKE A MIXED-UP ANIMAL BOOK

Use the following instructions to construct a "mixed-up" animal book.
(See **Mixed-Up Critters,** July 1–3). You will need 11" x 17" paper, scissors, a hole-punch,
pencils, yarn or shoestring, crayons or magic markers, a ruler, tape, and oaktag.

1. *Make a photocopying master using an 11" x 17" piece of paper.*
Draw a line down the center of the paper the long way so
that it is divided into two equal strips, 5 1/2" x 17". Draw lines
that divide each 17" strip into thirds. Make copies on white paper
and cut them in half the long way. Give each child one 17" strip.

2. *Children can draw animals on the strip, putting the head in the left cell,*
the body in the middle cell, and the tail in the right cell. Children can
then color the animal.

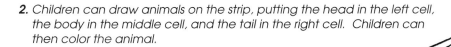

3. *Reinforce the top edge of each strip with clear tape. Put the pages*
between oaktag covers, punch holes along the top edge, and tie a piece
of yarn or shoestring through each hole. Then, cut each page of the book
in thirds along the cell lines.

As children turn the pages of the book, they can create mixed-up
combinations of animal body parts.

When the sun comes up

I set out

for the _____

when the sun comes up,

for I am the _____

the working _____

when the sun comes up.

© Hampton-Brown Books

The United States and Spanish-Speaking Countries of Latin America

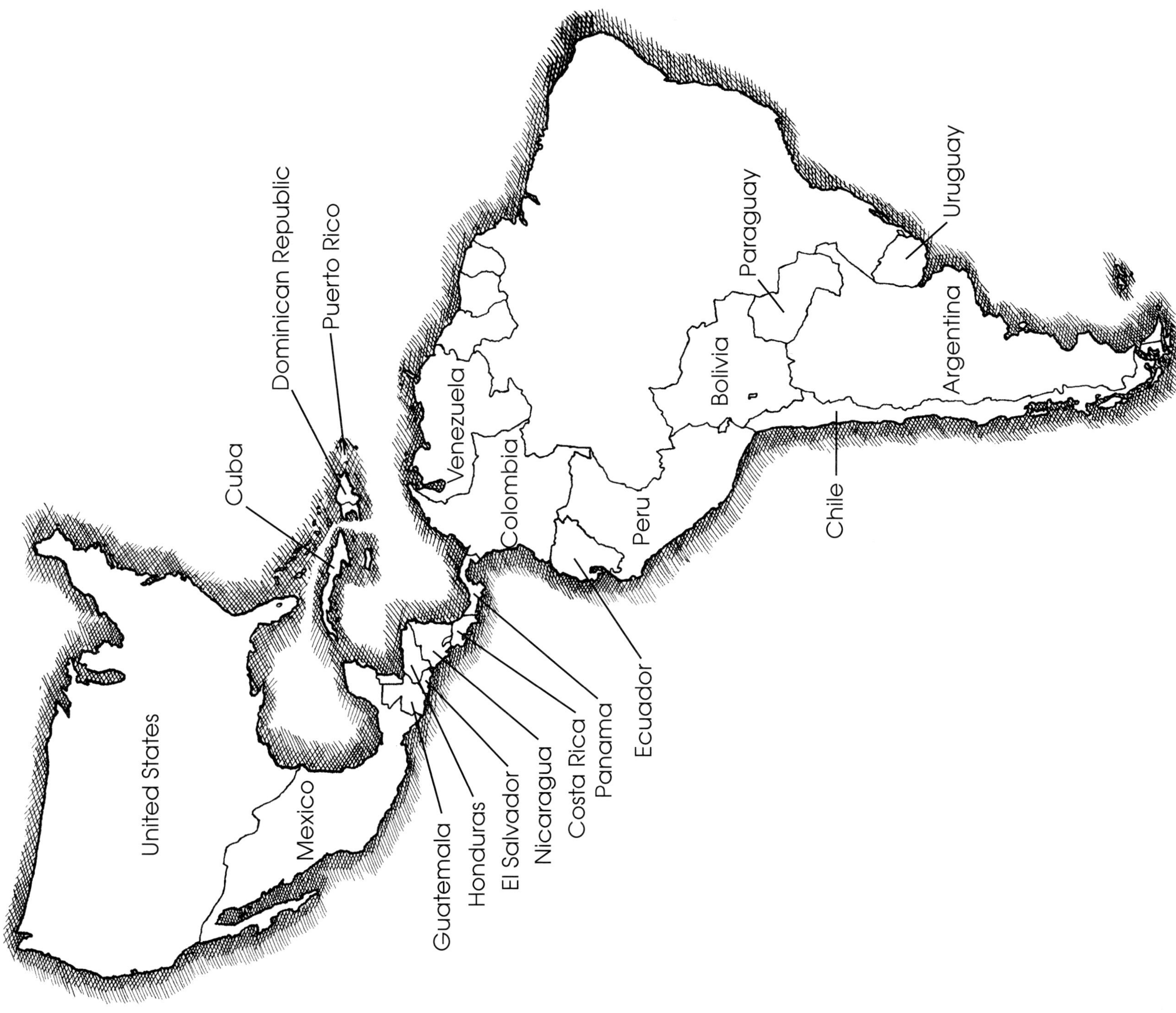

© Hampton-Brown Books

United States

Mexico

Cuba

Dominican Republic

Puerto Rico

Guatemala

Honduras

El Salvador

Nicaragua

Costa Rica

Panama

Ecuador

Venezuela

Colombia

Peru

Bolivia

Paraguay

Chile

Argentina

Uruguay

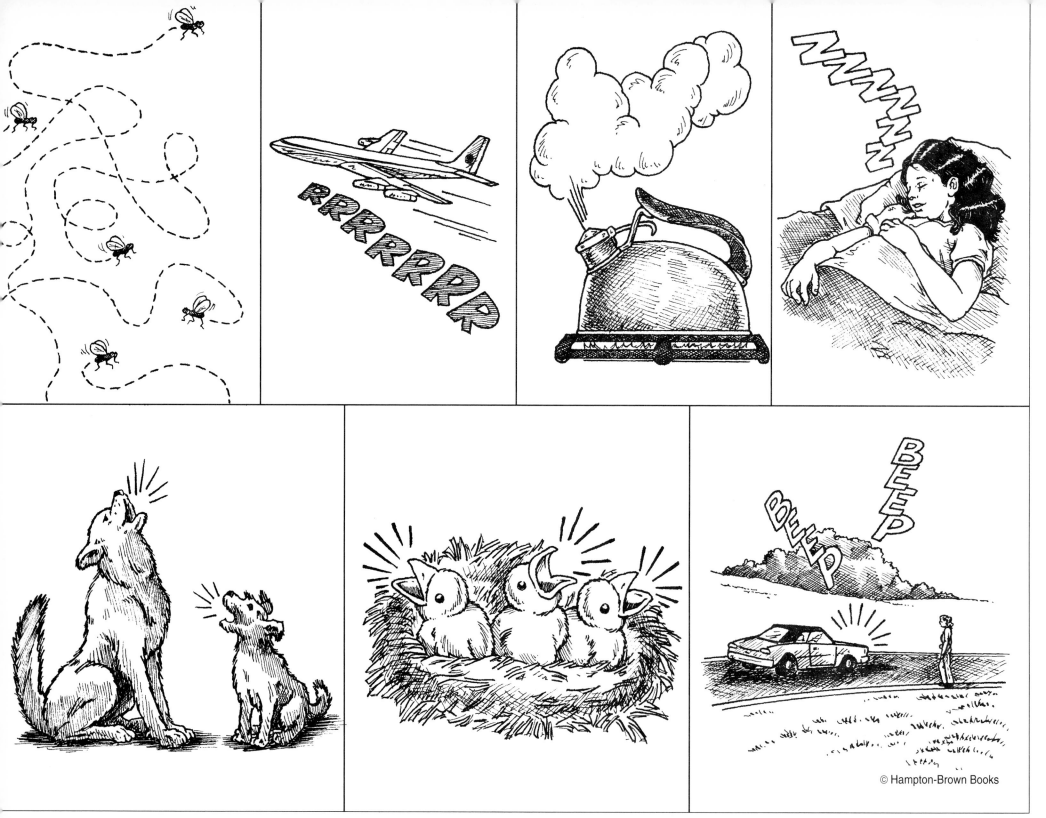

© Hampton-Brown Books

© Hampton-Brown Books

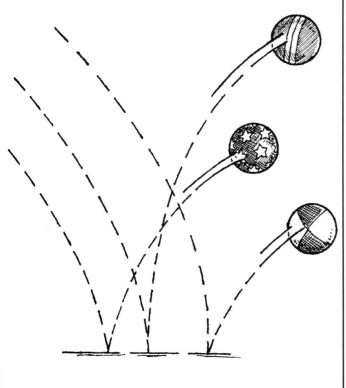
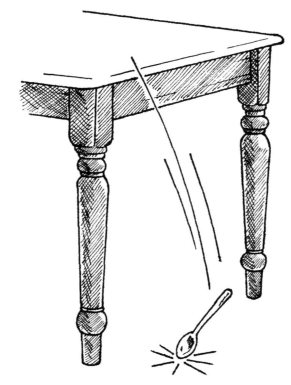

© Hampton-Brown Books

I'm getting a

And I'm getting a

And I'm getting to

And I'm getting to

And I'm getting to

And I'm getting to think that _____ could be hard.

Sunny

Rainy

Snowy

Cloudy

Foggy

Windy

© Hampton-Brown Books

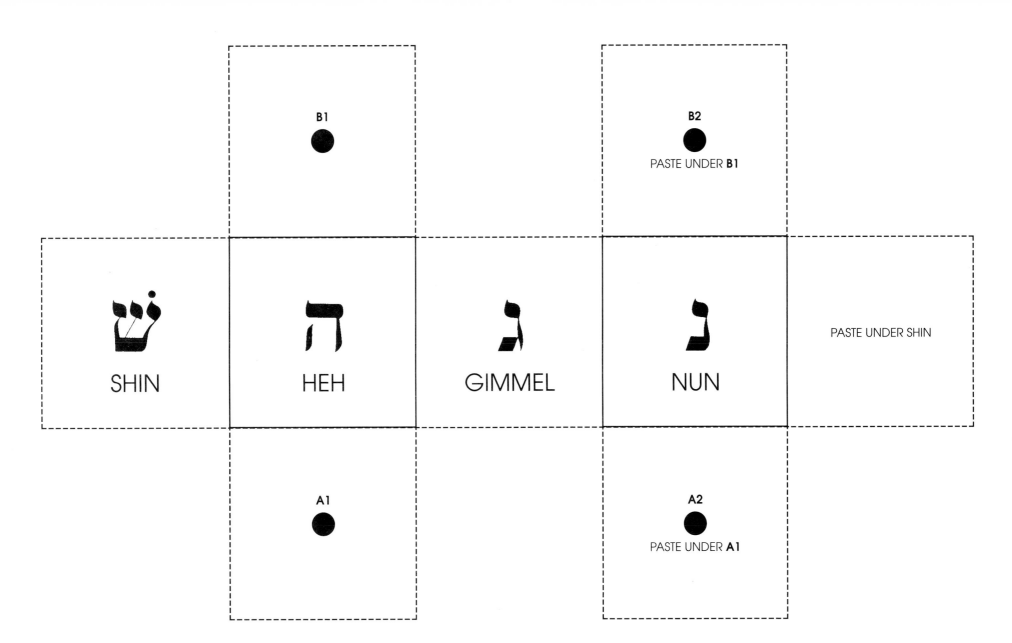

NOTE: For best results, copy the pattern onto lightweight card stock.

1. *Carefully cut out the pattern on the dotted lines.*
2. *Make holes at both spots marked A and both spots marked B.*
3. *Fold the dreydel on the solid lines and paste it together.*
4. *Gently push a pencil through holes A and B.*

© Hampton-Brown Books

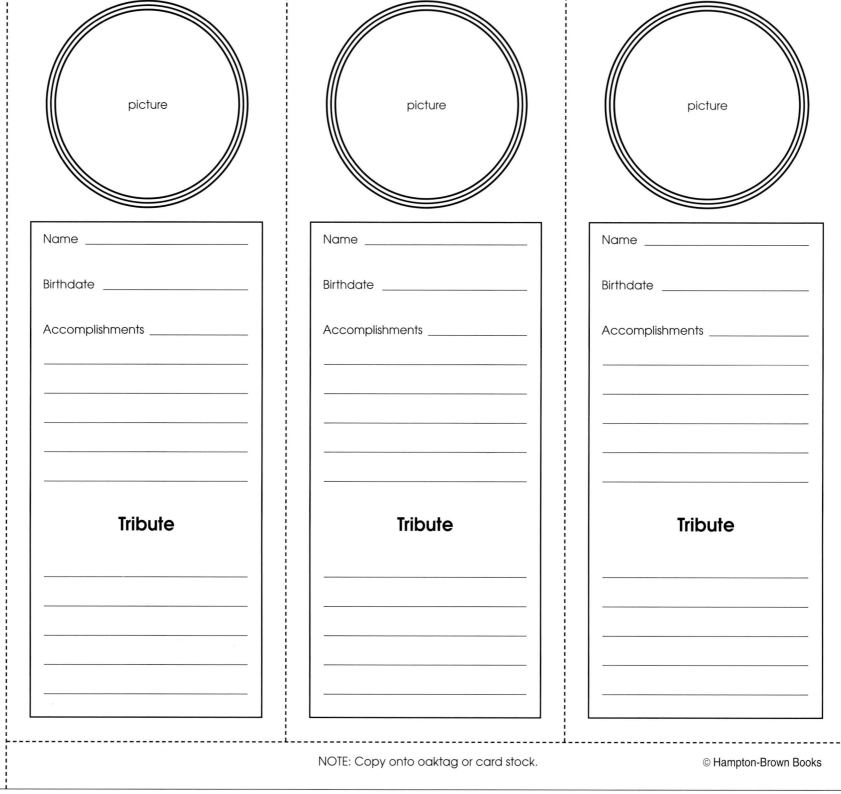

picture   picture   picture

Name _____   Name _____   Name _____

Birthdate _____   Birthdate _____   Birthdate _____

Accomplishments _____   Accomplishments _____   Accomplishments _____

_____   _____   _____

_____   _____   _____

_____   _____   _____

_____   _____   _____

Tribute   **Tribute**   **Tribute**

_____   _____   _____

_____   _____   _____

_____   _____   _____

_____   _____   _____

NOTE: Copy onto oaktag or card stock.

© Hampton-Brown Books

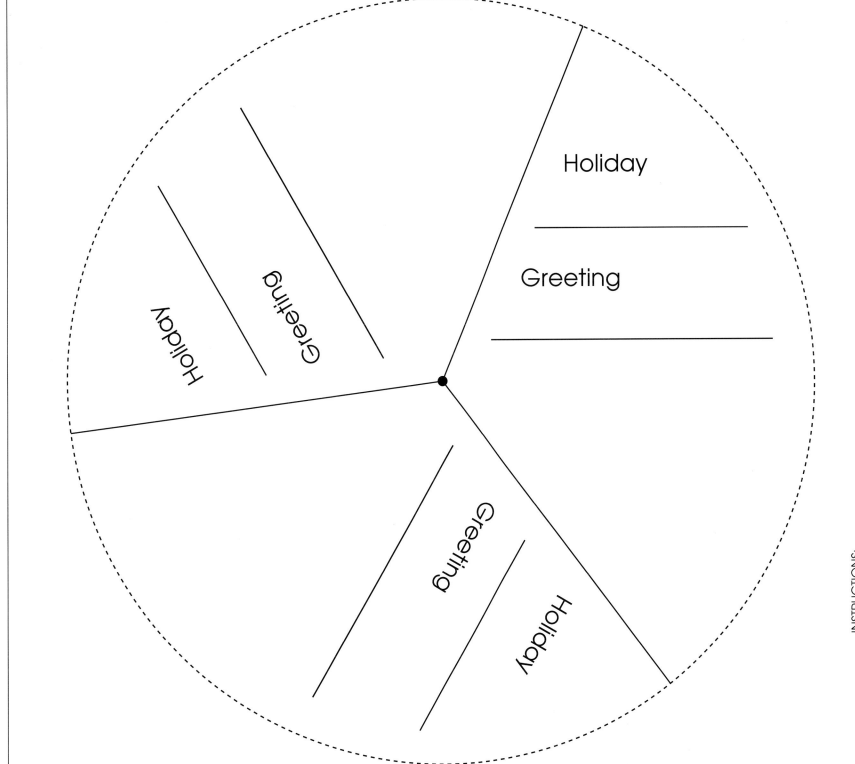

Holiday

Greeting

Greeting

Holiday

Greeting

Holiday

INSTRUCTIONS:
1. Copy this pattern and the one on **Activity Sheet 11** onto card stock.
2. Cut out both pieces and cut a small hole in the center of each, for a brad.
3. Fill in the blanks and add art or sentences in each section of this pattern.
4. Put the partial circle over the full circle, align the holes, and insert a brad, to create a "culture wheel."

© Hampton-Brown Books

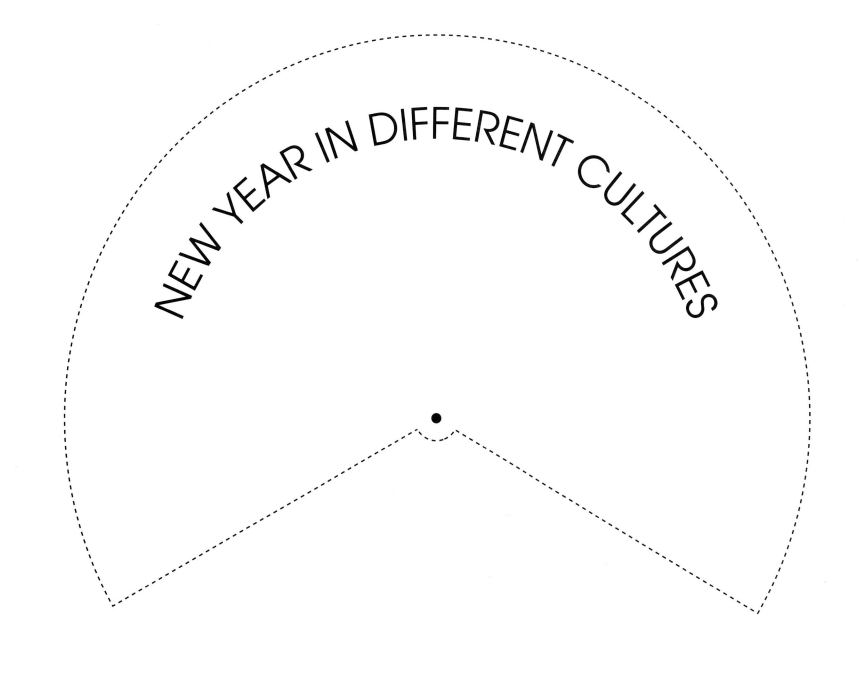

NEW YEAR IN DIFFERENT CULTURES

© Hampton-Brown Books

ACTIVITY SHEET 11 *LUNAR NEW YEAR ✦ February 11–13*

MAKE-A-NEW-FRIEND BINGO
Find someone who . . . .

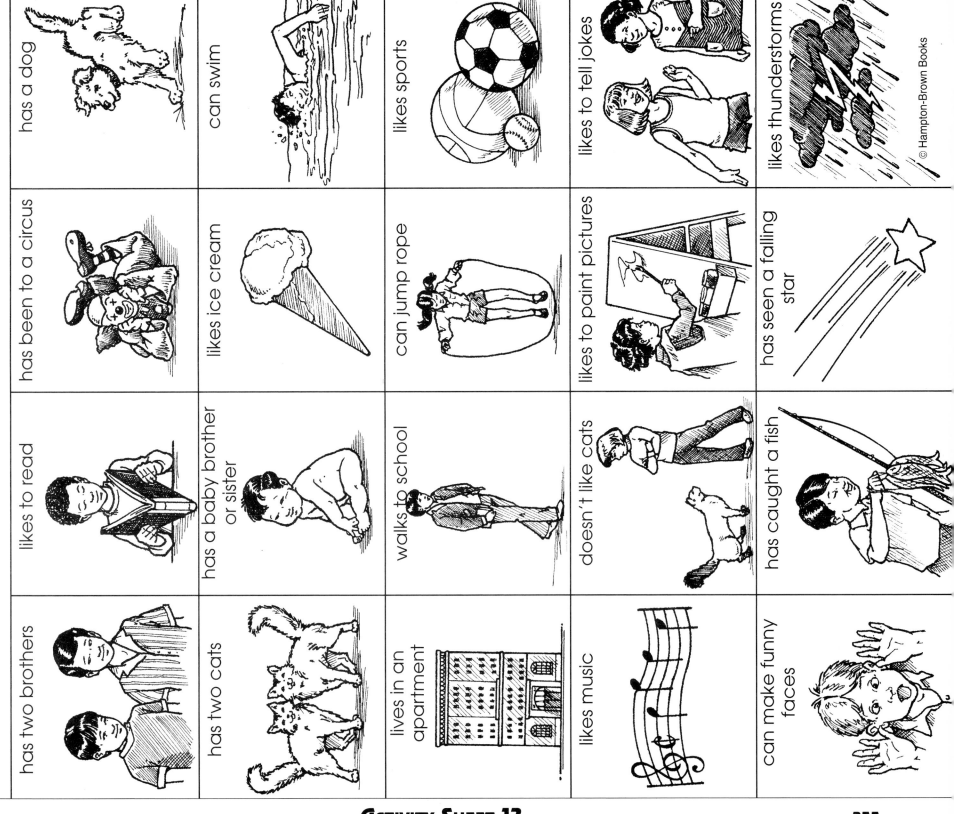

has a dog	can swim	likes sports	likes to tell jokes	likes thunderstorms
has been to a circus	likes ice cream	can jump rope	likes to paint pictures	has seen a falling star
likes to read	has a baby brother or sister	walks to school	doesn't like cats	has caught a fish
has two brothers	has two cats	lives in an apartment	likes music	can make funny faces

© Hampton-Brown Books

YELLOW

Green is _____

and red is _____

and yellow is _____

_____ is brown,

yellow _____ .

and blue is _____ ;

yellow _____ .

_____ are white,

black, pink, or mocha;

yellow's _____ .

© Hampton-Brown Books

INTERVIEW SHEET

Here are some questions to ask during your interview.

Name _____

How old are you? _____

When you were my age, what did you hope to do or
accomplish when you grew up?

_____

_____

_____

_____

(Remember to thank the person you interviewed for taking
the time to talk to you.)

© Hampton-Brown Books

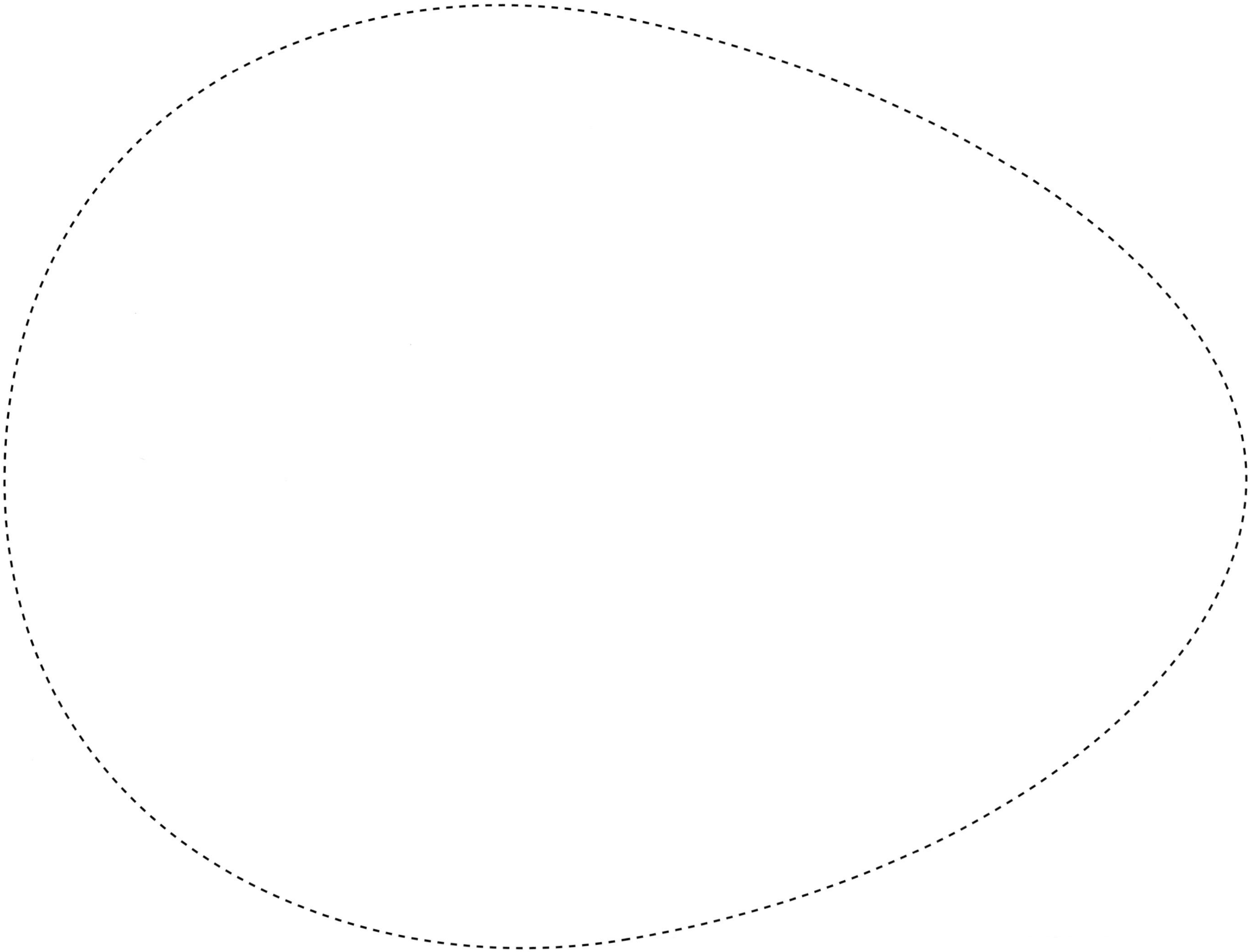

© Hampton-Brown Books

ACTIVITY SHEET 15

ON WHEELS

IN THE AIR

bicycle

car

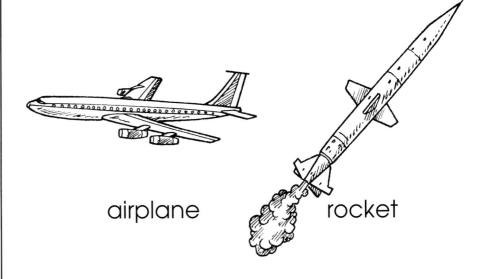

airplane   rocket

motorcycle

wheelchair

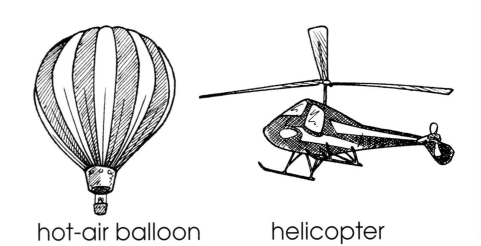

hot-air balloon   helicopter

© Hampton-Brown Books

ON OR IN THE WATER

ON TRACKS

submarine

ship

tug boat

inner tube

subway

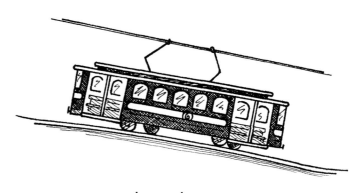

street car

train

© Hampton-Brown Books

OBSERVATION SHEET

The bug I saw looked like this:

It had _____ legs.
(number)

It had _____ wings.
(number)

Its body had _____ segments, or parts.
(number)

It _____ have antennae.
(did/did not)

© Hampton-Brown Books

CALENDAR CORRELATIONS

A Chorus of Cultures is organized around the Gregorian calendar. Named for Pope Gregory XII, who modified the Julian calendar that had been used in Europe since 46 C.E., the Gregorian calendar is by far the most commonly used for business and international matters. However, many religious and cultural commemorations are based on calendars other than the Gregorian. As a result, the exact dates of these commemorations on the Gregorian calendar change from year to year. The charts on page 265 show the dates on the Gregorian calendar when the holidays that appear in this book occur for the years 1993–2003. Dates for other commemorations can be obtained through the library or local religious or cultural organizations.

First, a note about some of the terminology:

◆ **A "lunar" calendar** is one that follows the cycles of the moon. The moon takes about 29½ days to complete its cycle from new to full to new. Twelve of these cycles, or lunar months, take 354 days. Therefore, a calendar that is strictly lunar records a 354-day year. The Islamic calendar is a lunar calendar.

◆ **A "solar" calendar** is based on the amount of time it takes the earth to make one complete revolution around the sun—just slightly more than 365 days. The Gregorian calendar is a solar calendar.

◆ **A "luni-solar" calendar** has months based on the moon's cycle—i.e. 29 or 30 days—with a periodic correction of extra days or months (in **leap years**) to bring the lunar measurement in line with the solar cycle. The Chinese and Hebrew calendars are both luni-solar.

THE CHINESE CALENDAR

Currently about 4,700 years old, the Chinese calendar is history's longest continuously used calendar. Made up of 12-year patterns (which themselves make up 60-year cycles), the Chinese calendar has a leap year every 2–3 years, with an extra month being added to the usual 12 so the new year always starts with the second new moon after the beginning of winter. The Chinese calendar is used today to determine the dates for traditional holidays and festivals of the Chinese culture and for those of the various other Asian cultures historically influenced by China: Korean, Vietnamese, and Japanese cultures, for example.

1981	1993	Rooster	(Yu)
1982	1994	Dog	(Siuh)
1983	1995	Pig	(Hai)
1984	1996	Rat	(Tse)
1985	1997	Ox	(Chau)
1986	1998	Tiger	(Yin)
1987	1999	Rabbit	(Mau)
1988	2000	Dragon	(Shin)
1989	2001	Snake	(Se)
1990	2002	Horse	(Wu)
1991	2003	Sheep	(Wi)
1992	2004	Monkey	(Shin)

More to Know

Each year in the Chinese calendar's 12-year pattern is named for an animal. Traditionally, it is believed that people's personalities reflect the characteristics of the animal of the year of their birth. Listed to the right are the animals (and their Chinese names) corresponding to the years 1981–2004 on the Gregorian calendar.

THE HEBREW CALENDAR

The Hebrew (or Jewish) calendar takes as its reference point the creation of the world, which, according to Jewish tradition, was 3,760 years and 3 months B.C.E. Many calendars distributed by synagogues and Jewish organizations have both the Gregorian and Hebrew years, months, and days listed on them; Jewish holidays are determined by the luni-solar calendar (which, like the Chinese calendar, adds a month every 2–3 years to account for the discrepancy between lunar and solar cycles). The months of the Hebrew calendar are:

Tishri (TISH-ree)
Heshvan (hesh-VON)
Kislev (kiss-LEHV)
Tevet (TAY-vess)
Shebat (sheh-BOT)
Adar (ah-DAHR)
 (**Ve-Adar** (VAY-ah-DAHR), or
  Adar II, in leap years)

Nisan (nee-SAHN)
Iyyar (ee-YAHR)
Sivan (SIV-on)
Tammuz (tah-MOOZ)
Av (awv, ahv)
Elul (eh-LOOL)

More to Know

Days in the Jewish tradition start at sundown. This means the dates given in the chart on page 265 are for the first *full* day of commemoration. For example, in 1993, the first *seder* for Passover was held on the evening of April 5, 1993, even though the first full day of observance is listed as April 6.

THE ISLAMIC CALENDAR

The traditional date of Mohammed's flight to freedom from Mecca to Medina provides the reference point for the Islamic calendar. Called the *Hejira* (heh-JY-ruh), this flight is said to have ended at sunset, July 16, 622 C.E. Islamic-calendar years are referred to as "the year (or *era*) of the Hejira." There is one day added for leap years; like the Chinese and Hebrew calendars, it appears every 2–3 years, and it comes at the end of the last month of the Moslem year. The Islamic-calendar months are listed at the left.

Muharram (moo-HAHR-em)
Safar (suh-FAHR)
Rabi I (RUH-bee)
Rabi II
Jumada I (joo-MOD-uh)
Jumada II
Rajab (RUH-job)
Sha'ban (sheh-BON)
Ramadan (RAM-uh-dan)
Shawwal (sheh-WAHL)
Dhu al-Qada (dool-KOD-ah)
Dhu al-Hijjah (dool-HIDJ-ah)

More to Know
The Muslim day, like the Jewish day, runs from sundown to sundown. Also, because the Muslim calendar is strictly a lunar one, the year is 354 days long (355 in leap years). This means that each date on the Islamic calendar corresponds to an earlier Gregorian date each succeeding year, taking about 33 years to travel backward completely through the Gregorian calendar.

EASTER

The Julian calendar was the official calendar of the Roman government when Christianity gained prominence. Therefore, most Christian religious holidays have fixed dates on the Julian-based Gregorian calendar. However, Easter is one of the Christian Church's "moveable feasts," meaning that it falls on a different day each year; specifically, the first Sunday after the first full moon on or after March 21.

More to Know
The dates listed on the chart are the dates that a majority of Christians will celebrate Easter. The calendars of Eastern Orthodox churches often differ, however, and may vary from these dates.

Chinese-Calendar Holidays, 1993–2003

	1993	1994	1995	1996	1997	1998	1999	2000	2001	2002	2003
Tet Trung Thu	9/30	9/20	9/9	9/27	9/16	10/5	9/24	9/12	10/1	9/21	9/11
Lunar New Year	1/24	2/11	1/31	2/19	2/7	1/28	2/15	2/4	1/24	2/12	2/1
Dragon Boat Festival	6/24	6/13	6/2	6/20	6/9	5/30	6/18	6/6	6/25	6/15	6/4

Hebrew-Calendar Holidays, 1993–2003 (Hebrew years 5754–5764)

	1993 5754	1994 5755	1995 5756	1996 5757	1997 5758	1998 5759	1999 5760	2000 5761	2001 5762	2002 5763	2003 5764
Rosh Hashanah 1 TISHRI	9/16	9/6	9/25	9/14	10/2	9/21	9/11	9/30	9/18	9/7	9/27
Yom Kippur 10 TISHRI	9/25	9/15	10/4	9/23	10/11	9/30	9/20	10/9	9/27	9/16	10/6
Hanukkah 25 KISLEV	12/9	12/28	12/18	12/6	12/24	12/14	12/4	12/22	12/10	11/30	12/20
Purim 14 ADAR or 14 ADAR II	3/7	2/25	3/16	3/5	3/23	3/12	3/2	3/21	3/9	3/26	3/18
Passover (Pesach) 15 NISAN	4/6	3/27	4/15	4/4	4/22	4/11	4/1	4/20	4/8	3/28	4/17

Islamic-Calendar Holidays, 1993–2003 (Years of Hejira 1413–1424)

Ramadan (See also below)	1993 1413 2/22	1994 1414 2/11	1995 1415 1/31	1996 1416 1/21	1997 1417 1/10						
						1998	1999	2000	2001	2002	2003
Eid al-Adha 10 DHU AL-HIJJAH	1413 5/31	1414 5/20	1415 5/9	1416 4/28	1417 4/17	1418 4/7	1419 3/27	1420 3/16	1421 3/5	1422 2/22	1423 2/11
Mawlid al-Nabi 12 RABI I	1414 8/30	1415 8/20	1416 8/9	1417 7/28	1418 7/17	1419 7/6	1420 6/26	1421 6/14	1422 6/4	1423 5/24	1424 5/14
Ramadan						1418 12/30	1419 12/9	1420 12/8	1421 11/26	1422 11/16	1423 11/5	1424 10/26

Easter Dates, 1993–2003

	1993	1994	1995	1996	1997	1998	1999	2000	2001	2002	2003
Easter	4/11	4/3	4/16	4/7	3/30	4/12	4/4	4/23	4/15	3/31	4/20

INDEX OF POEMS APPROPRIATE FOR ESL INSTRUCTION

Students acquiring English may be at any one of four stages in their progression toward fluency. This index lists the poems from *A Chorus of Cultures* appropriate to each of these stages of language acquisition: Pre-Production (Level 1), Early Production (Level 2), Speech Emergence (Level 3), and Intermediate Fluency (Level 4).

POEMS ESPECIALLY APPROPRIATE FOR LEVELS 1 AND 2

Poems in this category have simple language and concrete content.

Y	10/2	Take One Apple
Y	10/19	Ears Hear
	10/29	Wouldn't You?
♪	2/16	I Love Everybody
	2/25	Birthday Candles
	3/5	Yellow
	4/17	The Rabbit
B	4/25	I Love the World
Y	5/1	Maytime Magic
Y	7/23	Sleeping Outdoors
Y	8/26	Ravioli
	8/28	Chocolate Rhyme

Poems in this category have predictable text and a regular rhythm and rhyme scheme that makes them easy to memorize and recite. Many songs and raps fall into this category.

Y	9/5	One, Two, Three, Four, Five
♪	9/6	The Elephants
	9/10	Abuelito
	9/12	Piggy-Back
B	10/18	Sampan
Y	10/20	Song of the Train
♪	10/24	Under One Sky
	10/28	Brooms
	11/1	Cold November
	11/9	Good-Bye, Six—Hello, Seven
Y	11/14	Books to the Ceiling
Y	11/28	Polar Bear
	11/29	The Mitten Song
	12/11	Star-Light, Star-Bright
♪	12/15	Great Big Stars
Y	12/19	Bursting
♪	12/23	My Dreydel
	12/25	Must Be Santa
	12/28	Black Is Beautiful
	1/22	Snow! Snow! Snow!
	1/23	January
	1/24	Snow, Snow
Y	2/14	I Love You Little
	2/27	My First Birthday Gift
♪	3/13	We've Come to the Land
	4/6	April
♪	4/16	Little Spring
B	4/22	The Beautiful
	5/3	Did I Tell You?
	5/8	Rainbows

♪	5/19	Train Is a-Comin'
	5/22	Growing Old
♪	6/7	Jump Shamador
	6/10	I Like To . . .
Y	6/19	Daddy
	6/26	The Dragon Boats
	7/5	I Am Freedom's Child
♪	7/21	Rabbit
	8/16	August Heat
Y	8/17	I'll Tell You Something
	8/17	Bees

Y = Included in the Language Development Chart Set (Yellow Cover) **B** = Included in the Cultural Heritage Chart Set (Brown Cover) ♪ = Included in the Music Tapes

POEMS ESPECIALLY APPROPRIATE FOR LEVEL 3

During the Speech Emergence stage, students "spread their wings" with language, innovating on the patterns they hear, and trying out new ways of expressing themselves. Therefore, poems that allow patterned writing and oral composing are especially useful at this stage. Most of those listed on page 266 as well as these new ones lend themselves to these techniques.

	9/4	Chant of the Working People
	9/7	One, Two, Grow Tall
B	9/24	Little Sister
B	9/27	Borinquen
	10/9	I Am Sun Shining
B	10/13	Pride
	10/23	Hug O' War
Y	11/15	Good Books, Good Times!
	11/23	Opening Corn
	11/25	November
B	12/1	Home
	12/4	Just a Fire
	12/6	Not One Frown
	12/14	De Koven
	12/21	I Am Winter
	12/29	Wrapping Presents
	1/16	Martin Luther King, Jr.
B	2/18	The New Girl
Y	2/26	The Wish
Y	4/2	Way Down South
	4/10	A Spike of Green
	4/11	The Flowers
B ♪	4/12	The Day You Were Born
	5/10	Tommy's Mommy
	5/31	Sunday Morning Lonely
	6/1	M-I-S-S-I-S-S-I-P-P-I
	6/9	What I'll Be When I Grow Up
Y	6/15	Goodnight, Juma
	6/24	June Sunset
	6/29	A Modern Dragon

Y		7/2	Tails
Y	♪	7/25	I Live in a City
Y		8/4	Where Did the Baby Go?
		8/6	When Annie Was Adopted
		8/9	Name Poem

POEMS ESPECIALLY APPROPRIATE FOR LEVEL 4

Poems in this category include some figurative language and more-complex, less obvious patterns, suitable for the increasing sophistication of the intermediate English speaker. These poems also offer more opportunities for structured discussion and continued progress toward more complex writing.

	9/1	Time for School
	9/2	September
Y	9/21	Ooo-Ah, Wanna Piece of Pie
	10/10	Okay Everybody
	10/30	Autumn
B	11/3	Haiku
B	11/6	Family Gifts
	12/26	Kwanzaa Is . . .
B	12/27	My People
Y	12/31	The Year
B	1/1	The New Year
	1/3	I Have a Future
	1/4	Beginning a New Year Means
	1/21	A Winter Song
	1/29	Teasing
	1/30	It's All Around
	2/20	Poem
	3/1	Being Bilingual
	3/3	Crayons
	3/6	Rhinos Purple, Hippos Green
	3/10	Last Laugh
Y	3/12	Tommy
♪	3/18	Many Colors
	3/24	Image

B	3/25	If They Hate Me
Y	4/4	I Am Running in a Circle
Y	4/7	Spring Rain
	5/15	Preferred Vehicles
Y	5/18	Subways Are People
	5/23	Old Friends
	5/27	I Wasn't Born in My Country
B	6/12	Two Little Sisters
B	6/18	My Father
	7/3	The Elephant
	7/16	Another Kid
B	7/17	The Palet Man
	7/24	The Prairie
Y	7/26	Sunrise
	7/29	Rudolph Is Tired of the City
	8/15	The Feast of Lanterns

INDEX OF TITLES

INDEX OF FIRST LINES AND PHRASES

Hooting   10/31
Hurricane come   8/23
I already know where Africa is   9/2
I always like summer   6/22
I am a shell dancer   8/22
I am beside myself   12/20
I am hewn from   7/6
Y I am running in a circle   4/4
I am Sansei.   5/28
I am sun shining.   10/9
I believe in skateboarding   5/17
B I can feel   2/18
I can picture my   12/10
I cannot be hurt anymore.   3/24
Y I cannot remember—   8/4
I don't care if this man is black, blue,   10/22
I dream   9/19
I feel inside   10/14
I have a future in the bottom of my
    heart.   1/3
I have a half-sister   8/7
♪ I have a little dreydel   12/23
B i have looked into   11/3
B I hear Ah-Pau in the kitchen   8/25
I hear the school bell ringin'   6/4
I like me,   7/5
♪ **Y** I live in a city   7/25
♪ I love everybody, I love everybody,   2/16
Y I love you little,   2/14
B I love you, Big World.   4/25
I loved my friend.   2/20
I may be silent, but   10/11
I met a little country girl,   3/9
Y I put a seed into the ground   3/12
I ran a race   4/3
I remember the day   3/11
I say it and feel it's true: 3/1
B I see her in the morning   9/24
I see my future   6/8
B I shall dance tonight.   12/16
I shouldn't tell you this, BUT   12/22
I slip and I slide   2/7

I splash in the ocean   8/20
I stand in the woods   3/28
I stood in front of the class   11/10
I think I can succeed in anything   10/6
I was just another kid   7/16
I washed   3/23
I wasn't born in my country.   5/27
I will not play at tug o' war.   10/23
I wouldn't like it   7/12
I'd like to have a party   12/17
B If children were   1/1
If I could go   10/29
If I were a rope   12/13
If I were the cold weather   1/21
If there's one woman who I've loved in
    my life   4/29
B If they hate me   3/25
If you had a trunk instead of a nose   7/3
Y I'll tell you something   8/17
I'm getting a higher bunk bed.   11/9
In August, when the days are hot,   8/16
In early spring when Samuel plows   11/22
In January   1/23
In our one family, around   12/7
In the morning the city   7/26
♪ In the mountains there's a little spring   4/16
in springtime the violets   3/20
Into Mother's slide trombone   7/19
It is little children like you who will   9/16
It is only with this dancing,   7/13
It is the silence that frightens me so   4/28
It looks like any building   4/19
It must be odd   3/22
It ought to come in April,   3/17
It takes more than saying   2/17
B It's a place   12/1
It's all around us   1/30
It's bedtime and I dream   1/18
It's Christmas time here in my barrio   12/24
It's funny how a fire   12/4
It's Nathaniel talking   8/14
It's small   9/26

I've colored a picture with crayons.   3/3
John be playin'   3/31
Johnny, Johnny Appleseed   10/3
♪ Kakurenbo, suru mono yotto ii de   9/22
♪ **B** Kayitz, kayitz, konchiyah   6/21
Last night at bedtime   1/10
Let me tell you all about me.   6/28
Let the rain kiss you.   4/8
Let's start at the very beginning   3/26
Light is the ink we use   8/19
listen children   2/5
Long ago everything in the world was   3/4
Look down to the ground   7/31
Look out! Look out! You've spilt the ink.   4/1
Lotus seed candy   2/13
Love don't mean all that kissing   12/8
M-i-s-s-i-s-s-i-p-p-i   6/1
B Mama was funny   5/13
♪ Many colors, many colors we see in the
    fields   3/18
Mari and the moon   7/20
Mawlid is a very happy day.   8/24
Me and my Dad   6/16
me and my brother   8/5
Meg, yergoo, yergunnas;   9/7
Mom is simmering brisket on the stove   8/27
Mommy did you bring my flippers   5/10
Mommy,   1/28
Mommy, when I'm big and tall   5/11
Music always playin'   3/29
My ancestors can't see me   11/4
My breath is like mint   12/21
My child, there is much   9/3
My class sang at the retirement home   5/23
My country! Mid-ocean garden,   11/19
My daddy rides me piggy-back.   9/12
B my dark grandmother   5/25
My dream of America   10/27
B My father doesn't live with us.   6/18
My great aunt Marcella   5/24

Y = Included in the Language Development Chart Set (Yellow Cover)   **B** = Included in the Cultural Heritage Chart Set (Brown Cover)   ♪ = Included in the Music Tapes

My hair is as long as a pony's tail   7/14
My horse, fly like a bird   5/16
My love is   2/15
My name is like a music breeze   8/11
My name sounds like a   8/9
My nipa hut is very small,   3/14
B My sister and I are almost the same   8/8
My sister says   3/6
My Tota Man,   9/13
B My tribe is Choctaw and the name   8/13
B Native country like a branch of starfruit
      5/29
♪ **B** Nicely, nicely, nicely, nicely,   11/21
♪ Night from a railroad car window   5/19
9:10 p.m.   12/12
No more swimming   9/1
No one owns   1/31
No quiero oro,   12/18
No sky at all;   1/25
Not just a food—   8/29
♪ O ka leo   5/30
♪ Oh, rabbit on the moon,   7/21
♪ Oh, the voices   5/30
Okay everybody, listen to this: 10/10
Old Man Coyote was going along.   1/6
On stormy days   10/28
On the first day of school the teacher
      asked me   8/12
on paper   11/17
Once a present's wrapped   12/29
once a snowflake fell   2/8
Once after Ramadan,   5/20
Once upon a time there was a fly   8/18
One day after Christmas comes,   12/26
one day I was dumb enough   9/17
♪ One elephant went out to play   9/6
One night, a long, long time ago,   9/14
One, two three, cho-   8/28
One, two, grow tall.   9/7
Y One, two, three, four, five,   9/5
Only those that have traveled the   5/21
Y Ooo-ah, wanna piece of pie,   9/21
Y **B** Orgullosa de mi familia   10/13
Out of a land   4/5

Outside the night sneaks up with cat
      feet.   12/5
Over the river and through the wood,
      11/24
¡Patria!, jardín de la mar,   11/19
Pencil   11/18
people always ask what   11/8
B People keep asking where I come from
      7/9
Pin wheels whirling round   7/4
Plump and golden   12/9
Poetry is like a cascade   10/17
Prairie   7/24
Praying together, we made a new start.
      9/25
B Proud of my family   10/13
¡Qué divertido   12/29
Rabbit in your little hole   4/17
Rain is good   4/6
Rainbows, rainbows everywhere,   5/8
Y Ravioli, ravioli—   8/26
Real friends will share even   2/22
Ride, Sally Ride   3/10
Sakura! sakura! Yayo-i no sora wa   4/18
See the dragon come on a hundred
      legs!   6/30
See the spring sky   3/7
seven snakes   5/9
She begins, and my grandmother joins
      her.   4/9
She came to take   5/12
B Si los niños fuéramos   1/1
Six sad salamanders   8/3
Snow, snow, fly away   1/24
"So what if our parents and you came
      from China?   5/26
So you haven't got a drum, just beat
      your belly.   3/27
Someday   10/21
Sometimes in the cool summer dusk
      7/28
sounds like pulling down a zipper   11/23
B "Soursop, coconut, mango, lime!"   7/17
Splash! Afternoon tide roll in.   8/21

Stale moon, climb down.   9/15
standing before   7/10
Star-light, star-bright   12/11
Y Subways are people—   5/18
Summer's laughter, red and cool   6/23
♪ **B** Summer, summer and a shell,   6/21
Sunshine and weiners and pickles and
      ham,   6/14
Y Take one apple   10/2
Tangled hair, use a comb to unsnarl it.
      5/21
Teasing is being laughed at.   1/29
Tell me something, Grandpa,   9/10
Thank you for the things we have,   11/25
♪ **B** The beautiful things that are in this world
      4/12
Y The city yawns   7/26
The dancers come in the round house.
      7/15
The day is wrapping   6/24
The dragon boats! There they go!   6/26
♪ The earth is my mother—she's good to
      me—   4/26
The first day I came to America,   7/7
The flowers   4/11
The joy of seeing   11/16
The man said,   10/15
The mouth tastes food;   4/20
B The night is beautiful,   12/27
The old man   4/24
The other day   11/11
The reason I like chocolate   11/13
Y The secret of the polar bear   11/28
Y The storm came up so very quick   4/7
The summer started, I played. Soon   3/2
The way I see any hope for later,   1/26
The wind is cool and swift.   9/23
Y The year   12/31
B There are a lot of kids   2/21
B There is a place   9/9
There is no milk   4/3
There is no swimming   6/25
There were so many people   2/3
There's an orange tree out there,   9/29

These buildings are too close to me.
  7/29
They all laughed when I told them   3/10
They didn't give me   2/27
they make   3/16
Thirty days hath September,   9/30
This is the way I like to swim,   6/10
This summer we dare—we climb   we
  6/13
Three stripes   5/2
Through moonlight's milk   7/22
"Thumbs in the thumb-place   11/29
To become a teacher   6/5
Today   6/3
Tommy sits behind me   6/9
Tonight   8/15
♪ Train is a-comin', oh yes,   5/19
Two celebrations   5/20
B Two little sisters went walking one day,
  6/12
♪ Un elefante se balanceaba   9/6
Under my hood I have a hat   11/30
Y Under the dark is a star,   7/23
Uno, dos, tres, cho-   8/28
♪ Usagi, Usagi   7/21
B Waves lap lap   10/18
Y Way down south where bananas grow,
  4/2
We have a secret, just we three,   4/15
♪ We shall overcome, we shall overcome,
  9/18
Wealthy the man who has true friends.
  2/22
Wear it   3/21
Went to the corner   10/16
♪ We're all a family under one sky   10/24
♪ We're proud we can sing our family's
  songs   10/25
♪ We've come to the land   3/13
Y We've laughed until my cheeks are
  tight.   12/19
What a wonderful   6/11
What did the musician do when   3/31
What your mother tells you now   5/14

When Annie was adopted,   8/6
When his son-in-law   3/30
When I grow old I hope to be   5/22
When I look at you   10/26
When I was a child in the city   7/30
When I went out   4/10
When I'm by myself   10/7
When my daddy comes in from work
  6/17
When spider webs unite,   1/12
When the day is cloudy,   2/9
When the sun comes up   9/4
When we look out the window,   1/22
When we used to go to synagogue
  4/30
Where my grandmother lived   2/2
Where the back of my throat meets the
  bottom of my brain   7/18
Whether the weather be fine   2/10
Who I am is who they were   2/1
Who is mighty? One who makes   2/22
Who's got a beard that's long and
  white?   12/25
Why are 1996, 2000,   2/29
Why do they stare at me?   1/27
You are a dancy little thing,   12/14
You don't have to be bigger to be
  important.   5/5
B You whose day it is   1/2
Your birthday cake is made of mud
  2/28
Your teacher can lead you to learning;
  6/5

INDEX OF AUTHORS

This index can help you locate works by the various poets and writers included in *A Chorus of Cultures*. For each entry (other than the **Young Voices** entries, indicated by the **YV** label), life dates and a very brief indication of professional data are provided when known.

Ada, Alma Flor (1938–)
Professor, author, translator, poet, literary critic.
	9/10	Abuelito
B	10/13	Orgullo/Pride
	12/29	Envolviendo regalos
	3/1	Being Bilingual
Y	6/19	Daddy

Adams, Lee (1924–)
Lyricist, author.
| ♪ | 8/1 | Put On a Happy Face |

Adler, Susan Matoba (1947–)
Educator, writer, poet.
| | 5/28 | I Am Sansei |

Adoff, Arnold (1935–)
Poet, teacher, counselor, anthologist.
B	9/9	There Is a Place
Y	10/2	Take One Apple
	11/5	Still Finding Out
	12/7	In Our One Family
	1/26	The Way I See Any Hope for Later
	1/31	Afternoons: Two
	3/15	After All the Digging
B	3/25	If They Hate Me
	7/11	Borders

Alarcón, Francisco X. (1954–)
Writer, poet, critic, translator, teacher.
	11/20	Chicome-Coatl/Seven-Snake
B	1/9	Listen
	3/16	Ode to Tomatoes
	3/23	Shame
	5/9	Rainbow
B	5/25	Matriarch
	7/10	First Day of School

Aldis, Dorothy (1896–1966)
Writer, poet.
	10/28	Brooms
Y	12/19	Bursting
	7/4	Fourth of July Night

Allen, Marie Louise
Poet.
| | 11/29 | The Mitten Song |

Angelou, Maya (1928–)
Writer, poet, playwright, lecturer, journalist, editor.
| | 1/20 | On the Pulse of Morning |

Antin, Esther
Poet.
| | 11/22 | Corn |

Asch, Frank (1946–)
Author, illustrator, poet, teacher.
| Y | 7/26 | Sunrise |

Awiakta, Marilou (1936–)
Poet, writer, children's librarian.
| | 2/17 | Patchwork |

Bacmeister, Rhoda W. (1893–1991)
Educator, writer, poet.
| | 2/7 | Icy |

Baker, Barbara
Poet.
| | 4/10 | A Spike of Green |

Batulis, Melissa YV
| | 9/1 | Time for School |

Bennett, Rowena Bastin
Poet.
| | 6/29 | A Modern Dragon |

Boland, Aaron YV
| | 1/3 | I Have a Future |

Brooks, Gwendolyn (1917–)
Poet, novelist, lecturer.
	12/14	De Koven
Y	3/12	Tommy
	7/29	Rudolph Is Tired of the City

Bruchac, Joseph (1942–)
Storyteller, poet, novelist, journalist, publisher, teacher.
| | 1/6 | Old Man Coyote and the Rock |
| | 4/24 | Birdfoot's Grampa |

Bryan, Ashley (1923–)
Author, illustrator, professor, storyteller, poet.
| | 8/20 | Ancestry |

Bui, Nhung YV
| | 6/3 | E.S.O.L |

Bulich, Chad YV
| B | 12/1 | Home |

Campbell, Tony YV
| | 2/1 | Who I Am Is Who They Were |

Carawan, Guy, Jr. (1927–)
Musician, folk singer.
| ♪ | 9/18 | We Shall Overcome |

Carvalho, Joseph YV
| | 5/8 | Rainbows |

Cason, Julie (1963–)
Editor, poet.
| | 3/8 | So That's What Girls Are Made Of |
| | 4/13 | Easter Basket |

Chan, Sarah (1968–)
Poet.
	12/5	The Outside/Inside Poem
	7/28	Punchball
B	8/25	Grandma and the Thunder

Chávez, Felipe YV
| | 12/21 | I Am Winter |

Cherícián, David (1940–)
Translator, poet.
| | 9/4 | Chant of the Working People |

Child, Lydia Maria (1802–1880)
Abolitionist, feminist, teacher, writer, editor.
    11/24   *Over the River and Through the Wood*

Ching, Sandy **YV**
    5/8   *How to Get a Rainbow in Your Pocket*

Choe, Lena Domyung
Poet.
    11/10   *When I Am President . . .*

Chou, Johnny **YV**
    8/11   *When I Hear the Music in My Name*

Chute, Marchette (1909–)
Writer, poet.
    3/3   *Crayons*
Y *4/7*   *Spring Rain*
    6/14   *Picnics*
Y *7/23*   *Sleeping Outdoors*

Ciardi, John (1916–1986)
Professor, critic, lecturer, poetry editor, writer, poet.
    10/29   *Wouldn't You?*

Clifton, Lucille (1936–)
Poet, writer, teacher.
    9/2   *September*
    11/25   *November*
    2/5   *Listen Children*
    4/6   *April*
    4/21   *Elevator*
    5/31   *Sunday Morning Lonely*

Cockburn, Victor (1949–)
Musician, singer, teacher.
♪ *10/25*   *Something New*
B *11/6*   *Family Gifts*

Columbus, Christopher (c. 1451–1506)
Explorer, navigator.
    10/12   *Friday, 12 October 1492*

Crain, Suzanne (1952–)
Editor, poet.
♪ **B** *4/12*   *The Day You Were Born*
    4/17   *The Rabbit*
    5/23   *Old Friends*
    7/12   *I Wouldn't Like It*
    8/3   *Six Salamanders*

Crawford, Karen **YV**
    10/6   *Being Nobody*

Culver, Casse
Lyricist, composer.
    3/10   *Ride, Sally Ride*

Cumpiano, Ina (1941–)
Author, poet, translator.
    11/27   *What Flies Free*

Dickinson, Emily (1830–1886)
Poet.
    4/14   *Bee! I'm Expecting You!*

Dodge, Mary Mapes (1831–1905)
Writer, editor, poet.
    4/15   *The Secret*

Doty, Roy (1922–)
Writer, artist, cartoonist, illustrator.
    3/31   *Blowing Cold*

Drennen, M. Olive
Lyricist.
    3/9   *I Am a Suffragette*

Dumas, Henry (1934–1968)
Editor, publisher, educator, writer, poet.
    3/24   *Image*

E-Yeh-Shure
Poet.
    5/6   *Beauty*

Erickson, Jennifer **YV**
    12/2   *Dust in the City*

Esbensen, Barbara Juster (1925–)
Teacher, artist, writer, poet.
    3/7   *The Fourteenth Day of Adar*
    6/13   *At the Pool*

Fatchen, Max (1920–)
Poet, journalist, editor.
    2/11   *Dragon Dance*

Ferderber, Jenny **YV**
    5/24   *My Great Aunt*

Fernández, Norberto **YV**
    8/9   *Name Poem*

Fisher, Aileen (1906–)
Writer, poet, playwright.
    3/17   *Wearing of the Green*

Flakoll, Darwin J.
Translator.
    9/29   *There's an Orange Tree Out There*

Fleischman, Paul (1952–)
Writer, poet.
    8/19   *Fireflies*

Fleming, Jamie **YV**
    1/8   *As We Sit Around Grandpa's Chair*

Frank, Anne (1929–1945)
Diarist.
    4/28   *The Diary of Anne Frank*

Frank, Tanu
    9/23   *The Wind Is Cool and Swift*

Frazier, Kori **YV**
    1/22   *Snow! Snow! Snow!*

Fredericks, Bill
Musician, lyricist.
    12/25   *Must Be Santa*

Freire de Matos, Isabel (1915–)
Professor, poet.
B *9/27*   *Borinquen*

Friday, Ann
Poet.
Y 2/26   *The Wish*

Frieden, Melissa YV
    3/2   *The Loss of Something Very Special*

Fufuka, Karama (1951–)
Writer, editor, poet.
    12/3   *The Park People*
    6/17   *My Daddy Is a Cool Dude*

Fuller, Sean YV
    5/17   *Skateboarding*

Fuson, Robert H. (1927–)
Writer, educator, translator.
    10/12   *Friday, 12 October 1492*

Galarza, Ernesto (1905–1984)
Poet, historian, civil rights leader.
    4/3   *Three Silly Poems*
    7/3   *The Elephant*
Y 8/17   *I'll Tell You Something*
    8/17   *Bees*

Gali, Loyen Redhawk YV
    7/14   *My Hair Is Long*

Gall, Justin YV
    1/18   *In Dreams*

Gandhi, Mohandas K. (1869–1948)
Political and spiritual leader.
    9/16   *"It is little children like you . . ."*

Gautier Benítez, José (1851–1880)
Poet.
    11/19   *A Puerto Rico*

Gibson, Douglas
Poet.
    7/22   *Cat in Moonlight*

Giovanni, Nikki (1943–)
Professor, poet, lecturer.
B 10/8   *The Drum*

    11/8   *Poem for Rodney*
    11/13   *The Reason I Like Chocolate*
    2/8   *Winter Poem*
    3/20   *Springtime*
    5/10   *Tommy's Mommy*
    6/22   *Knoxville, Tennessee*

Glaser, Isabel Joshlin (1929–)
Teacher, writer, poet.
    10/21   *Prediction: School P.E.*

Goldfarb, S.E.
Musician.
♪ 12/23   *My Dreydel*

Greenfield, Eloise (1929–)
Writer, poet, teacher.
    9/17   *Education*
B 9/20   *Rope Rhyme*
    10/7   *By Myself*
    10/16   *Things*
    12/8   *Love Don't Mean*
    2/4   *Harriet Tubman*
B 5/13   *Mama*
    6/8   *I See My Future*
Y 6/15   *Goodnight, Juma*
    8/14   *Nathaniel's Rap*

Greeson, Laura YV
    4/23   *The Price*

Grossman, Sam
Musician.
♪ 12/23   *My Dreydel*

Hamilton, Frank
Musician, lyricist.
♪ 9/18   *We Shall Overcome*

Hammerstein, Oscar (1895–1960)
Lyricist, composer, stage manager, scriptwriter.
    3/26   *Do Re Mi*

Hanlon, Bert
Lyricist.
    6/1   *M-I-S-S-I-S-S-I-P-P-I*

Harris, William J. (1942–)
Professor, writer, poet.
    10/15   *An Historic Moment*
    1/21   *A Winter Song*

Hashin (20th century)
Poet.
    1/25   *Loneliness*

Hayashi, Ryuha
Lyricist.
♪ 9/22   *Kakurenbo*

Hearn, Michael Patrick
Poet.
    3/6   *Rhinos Purple, Hippos Green*

Henderson, Harold G. (1889–1974)
Educator, translator, author.
    1/25   *Loneliness*

Henderson, Rose
Poet.
    5/22   *Growing Old*

Henríquez, Daniel YV
    2/15   *My Love*

Hoberman, Mary Ann (1930–)
Writer, poet.
B 6/18   *My Father*
    8/6   *When Annie Was Adopted*
    8/7   *Half-Whole-Step*

Holder, Julie
Poet.
Y 8/4   *Where Did the Baby Go?*

Holman, Felice (1919–)
Writer, poet.
Y 12/31   *The Year*

Hopkins, Lee Bennett (1938–)
Teacher, writer, poet, anthologist.
Y 11/15   *Good Books, Good Times!*
    3/10   *Last Laugh*
Y 5/18   *Subways Are People*

Horton, Zilphia
Musician, lyricist.
♪ 9/18   *We Shall Overcome*

Hru, Dakari Kamau
Poet, storyteller, teacher.
     3/31   *John Coltrane Ditty*

Huff, Barbara A. (1929–)
Editor, writer, poet.
     4/19   *The Library*

Hughes, Langston (1902–1967)
Poet, writer, lecturer, playwright, lyricist, journalist.
     9/12   *Piggy-Back*
B 12/27   *My People*
     1/7   *Aunt Sue's Stories*
     1/19   *Dreams*
     2/20   *Poem*
     3/21   *Color*
     4/8   *April Rain Song*
     7/26   *City*

Hughes, Leslie
Teacher, poet.
     10/26   *To My Students*

Huynh, Phuc YV
B 8/8   *My Sister's Just Like Me*

Hwang, Yi (1501–1570)
Poet.
     11/4   *The Path*

Hymes, James L., Jr.
Professor, writer, poet.
   Y 10/19   *Ears Hear*

Hymes, Lucia (1907–)
Writer, poet.
   Y 10/19   *Ears Hear*

Imrie, Alex YV
     9/13   *Tota Man*

Ipcar, Dahlov (1917–)
Artist, author, illustrator, poet.
     5/4   *Fishes' Evening Song*

Israeli, Ilana
Poet.
♪ **B** 6/21   *Shir Kaytzi*

Jacobs, Leland B. (1907–1992)
Professor, lecturer, author, editor, poet.
     5/15   *Preferred Vehicles*

Jaret, Mazal
Musician, lyricist.
♪ **B** 6/21   *Summer Song*

Jeffrey, Formikia YV
     2/3   *Black History*

Jiménez, José YV
     1/29   *Teasing*

Jinto, Yoshimura   See Yoshimura, Jinto.

Johnson, Carol
Lyricist, composer.
♪ 4/26   *The Earth Is My Mother*

Joseph, Lynn
Poet, writer, lawyer.
     3/29   *Steel Drum*
     6/4   *Miss Teacher*
B 7/17   *The Palet Man*
     8/21   *Pullin' Seine*

Katz, Bobbi (1933–)
Writer, poet.
     8/30   *What Shall I Pack in the Box Marked "Summer"?*

Kennedy, X. J. (1929–)
Professor, lecturer, writer, poet, anthologist.
     7/19   *Slide Trombone*

King, Joanie YV
     1/30   *It's All Around*

Kraus, Ruth (1911–)
Playwright, screenwriter, poet.
     11/17   *Beginning on Paper*

Kredenser, Gail (1936–)
Editor, journalist, writer, poet.
   Y 11/28   *Polar Bear*

Kuskin, Karla (1932–)
Writer, poet, illustrator.
     10/10   *Okay Everybody*
     11/30   *Winter Clothes*
     12/20   *I Am Beside Myself*
     6/28   *Let Me Tell You All About Me*

LaRock, Christine YV
     3/4   *Why the Sun Is Yellow*

Lear, Edward (1812–1888)
Artist, author, poet.
     10/1   *A. Apple Pie*

Lee, Li-Young (1957–)
Poet, artist.
     4/9   *I Ask My Mother to Sing*

Liatsos, Sandra
Poet.
     2/27   *My First Birthday Gift*

Lillegard, Dee
Writer, poet, teacher.
     12/4   *Just a Fire*

Ling, Amy (1939–)
Editor, professor, poet.
     1/28   *Slit Eyes*
     5/26   *Sister*

Livingston, Myra Cohn (1926–)
Poet, anthologist, professor.
     4/5   *Passover*
   Y 7/2   *Tails*

Lobel, Arnold (1933–1987)
Writer, poet, illustrator.
   Y 11/14   *Books to the Ceiling*

Lomatewama, Ramson
Poet.
♪ 1/13   *Cloud Brothers*

Long, Doughtry (1942–)
Writer, poet.
    2/2   *Where My Grandmother Lived*

Long, Sheron
Publisher, educator, poet.
    7/31   *Flying over Kansas*

Lopez, Alonzo
Poet.
  B *12/16*   *Celebration*

Loureiro, James YV
    11/18   *Pencil*

Lum, Wing Tek
Poet.
    10/27   *Chinese Hot Pot*

Lyon, Amanda YV
    12/2   *Dust in the City*

Maji, Tianah Awezi YV
    1/15   *Peace Starts at Home*

Mark, Diane Mei Lin
Filmmaker, journalist, writer, poet.
    3/11   *Rice and Rose Bowl Blues*

Marks, R. H.
Poet.
    5/12   *New Mother*

Martí, José (1853-1895)
Writer, journalist, patriot.
    10/5

Martin, Bill, Jr (1916–)
Teacher, lecturer, storyteller, writer, poet.
    7/5   *I Am Freedom's Child*

McClester, Cedric (1946–)
Journalist, writer, poet.
    12/26   *Kwanzaa Is . . .*

McCord, David (1897–)
Poet, editor, humorist, professor.
  Y *10/20*   *Song of the Train*
     3/5   *Yellow*

Merriam, Eve (1916–1992)
Poet, playwright, writer.
    9/19   *Fantasia*

Millum, Trevor (1945–)
Writer, poet, teacher.
 ♪ *2/12*   *Lion Dance*

Mir, Sophia (1970–)
Writer.
    2/23   *Our First Fast*

Mitchell, Monique YV
    7/24   *The Prairie*

Mitsui, Jim
Poet.
    3/30   *Shakuhachi*

Montoya, Laurie Y. YV
    10/14   *I Live Free*

Moore, Hal
Musician, lyricist.
    12/25   *Must Be Santa*

Moore, Lilian (1909–)
Teacher, editor, writer, poet.
    2/6   *Dragon Smoke*

Moss, Jeff
Songwriter, poet.
  B *2/21*   *A Lot of Kids*
    7/18   *The Ice Cream Pain*

Nez, Daryl YV
    12/10   *Family*

Nguyen, Emily (1947–)
Poet.
    2/13   *Tet*
    6/24   *June Sunset*

Nguyen, Trang YV
  B *5/29*   *My Beloved Country*

Nichols, Grace
Poet.
    8/23   *Sea Timeless Song*

O'Connor, James YV
    6/16   *Me and My Dad*

O'Dea, Adam YV
    3/28   *Drums*

O'John, Calvin (1946–)
Painter, poet.
  B *5/7*   *Dirt Road*

Palacios, Argentina (1938–)
Writer, translator, storyteller.
    12/6   *Not One Frown*

Pee, Tao Lang
Poet.
  B *10/18*   *Sampan*

Pelham, Ruth (1949–)
Performer, educator, songwriter.
 ♪ *10/24*   *Under One Sky*
    4/29   *The Grandma Song*

Perkins, Useni Eugene
Poet, playwright, editor, sociologist.
    1/16   *Martin Luther King, Jr.*

Perry, Phyllis J. (1933–)
Teacher, educator, writer, poet.
    10/31   *Halloween*

Pham, Tuyen YV
    7/8   *Drifting on the Ocean*

Philabaum, April YV
    1/22   *Snow! Snow! Snow!*

Philip, Harry
Poet.
    9/15   *Rosh Ha-Shanah Eve*

Po, Kien YV
    10/17   *What Is Poetry?*
    12/12   *Snowflakes*

Pomerantz, Charlotte (1930–)
Writer, poet, editor.
    8/10   *The Four Brothers*

Pomeroy, Marnie
Poet.
    4/1   *April Fools' Day*

Prelutsky, Jack (1940–)
Poet, singer, anthologist.
  Y 4/4   *I Am Running in a Circle*

Provost, Orren YV
    12/13   *If I Were a Rope*

Quijada Urías, Alfonso (1940–)
Poet.
    9/29   *There's an Orange Tree Out There*

Quintana, Juan (1954–)
Editor, translator, poet.
    9/4   *Chant of the Working People*
  B 9/27   *Borinquen*
    11/19   *To Puerto Rico*
    12/18   *Piñata*
    12/29   *Wrapping Presents*
    2/24   *Dream America*
    3/18   *Many Colors*
    5/11   *Mommy, When I'm Big and Tall*
    6/23   *Watermelon*

Quintana, Leroy (1944–)
Writer, poet, professor, editor.
    1/11   *A Fairy Tale*

Raffi (Raffi Cavoukian; 1948–)
Singer, songwriter, environmental activist.
♪   1/5   *Anansi*

Reese, Pee Wee
Baseball player.
    10/22   *What Counts*

Reichin, Susan L. (1942–)
Teacher, musician, singer.
    6/6   *Why I Teach*

Rendón, María YV
    2/19   *Friends*

Reynolds, Malvina (1900–1978)
Singer, guitarist, composer, lyricist.
♪ Y 7/25   *I Live in a City*

Rohrbough, Katherine F.
Lyricist.
    4/18   *Cherry Trees*

Rojas, Ricardo YV
    11/26   *As I Walk This Road*

Roston, Ruth
Poet.
    12/22   *First Night of Hanukkah*

Rountree, Wendy YV
    1/27   *Why Do They Stare?*

Ryan, Benny
Lyricist.
    6/1   *M-I-S-S-I-S-S-I-P-P-I*

Sánchez, Paola YV
    4/11   *The Flowers*

Sanchez, Sonia (1934–)
Writer, playwright, screenwriter, poet.
  B 11/3   *Haiku*

Sandburg, Carl (1878–1967)
Poet, biographer, historian, folklorist.
♪   5/19   *Window*

Savren, Shelly
Poet.
    12/9   *Bubie Annie*

Seale, Doris (1936–)
Poet, writer, children's librarian.
  B 9/24   *Little Sister*
    7/13   *Pow Wow*

Seeger, Pete (1919–)
Songwriter, musicologist, banjo player.
♪   9/18   *We Shall Overcome*

Sendak, Maurice (1928–)
Writer, illustrator.
    1/23   *January*

Shamma, Riyad
Engineer, teacher, poet.
    5/20   *Eid*

Shigeji, Tsuboi   *See Tsuboi, Shigeji.*

Shiki (1867–1902)
Critic, poet, essayist.
    6/11   *Wonderful Day*

Shimofusa, Kan'ichi
Musician, composer.
♪   9/22   *Kakurenbo/Hide and Seek*

Silverstein, Shel (1932–)
Writer, poet, humorist, composer, songwriter.
    10/23   *Hug O' War*
    3/27   *Ourchestra*

Simpson, Bert
Lyricist.
♪   1/5   *Anansi*

Skidders, Tara YV
    8/5   *Me and My Brother*

Smith, William Jay (1918–)
Poet, translator, professor.
    6/27   *Dragon*

Sneve, Virginia Driving Hawk (1933–)
Teacher, writer, poet.
    5/16   *My Horse, Fly Like a Bird*
    7/16   *Another Kid*

Soto, Gary (1952–)
Writer, poet, professor.
    9/26   *Ode to My Library*
    5/2   *Ode to My Kitten*
    6/25   *Ode to the Sprinkler*

Southivongnorath, Kaykham YV
　　5/27　　I Wasn't Born in My Country

Sperling, Karam YV
　　8/24　　Mawlid al-Nabi

Steinbergh, Judith W. (1943–)
Poet, lyricist, teacher.
♪　10/25　　Something New
B　11/6　　Family Gifts
♪ B　6/21　　Summer Song
　　8/27　　Cooking for Shabbas with My
　　　　　　Family

Strouse, Charles
Composer.
　　8/1　　Put On a Happy Face

Suárez, Eloy
　　9/8　　Instructions on How to Read

Tablada, José Juan (1871–1945)
Poet.
　　6/23　　Sandía

Tafolla, Carmen (1951–)
Professor, poet, writer.
　　9/3　　Much to Learn
　　12/24　　No Room! No Room!
　　5/5　　You Don't Have to Be Bigger to Be
　　　　　　Important
　　7/20　　Mari and the Moon

Tagliabue, John (1923–)
Professor, poet, translator.
　　11/16　　Japan Poem

Thomas, Joyce Carol (1938–)
Lecturer, professor, poet, writer, editor.
　　7/6　　Black Child

Townsend, Albert YV
　　7/15　　Round House Dancing

Tsuboi, Shigeji (1898–1975)
Poet.
　　10/11　　Silent, But . . .

Underhill, Sarah YV
　　7/27　　Going to School on the Subway

Vando, Gloria
Poet, teacher, publisher.
　　6/20　　Puerto Rican Day Parade
　　7/30　　Childhood Country

Vargas, Christopher YV
　　11/7　　"Dear Mr. President . . ."

Veiga, Marisella (1960–)
Poet, writer, translator.
　　9/28　　Two in One

Viorst, Judith (1931–)
Writer, poet, editor, journalist.
　　11/9　　Good-Bye, Six—Hello, Seven

Vo, Bay YV
　　7/7　　Poem

Want, Marla YV
　　10/9　　I Am Sun Shining

Watson, Clyde (1947–)
Writer, poet, composer.
　　11/12　　A Book Is a Place

Watts, Mabel (1906–)
Writer, poet.
Y　5/1　　Maytime Magic

Weeks, Gladys
Poet.
　　5/3　　Did I Tell You?

Weinstein, Josh (1965–)
Musician, singer, songwriter, writer, poet.
　　10/3　　Johnny Appleseed
　　10/30　　Autumn
♪　11/2　　Death Went and Sat Down One Day
　　11/11　　Dear Uncle Gregg
　　12/17　　I'd Like to Have a Party
　　1/10　　"Fairily Worried"?
　　1/17　　Dreams Are
B　4/27　　Being Jewish
　　4/30　　Social Services
♪　5/30　　Oh, the Voices

Wells, Rosemary (1943–)
Writer, poet, illustrator.
　　2/28　　Your Birthday Cake

WhiteBear, Beverly YV
　　8/22　　I Am a Shell Dancer

Whitman, Ruth (1922–)
Poet, translator, professor.
　　1/4　　Beginning a New Year Means

Wilson, Victoria YV
B　8/13　　My Tribe Is Choctaw
　　8/18　　How Fireflies Got Their Light

Wollner, Paul YV
B　4/25　　I Love the World

Wong, Nellie (1934–)
Poet, writer.
　　8/12　　How a Girl Got Her Chinese Name

Worth, Valerie (1933–)
Poet.
　　8/31　　Crickets

Xu, Zheng YV
　　9/11　　Grandfather Is a Chinese Pine

Yamada, Mitsuye (1923–)
Poet, anthologist.
　　3/22　　Looking Out
　　5/14　　What Your Mother Tells You
B　7/9　　Mirror Mirror

Yoon, Suk-Joong (1911–)
Poet, essayist, professor, publisher
♪　4/16　　Little Spring

Yoshimura, Jinto YV
　　8/15　　The Feast of Lanterns

Yunque, Álvaro (1889–1982)
Novelist, poet.
　　5/11　　Mommy, When I'm Big and Tall

Zolotow, Charlotte (1915–)
Editor, poet, writer.
B　2/18　　The New Girl

INDEX OF GENRES

You can use this index to help you find examples of:

◆ **Poetic Forms,** such as acrostics, concrete poems, or haiku
◆ **Literary Genres,** such as counting rhymes, folktales, letters, or songs and lyrics
◆ **Unique Authorship,** such as group poems

ACROSTIC

	9/28	Two in One

CINQUAIN

	11/18	Pencil

CONCRETE POETRY

Y	12/31	The Year
	7/31	Flying Over Kansas

COUNTING RHYMES

Y	9/5	One, Two, Three, Four, Five TRADITIONAL
♪	9/6	Los elefantes/The Elephants TRADITIONAL
	9/7	Meg, Yergoo, Yergunnas/One Two, Grow Tall TRADITIONAL
	11/1	Cold November

DIARY ENTRIES

	10/12	Friday, 12 October 1492
	4/28	The Diary of Anne Frank

FOLKTALES

	9/14	The Emperor's Dream
	10/3	Johnny Appleseed
♪	1/5	Anansi
	1/6	Old Man Coyote and the Rock
	3/4	Why the Sun Is Yellow
	8/18	How Fireflies Got Their Light

FOLK RHYMES

Y	9/5	One, Two, Three, Four, Five
	9/7	Meg, Yergoo, Yergunnas/One, Two, Grow Tall
	9/30	Thirty Days Hath September
	12/11	Star-Light, Star-Bright
	12/18	Piñata
	2/9	When the Day Is Cloudy
	4/17	Arnab/The Rabbit
B	6/12	Two Little Sisters
	6/26	The Dragon Boats
	8/28	Rima de chocolate/Chocolate Rhyme
	8/29	A Riddle to Chew On

GAMES

Y	9/5	One, Two, Three, Four, Five TRADITIONAL
♪	9/6	Los elefantes/The Elephants TRADITIONAL
B	9/20	Rope Rhyme
Y	9/21	Ooo-Ah, Wanna Piece of Pie
♪	6/7	Jump Shamador TRADITIONAL

GROUP POEMS

	11/23	Opening Corn
B	1/1	El año nuevo/The New Year

HAIKU

B	11/3	Haiku
	1/17	Dreams Are
	1/25	Loneliness
	6/11	Wonderful Day

LETTERS

	11/7	"Dear Mr. president . . ."
	11/11	Dear Uncle Gregg

LIMERICKS

	6/27	Dragon

LYRICS See Songs & Lyrics

NARRATIVE POETRY See Story Poems/Narrative Poetry

NONSENSE

Y	4/2	Way Down South
	4/3	Three Silly Poems
	6/2	Constantinople
	6/2	Chicago
	7/19	Slide Trombone

ONOMATOPOEIA/SOUND POEMS
See also **Tongue Twisters**

B	9/20	Rope Rhyme
	10/1	A. Apple Pie
B	10/18	Sampan
Y	10/19	Ears Hear
Y	10/20	Song of the Train
	10/31	Halloween
	12/20	I Am Beside Myself
	1/22	Snow! Snow! Snow!
♪	2/12	Lion Dance
	3/29	Steel Drum
	5/4	Fishes' Evening Song
	8/10	The Four Brothers
	8/21	Pullin' Seine

POEMS FOR TWO VOICES

♪	2/12	Lion Dance
	8/19	Fireflies

PROVERBS

	10/4	"A stone from the hand . . ."
B	12/30	Giving
	1/12	"When spider webs unite . . ."
	2/22	Friendship
	4/20	"The mouth tastes food . . ."
	5/21	The Wisdom of the Ages
	6/5	Teachers
	8/2	"Everyone in the world . . ."

Y = Included in the Language Development Chart Set (Yellow Cover)   **B** = Included in the Cultural Heritage Chart Set (Brown Cover)   ♪ = Included in the Music Tapes

INDEX OF THEMES

Y = Included in the Language Development Chart Set (Yellow Cover)   **B** = Included in the Cultural Heritage Chart Set (Brown Cover)   ♪ = Included in the Music Tapes

COUNTRYSIDE

11/5	*Still Finding Out*
7/24	*The Prairie*
7/29	*Rudolph Is Tired of the City*
7/30	*Childhood Country*
7/31	*Flying over Kansas*

CULTURAL CELEBRATIONS

	9/14	*The Emperor's Dream* TET TRUNG-THU
	9/15	*Rosh Ha-Shanah Eve* ROSH HASHANAH
	9/25	*A New Start* YOM KIPPUR
	9/26	*Ode to My Library* HISPANIC HERITAGE MONTH
B	10/13	*Orgullo/Pride* DÍA DE LA RAZA
♪	11/2	*Estaba la Muerte un día/Death Went and Sat Down One Day* DÍA DE LOS MUERTOS/DAY OF THE DEAD
	11/19	*A Puerto Rico/To Puerto Rico* PUERTO RICO DISCOVERY DAY
	11/24	*Over the River and Through the Wood* THANKSGIVING
	12/22	*First Night of Hanukkah* HANUKKAH
♪	12/23	*My Dreydel* HANUKKAH
	12/24	*No Room! No Room!* CHRISTMAS, POSADAS
	12/25	*Must Be Santa* CHRISTMAS
	12/26	*Kwanzaa Is . . .* KWANZAA
	2/1	*Who I Am Is Who They Were* BLACK HISTORY MONTH
	2/11	*Dragon Dance* LUNAR NEW YEAR
♪	2/12	*Lion Dance* LUNAR NEW YEAR
	2/13	*Tet* TET
	2/23	*Our First Fast* RAMADAN
	3/7	*The Fourteenth Day of Adar* PURIM
	4/5	*Passover* PASSOVER
	4/13	*Easter Basket* EASTER
	4/18	*Sakura/Cherry Trees* CHERRY BLOSSOM FESTIVAL
B	4/27	*Being Jewish* JEWISH HERITAGE WEEK
	5/5	*You Don't Have to Be Bigger to Be Important* CINCO DE MAYO
	5/20	*Eid* EID AL-ADHA
	5/26	*Sister* ASIAN AND PACIFIC AMERICAN HERITAGE MONTH

	6/26	*The Dragon Boats* DRAGON BOAT FESTIVAL
	6/30	*Song of the Dragon* LUNAR NEW YEAR
	8/15	*The Feast of Lanterns* O-BON
	8/24	*Mawlid al-Nabi* MAWLID AL-NABI

CULTURAL TRADITIONS

Folk Songs and Traditional Songs

♪	9/6	*Los elefantes/The Elephants*
♪	11/2	*Estaba la Muerte un día/Death Went and Sat Down One Day*
	11/24	*Over the River and Through the Wood*
♪	12/15	*Great Big Stars*
B	1/2	*You Whose Day It Is*
♪	1/14	*Hineh Ma Tov /Oh, How Good*
	2/9	*When the Day Is Cloudy*
♪	3/13	*Artza Alinu /We've Come to the Land*
	3/14	*My Nipa Hut*
	3/19	*Spring Song*
♪ **B**	4/12	*El día en que tú naciste/The Day You Were Born*
♪	4/16	*Ong Dal Sam/Little Spring*
	4/18	*Sakura/Cherry Trees*
B	4/22	*The Beautiful*
♪	5/19	*Train Is a-Comin'*
♪	5/30	*O Ka Leo/Oh, the Voices*
♪	6/7	*Jump Shamador*
♪	6/30	*Song of the Dragon*
♪	7/21	*Usagi/Rabbit*

Folklore and Folktales

	9/14	*The Emperor's Dream*
	10/3	*Johnny Appleseed*
	12/25	*Must Be Santa*
♪	1/5	*Anansi*
	1/6	*Old Man Coyote and the Rock*
	1/10	*"Fairily Worried"?*
	3/4	*Why the Sun Is Yellow*

Oral History

	1/7	*Aunt Sue's Stories*
	1/8	*As We Sit Around Grandpa's Chair*

Proverbs

	10/4	*"A stone from the hand . . ."*
B	12/30	*Giving*
	1/12	*"When spider webs unite . . ."*
	2/22	*Friendship*
	4/20	*"The mouth tastes food . . ."*
	5/21	*The Wisdom of the Ages*
	6/5	*Teachers*
	8/2	*"Everyone in the world . . ."*

Rhymes and Riddles

Y	9/5	*One, Two, Three, Four, Five*
	9/7	*Meg, Yergoo, Yergunnas/One, Two, Grow Tall*
	12/11	*Star-Light, Star-Bright*
	12/18	*Piñata*
	4/17	*Arnab/The Rabbit*
B	6/12	*Two Little Sisters*
	6/26	*The Dragon Boats*
	8/28	*Rima de chocolate/Chocolate Rhyme*
	8/29	*A Riddle to Chew On*

DANCING See under **Activities**

DAY OF THE DEAD See *Cultural Celebrations*

DEATH

♪	11/2	*Estaba la Muerte un día/Death Went and Sat Down One Day*
	5/31	*Sunday Morning Lonely*
	8/15	*The Feast of Lanterns*

DÍA DE LA RAZA See *Cultural Celebrations*

DÍA DE LOS MUERTOS See *Cultural Celebrations*

DISCRIMINATION

10/22	*What Counts*
1/26	*The Way I See Any Hope for Later*
1/27	*Why Do They Stare?*
1/28	*Slit Eyes*
1/30	*It's All Around*
3/9	*I Am a Suffragette*
3/10	*Last Laugh*
3/10	*Ride, Sally Ride*
3/11	*Rice and Rose Bowl Blues*

Y = Included in the Language Development Chart Set (Yellow Cover)   **B** = Included in the Cultural Heritage Chart Set (Brown Cover)   ♪ = Included in the Music Tapes

Y = Included in the Language Development Chart Set (Yellow Cover)   **B** = Included in the Cultural Heritage Chart Set (Brown Cover)   ♪= Included in the Music Tapes

	1/20	On the Pulse of Morning
	1/26	The Way I See Any Hope for Later
♪	2/16	I Love Everybody
B	4/25	I Love the World
♪	5/30	O Ka Leo/Oh, the Voices
	7/5	I Am Freedom's Child

VALENTINE'S DAY See **Holidays**

VETERANS' DAY See **Holidays**

WEATHER AND SEASONS

2/10	Weather

Fall

9/23	The Wind Is Cool and Swift
10/28	Brooms
10/29	Wouldn't You?
10/30	Autumn
11/1	Cold November
11/24	Over the River and Through the Wood
11/26	As I Walk This Road
8/31	Crickets

Ice

1/23	January
2/7	Icy

Rain

	9/23	The Wind Is Cool and Swift
	10/28	Brooms
	2/9	When the Day Is Cloudy
	3/20	Springtime
	4/6	April
Y	4/7	Spring Rain
	4/8	April Rain Song
	4/9	I Ask My Mother to Sing
	5/8	Rainbows
	5/8	How to Get a Rainbow in Your Pocket

Rainbows

5/8	Rainbows
5/8	How to Get a Rainbow in Your Pocket
5/9	Rainbow

Snow

11/24	Over the River and Through the Wood
11/26	As I Walk This Road
1/22	Snow! Snow! Snow!
1/24	Snow, Snow
1/25	Loneliness
2/8	Winter Poem

Spring

	2/8	Winter Poem
	3/17	Wearing of the Green
♪	3/18	De colores/Many Colors
	3/19	Spring Song
	3/20	Springtime
	4/6	April
Y	4/7	Spring Rain
	4/8	April Rain Song
	4/14	Bee! I'm Expecting You!
	4/15	The Secret
	4/18	Sakura/Cherry Trees

Summer

	6/11	Wonderful Day
	6/13	At the Pool
	6/14	Picnics
♪ B	6/21	Shir Kaytzi/Summer Song
	6/22	Knoxville, Tennessee
	6/23	Sandía/Watermelon
	6/24	June Sunset
	6/25	Ode to the Sprinkler
Y	7/23	Sleeping Outdoors
	7/28	Punchball
	8/16	August Heat
	8/30	What Shall I Pack in the Box Marked "Summer"?
	8/31	Crickets

Thunder

2/9	When the Day Is Cloudy

Wind

9/23	The Wind Is Cool and Swift
10/28	Brooms
10/29	Wouldn't You?

Winter

11/30	Winter Clothes

12/21	I Am Winter
1/21	A Winter Song
1/22	Snow! Snow! Snow!
1/23	January
1/24	Snow, Snow
1/25	Loneliness
2/6	Dragon Smoke
2/7	Icy
2/8	Winter Poem
2/9	When the Day Is Cloudy

WIND See under **Weather and Seasons**

WINTER See under **Weather and Seasons**

WOMEN See **Equal Rights for Women**

WOMEN'S HISTORY MONTH See **Holidays**

WORK / WORKERS See **Activities: Working; Careers**

WRITING

10/16	Things
11/16	Japan Poem
11/17	Beginning on Paper
11/18	Pencil
6/1	M-I-S-S-I-S-S-I-P-P-I SPELLING
6/2	Chicago SPELLING
6/2	Constantinople SPELLING

YEAR See also **New Year**

	9/30	Thirty Days Hath September
Y	12/31	The Year
	2/29	Riddle LEAP YEAR

YOM KIPPUR See **Cultural Celebrations; New Year**

ZOO See **Animals**

Y = Included in the Language Development Chart Set (Yellow Cover) **B** = Included in the Cultural Heritage Chart Set (Brown Cover) ♪ = Included in the Music Tapes

ACTIVITIES INDEX

Page numbers appearing in **boldface type** indicate an activity with a multicultural focus.

Acknowledgments continued from page 2

"Fourth of July Night" by Dorothy Aldis from HOP, SKIP AND JUMP! Copyright 1934, renewed © 1961 by Dorothy Aldis. Reprinted by permission of the author.

"Did I Tell You" by Gladys Weeks, edited by Sylvia Cavazos Peña is reprinted with permission from the Publisher of KIKIRIKÍ (Houston: Arte Público Press—University of Houston, 1987).

"Patchwork" by Marilou Awiakta from ABIDING APPALACHIA: WHERE MOUNTAIN AND ATOM MEET. Iris Press, 1992 (Seventh Edition). Reprinted by permission of Iris Press on behalf of Marilou Awiakta.

"The Beautiful" is from FOLK SAYINGS FROM THE HAWAIIAN (OLELO NO'EAU A KA HAWAII). All rights reserved. © 1961. Copyright by Jane Lathrop Winne and Mary Kawena Pukiu. Reprinted with permission of Patience Bacon, agent for the estate of Mary Kawena Pukiu.

"A Spike of Green" by Barbara Baker is from READ-ALOUD RHYMES FOR THE VERY YOUNG selected by Jack Prelutsky. Extensive research failed to locate the copyright holder of this work.

"Celebration" by Alonzo Lopez and "Dirt Road" by Calvin O'John are from WHISPERING WIND by Terry Allen. Copyright © 1972 by the Institute of American Indian Arts. "Loneliness" by Hashin from AN INTRODUCTION TO HAIKU by Harold G. Henderson. Copyright © 1958 by Harold G. Henderson. Excerpt from ANNE FRANK: THE DIARY OF A YOUNG GIRL by Anne Frank. Copyright 1952 by Otto Frank. All used by permission of Doubleday, a division of Bantam Doubleday Dell Publishing Group, Inc. "A Lot of Kids" and "The Ice Cream Pain" are from THE BUTTERFLY JAR by Jeff Moss. Copyright © 1989 by Jeff Moss. Used by permission of Bantam Books, a division of Bantam Doubleday Dell Publishing Group, Inc.

"A New Start" is from THE HIGH HOLY DAYS MACHZOR. All rights reserved. Reprinted by permission of Behrman House, Inc., 235 Watchung Avenue, W. Orange, NJ 07052.

"A Modern Dragon" by Rowena Bastin Bennett is from READ-ALOUD RHYMES FOR THE VERY YOUNG compiled by Jack Prelutsky. All rights reserved. © 1986. Reprinted by permission of Kenneth C. Bennett, agent for the estate of Rowena Bastin Bennett.

"listen children," copyright © 1987, by Lucille Clifton. Reprinted from GOOD WOMAN: POEMS AND A MEMOIR 1969–1980, by Lucille Clifton, and "I Ask My Mother to Sing," copyright © 1986 by Li-Young Lee. Reprinted from ROSE, by Li-Young Lee. Used with the permission of BOA Editions, Ltd., 92 Park Ave., Brockport, NY 14420.

"My Dreydel" by S.E. Goldfarb and Sam Grossman is from THE SONGS WE SING. All rights reserved. © 1950. Reprinted by permission of the Board of Jewish Education of Greater New York.

"I Have a Future" by Aaron Boland is from THE VOICE IS ME/LA VOZ ES MÍA edited by Patrice Vecchione. All rights reserved. © 1992. Reprinted by permission.

"Orgullo" by Alma Flor Ada. All rights reserved. Copyright © 1993 Alma Flor Ada. Used with permission from BookStop Literary Agency.

"One, two, grow tall" from STREET RHYMES AROUND THE WORLD edited by Jane Yolen. Copyright © 1992 by Jane Yolen. Reprinted by permission of Wordsong, Boyds Mill Press, Inc. All rights reserved.

"Mama," "I See My Future," "Nathaniel's Rap," and "Education" are from NATHANIEL TALKING by Eloise Greenfield. Copyright © 1988 by Eloise Greenfield. Reprinted by permission of Marie Brown Associates.

"Opening Corn" by Mr. Perucki's Fourth Grade Class, "Who I Am Is Who They Were" by Tony Campbell, and "Skateboarding" by Sean Fuller are from REMEMBERING WHAT HAPPENED edited by Daryl Ngee Chinn. All rights reserved. © 1991. "Tota Man" by Alex Imrie and "A Word from the Poet-Teacher" by Susan Terence are from THE BOY WHO HEARD A VOICE edited by Karin Faulkner, et al. All rights reserved. © 1989. "El año nuevo" by Margot Pepper's First Grade Class, "A Word from the Poet-Teacher" by Margot Pepper, and "Drifting on the Ocean" by Tuyen Pham are from SNOW WE MIGHT SEE IN THE DESERT edited by Daryl Chinn, et al. All rights reserved. © 1992. "Drums" by Adam O'Dea and "I Am a Shell Dancer" by Beverly WhiteBear are from A CHANT A MILE LONG edited by Karin Faulkner and Daryl Chinn. All rights reserved. © 1990. All reprinted by permission of California Poets in the Schools.

"Rainbows" by Joseph Carvalho, Jr. All rights reserved. © Joseph Carvalho, Jr. Reprinted by permission of the author.

"Grandma and the Thunder" and "Punchball" are by Sarah Yim Hong Chan. All rights reserved. © Sarah Chan. Reprinted by permission of the author.

"Just a Fire" from SEPTEMBER TO SEPTEMBER: POEMS FOR ALL YEAR ROUND by Dee Lillegard. Copyright © 1986 by Regensteiner Publishing Enterprises, Inc. Reprinted by permission of Childrens Press.

"How to Get a Rainbow in Your Pocket" by Sandy Ching is from POETRY IN PERFORMANCE 15. All rights reserved. © 1987. Reprinted by permission.

"When I Hear the Music in My Name" by Johnny Chou is from BEFORE AND AFTER MY CRY edited by Carolyn Lau. All rights reserved. © 1987. Reprinted by permission of the author.

"Chicome-Coatl/Seven-Snake," "Listen," "Ode to Tomatoes," "Shame," "Rainbow," and "Matriarch" by Francisco X. Alarcón are from SNAKE POEMS by Francisco X. Alarcón. © 1992. "First Day of School" by Francisco X. Alarcón is from BODY IN FLAMES/CUERPO EN LLAMAS by Francisco X. Alarcón. © 1990. All reprinted by permission of Chronicle Books.

"Something New" by Victor Cockburn and Judith Steinbergh. All rights reserved. © 1993 Victor Cockburn and Judith Steinbergh. Used by permission of the authors.

"In Dreams" by Justin Gall is from THE RAGGED HEART edited by Norita Dittberner-Jax. All rights reserved. © 1989. Reprinted by permission of COMPAS, Inc.

English lyrics for "The Elephants" from EVERYBODY SINGS! compiled by Deborah K. Coyle. © 1983. All rights reserved. Reprinted by permission of the author.

"M-I-S-S-I-S-S-I-P-P-I" by Bert Hanlon, Benny Ryan and Harry Tierney. Copyright © 1916, 1944 (Renewed 1972) c/o EMI FEIST CATALOG INC. World print rights controlled and administered by CPP/BELWIN, INC., Miami, FL. All rights reserved. "Put On a Happy Face" by Lee Adams and Charles Strouse. Copyright © 1960 (Renewed 1988) LEE ADAMS and CHARLES STROUSE c/o THE SONGWRITERS GUILD. Used by Permission of CPP/BELWIN, INC, Miami, FL. All rights reserved.

"The Price" by Laura Greeson and "Snow! Snow! Snow!" by Kori Frazier and April Philabaum reprinted by permission of the authors and CREATIVE KIDS magazine. © 1992. All rights reserved.

"There's An Orange Tree Out There" from the book of poems THEY COME AND KNOCK ON THE DOOR by Alfonso Quijada Urías. Translated by Darwin J. Flakoll. Published by Curbstone Press, 1991. Copyright © 1991 by Alfonso Quijada Urías. Translation Copyright © 1991 by Darwin J. Flakoll. Reprinted by permission of Curbstone Press.

Curtis Brown, Ltd., for "Spring," "Summer," "Fall," and "Winter" by Lee Bennett Hopkins. Copyright © 1993 by Lee Bennett Hopkins. "Last Laugh" by Lee Bennett Hopkins is from KIM'S PLACE AND OTHER POEMS by Lee Bennett Hopkins. Copyright © 1974 by Lee Bennett Hopkins. "April" by Lucille Clifton is from EVERETT ANDERSON'S YEAR by Lucille Clifton. Copyright © 1974 by Lucille Clifton. "Elevator" by Lucille Clifton is from HOME by Michael Rosen. Copyright © 1992 by Lucille Clifton. "Subways Are People" by Lee Bennett Hopkins is from POETRY ON WHEELS. Copyright © 1974 by Lee Bennett Hopkins. "Good Books, Good Times" by Lee Bennett Hopkins is from GOOD BOOKS, GOOD TIMES. Copyright © 1985 by Lee Bennett Hopkins. "A Book Is a Place" by Clyde Watson. Copyright © 1980 by Clyde Watson; 1980 Children's Book Week Poem, written for Children's Book Council, Inc. All reprinted by permission of Curtis Brown, Ltd.

"Sea Timeless Song" is from COME ON INTO MY TROPICAL GARDEN by Grace Nichols. Reproduced with permission of Curtis Brown Group Ltd, London. Copyright © Grace Nichols 1988.

"I think I can succeed . . ." is from LOOK AT ME! published by the Dallas Public Library. All rights reserved. © 1973. Reprinted by permission of the publisher.

"Blowing Cold" by Roy Doty is from PUNS, GAGS, QUIPS, AND RIDDLES compiled by Roy Doty. All rights reserved. © 1974 Doubleday & Company, Inc. Reprinted by permission of the author.

"The Fourteenth Day of Adar" by Barbara Juster Esbensen is from POEMS FOR JEWISH HOLIDAYS compiled by Myra Cohn Livingston. All rights reserved. © 1986 Barbara Juster Esbensen. Reprinted by permission of the author.

The illustration for "Old Man Coyote and the Rock" (January 6) is by John Kahionhes Fadden. It first appeared in NATIVE AMERICAN STORIES by Joseph Bruchac (Golden, CO: Fulcrum Press, 1991). The illustration is © John Kahionhes Fadden. All rights reserved. Used by permission.

"Crickets" from SMALL POEMS by Valerie Worth. Copyright © 1972 by Valerie Worth. "Dragon" is from LAUGHING TIME by William Jay Smith. All rights reserved. © 1980. Both reprinted by permission of Farrar, Straus and Giroux, Inc. "the drum," "poem for rodney," and "springtime" from SPIN A SOFT BLACK SONG by Nikki Giovanni. Copyright © 1971 by Nikki Giovanni. Reprinted by permission of Hill and Wang, a division of Farrar, Straus and Giroux, Inc.

"Wearing of the Green" by Aileen Fisher. Reprinted from YEAR-ROUND PROGRAMS FOR YOUNG PLAYERS by Aileen Fisher. Copyright © 1985, 1986 by Aileen Fisher.

"Estaba la Muerte un día" is from LÍRICA INFANTIL DE MÉXICO compiled by Vincente T. Mendoza. All rights reserved. © 1980 Fondo de Cultura Económica. Reprinted by permission.

"The Loss of Something Very Special" by Melissa Frieden is from THE BOY WHO HEARD A VOICE edited by Karin Faulkner, et al. All rights reserved. © 1989. Reprinted by permission of Joan Frieden.

"Old Man Coyote and the Rock" is from NATIVE AMERICAN STORIES by Joseph Bruchac. All rights reserved. © 1991 Joseph Bruchac. Reprinted by permission of Fulcrum Publishing, 350 Indiana Street, #350, Golden, CO 80401 (303) 2770-1623 on behalf of the author.

"Bees," "I'll Tell You Something," and "Three Silly Poems" by Ernesto Galarza are from POEMAS: PE-QUE PE-QUE PE-QUE-ÑITOS. All rights reserved. © 1972 Ernesto Galarza. "The Elephant," by Ernesto Galarza is from ZOO FUN. All rights reserved. © 1971 Ernesto Galarza. All reprinted by permission of Mae Galarza.

"Cat in Moonlight" by Douglas Gibson is from WHEN THE DARK COMES DANCING compiled by Nancy Larrick. All rights reserved. © Douglas Gibson. Reprinted by permission of Dorothy Gibson, agent for the estate of Douglas Gibson.

"Prediction: School P.E." by Isabel Joshlin Glaser from CRICKET 1990. All rights reserved. © 1990 Isabel Joshlin Glaser. Reprinted by permission of the author, who controls all rights.

"Snow, Snow, Fly Away" from ONE POTATO, TWO POTATO, THREE POTATO, FOUR compiled by Mary Lou Colgin. All rights reserved. © 1982 by Mary Louise N. Colgin. Published by Gryphon House, Mt. Rainier, MD 20712. Reprinted by permission of Gryphon House on behalf of Mary Lou Colgin.

"What Counts" excerpt from TEAMMATES by Peter Golenbock, copyright © 1990 by Golenbock Communications, Inc. "Ode to

My Library" and "Ode to the Sprinkler" from NEIGHBORHOOD ODES, copyright © 1992 by Gary Soto. "The New Girl" from EVERYTHING GLISTENS AND EVERYTHING SINGS: NEW AND SELECTED POEMS, copyright © 1987 by Charlotte Zolotow. "The Dragon Boats" from DRAGON KITES AND DRAGONFLIES, copyright © 1986 by Demi. "Window" from CHICAGO POEMS by Carl Sandburg. All reprinted by permission of Harcourt Brace & Company.

"By Myself," "Love Don't Mean," "Rope Rhyme," and "Things" are from HONEY, I LOVE by Eloise Greenfield. Copyright © 1978 by Eloise Greenfield. "De Koven," "Tommy," and "Rudolph Is Tired of the City" are from BRONZEVILLE BOYS AND GIRLS by Gwendolyn Brooks. Copyright © 1956 by Gwendolyn Brooks Blakely. "The Mitten Song" is from A POCKETFUL OF POEMS by Mary Louise Allen. Text copyright © 1957 by Marie Allen Howarth. "Okay Everybody" is from NEAR THE WINDOW TREE by Karla Kuskin. Copyright © 1975 by Karla Kuskin. "Winter Clothes" is from THE ROSE ON MY CAKE by Karla Kuskin. Copyright © 1964 by Karla Kuskin. "Wouldn't You?" is from YOU READ TO ME, I'LL READ TO YOU by John Ciardi. Copyright © 1962 by John Ciardi. "Hug O'War" and "Ourchestra" are from WHERE THE SIDEWALK ENDS by Shel Silverstein. Copyright © 1974 by Evil Eye Music, Inc. "I Am Beside Myself" is from SOAP SOUP AND OTHER VERSES by Karla Kuskin. Copyright © 1992 by Karla Kuskin. "January" is from CHICKEN SOUP WITH RICE: A BOOK OF MONTHS by Maurice Sendak. Copyright © 1962 by Maurice Sendak. "Afternoons: 2" is from SPORTS PAGES by Arnold Adoff. Copyright © 1986 by Arnold Adoff. "Harriet Tubman" is from HONEY, I LOVE by Eloise Greenfield. Copyright © 1978 by Eloise Greenfield. "At the Pool" is from COLD STARS AND FIREFLIES: POEMS OF THE FOUR SEASONS by Barbara Juster Esbensen. Copyright © 1984 by Barbara Juster Esbensen. "Let Me Tell You All About Me" is from DOGS & DRAGONS, TREES & DREAMS by Karla Kuskin. Copyright © 1980 by Karla Kuskin. "Ancestry" is from SING TO THE SUN by Ashley Bryan. Copyright © 1992 by Ashley Bryan. "Fireflies" is from JOYFUL NOISE: POEMS FOR TWO VOICES by Paul Fleishman. Copyright © 1988 by Paul Fleishman. All reprinted by permission of HarperCollins Publishers.

"An Historic Moment" and "A Winter Song" are by William J. Harris. All rights reserved. © William J. Harris. Reprinted by permission of the author.

"Bee! I'm Expecting You" by Emily Dickinson reprinted by permission of the publishers and the Trustees of Amherst College from THE POEMS OF EMILY DICKINSON, Thomas H. Johnson, ed., Cambridge, Mass., The Belknap Press of Harvard University Press, Copyright © 1951, 1955, 1979, 1983 by the President and Fellows of Harvard College.

"My Love" is by Daniel Henríquez from POETRY IN PERFORMANCE 15. © 1987. Reprinted by permission.

"Where Did the Baby Go?" by Julie Holder is from ANOTHER FIRST POETRY BOOK edited by John Foster. © Julie Holder. Reprinted by permission of H. B. Holder on behalf of Julie Holder.

"My Horse, Fly Like a Bird" by Virginia Driving Hawk Sneve. Copyright © 1989 by Virginia Driving Hawk Sneve. Reprinted from DANCING TEEPEES: POEMS OF AMERICAN INDIAN YOUTH by permission of Holiday House.

"September" and "November" are from EVERETT ANDERSON'S YEAR by Lucille Clifton. Copyright © 1974 by Lucille Clifton. "The Path" by Yi Hwang is from SUNSET IN A SPIDER WEB, adapted by Virginia Olsen Baron. Copyright © 1974 by Virginia Olsen Baron. "Sunday Morning Lonely" is from SOME OF THE DAYS OF EVERETT ANDERSON by Lucille Clifton. Copyright © 1970 by Lucille Clifton. All reprinted by permission of Henry Holt and Company, Inc.

"You Whose Day It Is" is from SONGS OF THE DREAM PEOPLE: CHANTS AND IMAGES FROM THE INDIANS AND ESKIMOS OF NORTH AMERICA. Edited and illustrated by James Houston. Atheneum, New York, copyright © 1972 by James Houston. Reprinted by permission of the author.

"John Coltrane Ditty" by Dakari Hru is from A JOYFUL SOUND edited by Deborah Slier. All rights reserved. © 1990 Dakari Hru. Reprinted by permission of the author.

"The Library" by Barbara A. Huff is from THE RANDOM HOUSE BOOK OF POETRY FOR CHILDREN selected by Jack Prelutsky. All rights reserved. © Barbara A. Huff. Reprinted by permission of the author.

"To My Students" by Leslie Hughes is from HEROES: AND STILL IT MOVES, 1990, a publication of the Galileo High School Creative Writing Project, now the McAteer Creative Writing Project, and California Poets in the Schools. For information about current student publications, contact J. Bebelaar, McAteer High School, 555 Portola Drive, San Francisco, CA 94131. Reprinted by permission of the author.

"Our First Fast" by Sophia Mir. All rights reserved. © 1993 Sophia Husain. Reprinted by permission of the author.

"My Sister's Just Like Me" by Phuc Huynh is from WATCH OUT FOR POEMS THAT FLY OUT OF YOUR MIND edited by Mary Carden. All rights reserved. © 1992. Reprinted by permission.

"Must Be Santa" by Hal Moore and Bill Fredericks. Copyright © 1960 Hollis Music Inc. All rights for the United States of America controlled jointly by: Woodwyn Music, 261 Woodbine Road, North Stamford, CT 06903 and Intuitive Music, 256 Ohayo Mountain Road, Woodstock, NY 12498. All rights for the world outside the United States of America controlled by: Hollis Music Inc., New York, NY. Used by permission.

"Summer Song" from THE RED TAIL OF THE RAINBOW, © 1983 by Ilana Even-Tov Israeli, winner of the "Zeev" Prize for Children's Literature in 1983/84, printed in Israel. English translation by Mazal Jaret. Used by permission of the author.

"Hide and Seek" and "Rabbit" reprinted from 101 FAVORITE SONGS TAUGHT IN JAPANESE SCHOOLS, International Edition. English translation by Ichiro Nakano. Published by the Japan Times, Ltd., Tokyo. Used by permission of the publisher.

"Black History" by Formikia Jeffrey is from POETRY IN PERFORMANCE 18. All rights reserved. © 1990 Formikia Jeffrey. Reprinted by permission.

"Teasing" by José Jiménez is from WATCH OUT FOR POEMS THAT FLY OUT OF YOUR MIND edited by Mary Carden. All rights reserved. © 1992. Reprinted by permission.

"The Earth Is My Mother" © Copyright 1981, Carol A. Johnson, Noeldner Music (BMI), All rights reserved. P.O. Box 6351, Grand Rapids, MI 49506. From recording titled MIGHT AS WELL MAKE IT LOVE. Reprinted by permission of the author.

"Dragon Dance" by Max Fatchen. All rights reserved. Copyright © 1989 Max Fatchen. Reprinted by permission of John Johnson Ltd., London.

"What Shall I Pack in the Box Marked 'Summer'?" by Bobbi Katz. Copyright © 1970 by Bobbi Katz. Reprinted with permission of the author.

"April Rain Song," "Dreams," and "Poem" from THE DREAM KEEPER AND OTHER POEMS by Langston Hughes. Copyright 1932 by Alfred A. Knopf, Inc. and renewed 1960 by Langston Hughes. "Aunt Sue's Stories" and "My People" from SELECTED POEMS by Langston Hughes. Copyright 1926 by Alfred A. Knopf, Inc. and renewed 1954 by Langston Hughes. "Color" from THE PANTHER AND THE LASH by Langston Hughes. Copyright © 1967 by Arna Bontemps and George Houston Bass. All reprinted by permission of Alfred A. Knopf, Inc.

"Beginning on Paper" is from SOMEBODY SPILLED THE SKY by Ruth Krauss. All rights reserved. © 1976, 1979 Ruth Krauss. Reprinted by permission of Stewart I. Edelstein on behalf of the author.

"Polar Bear" is from THE ABC OF BUMPTIOUS BEASTS by Gail Kredenser. © 1966 by Gail Kredenser. Extensive unsuccessful attempts were made to contact the copyright holder of this work.

"Sister" is from CHINAMERICA REFLECTIONS by Amy Ling. All rights reserved. © 1984 Amy Ling. "Slit Eyes" and "A Word from the Poet" by Amy Ling. All rights reserved. © Amy Ling. All reprinted by permission of the author.

"Half-Whole-Step," "My Father," and "When Annie Was Adopted" are from FATHERS, MOTHERS, SISTERS, BROTHERS: A COLLECTION OF FAMILY POEMS by Mary Ann Hoberman. Text copyright © 1991 by Mary Ann Hoberman. "Yellow" is from ONE AT A TIME by David McCord. Copyright © 1974 by David McCord. "Song of the Train" from ONE AT A TIME is by David McCord. Copyright 1952 by David McCord. All by permission of Little, Brown and Company.

"Cloud Brothers" is from SILENT WINDS: POETRY OF ONE HOPI by Ramson Lomatewama © 1981. Reprinted by permission of the author.

"Where My Grandmother Lived" by Doughtry Long is from MAKE A JOYFUL SOUND edited by Deborah Slier. All rights reserved. © Doughtry Long. Reprinted by permission of the author.

"Pencil" by James Loureiro is from WE ARE POETS, TOO! edited by Brigitta Geltrich-Ludgate. Extensive research failed to locate the copyright holder of this work.

"Chinese Hot Pot" by Wing Tek Lum is from THE BEST OF BAMBOO RIDGE edited by Eric Chock and Darrell H.Y. Lum. All rights reserved. © 1986 Wing Tek Lum. Reprinted by permission of the author.

"Good-bye, Six—Hello, Seven" by Judith Viorst. Reprinted with permission of Atheneum Publishers, an imprint of Macmillan Publishing Company, from IF I WERE IN CHARGE OF THE WORLD AND OTHER WORRIES by Judith Viorst. Copyright © 1981 by Judith Viorst. "Great Big Stars" is reprinted and recorded with the permission of Atheneum Publishers, an imprint of Macmillan Publishing Company, from ALL NIGHT, ALL DAY: A CHILD'S FIRST BOOK OF AFRICAN-AMERICAN SPIRITUALS selected and illustrated by Ashley Bryan. Musical arrangements by David Manning Thomas. Copyright © 1991 Ashley Bryan. "Into Mother's Slide Trombone" by X. J. Kennedy. Reprinted with permission of Margaret K. McElderry Books, an imprint of Macmillan Publishing Company, from BRATS by X. J. Kennedy. Copyright © 1986 by X. J. Kennedy. "The Year" by Felice Holman. Reprinted with permission of Charles Scribner's Sons, an imprint of Macmillan Publishing Company, from THE SONG IN MY HEAD AND OTHER POEMS by Felice Holman. Copyright © 1985 Felice Holman.

"Peace Starts at Home" by Tianah Awezi Maji is from I HAVE SOMETHING TO SAY ABOUT THIS BIG TROUBLE: CHILDREN OF THE TENDERLOIN SPEAK OUT compiled by Reverend Cecil Williams and Janice Mirikitani. All rights reserved. © 1989 Glide Memorial United Methodist Church. Reprinted by permission of the author.

"Rosh Ha-Shanah Eve" by Harry Philip is from POEMS FOR JEWISH HOLIDAYS selected by Myra Cohn Livingston. All rights reserved. © 1986 Harry Philip. Reprinted by permission of Diane Margolis on behalf of Richard J. Margolis.

"Rice and Rose Bowl Blues" by Diane Mei Lin Mark is from BREAKING SILENCE, AN ANTHOLOGY OF CONTEMPORARY ASIAN AMERICAN POETS edited by Joseph Bruchac. All rights reserved. © Diane Mei Lin Mark. Reprinted by permission of the author.

"Hide and Seek" by Kan'ichi Shimofusa and Ryuha Hayashi. Copyright © 1960 Edward B. Marks Music Company. Copyright renewed. International copyright secured. All rights reserved. Used by permission.

"Jump Shamador," an adaptation of a traditional Jamaican song transcribed by Edna Edet, is reprinted by permission of Cheryl Warren Mattox from SHAKE IT TO THE ONE THAT YOU LOVE THE BEST © 1989.

"Kwanzaa Is . . ." by Cedric McClester is from MAKE A JOYFUL SOUND edited by Deborah Slier. All rights reserved. © 1990 Cedric McClester. Reprinted by permission of the author.

"Friday, 12 October 1492" is reprinted, with permission, from THE LOG OF CHRISTOPHER COLUMBUS, by Robert H. Fuson. Copyright 1987 by Robert H. Fuson. Published by International Marine, an imprint of TAB Books, a Division of McGraw-Hill Inc., Blue Ridge Summit, PA 17294-0850 (800-233-1128).

"Fishes' Evening Song" by Dahlov Ipcar. Copyright © 1967 by Dahlov Ipcar. From the book WHISPERINGS AND OTHER THINGS. "Rhinos Purple, Hippos Green" by Michael Patrick Hearn. Copyright © 1981 by Michael Patrick Hearn. From the book, BREAKFAST BOOKS AND DREAMS. Both reprinted by permission of McIntosh and Otis, Inc.

"Lion Dance" by Trevor Millum. First published in LET'S CELEBRATE published by Oxford University Press, 1989. © Trevor Millum. Reprinted by permission of the author.

"As I Walk This Road" by Ricardo Rojas and "I Live Free" by Laurie Y. Montoya are from ANGWAMAS, MINOSEWAG, ANISHINABEG: TIME OF THE INDIAN by David Martinson. All rights reserved. © 1979 The Minnesota Chippewa Tribe. Reprinted by permission of The Minnesota Chippewa Tribe and COMPAS, Inc.

"The Prairie" by Monique Mitchell is from WHAT IS MY HEART SINGING TO ME edited by Carolyn Lau. All rights reserved. © 1988 Monique Mitchell. Reprinted by permission of the author.

"Shakuhachi" by James Masao Mitsui. All rights reserved. © James Masao Mitsui. Reprinted by permission of the author.

"Borders," "If They Hate Me," "In Our One Family," "Still Finding Out," and "The Way I See Any Hope for Later" from ALL THE COLORS OF THE RACE by Arnold Adoff. Copyright © 1982 by Arnold Adoff. "After All the Digging," "Take One Apple," and "There Is a Place" from EATS by Arnold Adoff. Copyright © 1979 by Arnold Adoff. "Miss Teacher," "The Palet Man," "Pullin' Seine," and "Steel Drum" from COCONUT KIND OF DAY by Lynn Joseph. Copyright © 1990 by Lynn Joseph. All by permission of Lothrop, Lee & Shepard Books, a division of William Morrow & Co., Inc. "Beauty" from BEAUTY by E-Yeh-Shure. Copyright © 1939 William Morrow & Co., Inc. Copyright renewed 1967 by Louise Abeita Chiwiwi. "Knoxville, Tennessee" from BLACK FEELING, BLACK TALK, BLACK JUDGMENT by Nikki Giovanni. Copyright © 1968, 1970 by Nikki Giovanni. "The Reason I Like Chocolate" and "Tommy's Mommy" from VACATION TIME by Nikki Giovanni. Copyright © 1980 by Nikki Giovanni. "Winter Poem" from MY HOUSE by Nikki Giovanni. Copyright © 1972 by Nikki Giovanni. All by permission of William Morrow & Co., Inc. "Books to the Ceiling" from WHISKERS AND RHYMES by Arnold Lobel. Copyright © 1985 by Arnold Lobel. "The Four Brothers" from THE TAMARINDO PUPPY by Charlotte Pomerantz. Copyright © 1980 by Charlotte Pomerantz. "I Am Running in a Circle" from NEW KID ON THE BLOCK by Jack Prelutsky. Copyright © 1984 by Jack Prelutsky. "Sunrise" from CITY SANDWICH by Frank Asch. Copyright © 1978 by Frank Asch. All by permission of Greenwillow Books, a division of William Morrow & Co., Inc.

"Japan Poem," (originally untitled) is from THE DOORLESS DOOR by John Tagliabue. All rights reserved. © 1970. Reprinted by permission of Mushinsha Limited.

"It is little children like you . . ." by Mahatma Gandhi is from THE DIARY OF MAHADEV DESAI edited by Valji Govindji Desai. All rights reserved. © 1953. Reprinted by permission of the Navajivan Trust.

"June Sunset" and "Tet" by Emily Nguyen. All rights reserved. © Emily Nguyen. Reprinted by permission of the author.

"Piggy-Back" and "City" are from THE LANGSTON HUGHES READER (Braziller, 1958). Copyright © 1958 by Langston Hughes. Copyright renewed 1986 by George Houston Bass. Reprinted by permission of Harold Ober Associates Incorporated.

"I Like To . . ." is from FINGER FROLICS compiled by Liz Cromell, et al. All rights reserved. © 1983. Reprinted by permission of Partner Press.

"Sampan" by Tao Lang Pee is from WHEEL AROUND THE WORLD edited by Chris Searle. Extensive reserach failed to locate the copyright holder of this work.

"Under One Sky" (words and music) and "The Grandma Song" (words) from UNDER ONE SKY by Ruth Pelham. © 1982 Ruth Pelham Music ASCAP, P.O. Box 6024, Albany, NY 12206. Reprinted by permission of the author. "The Grandma Song" is recorded on Ruth Pelham's recordings UNDER ONE SKY (Gentle Wind 1012) and LOOK TO THE PEOPLE (Flying Fish 399) and can be ordered by writing to the author at the address above.

"Silent But . . . . " by Tsuboi Shigeji from THE PENGUIN BOOK OF JAPANESE VERSE translated by Geoffrey Bownas and Anthony Thwaite (Penguin Books, 1964) translation copyright © Geoffrey Bownas and Anthony Thwaite, 1964. Reprinted by permission of Penguin Books Ltd, London.

"Goodnight, Juma" is from NIGHT ON NEIGHBORHOOD STREET by Eloise Greenfield. Copyright © 1991 by Eloise Greenfield. Used by permission of Dial Books for Young Readers, a division of Penguin Books USA Inc. The excerpt that appears in "As a Matter of Fact" for July 8 is from "Mojados (Wetbacks)" from NEW AMERICANS: AN ORAL HISTORY by Al Santoli. Copyright © 1988 by Al Santoli. Used by permission of Viking Penguin, a division of Penguin Books USA Inc. "My Daddy Is a Cool Dude" and "The Park People" from MY DADDY IS A COOL DUDE AND OTHER POEMS by Karama Fufuka. Copyright © 1975 by Karama Fufuka. Used by permission of Dial Books for Young Readers, a division of Penguin Books USA Inc. "Icy" from STORIES TO BEGIN ON by Rhoda W. Bacmeister. Copyright 1940 by E.P. Dutton, renewed © 1968 by Rhoda W. Bacmeister. Used by permission of Dutton Children's Books, a division of Penguin Books USA Inc.

"Martin Luther King Jr." is from WHEN YOU GROW UP: POEMS FOR CHILDREN by Useni Eugene Perkins. All rights reserved. © 1982 Useni Eugene Perkins. Reprinted by permission of the author.

"Two Little Sisters . . ." reprinted by permission of Philomel Books from CHINESE MOTHER GOOSE RHYMES, selected and edited by Robert Wyndham, copyright © 1968 by Robert Wyndham.

"A Puerto Rico" by José Gautier Benítez is from LITERATURA DEL CARIBE ANTOLOGÍA. All rights reserved. © 1988. Reprinted by permission of Patricia Gutiérrez, Editorial Plaza Mayor.

"What Is Poetry?" by Kien Po is from HEROES: AND STILL IT MOVES, 1990, a publication of the Galileo High School Creative Writing Project, now the McAteer Creative Writing Project, and California Poets in the Schools. For information about current student publications, contact J. Bebelaar, McAteer High School, 555 Portola Drive, San Francisco 94131, phone 415-695-5700. Reprinted by permission of the poet.

"April Fool's Day" by Marnie Pomeroy is from POEMS FOR SEASONS AND CELEBRATIONS edited by William Cole. All rights reserved. © Marnie Pomeroy. Reprinted by permission of the author.

"Mommy, When I'm Big and Tall" by Álvaro Yunque. © Álvaro Yunque. Reprinted by permission of Ediciones Preescolar.

"Borinquen" by Isabel Freire de Matos and "Sandía" by José Juan Tablada from NIÑOS Y ALAS, edited by Ismael Rodríguez Bou. All rights reserved. © 1958. Reprinted by permission of the Puerto Rico Council on Higher Education.

"Brooms" by Dorothy Aldis reprinted by permission of G. P. Putnam's Sons from EVERYTHING AND ANYTHING, copyright 1925–27, © renewed 1953–55 by Dorothy Aldis. "Bursting" by Dorothy Aldis reprinted by permission of G. P. Putnam's Sons from ALL TOGETHER by Dorothy Aldis, copyright 1952 by Dorothy Aldis, © renewed 1980 by Roy E. Porter.

"A Fairy Tale" is from SANGRE by Leroy V. Quintana. Copyright © 1981 by Leroy V. Quintana. Published by Prima Agua Press. Reprinted by permission of the author.

Fragment from ON THE PULSE OF MORNING by Maya Angelou. Copyright © 1993 by Maya Angelou. Reprinted by permission of Random House, Inc.

"Why I Teach" by Susan L. Reichin. © 1993 Susan L. Reichin. Used by permission of the author. All rights reserved.

"Dragon Smoke" is from I FEEL THE SAME WAY by Lilian Moore. Copyright © 1967 by Lilian Moore. "Fantasia" is from FINDING A POEM by Eve Merriam. Copyright © 1970 by Eve Merriam. "Passover" is from CELEBRATIONS by Myra Cohn Livingston. Copyright © 1985 by Myra Cohn Livingston. Holiday House, New York. "Tails" is from WHISPERS AND OTHER POEMS by Myra Cohn Livingston. Copyright © 1958, © renewed 1986 Myra Cohn Livingston. Originally published by Harcourt Brace & Company. "Wonderful Day" is from CRICKET SONGS: JAPANESE HAIKU translated by Harry Behn. © 1964 Harry Behn. Copyright © renewed 1992 Prescott Behn, Pamela Behn Adam, and Peter Behn. "My First Birthday Gift" by Sandra Liatsos. Copyright © 1991 by Sandra Liatsos. "New Mother" by R. H. Marks first appeared in POEMS FOR MOTHERS edited by Myra Cohn Livingston. Copyright © 1988 by R. H. Marks. All reprinted by permission of Marian Reiner for the authors.

"Friends" by María Rendón is from POETRY IN PERFORMANCE 20. All rights reserved. © 1992. Reprinted by permission of Raquel Rendón on behalf of her daughter, María Rendón.

"We Shall Overcome" Musical and lyrical adaptation by Zilphia Horton, Frank Hamilton, Guy Carawan and Pete Seeger. Inspired by African American gospel singing, members of the Food & Tobacco Workers Union, Charleston, SC, and the southern Civil Rights Movement. TRO– Copyright © 1960 (renewed) and 1963 (renewed) Ludlow Music, Inc., New York, NY. Royalties derived from this composition are being contributed to the We Shall Overcome Fund and The Freedom Movement under the Trusteeship of the writers. Used by permission of The Richmond Organization.

"Crayons" and "Sleeping Outdoors" are from RHYMES ABOUT US by Marchette Chute. Published 1974 by E.P. Dutton. Copyright 1974 by Marchette Chute. "Picnics" and "Spring Rain" are from AROUND AND ABOUT by Marchette Chute, copyright 1957 by E.P. Dutton. Copyright renewed 1984 by Marchette Chute. All reprinted by permission of Elizabeth Roach.

"First Night of Hanukkah" by Ruth Roston is from POEMS FOR JEWISH HOLIDAYS selected by Myra Cohn Livingston. All rights reserved. © 1986 Ruth Roston. Reprinted by permission of the author.

"Why Do They Stare?" by Wendy Rountree is from I HEARD A SCREAM IN THE STREET: POEMS BY YOUNG PEOPLE IN THE CITY selected by Nancy Larrick. Extensive research failed to locate the copyright holder of this work.

"The Flowers" by Paola Sanchez is from POETRY IN PERFORMANCE 19. All rights reserved. © 1991. Reprinted by permission.

"Bubie Annie" by Shelley Savren is from REMEMBERING WHAT HAPPENED edited by Daryl Ngee Chin. All rights reserved. © 1991 Shelley Savren. Published by California Poets in the Schools. Reprinted with permission of the author.

"Halloween" by Phyllis J. Perry is from INSTRUCTOR 1971. All rights reserved. © 1971 Instructor Publications. Reprinted by permission of Scholastic, Inc. "Preferred Vehicles" by Leland B. Jacobs. Reprinted from INSTRUCTOR, © copyright September 1966, Instructor Publications, Inc., used by permission.

"I Live in a City" words and music by Malvina Reynolds. © 1960 Schroder Music Co., Renewed 1988. Used by permission. All rights reserved.

"Little Sister" and "Pow Wow" are from BLOOD SALT by Doris Seale. All rights reserved. © Doris Seale. Reprinted by permission of the author.

"Arnab (The Rabbit)" (page 170): From THE ARABS: ACTIVITIES FOR THE ELEMENTARY SCHOOL LEVEL by Audrey Shabbas, Carol El-Shaieb, Ahlam Nabulsi. © 1991 by A. Shabbas. By permission of the authors.

"Eid" by Riyad Shamma. All rights reserved. © Riyad Shamma. Reprinted by permission of the author.

"Song of the Dragon" Traditional Chinese Folk Song from FUN, FOOD AND FESTIVALS by Kathryn G. Obenshain, Alice D. Walker and Joyce Merman. Copyright © 1978 Shawnee Press, Inc. (ASCAP). International Copyright Secured. All Rights Reserved. Used by permission.

"If I were a rope . . ." by Orren Provost is from PHOTOGRAPHS AND POEMS BY SIOUX CHILDREN FROM THE PORCUPINE DAY SCHOOL, PINE RIDGE INDIAN RESERVATION by Arthur Amiotte and Miles Libhart. © 1971. Reprinted by permission of the Sioux Indian Museum.

"Another Kid" by Virginia Driving Hawk Sneve. All rights reserved. © Virginia Driving Hawk Sneve. Reprinted by permission of the author.

"Ode to My Kitten" is copyrighted © 1993 by Gary Soto. Used by permission of the author.

"Home" by Chad Bulich is from POETRY SHELL: A MAGAZINE OF VERSE, Vol. XVII, No. 1, edited by Paul Spencer. All rights reserved. © 1989. Reprinted by permission of Paul Spencer.

"I Love You Little," "The Secret" by Mary Mapes Dodge, and "I Am Freedom's Child" by Bill Martin Jr are from BILL MARTIN JR'S TREASURE CHEST OF POETRY. © 1986 DLM Teaching Resources. Reprinted by permission of SRA School Division.

"I Am a Suffragette" from SONGS AMERICA VOTED BY by Irwin Silber. Copyright © 1971 by Stackpole Books. All rights reserved. Used by permission.

"Cooking for Shabbas with My Family" by Judith Wolinsky Steinbergh. © 1993 Judith Wolinsky Steinbergh. Reprinted by permission of the author.

"Instructions on How to Read" by Eloy Suárez is from POETRY IN PERFORMANCE 15. All rights reserved. © 1987. Reprinted by permission.

"Dear Mr. president" by Christopher Vargas is from DEAR MR. PRESIDENT by the students of Sunny Sands Elementary School. All rights reserved. ©1991. Reprinted by permission of Molly Schecter, Sunny Sands Elementary School.

"Ride, Sally Ride" is the lyrics to a song by Casse Culver, © 1983 by Shuttle Songs Ltd., a division of Sweet Alliance Music BMI, Silver Springs, MD. All rights reserved. Used by permission of the author.

"Mari and the Moon," "Much to Learn," "You Don't Have to Be Bigger to Be Important," and "No Room! No Room!" by Carmen Tafolla. All rights reserved. © Carmen Tafolla. Reprinted by permission of the author.

"Family Gifts" © 1991 by Victor Cockburn, Judith Steinbergh from: WHERE I COME FROM! SONGS AND POEMS FROM MANY CULTURES. Talking Stone Press, 1992, Boston.

Reprint permission for "Haiku" from I'VE BEEN A WOMAN,

Copyright 1978 by Sonia Sanchez. Published 1985 by Third World Press, Chicago, IL.

"Black Child" Copyright © 1981 Joyce Carol Thomas. Reprinted by permission of the author.

"Image" by Henry Dumas is from the book KNEES OF A NATURAL MAN by Henry Dumas. Copyright © 1989 by Loretta Dumas and Eugene B. Redmond. Used by permission of the publisher, Thunder's Mouth Press.

"Being Nobody" by Karen Crawford and "I Love the World" by Paul Wollner are from MIRACLES: POEMS BY CHILDREN OF THE ENGLISH-SPEAKING WORLD. Edited by Richard Lewis. Reprinted by permission of Richard Lewis. All rights reserved. © 1966 by Richard Lewis. Distributed by The Touchstone Center, New York, NY. "The Feast of Lanterns" by Yoshimura Jinto is from THERE ARE TWO LIVES edited and translated by Richard Lewis and Haruna Kimura. © Richard Lewis and Haruna Kimura, 1970. Originally published by Simon and Schuster, 1970. Reprinted by permission of Richard Lewis on behalf of the Touchstone Center.

"Anansi" Music by Raffi/Words by Bert Simpson. © 1979 Homeland Publishing, a division of Troubadour Records, Ltd. All rights reserved. Used by permission.

"Bahay Kubo/My Nipa Hut" from FOLK SONGS HAWAII SINGS compiled by John M. Kelly. © Charles E. Tuttle Co., Inc. 1962, Rutland, VT, Boston, MA, Tokyo, Japan. All rights reserved. Reprinted by permission of publisher.

"Dust in the City" by Jennifer Erickson and Amanda Lyon, "Round House Dancing," by Albert Townsend, and "The Wind Is Cool and Swift" by Tanu Frank are from DAYBREAK STAR INDIAN READER. Seattle. Reprinted by permission of United Indians of All Tribes Foundation.

"Corn" by Esther Antin from RAINBOW IN THE SKY, an anthology compiled by Louis Untermeyer, has been published with permission by the Estate of Louis Untermeyer c/o Professional Publishing Services.

"Childhood Country" and "Puerto Rican Day Parade" by Gloria Vando. All rights reserved. © Gloria Vando. Reprinted by permission of the author.

"Maytime Magic" by Mabel Watts is from THE RANDOM HOUSE BOOK OF POETRY FOR CHILDREN selected by Jack Prelutsky. All rights reserved. © Mabel Watts. Reprinted by permission of Patricia Watts Babcock on behalf of Mabel Watts.

"Your Birthday Cake" by Rosemary Wells is from TO RIDE A BUTTERFLY edited by Nancy Larrick and Wendy Lamb. All rights reserved. © 1991. Reprinted by permission of the author.

"Birdfoot's Grampa" is from NEAR THE MOUNTAINS by Joseph Bruchac. © White Pine Press. Reprinted by permission of the publisher.

"Beginning a New Year Means . . ." by Ruth Whitman. Copyright © 1987 by Ruth Whitman. Reprinted by permission of the author.

"Do-Re-Mi" (p. 159). Copyright © 1959 by Richard Rodgers and Oscar Hammerstein II. WILLIAMSON MUSIC, owner of publication and allied rights throughout the world. Copyright renewed. International copyright secured. Used by permission. All rights reserved.

"Looking Out," "Mirror, Mirror," and "What Your Mother Tells You" by Mitsuye Yamada are from CAMP NOTES AND OTHER POEMS. Copyright © 1992 by Mitsuye Yamada. Used with permission of the author and Kitchen Table: Women of Color Press, P.O. Box 908, Latham, NY 12110.

"How a Girl Got Her Chinese Name" by Nellie Wong from DREAMS IN HARRISON RAILROAD PARK. Reprinted by permission of Nellie Wong.

"Sakura (Cherry Trees)" English version by Katherine F. Rohrbough. English © 1956 World Around Us Songs, Inc. Used by permission. In BRIGHT MORNING STARS (WAS).

"Grandfather Is a Chinese Pine" by Zheng Xu is from POETRY IN PERFORMANCE 19. All rights reserved. © 1991. Reprinted by permission.

"Ong Dal Sam/Little Spring" by Suk-Joong Yoon in HALF PAST FOUR (translated from Korean by Francis Taewon Yoon and David Lapham). Los Angeles: F.T. Yoon Co., 1978. Reprinted by permission of the publisher.

"Weather" (author unknown) is from RANDOM HOUSE BOOK OF POETRY FOR CHILDREN selected by Jack Prelutsky. "What I'll Be When I Grow Up" (author unknown) is from SOME PEOPLE I KNOW by Beverly J. Armento, et al. "Black is Beautiful" (author unknown) is from I HEARD A SCREAM IN THE STREET: POEMS BY YOUNG PEOPLE IN THE CITY selected by Nancy Larrick. "I Love Everybody" (author unknown) is from EVERYBODY SAYS FREEDOM by Pete Seeger and Bob Reiser. Extensive research failed to locate the copyright holders of these works.

PHOTO CREDITS: The Bettmann Archive, pp. 134, 149; Comstock, Inc., p. 139; FPG International, p. 80; The Gamma Liaison Network, p. 234; Grant Huntington, pp. 14, 123; Lawrence Migdale, pp. 41, 58, 63, 64, 75, 92, 100, 105, 109 (both), 114, 125, 130, 140, 144, 146, 192, 197, 209, 211, 214, 227; Superstock, Inc., pp. 167, 187; UNIPHOTO/PICTOR, pp. 74, 135, 157, 174, 188, 189 (Michael Yada), 194 (Charles Gupton), 202; Annie Valva, p. 158.

A Chorus of CULTURES

Poem for Two or More Voices

To America's voices, singing along,

Composing our verses,

Listen now with me and sing.

To our chorus of cultures

To our voices so strong

All part of the chorus,

Listen now with me and sing.

Listen now with me and sing.

Composing our song,

To our chorus of cultures

Listen now with me and sing.

All part of the song.

Listen now with me and sing.

ADD YOUR VOICES TO THE CHORUS!

Hampton-Brown Books invites you to "sing along" with *A Chorus of Cultures* by creating your own improvisation on the "Dedication" poem (see inside front cover).

The Poem for Two or More Voices to the left is one improvisation idea (see page 34 for a description of this technique). Here are some others:

✦ Add your own line to the poem—and then give your own twist to reading it! Perhaps one group will recite the poem while another whispers the new line over and over. Or, what could be more appropriate for a poem about *A Chorus of Cultures* than a choral reading?

✦ How about truly making the poem a "chorus"—the chorus to a song, that is! Children can "compose their verses," then the poem itself can be the chorus.

✦ Because "America's voices" speak in many languages, perhaps your students can help you translate the dedication and present it in Spanish, or Vietnamese, or Hebrew, or Russian, or Sign Language, or . . . ?

You might write your improvisation on a banner, make it into a Big Book, record it on audio or video, turn it into a take-home bookmark, or . . . well, the sky's the limit! One thing we hope, though, is that you'll share your improvisations with us at:

Hampton-Brown Books
Attn: Cara Lieb
26385 Carmel Rancho Blvd.
Carmel, CA 93923

Permission is hereby granted to duplicate text from the dedication poem (for classroom use only) to create and share improvisations.

To order more copies of *A Chorus of Cultures* Anthology, Music Tapes, Poetry Charts, or Small Books
✦ Call Toll Free: 1-800-333-3510 ✦ Fax: 408-384-8940
or ✦ Complete this form and mail to
Hampton-Brown Books ✦ P.O. Box 223220 ✦ Carmel, CA 93922

TITLE	QUANTITY	x	PRICE*	=	AMOUNT
Anthology	_____		_____		_____
Music Tapes	_____		_____		_____
Poetry Charts	_____		_____		_____
Small Books	_____		_____		_____
Complete Program	_____		_____		
			SUBTOTAL		_____
		Add 10% for Shipping & Handling			_____
		Plus Sales Tax if in California			_____

* Call toll free or see our latest catalog for current price and sales tax information. **TOTAL** _____

METHOD OF PAYMENT (no cash please)

1. Payment enclosed ☐ Check payable to Hampton-Brown Books
☐ Money Order

2. Charge to my credit card

☐ Mastercard ☐ Visa Card Number _____

Expiration date _____ Daytime phone _____

Signature _____

3. School Purchase Order Attached: _____

BILL TO

Name _____

Title _____ Grade(s) _____

School _____

Street _____

City _____ Telephone _____

State _____ Zip _____

SHIP TO (if different)

Name _____

Title _____ Grade(s) _____

School _____

Street _____

City _____ Telephone _____

State _____ Zip _____

To order more copies of *A Chorus of Cultures* Anthology, Music Tapes, Poetry Charts, or Small Books
✦ Call Toll Free: 1-800-333-3510 ✦ Fax: 408-384-8940
or ✦ Complete this form and mail to
Hampton-Brown Books ✦ P.O. Box 223220 ✦ Carmel, CA 93922

TITLE	QUANTITY	x	PRICE*	=	AMOUNT
Anthology	_____		_____		_____
Music Tapes	_____		_____		_____
Poetry Charts	_____		_____		_____
Small Books	_____		_____		_____
Complete Program	_____		_____		
			SUBTOTAL		_____
		Add 10% for Shipping & Handling			_____
		Plus Sales Tax if in California			_____

* Call toll free or see our latest catalog for current price and sales tax information. **TOTAL** _____

METHOD OF PAYMENT (no cash please)

1. Payment enclosed ☐ Check payable to Hampton-Brown Books
☐ Money Order

2. Charge to my credit card

☐ Mastercard ☐ Visa Card Number _____

Expiration date _____ Daytime phone _____

Signature _____

3. School Purchase Order Attached: _____

BILL TO

Name _____

Title _____ Grade(s) _____

School _____

Street _____

City _____ Telephone _____

State _____ Zip _____

SHIP TO (if different)

Name _____

Title _____ Grade(s) _____

School _____

Street _____

City _____ Telephone _____

State _____ Zip _____